Parliaments and Legislatures Series

Parliaments and Legislatures Series
General Advisory Editor
Samuel C. Patterson, Ohio State University, USA

The aims of this series are to enhance knowledge about the well-established legislative assemblies of North America and western Europe and to publish studies of parliamentary assemblies worldwide—from Russia and the former Soviet bloc nations to Asia, Africa, and Latin America. The series is open to a wide variety of theoretical applications, historical dimensions, data collections, and methodologies.

Beyond Westminster and Congress: The Nordic Experience

Edited by
Peter Esaiasson
Knut Heidar

Ohio State University Press
Columbus

Library of Congress Cataloging-in-Publication Data

Beyond Westminster and Congress : the Nordic experience / edited by Peter
Esaiasson and Knut Heidar.
     p. cm.—(Parliaments and legislatures series)
     Includes bibliographical references and index.
     ISBN 0-8142-0839-8 (alk. paper)
     1. Legislative bodies—Scandinavia. 2. Representative government and
representation—Scandinavia. 3. Comparative government. I. Esaiasson, Peter.
II. Heidar, Knut, 1949– III. Series.
JN7056 .B49 2000
328'.0948—dc21
                                              99-050071

Type set in Adobe Caslon with Gill Sans by Graphic Composition, Inc.
Printed by Thomson-Shore, Inc.

9 8 7 6 5 4 3 2 1

Contents

Foreword

The comparative study of parliamentary institutions generally comes in two forms. The first and more common is the analysis of individual legislatures or parliaments, constituting a case study or series of case studies. These studies describe and analyze the environment, development, institutional structure, and representative behavior of parliaments. Understanding how parliaments work is greatly enhanced by such inquiries when their rich detail, their "thick description," exposes the performance of representative assemblies in their historical, cultural, and political contexts. The second mode of comparative research on parliaments takes the properties of parliamentary institutions and their members as the basis for cross-institutional measurement of dependent and independent variables, ultimately suitable for modeling free of interference from country-specific, unique factors. Although *Beyond Westminster and Congress* draws much from both lines of inquiry, its authors lean conspicuously in the direction of truly comparative analysis of parliamentary institutions. In doing so, they make this book something of a rarity, and an unusually important contribution to knowledge about parliamentary life.

The Nordic parliaments are, of course, the national legislative assemblies of Denmark, Finland, Iceland, Norway, and Sweden. These five parliaments are kindred in many ways. All are democratically elected bodies, their members chosen by proportional representation. All are unicameral in their inception, although the Norwegian Storting forms a kind of second chamber after it convenes. At the same time, these five parliaments differ in important ways—in their historic political development, their modes of election, and their internal structures. Sharing many cultural attributes and similar institutional arrangements, but exhibiting important political differences, these five Nordic countries present interesting possibilities for comparative parliamentary analysis.

In the course of investigating the effects of institutional differences among Nordic parliaments, Peter Esaiasson and Knut Heidar and their fellow contributors draw comparisons with the national legislative assemblies in the United States and the United Kingdom. The U.S. Congress and the Westminster Parliament provide comparative exemplars as the most studied, and most emulated, parliaments of the world. The Congress and Westminster cases provide the authors with benchmarks against which to assay institutional similarities and differences among the Nordic parliaments.

This study is a landmark in various respects. Cross-national comparison of political institutions is not an easy task, as these authors are well aware. Developing measurements that are equivalent across complex institutions presents daunting methodological problems. Data collection in multinational research may involve great difficulties in organization, conceptualization, retrieval, and analysis. Accordingly, research genuinely comparing political institutions in different national settings is uncommon. These authors have formed a research team in order to face the challenges of cross-national analysis, collecting and analyzing comparable sets of empirical data in the five Nordic systems. The core data for this comparative effort derive from two surveys—of members of parliament and of citizen voters—conducted in the mid-1990s. But the authors deploy a variety of other data as well, including roll-call voting and committee assignments.

This truly collaborative research project, coordinating the efforts of more than a dozen political scientists, provides an important contribution to understanding how parliaments work. At a minimum, we learn that parliaments in the Nordic countries are not trivial, insignificant, or superannuated bodies, mere puppets at the beck and call of political executives or other outside forces. Rather, as these authors demonstrate, the Nordic parliaments are "working parliaments," all active and influential in formulating and enacting public policies.

Samuel C. Patterson

Acknowledgments

Despite repeated pleas for increased Nordic cooperation among social scientists, Nordic five-nation comparisons are relatively rare undertakings. Looking back on the project, we must acknowledge that cross-country comparisons increase the workload. Still, they are well worth the extra effort.

The project began at a conference of the Nordic Political Science Association in Oslo in 1993, when several of the contributors to this book discussed the possibility of coordinating parliamentary surveys already under way in some of the Nordic countries. The five-nation project on "Nordic Legislatures and Legislators" (or NORDLEG for short) was started shortly thereafter.

The research group met on seven different occasions in order to plan, prepare, and discuss. It first met in Turku, Finland, at the initiative of Matti Wiberg. Subsequently, it met in 1994 in Århus, Denmark; in 1995 in Göteborg, Sweden, and Oslo, Norway; in 1996 at the Nordic Political Science Association conference in Helsinki, Finland; in January 1997 in Göteborg; and finally in June 1997 in Skagen, Denmark.

This project has enjoyed support from each of the five nations involved, as well as from the Nordic community as a whole. Its various national components have in most cases been funded by each country's national research council. Local institutes have assisted as well.

The Danish study was supported by the Danish Social Science Research Council and by Århus University Research Foundation. Birgit Møller and Peter Feilberg Schjødt did the coding of the questionnaire and of biographical data.

The Icelandic Research Council and the University of Iceland Research Fund helped finance the Icelandic surveys. Johanna S. Palsdottír assisted with the parliamentary survey, while the voter survey was conducted by the Social Science Research Institute at the University of Iceland.

In Finland, the field work of the survey was carried out by Pentti Kiljunen at Yhdyskuntatutkimus.

In Norway, the major support came from the Norwegian Research

Council. The voter study was conducted and mostly financed by Statistics Norway. Hanne Marthe Narud received a grant from the Nordic Council of Ministers under the program The Nordic Countries and Europe, which enabled her to work full-time with the project. Frode Berglund helped in the practical administration of the Norwegian parliamentary survey, as well as doing the coding and preparing the data for analysis.

The Bank of Sweden Tercentenary Foundation funded the Swedish Riksdag Study, while the voter survey was the traditional election study, carried out in cooperation with the Swedish Central Bureau of Statistics. Martin Brothén was responsible for administration and data management in the Riksdag survey.

Since 1995, moreover, the Joint Committee of the Nordic Social Science Research Councils (NOS-S) has provided support for the Nordic cooperation involved in this project. The assistance of the NOS-S committee has been crucial to the comparative effort; otherwise, we would have been left with two or three uncoordinated national projects. And without the extraordinary efforts of Martin Brothén, the coordination of the data would have been much more difficult for all participants in the NORDLEG group.

We would also like to thank Peter Mayers for his engaged work in improving the English language of the contributors, and the Ohio State University Press reviewers for their good advice. Knut Heidar wishes also to thank the Fulbright Foundation in Norway for its support and the Department of Political Science at the University of Denver for its hospitality during his sabbatical there in the autumn of 1998.

Finally, our thanks go to the parliamentarians and voters who took the time to answer our questionnaires. It is they who made this study possible in the most basic sense.

The Age of Representative Democracy

Peter Esaiasson and Knut Heidar

We are living in the age of representative democracy. For most practical purposes, the distinction between "democracy" and "representative democracy" is today a superfluous one. We may argue about the nature of representative democracy. Radicals who champion citizen participation in public decision-making may consider it a poor substitute for the real thing. Others may claim that we have witnessed a two-step process toward the democratic governance of modern societies: the old Greeks did the first part of the job, but it was not until the original idea of rule by the people was joined to the notion of representation in the eighteenth century that the democratic doctrine became relevant to large-scale nation-states. Yet others may argue that representative democracy is a system of governance in its own right, distinctly different from classical democracy.[1] Whatever position we take on these matters, however, reformers of authoritarian political systems always rely—when push comes to shove—on the principles of representative democracy.

A core idea of democratic representative government is to entrust, for a limited period of time, a chosen few with the right to make binding decisions on behalf of the many. As a collective, these trusted representatives form an institution referred to as "parliament," the "legislature" or, most generally, the "assembly."[2] In order to facilitate the conduct of government, practicing representative democracies have certainly developed complex arrangements of complementary political institutions. None of these, however, have been more central than parliament. If we wish to understand the workings of politics in the age of representative democracy, we must confront the major questions about the arena in which the selected few meet and decide. How does parliament operate, why does it operate as it does, and what are the consequences thereof?

Although all representative democracies share the principle that those granted the right to govern must be elected at regular intervals, parliaments vary considerably in their precise institutional setup (see, e.g., Lijphart 1984). Indeed, no two real-world polities can be found with identical constitutional rules for their parliament. Consider, for example, the well-known difference between legislative assemblies in presidential systems and those in parliamentary systems. Another difference plain to political scientists exists between the role of parliament in a majoritarian type of government and its role in a system with proportional elections.

Where finer institutional arrangements are concerned, the differences are almost innumerable. To name just a few: parliaments vary in regard to seating arrangements, voting procedures, committee structure, number of seats, rules for parliamentary debate, and degree of staff support for individual representatives. The designers of democratic polities have clearly taken pluralism seriously.

The unexpected overturn of authoritarian regimes in eastern Europe following the fall of the Soviet empire put the political-science discipline to a test. What well-founded advice based on the experience of Western democracies could be offered reformers about how to design a constitution making for a well-functioning parliament? Which institutional arrangements have what effects on the operations of parliaments? What matters and what doesn't? Developments have made clear that, as a discipline, we do not know enough about the precise effects of institutional arrangements (if indeed there are precise effects; cf. Judge 1995).

Given the complexity of the topic, it is hardly surprising that political scientists have had a problem providing authoritative answers as to how and why parliaments operate the way they do, and with what consequences. Now the building of new democracies in eastern Europe and elsewhere has created an urgent need for such answers. In our judgment, there is no better way to progress than to continue scrutinizing the workings of parliaments in different contexts. Yet we think it reasonable to try—even while acknowledging the need for more systematic empirical research—to examine the topic from new angles. We need something fresh, not more of the same.

THE NORDIC FOCUS

This study of the five Nordic parliaments has been designed to overcome what we believe are three shortcomings in the scholarly debate on the workings of legislatures. The first is the well-known *bias in the selection of cases*. While each representative democracy has its own unique history and institutional setup, much of our shared understanding of the workings of parliaments is still shaped by the experiences of just two institutions: the British House of Commons and the U.S. Congress.

The second shortcoming reflects the inclination of political scientists *to care mostly about differences*. This inclination often makes sense methodologically; however, a relentless search for differences may mean that basic similarities between parliaments are overlooked. In metaphysical terms, we run the risk of missing the *essence* of the workings of democratic parliaments.

The third shortcoming lies in a failure to formulate *fruitful definitions of the dependent variable*. The problem here is twofold. First, many sophisticated studies on the effects of various institutional arrangements spend surprisingly little time discussing the validity of the dependent variables chosen. If we are to understand democratic parliaments more fully, we must be as careful in what we study as we are in explaining what we are studying. Second, many studies focus on a single aspect of the complex operations of parliaments. Taken to their extreme, such research strategies run the risk of producing increasingly compartmentalized knowledge of the operations of parliaments.

Our approach in this book has three matching features. First, to adjust for previous bias in the selection of cases, we direct our attention to the parliamentary experience of the five Nordic countries: Denmark, Finland, Iceland, Norway, and Sweden. Second, to enrich our general understanding of the workings of parliaments, we watch carefully not only for differences between parliaments but also for universals uniting democratic assemblies in a variety of institutional settings. Third, in an effort to devise fruitful definitions of dependent variables, we have looked for operationalizations that provide meaningful descriptive information. In addition, our dependent variables cover—owing to the complexity of the phenomena under review—a broad array of parliamentary relations (internal parliamentary affairs, for example, as well as relations with other actors and structures such as voters, competing national elites, and the new internationalized world order).

A final characteristic of our approach is its truly comparative character: from planning to final report, this study has been carried out in a collective spirit and with a strong commitment to standardization.

We want to make clear from the outstart that believers in quick fixes will likely be disappointed with the general findings that will be presented in the following. First, there is not much left of a Nordic *model* in our concluding chapter. To the extent that all Nordic parliaments operate in a similar fashion, these ways are usually also found (a) among most democratic parliaments (a universal model), or (b) among most parliaments in parliamentary regimes (a parliamentary system model as opposed to a presidential system model), or (c) among most parliaments in parliamentary regimes based on proportional representation (PR) voting systems (a Continental model as opposed to the Westminster model).

Second, and even more important, we will argue that the Nordic experience indicates that institutional arrangements are not overly effective tools for controlling the operations of parliaments. Reformers of representative democracies may have an almost unlimited number of constitutional options at their disposal, but they can count on relatively few precise effects. There are two reasons for this. One is that all democratically elected legislatures function, in some respects, in a similar fashion. No matter what the specific institutional arrangements, the chosen few will act in a particular way. The other reason that constitutional engineers are crippled is that political-cultural factors play a crucial role for important aspects of the operations of parliaments. How parliaments operate is determined to a great extent by factors that are not easily changed.

A LESS-BIASED SELECTION OF CASES

Empirical studies on macropolitical phenomena like the workings of democratic parliaments usually follow the logic of traditional case-study research (countless variables, but just one case) or traditional quantitative research (many cases, relatively few variables).[3] Each research design has well-known strengths and weaknesses.

One advantage of quantitative studies is that they tend to minimize the risk that findings will be distorted by bias in the selection of cases. Such an approach has the drawback, however, that the measurements of variables employed are quite often crude. Qualitative case studies, on the other hand, have the converse characteristics: they are potentially strong in the validity of their measurements but weak in the generalizability of their findings. The difficulty of obtaining valid measurements of the workings of parliaments will be addressed later on. We shall begin here with a discussion of how the generalizability of empirical findings in the field can be improved.

This book is part of a growing trend of comparative empirical studies of parliaments outside the Anglo-Saxon core countries, studies conceived in an effort to overcome the selection bias within this field of research (e.g., Döring 1995; Schmitt and Thomassen 1999; Katz and Wessels 1999;

Miller et al. 1999). Yet despite recent positive developments, too much of our thinking on the workings of parliaments and parliamentarians is still influenced by the experience of legislative assemblies in the style of Westminster and the U.S. Congress.

The British dominance, of course, has historical roots. Victorian England, with its enormous self-confidence, persuaded the world that the British parliament is "the mother of all parliaments." That this mind control is still in place can be seen in the terminology used in the literature on parliaments and parliamentarians. Widely used terms such as "party whip" and "backbencher" have concrete meaning only for specific British arrangements.

A more important example of British dominance can be seen in the fact that the lively debates in the House of Commons have set an implicit standard for viable parliamentary debate. When the often pedestrian performance of other elected representatives is compared with the verbal fireworks of artful British orators, the functional difference between working and deliberative parliaments is typically neglected. In simplified terms, we may say that British members of parliament are there to talk, whereas the members of working parliaments are there to do legislative work.

A still more important example of dominance is the fact that the British doctrine on the proper relationship between government and opposition long kept us from the full realization that there are other and less adversarial models for parliamentary opposition (Strøm 1986; 1990; Lewin 1996).

The dominance of the United States over our common understanding of the workings of parliaments and parliamentarians is obvious to anyone even remotely acquainted with the scholarly literature. When social-science research in the field was last summarized in an internationally comprehensible language—in the *Handbook of Legislative Research*—about eight in ten (76 percent) of the references were to studies of the U.S. case.[4] Given that the U.S. Congress is traditionally portrayed as an outlier among democratic legislatures, it is likely that such a dominance is a hindrance to our general understanding of parliaments.

We are not saying that research on the workings of parliaments and parliamentarians is necessarily more biased than other areas of the social sciences. On the contrary, leading scholars in the field are well aware of the dangers of cultural blindness (e.g., Mezey 1979; Loewenberg and Patterson 1979; Copeland and Patterson 1994). The problem is not that Anglo-Saxon scholarship is strong but rather that other voices are so weak. If we are serious about coming to grips with the phenomenon in question, we should try to learn from as many representative democracies as possible.

By this reasoning, it would be beneficial to bring into the picture *any* democratic parliament from outside the spheres of Westminster and Congress. For a couple of reasons, however, there is much to be said for a comparative study of the five Nordic parliaments in particular. These reasons bear on *how* parliaments work and on *why* they work as they do.

ON THE LOOK-OUT FOR SIMILARITIES AS WELL AS DIFFERENCES

It would be wise to be humble about the prospects for devising an irrefutable explanation of why parliaments work as they do. We must study these complex processes in a setting that is anything but experimental. We must bear in mind constantly that comparative social science is limited by such methodological problems as "too many variables, too few cases" (Lijphart 1971), and "Galton's problem" of diffusion between countries (Naroll 1965).

In order to simplify this task somewhat, our primary analytical focus in this study will be on the effects of *institutional arrangements*. Our definition of institutional arrangements is a fairly narrow one. We take it to refer to such concrete features of "governmental structures" as the type of voting system and the number of seats in parliament (cf. Weaver and Rockman 1993:8). In chapter 2, we shall give a more detailed exposition of the relevant institutional variables.

We use institutional arrangements as our main "sparring partner" simply because most political scientists are convinced that institutional arrangements are important (few of us are free from early Weberian impressions; cf. Rothstein 1996). As defined in this study, moreover, institutions are relatively easy to change. By learning more about which institutional arrangements matter in what way, we will be in a better position, when our services are summoned, to advise reformers of democratic societies.

For our purposes, the five Nordic parliaments facilitate flexible analysis. In one respect, the Nordic polities are both institutionally homogeneous and different from the Congress and Westminster models; they are all, that is, parliamentary democracies with proportional representation.[5] As such, they offer an alternative to the separation between executive and legislative branches characteristic of the Congress model, and to majoritarian parliamentary democracies based on single-member districts typified by the Westminster model. By comparing the experience of the Nordic parliaments to what is known about Congress and Westminster, we can assess the effects of basic governmental structures.

Of course, we cannot be sure that we are actually observing the effects of basic governmental structures. The Nordic countries are not only quite homogeneous in terms of type of parliamentary system, they are also fairly similar in terms of political culture (e.g., Elder et al. 1988; Graubard 1986; Stenelo and Jerneck 1996). In order to help us sort out the effects of political culture from those of basic governmental structures, we will make an effort to extend our comparisons outside the Westminster and Congress types to include also other parliamentary systems with proportional representation. These comparisons include, in particular, the polities frequently discussed under the label of the "Continental model"—for example, Germany and the Netherlands.[6]

In assessing the effects of basic governmental structures, we thus utilize intra-Nordic similarities in institutional arrangements. (Of course, our assessment draws as well on the existing body of knowledge about Congress and Westminster, as well as about parliaments of other types.) When assessing the effects of specific institutional arrangements, however, we shall make use of internal Nordic *differences*.

The five Nordic countries have adopted differing institutional arrangements in several respects. These differences bear on voting system (personal-preference voting versus party-list voting), nomination processes (with their varying degrees of centralization), and parliamentary organization (e.g., differences in size, committee structure, and standing orders).[7] The Nordic setting makes for a rather strict test of the thesis that specific institutional arrangements are important. If specific institutional arrangements have strong and consistent effects, these effects should be visible even within the relative cultural uniformity of the five Nordic parliamentary democracies.

When we emphasize the differences among the Nordic countries, though, we still cannot be sure we are observing the effects of institutional arrangements. This is because Nordic polities vary in more than their specific institutional arrangements. They differ as well in their historical preconditions. In Stein Rokkan's "conceptual map of Europe"—which he drew up as a guide to the patterns of state building observed since the sixteenth century—the five Nordic countries were put in four different categories (Rokkan 1975). There is thus every reason to be careful in drawing conclusions.

To facilitate the analysis, we will apply certain rules of thumb when interpreting empirical findings. More precisely, we will look for a limited number of patterns in the data. The basic question is whether the five Nordic parliaments work in a similar fashion, or whether they somehow differ. If they work in essentially the same way, the central question is whether there is reason to believe that most parliaments work in this way (in accordance with a kind of democratic-legislative essence), or whether instead we have observed practices common to the Nordic parliaments alone, or perhaps shared only with Westminster or Congress. If, on the other hand, the Nordic parliaments prove to differ from one another, we will discuss to what extent these differences can be attributed to variations in institutional arrangements and to what extent other forces may be in play.

Upon having considered a broad array of parliamentary relationships, in other words, we will concentrate on the following three questions: Which parliamentary elements are common to all representative democracies? What is the common denominator of the Nordic parliaments distinguishing them from the Westminster and Congress models? In what way are the Nordic parliaments unique as compared with one another?

We find it particularly important to look for universal characteristics that are likely shared by all parliaments. Political scientists tend, as argued above, to care mainly about differences, thus overlooking aspects that unite the phenomena under scrutiny. This means, in the case of the workings of parliaments and parliamentarians, that we run the risk of overlooking what characterizes the political system in which we are actually living.[8] This is an unhappy state of affairs. For one thing, since dissatisfaction with politicians quite often runs high among citizens, it is important to have reasonable demands on the workings of parliaments. If the public knows what to expect, we may have an antidote to populist policy solutions. There are no quick fixes to the endemic features of democratic politics.

DEFINING WHAT TO STUDY

In comparative research, the descriptive characteristics of the phenomenon under study often play, surprisingly, a secondary role. Recent years have seen the publication of many impressive works on the political effects of such institutional arrangements as electoral systems and parliamentary versus presidential systems (e.g., Grofman and Lijphart 1986; Lijphart 1994; Taagepera and Shugart 1989; Shugart and Carey 1992; Sartori 1994). Illuminating as these studies are, they show a mysterious blind spot. They move ever so swiftly from the general question of the effects of political institutions to technical matters having to do with how to measure narrowly defined (and often rather esoteric) dependent variables. The stages wherein theoretical definitions are developed and the validity of measurements discussed are handled rather lightly. It is as if the question of good description were of secondary importance, and one consequence of an institutional arrangement just as good as another.

From the perspective of this study, comparative analysis that specifically addresses the workings of parliaments suffers from a different problem. The problem here is that the research mainly deals with a single aspect of parliamentary operations, such as the role of parliaments in the policy-making process (Blondel 1973; Mezey 1979; Olson and Mezey 1991), the relation between the legislature and the executive (King 1976; Damgaard 1992a), the workings of the committee system (Lees and Shaw 1979), or the function of parliamentary questions (Franklin and Norton 1993; Wiberg 1994a). Invaluable as these studies are, they highlight only one aspect of the complex workings of democratic parliaments.

It is our ambition to move beyond both simplified measurements and compartmentalized studies. In what follows, we take a broad approach to describing *how* parliaments operate, in the process disentangling what we consider to be the main dimensions of parliamentary operations.

Our reasoning proceeds from the two common denominators of democratic parliaments mentioned at the beginning of this chapter. The members of democratic parliaments (a) are elected for a limited term, and (b) must act together. On the basis of this conception of parliament, we claim that its mode of operation can be specified in terms of four distinct relationships: the *vertical* (toward the electorate), the *internal* (among MPs, i.e., the organization of parliament), the *horizontal* (toward other elite decision-makers and national institutions), and the *external* (toward the international community as well as the future). Put differently, a good answer to the how-question would address considerations of representation, internal organization, relations with competing political elites, and stance toward the outside world.[9]

The first relationship is an *electoral* one. It concerns the connection between representatives and represented. How does public opinion come into play when members take action in parliament, and to which collective of citizens, if any, are representatives responsive?

The involvement of citizens in the decision-making process via their elected representatives is ambiguous in democratic theory and uncertain in practice. Both academic and political efforts leave the core meaning of "responsive actions" by representatives basically contested. The fundamental bone of contention has to do with the conception of "the will of the people." While public opinion must be part of the picture somehow, representation is compatible both with following public opinion (representation from below) and with leading it (representation from above).

According to elitist conceptions of democracy, representatives should focus more or less exclusively on exercising leadership. The argument may be that the notion of a specific popular will is illusory, or (in the case of radically elitist views) that public opinion is shortsighted, narrow-minded, and not to be trusted with direct influence over public matters.

The contrary view is championed by advocates of participatory democracy. According to them, public opinion should have direct influence on public decision-making. The basic argument is that no other authority is better equipped to make binding decisions on behalf of the collective than are individual citizens themselves. Taken to its extreme, this argument runs counter to the very idea of representative democracy and turns into a plea for direct democracy and popular referenda.

The second major step in specifying how parliament works is describing its internal *organization*, and in particular its internal decision-making process. This internal description aims at opening up the "black box" in the transmission belt between individual representatives and the authoritative decisions taken by parliament. Where in the organizational and sociometric networks of parliament are the final decisions taken and by whom? By what norms are representatives' actions guided?

We see only part of the picture, however, if we concentrate exclusively on the vertical relationship between representatives and represented (as is often done in the specialized literature on political representation) and on the internal organization and power structures of parliament. Parliaments may well occupy the apex of the constitutional law-making pyramid in representative democracies, but they are clearly not the only institutional locus of power in real-world politics. If they were, we wouldn't bother debating "the decline of parliaments." We must also, therefore, look into the relationships with *other national decision-making actors and institutions*—irrespective of whether such relationships are codified in the constitution proper or not. What, in other words, is the position and power of parliament in the state; that is, its position in the overall scheme of national decision-making?

This type of relationship includes, first of all, the "parliamentary" relationship to the executive branch of government. It also include horizontal relationships to extra-parliamentary party organizations, to the state bureaucracy, to organized interest groups, and to the media. Analyzing these will help us map the position of parliament in the process of public policy-making in general.

The vertical, horizontal, and internal relationships of parliaments are traditional topics of parliamentary research. The emerging new world order has added another important type of relationship to the agenda. Parliaments as we know them are tightly enmeshed in the nation-state. The rapid internationalization of politics—under such labels as "Europeanization" and "globalization"—poses a challenge to national politics in general and to the operation of parliaments in particular. If, then, we are to understand parliaments in the modern world, we must take the *external* relationships of parliaments and parliamentarians into account as well. Part of this external dimension will also include, arguably, the attitudes of parliamentarians toward the *future*, particularly as regards the emerging new world order.

THE RESEARCH PROJECT

According to Heinz Eulau, "legislative scholars will increasingly turn to team research and comparative international or cross-national studies" (Eulau 1985:11). The project reported here is an example of that. Of course, Nordic scholars can learn from the early efforts of Stein Rokkan.[10] Furthermore, the focus on systemic institutional arrangements has already given way to a growing interest in comparative studies, and as comparative research have evolved, the number of studies employing standardized methods of measurement is increasing.

The obstacles to fully standardized measurements, however, are many. We argue that this study has an edge on many other comparative projects in two important respects. First, by committing ourselves to standardization from the initial planning of the project, and by studying five countries of which three (Denmark, Norway, and Sweden) have similar languages, we have managed to bring the number of idiosyncrasies down to an unusually low level. That some peculiarities still remain—some due to subtle differences in the connotation of words, others explicable only by reference to the human factor—shows just how difficult it is to carry out truly comparative social-science research. We dare say, however, that compared to almost all of the cross-country studies of which we are aware, this volume should occasion readers little worry over study effects.

Two data sets were generated through the project. The first covers the responses of elected representatives in all five countries to identical questions in a survey conducted between November 1994 (Sweden) and May 1996 (Iceland). All parliamentarians serving at the time received the questionnaire, and the response rate was 97 percent in Sweden, 88 percent in Norway, 70 percent in Iceland, 63 percent in Denmark, and 61 percent in Finland. The other data set is a representative national survey of the electorates in all of the countries but Finland. These voter surveys repeated some of the issue-position questions put to the representatives and were conducted in connection with the parliamentary survey. We have no reason to think that either the parliamentary or the electoral data are flawed in ways that would necessitate more than the standard caution called for by data of this kind.[11]

It bears emphasizing once more that, in our view, this study has the advantage over many others when it comes to giving precise answers to the descriptive how-questions. Indeed, diversely operationalized dependent variables unavoidably allow personal biases to play a role in one's judgment as to whether or not the same empirical pattern is present in the countries under scrutiny. Standardized measurements reduce the space for personal idiosyncrasies. But not even perfect measurements can help us make all the tough decisions. In working on this project, most participants have struggled to find appropriate criteria for the assessment of empirical results: Yes, there are statistically significant differences among the five Nordic polities. But are these polities also *substantively* different? It will take a lot of continued standardized effort before social scientists can honestly claim to be on firm ground when making decisions like this.

It bears stressing as well that, in presenting our broad conception of the subject matter, we have clearly had to make some choices regarding our research strategy. In order to achieve breadth in coverage, we have had to restrict our empirical approach. Our presentation of the four relationships is primarily survey based. Where our general presentation is concerned, we have mainly opted for a systematic tapping of the experiences and opinions of the people currently serving as parliamentary representatives. To a lesser extent, we have sought to present a systematic "picture of procedures" (such as the rules governing the institutions). The idea has been to generate data on "patterns of actions" (including legislative output) and to seek out relevant "historical events" that have shaped institutional practices.

CHAPTER OUTLINE

Chapter 2, which was written by Knut Heidar with the assistance of four country specialists, presents the main features of the five Nordic countries as these are relevant to the similarity/difference discussion, and it provides the reader with the contextual knowledge necessary for a critical evaluation of our findings. Heidar begins with the basic nation-building background, as understood in the Rokkanian tradition, and proceeds to discuss some general features of Nordic polities and parliamentary arrangements. This chapter serves as a reference for subsequent analysis of the effects of institutional arrangements.

The *first* substantive part of the book covers the "vertical" relationships of parliament; that is, the question of how well the electorate is represented at the parliamentary level. In chapter 3, Peter Esaiasson looks at how the individual member of parliament views his or her task as a representative. The object is to test the validity of the "task-definition approach." Do we gain insight into parliamentary life by assuming that elected representatives act to champion the interests they personally consider important to champion?

In chapter 4, Hanne Marthe Narud and Henry Valen take a new look at the old issue of descriptive representation. It is generally believed that Nordic polities are more egalitarian than almost any other. But how egalitarian are each of these countries in fact, and to what degree does the social background of representatives make a difference in terms of policy representation?

Chapters 5 and 6 focus on the relationship between elected representatives and specific electoral groups. In chapter 5, Henry Valen, Hanne Marthe Narud and Ólafur Th. Hardarson raise the question of geographic representation. In the literature, geographical representation is generally associated with single-member-district electoral systems. Narud, Valen, and Hardarson show, however, that geography is a highly relevant dimension in PR systems as well. Lena Wängnerud, for her part (in chapter 6), analyzes a phenomenon that makes the Nordic polities stand out among the representative democracies of the world—the fact that women are present in parliamentary life to an unusual degree. In particular, Wängnerud examines the empirical support for the notion of a unique Nordic "passion for equality," and she suggests a new interpretation of recent developments more focused on political mobilization than on culture.

Lastly in this part, Sören Holmberg analyzes in chapter 7 the degree of policy congruence between representatives and those represented. To what degree do voters and their representatives think alike on important policy matters? And does the degree of issue congruence vary among the Nordic countries? In analyzing this question, Holmberg draws upon data from both the parliamentary and the electoral level.

In the *second* substantive part of the book, we turn to the debates on internal features, which essentially concern the organization and practice of "the house" itself. All of the Nordic systems are "party-driven"; accordingly, the first chapter here—that by Knut Heidar (chapter 8)—deals with the position of party groups in parliament. How centralized is decision-making within parliamentary party groups in the Nordic parliaments, and how do the findings square with evidence from other polities?

Chapter 9, by Torben K. Jensen, follows up on this theme by concentrating on the norm of party discipline. Parliamentary systems are generally characterized by a virtually complete cohesiveness when it comes to roll-call voting, but Jensen shows there is much more to the picture than the final act of voting. Magnus Hagevi's analysis (in chapter 10) of parliamentary committees and committee assignments puts another important piece of the puzzle into place. In working parliaments like the Nordic ones, what is the role of committees in the internal hierarchy of power and what measure of control over their assignments do individual representatives possess?

The *third* substantive part focuses on the horizontal relationships of parliaments. Our purpose is to assess the role of parliament from a constitutional perspective, and to evaluate the decision-making potential of parliament relative to that of other national loci of power. Erik Damgaard starts out here (in chapter 11) with the traditional but still lively question of parliamentary-executive modes. What are the general characteristics of executive-legislative relations, and is there anything "Nordic" about how Denmark, Finland, Iceland, Norway, and Sweden organize this relationship?

In chapter 12, Ólafur Th. Hardarson examines the relationship between parliaments and a broad set of competing elites: interest organizations, party organizations, trade and industry, financial markets, the bureaucracy, the mass media, and the European Union. Who has power? Who should be more influential and who less? More precisely, Hardarson analyzes how elected representatives perceive the power structure, and how their ideal system of representation would work.

In the *fourth* and final substantive part, we turn to more distant affairs, with a look at the embryonic external relations of parliaments. In chapter 13, by Martin Brothén, the perspective is on the individual representative. This chapter discusses the international involvement of Nordic parliamentarians. Since parliaments were once developed to link the local with the national, international involvement on the part of elected representatives has always been problematic. Brothén asks which factors account for the international contacts of representatives. He suggests that, for one thing, truly personal factors are important for how representatives relate to the world outside their home constituencies.

Chapter 14, by Tapio Raunio and Matti Wiberg, focuses on the organization of parliaments as they attempt to cope with the internationalization of politics. The authors focus on how parliaments handle relations with that institution which, more than any other, has shaped European politics during recent decades—the European Union. Their analysis draws upon the varying experiences of the Nordic countries vis-à-vis the EU (Denmark is a long-time member, Finland and Sweden have recently joined, Norway voted down the option of joining in a recent referendum, and Iceland has never really considered membership). How have established parliaments dealt with the shock of having to surrender portions of their sovereignty to an external power like the European Union? Have different parliaments followed different strategies of adaptation?

In this part, moreover, we also discuss the future—its issues and its risks. The internationalized world order is generally considered to be a rather new development; by analyzing differing views on the years to come, we can learn both about what may happen in the future and about how things stand today. In chapter 15, Hanne Marthe Narud and Henry Valen analyze the extent to which representatives and voters hold similar views on future risks for representative democracies. In chapter 16, Torben K. Jensen reconstructs—with the help of cultural theory—the ideologies underlying representatives' views on future developments.

In chapter 17, finally, the editors sum up the findings and discuss the merits of the institutional perspective in explaining the workings of Nordic parliaments. We comb the intermediate chapters for indications of a Nordic *parliamentary model*—one diverging from both Congress and Westminster. What is the common denominator of Nordic parliaments? In what way are the Nordic parliaments unique as compared with one another? Furthermore, what can we learn from the Nordic experience regarding the explanatory potential of institutional factors like electoral systems and parliamentary size?

NOTES

1. This is Bernhard Manin's argument in his thought-provoking book *The Principles of Representative Government* (1997).

2. The terms "parliament" and "legislature" will be used interchangably. "Parliament" is the general term in a West European context (although it should not be taken to denote a parliamentary system); "legislature" is the common U.S. term.

3. For documentation of this tendency, see Sigelman and Gadbois (1983); Bollen et al. (1993). For a general discussion, see Ragin et al. (1996).

4. Loewenberg et al. (1985).

5. Of course, Finland, with its semi-presidential system, may be classified as an exception to the rule. Iceland, for its part, has a president also, but one without significant powers. For a further discussion, see chapter 2 below.

6. In particular, see chapters 2 and 17.

7. The institutional setup of the five Nordic parliamentary democracies is discussed in some detail in chapter 2 below.

8. Given that we are not comparing democratic parliaments to authoritarian parliaments, that is.

9. This analytical framework may be compared to one previously suggested by Loewenberg and Patterson (1979), which concentrates on three basic functions

performed by legislatures: "linkage," "recruitment of legislative and executive leaders," and "conflict management." Our perspective differs from theirs in that, among other things, we are interested in the workings of democratic parliaments. Most authoritarian regimes pride themselves on having some form of parliamentary institution, but we have no particular interest in understanding legislatures in general.

10. We do not wish to imply that this is the first comparative study of Nordic parliaments and parliamentarians. For some recent English-language books, see Arter (1984); Damgaard (1992a); and Wiberg (1994a).

11. Further details on each study are given in appendix 1.

2

Five Most Similar Systems?

*Knut Heidar with Erik Damgaard, Peter Esaiasson,
Ólafur Th. Hardarson, and Tapio Raunio*

The five Nordic countries—and in particular the three Scandinavian ones (Denmark, Norway, and Sweden)—are often grouped together in the comparative literature. They are labeled "working multiparty systems" (Rustow 1956) or "consensual democracies" (Elder et al. 1988), and they are considered a natural grouping in analyses of "Nordic democracy" (Koch and Ross 1949; Allardt 1981) and of common "nordicness" (Graubard 1986). It is little wonder, then, that they are often considered a suitable setting for the comparative analysis of parliaments. "At the national level," Damgaard writes, "a 'comparable-case' strategy . . . or a 'most similar systems' design . . . could hardly find better research conditions" (Damgaard 1992b:11; cf. Arter 1984).

However, whether phenomena or countries are to be placed in the same category or in different ones is a relative matter. If we use concepts at a low level of abstraction, and deploy measuring instruments that are fine and precise, we are likely to discover differences. If, on the other hand, our concepts are abstract and our methods of measurement rough, we will probably encounter similarities.

As mentioned in chapter 1, Stein Rokkan mainly noted the differences. This researcher—the comparativist par excellence in Nordic social science—placed the five Nordic countries in four different spaces in his "conceptual map" of state-building in western Europe (Rokkan 1975; Rokkan 1981; Rokkan and Urwin 1983). The two old nation-states of Denmark and Sweden were similar, in his view, in that both were strong empire states; they differed, however, in their distance from the city network and in their seaward versus landward attributes. As for the new states of Norway (independent in 1905), Iceland (1944), and Finland (1917), these fell into two different categories, inasmuch as the first two were seaward peripheries, while Finland was a landward buffer. All five countries were distinctively northern European in their cultural heritage, however, and all had a Protestant state church.

Comparative analysis requires that the causally relevant variables be identified. We need to know the relevant similarities and differences between the countries compared. In the language of comparative methodology, we must know which variables we control and which we do not. Only then will we be able to leave the inconsequential variables—those not affecting the parliamentary phenomena under examination—out of the study. The problem in practice, of course, is that we do not know which variables are the relevant ones (especially not in advance). The status of theory in the social sciences is such that our choices must be based, to a large extent, on an informed guess.

In general, variables of three types are singled out for closer causal analysis in comparative political studies: institutional variables, political variables, and sociocultural variables. In the following, we shall concentrate on institutional and political variables. This should not be taken to mean that differences in political culture do not exist or that such differences cannot be adduced in subsequent chapters to explain differences in parliamentary practice. We do expect, however, that political and institutional structures will be potentially more rewarding in an analytical sense, because the differences between the Nordic countries are more clearly identifiable within these categories of explanation.

MAPPING INSTITUTIONAL AND POLITICAL VARIATION: FIVE QUESTIONS AND TWO COMPARISONS

Damgaard (1994) has argued that the Nordic parliaments are basically party-directed, and that they contain important committees within which policy specialists operate—often with an eye to the interests in society with which they are sympathetic or aligned. Although parties are the driving force in parliament, committees structure the policy activities of members of parliament. Moreover, Nordic parliaments are more consensual than confrontational. In a recent comparison of the Danish Folketing with the Swedish Riksdag, Ingvar Mattson (1996a) speaks of "bargaining democracies and parliaments." The experience of the three Scandinavian countries with minority governments in recent decades strengthens this point. We also find extensive political bargaining between parties in Finland and Iceland, where majority coalitions have governed. Of course, Nordic parliaments also exhibit confrontation and intense competition between parties.

Confrontational styles arise mainly in connection with interparty conflicts during the process of government formation, and they usually turn on issues related to the competition for government office. Perhaps we could speak of a "nested game" in which the main objective is to capture government office, while the secondary aim is to pass some legislation from a position of parliamentary strength. The party system and the type of government are central factors for explaining how Nordic parliaments operate.

Mapping institutional and political variation requires a more detailed grid. Elements from Weaver and Rockman's "three-tier" approach to the comparative assessment of institutional effects may serve our purpose here. In their introduction to *Do Institutions Matter?* they focus on institutional differences influencing the process of decision-making and the political capabilities of political systems (Weaver and Rockman 1993:8–9). Their first tier of explanation deals with the difference between presidential and parliamentary systems. This difference, they argue, has consequences for party discipline, executive recruitment, cabinet centralization, and accountability. Their second tier deals basically with differences in governmental type (majority vs. minority, single-party vs. coalition, etc.). Such differences are thought to carry consequences for cohesion, stability, the autonomy of government elites, and the influence of interest groups. Third-tier factors combine lower-level organizational attributes of parliaments (bicameralism, voting rules) with political factors (past policy choices, political conditions, and goals) and other political institutions (judicial review, federalism, bureaucracy).

The Weaver and Rockman taxonomy is clearly conceived for comparing other countries with the United States. Its purpose is to reveal how other systems look as compared to the American standard. In addition, some of the (in our judgment) most significant factors highlighted by the two authors are what we would label political, not institutional factors (although that obviously depends on how we define "institution"—see chapters 1 and 17). When turning the tables and asking how the rest of the world looks as seen from a Nordic standpoint, and when investigating intra-Nordic differences, we need to reformulate their approach.

On the basis of Weaver and Rockman's analytical scheme, we would pose the following five questions for Nordic comparisons (both internally and externally):

1. What are the main political cleavages, and what characterizes the party systems? (Third tier: political factors)
2. What is the constitutional context in terms of the separation of powers and parliamentary-executive relations? (First tier)
3. How should we characterize the type of government? (Second tier)
4. What are the voting rules for deciding the composition of parliament? (Third tier: organizational attributes/institutions)
5. How are the Nordic parliaments organized internally? (Third tier: Organizational attributes)

Our aim in this chapter is to highlight the similarities and differences between the Nordic parliamentary systems and thereby to provide a background for subsequent chapters. We begin our presentation with a brief look at the general political history of the Nordic countries and at the growth of their party systems in particular (first question). We then take up the second and third questions: to wit, we sketch major events in the rise of the Nordic representative democracies, and we look at the parliament-executive story in particular. Our focus then shifts to the current situation (and the fourth question), starting with the voting rules/electoral system and the nominating process. A discussion of question 5 then follows: we examine the constitutional structure and internal organization of the five parliaments, including their different ways of handling foreign affairs (particularly relations with the European Union). In conclusion, finally, we consider similarities and differences in the overall institutional and political setup of the different Nordic parliaments and we discuss how Nordic arrangements compare with the two dominant representative models: the United Kingdom parliament at Westminster (the House of Commons) and the United States Congress (the House of Representatives).

In other words, answering the five questions will give us a basis for two comparisons: first, between the Nordic parliaments themselves; and second, between the Nordic parliaments on the one hand and Congress and Westminster on the other.

NATIONAL LEGACIES AND THE RISE OF PARTY SYSTEMS

Institutions grow in a symbiotic relationship with national history. Sweden entered "the age of revolutions" and mass politics with consolidated borders and a basically homogeneous population. Finland came under Russia in 1809 after six centuries of Swedish rule. Norway was forced into a union under the Swedish king in 1814, but won home rule in the post-Napoleonic turmoil. Denmark—although a consolidated nation-state early on—had to fight Prussia later in the nineteenth century before settling its southern borders through a referendum in 1920.

The Swedish constitution of 1809 marked the end of absolutism. The new parliament—the Riksdag—contained four chambers, one for each of the estates; in 1866 this was reduced to two. Politics in the late nineteenth century was dominated by the struggle between conservatives and liberals. The conservative elite of aristocrats, landed gentry, and top civil servants fought free trade, universal suffrage, and democratization, policies that were advanced by the urban bourgeoisie, the peasants, and the "popular movements" based in teetotaler and lay-church causes.

Industrialization came relatively late to Sweden, but working-class organizations and politics moved to the fore of the public agenda in the first third of the twentieth century. Universal suffrage was established in 1921, general male suffrage in 1909. Conservative and liberal groups organized parties just after the turn of the century, and the party system was shaped between 1890 and 1920.

In 1919, the Social Democrats became the largest party in the Riksdag, and between 1932 and 1991 the party never received less than 40 percent of the vote (see appendix 2 for the share of votes and seats by party). The Swedish Communist Party—from 1990 the Left Party—was created in 1921. The last party in the old five-party system—the Farmers' Party, later renamed the Center Party—was organized after a merger in 1921. No new party entered parliament during the postwar period until the Christian Democrats won a seat in 1985. The Greens entered parliament three years later, and the New Democracy Party (a right-wing populist grouping) was rather abruptly created before the election of 1991, only to disappear from parliament in the 1994 election.

Denmark was closer than Sweden to the old European trade routes and so developed strong cities financed by trade capitalism. Absolutist rule was based on an alliance with the urban bourgeoisie, while agriculture was dominated by the landed gentry (whereas in Sweden and Norway a free peasantry prevailed). The old regime had to give way following the Europe-wide revolutionary springtime of 1848, and the monarch was forced to accept a constitution reducing his power. A two-chamber parliament was created; the lowest chamber was elected by all men over thirty. Universal suffrage came in 1915.

Three waves of mobilization left their mark on Denmark's party system. The bourgeoisie, the farmers, and the workers all got a party of their own, so to speak, during the latter part of the nineteenth century. From the 1870s on, the liberal Left Party fought for parliamentarism, while the conservative party defended traditional elites. The Social Democrats made their electoral breakthrough just after the turn of the century, but their strength never equaled that of their sister parties in Sweden and Norway. The Left Party split into a rural and a more urban branch (the Radical Left). These four parties dominated Danish politics until the dramatic election of 1973, when the number of parliamentary parties doubled from five to ten. Prior to 1973, the party system came close to the five-party model, with a left socialist, a social democratic, a liberal, a farmers', and a conservative party. The left/right cleavage was dominant in Danish politics, although it was supplemented by an urban-rural conflict. More recently, conflict over foreign policy and the European Union has emerged as an important cleavage.

Norway was subject to Danish absolutist rule until 1814. A subsequent union with Sweden lasted till 1905. This was basically a monarchical union with a common foreign policy. Toward the latter part of the nineteenth century, the union became a potent source of political mobilization. Norway's nation-building process started as a reaction against the traditional Danish domination in matters of language, but it turned into a reaction against the influence of urban secular trends and finally ended up focusing on Swedish political control in foreign affairs. The country had a large free peasantry, but it was dominated economically by the trading cities of its seaboard. It was also the first Nordic country with a broad-based electoral system: in 1814, approximately 45 percent of all male citizens above the age of twenty-five got the vote (Kuhnle 1972). Universal suffrage, however, had to wait till 1913.

Organized parties entered Norwegian politics in the 1880s, with the liberal Left Party, representing rural movements and urban antiestablishment sectors, facing off against the conservative Right Party. The Norwegian Labor Party had to await the removal of the "national question" in 1905 before achieving electoral success. A five-party configuration appeared in the early 1920s, after the split in the labor movement had created the Communist Party and the old Left Party had produced an agrarian offspring. The Norwegian party system was later supplemented by a Christian People's Party (1933), and in 1973 the Danish-inspired right-wing populist Progress Party was added to the list.

A mixture of cleavages supplemented the left/right political dimension; in particular, the standoff between center and periphery—the latter with its "countercultures" based on language, teetotalism, and lay Christianity—contributed to the complex tapestry of Norwegian party politics.

The Finns have the most turbulent and violent political past among the Nordic peoples. The country was made a grand duchy by the tsar in 1809; it declared independence after the communists seized power in Russia in 1917. This was followed by an internal uprising, and a bloody civil war ensured between Reds and Whites. Harsh repression followed upon the victory of the Whites. The Communist Party was prohibited; even so, communist-controlled organizations provoked the formation of the (short-lived) extreme-right Lapua movement around 1930.

In the nineteenth century, the Russian authorities had forbidden popular movements to organize political parties; after independence, the old relationship to the Soviet Union continued to affect Finnish politics in general and party politics in particular. In cultural terms, Finland was the "outpost" of the Protestant West against the Orthodox East (Lindström and Karvonen 1987). Following the Russian Revolution of 1905, the Finns seized the opportunity to rewrite their constitution and became the first European country to establish universal suffrage (in 1906). At the same time, they changed their Swedish-style four-estate assembly into a one-chamber parliament, the Eduskunta.

Early political cleavages included the language issue—Swedish versus Finnish—and the question of how far to press national demands with the Russian authorities. The conservative party (now the National Coalition) originated with the more cautious "old Finn" movement. But, by and large, the strongest party on the center-right in the post-1945 era has been the agrarian Center Party. The party kept this position in spite of rural competition from the populist Rural Party from 1970.

The third large party, the Social Democrats, was organized around the turn of the century, and although weaker than its Swedish and Norwegian counterparts, it has been the largest party in parliament most of the time since 1945. The Communist Party (now the Left-Wing Alliance) was legalized after the war; up to the breakdown of the Soviet Union, it was among the most successful communist parties in western Europe.

The fourth of the original Finnish parties, the Swedish People's Party, is a typical ethnic party based on the Swedish-speaking population of the coastline. In the 1970s the Finns got their Christian Party, and after Chernobyl in 1986 a viable green party (the Green League) emerged as well; it has been one of the five parties in the "rainbow" government since 1995.

For centuries, the people of Iceland kept a strong sense of national identity, notwithstanding their political subordination to Denmark. The country was a "dependency" under Denmark until 1918. It was then in union with the latter country until 1944, at which point it declared its independence. The Danish written language made no inroads, nor was political mobilization nurtured by internal cultural cleavages as in Norway. Religious differences were neither significant nor politicized. The country obtained home rule in 1904, and Icelanders enjoyed *de facto* control over domestic affairs.

Universal suffrage came in 1915. The first political parties were organized at the turn of the century on the basis of the demand for independence; between 1916 and 1930 new parties started emerging out of the developing social tensions. A four-party system with conservative, agrarian, social democratic, and left socialist parties had developed by 1950, and was bolstered by regional differences and debates over foreign policy.

The Independence Party is the conservative party, and it is usually the largest party in electoral terms. It blends conservative and liberal elements with appeals to national unity over class interests. The Progress Party is an agrarian and rural-based party, although traditionally it has been both stronger and broader—in terms of its social profile—than the agrarian center parties of the other Nordic countries (excepting Finland). Since the left forces are split, the Social Democratic Party is fairly weak. The last of the traditional major parties is the People's Alliance, a party with left socialist tendencies and organizational roots in the old communist party. It has generally been the largest party on the left.

The 1980s saw a new arrival to the party system in the shape of the Women's Alliance. Thus, while the four old parties dominated the Althingi until 1971, the presence of five or six parties has been the more common pattern since then.

As viewed from the late twentieth century, the major point of divergence among the Nordic countries in terms of political history would appear to be the lateness of the state-building process in Norway, Finland, and Iceland. All three became fully independent only in this century. The Finns alone experienced a violent political period with a civil war.

The similarities in the party system are more striking than the differences, and the notion of a Scandinavian five-party system (Berglund and Lindström 1978) captures the essential story: to the left a strong social democratic party with a small communist or left socialist party, facing a conservative party joined by liberal and agrarian parties in the center. But there are also important differences among the Nordic countries. The relative strength of the parties varies, certain parties are influential only in certain countries (recall the Norwegian Christians), and the emergence of new parties in the 1970s and 1980s has complicated the picture further. The strongest social democrats are found in Sweden and Norway, the strongest agrarian parties in Finland, Denmark, and Iceland. In recent decades, the five-party character of the system has been softened by the emergence of new parties: the populist right in Denmark, Norway, and (briefly) Sweden, the greens in Finland and Sweden, and the Women's Alliance in Iceland.

PARLIAMENTS AND PARLIAMENTARY DEMOCRACY

In comparative terms, the Nordic countries have a long tradition of parliamentary democracy. They also have, as we shall see, a tradition of minority governments and close interparty cooperation. The breakthrough for parliamentarism—meaning an arrangement whereby the government of the day must be accepted as such (negatively or positively) by a majority in parliament—came in 1884 in Norway, 1901 in Denmark, 1904 in Iceland, and 1917 in Sweden and Finland.

The Norwegian constitution of 1814 was based on Montesquieu's teachings and American practice, and among its clauses was the separation of powers. The personal powers of the king disappeared gradually during the first half of the nineteenth century, and the semi-independence of the executive came under increasing attack from the 1860s onward. In 1884, the Storting forced the government to accept parliamentary confidence as the basis for executive authority. This upheaval was directed by the liberal party.

The new parliamentary system was a "party democracy" in which the cement of party ideology and organization tied the two branches of government together. In parliamentary terms, this led to one-party governments during the classic era of two-party politics up to 1905, coalition governments in the multiparty era from 1905 to 1935, and once again to one-party governments in the years of social-democratic dominance (1935–65).

Since 1965, Norwegian governments have alternated between one-party Labor minority governments and coalition governments based on "nonsocialist" (or "bourgeois") parties. However, no viable alternative to a minority Labor government existed between 1990—when the last nonsocialist coalition government disintegrated over EU policy—and 1997. The Labor government in office during those years based its power on shifting parliamentary alliances. The election of 1997 brought a minority coalition of middle parties to power.

Norwegian governments do not need a "positive" vote of confidence to survive, but they cannot survive a vote of no confidence. Well into the 1970s, the "accepted truth" in the political science literature was that the

Storting had lost power, while the executive branch, including the central state bureaucracy and the corporate power channels, had gained. The minority position of governments from 1971 onward, however, has forced ministers to listen more carefully to signals sent from parliament (Olsen 1983). Ministers have had to be more careful in handling their parliamentary committee if they wish to avoid trouble. This is a long way from the Labor parliamentarism of the 1950s, when no "situation" arose unless the parliamentary Labor Party group allowed it to.

The electoral period is constitutionally set at four years, and the government cannot dissolve parliament at will.

In Denmark, the upper house was abolished in 1953 when a new constitution was adopted. This constitution also codified some of the established parliamentary practices. Parliamentarism was established in 1901 after a prolonged confrontation between the lower chamber (the Folketing) and the king, who was allied with the upper chamber (the Landsting). The confrontation ended in a landslide victory for the Liberal Reform Party, which forced the king to appoint a government with a majority in the Folketing.

After 1906, no single party has ever commanded a majority in the Folketing. The period between 1913 and 1945 was distinguished by a "two-bloc parliamentary system" (Rasmussen 1972:244). The blocs followed the left-right dimension. They formed either coalition governments or minority governments relying on supporting parties in parliament. During the early postwar years, minority governments without permanent supporting parties were in power.

Later—from 1953 to 1964—the Danes more or less returned to the old two-bloc system. The multiplication of parties after the crucial 1973 election produced a system of minority governments formed either by the Social Democrats or by nonsocialist coalitions. A fairly stable "four-leaf" government stayed in power from 1982 to 1988, but it added a legacy of alternative majorities to Danish parliamentarism. This meant that the government decided to execute policies it opposed, most visibly so in the field of foreign affairs and defense. These policies were opposed by most of the parties in the coalition government, but they had a majority of the Folketing behind them. The government accepted numerous defeats without resigning or calling a new election: "Often the government was actually in opposition and the opposition was actually in government" (Damgaard 1992c:35).

What distinguishes Danish parliamentarism is the close cooperation of the Folketing parties and the importance of comprehensive parliamentary compromises. At the same time, the system has had a rather plastic two-bloc character, with the two main adversaries—the Social Democrats and the Liberals—forming the core of each bloc (disregarding a rather atypical coalition between the two parties from 1978 to 1979).

Despite their political fluidity, Danish governments have not been especially unstable. And although Denmark had a short-lived majority government from 1993 to 1994, the Folketing is clearly a strong parliament. Indeed, it has arguably increased its relative strength in recent decades (Damgaard 1992c:48).

The Icelandic Althingi was re-established in 1845, as a consultative assembly to the Danish king. It served an important function as a forum for Icelandic politicians and as a platform for nationalist demands. The Althingi was divided in 1874 into two chambers, but since 1991 it has been unicameral.

Icelandic home rule and parliamentarism were both established in 1904, as a by-product of the newly won parliamentarism in Denmark. The first cabinet was created in 1917, when the number of ministers was increased from one to three. From 1917 to 1932, one-party and minority governments were the most common. No single party has had a working majority in the Althingi since 1927, and majority coalitions have been the rule since 1932.

Coalition governments of three types have predominated during this period: right-wing governments, left-wing governments, and conservative–social democratic governments. Although this last is an unusual combination by Scandinavian standards, the first right-left coalition of this kind formed the longest-lived government in Icelandic history (1959–71). The same coalition ruled the country from 1991 to 1995.

The Icelandic coalition system is very open. The four old parties have all worked with each other, except that one combination has been missing: the left socialists and the conservatives have never, formally speaking, served together in a coalition. Ideological considerations seem to have had less impact on government formation in Iceland than in the Scandinavian countries, and there are no party blocs. This is probably related to the patronage system and the pragmatic nature of the parties (Kristinsson 1996).

Members of the Althingi serve a four-year term, but it can be dissolved by the president acting on the advice of the prime minister. In practice, the Althingi is dissolved only with the approval of all coalition partners in the cabinet. Since 1944, terms have lasted three and a half years on average (Hardarson 1997:1).

The Althingi is considered a rather strong and party-oriented parliament, inasmuch as most policy issues are resolved within the parliamentary parties, as are major decisions concerning the formation of coalition governments. According to Nordal and Kristinsson, "when parties are in government, the parliamentary parties are restrained by the need to maintain cohesion within the government. Even so, parliamentarians retain substantial power vis-à-vis the team of Ministers in their own parties. Government bills are presented to the parliamentary parties in government before being presented to the assembly" (Nordal and Kristinsson 1996:125–26).

The tradition of the Swedish Riksdag stretches back to the Middle Ages, when it emerged as a rather unusual parliament based on representation of four estates: the peasants, the clergy, the burghers, and the nobility. The two chambers introduced in 1866 were reduced to one in 1970 (von Sydow 1991).

After parliamentarism was established in 1917, a period of unstable minority governments followed, but in 1932 a long period of social democratic dominance began. The Social Democrats stayed in power either in coalition with the Agrarians (1936–39, 1951–57) or as strong minority governments relying on the parliamentary support of the Agrarians or the Communists (the Center Party changed its name to the Agrarian Party in late 1957).

After the one-chamber reform in 1970, confrontations between the two blocs—socialists and nonsocialists—got sharper (Sannerstedt and Sjölin 1992). The 1976 election resulted in a nonsocialist (coalition) government for the first time in forty-four years. Since then, government power has by and large alternated between minority social democratic governments and nonsocialist majority coalitions.

In spite of the confrontations between the two blocs, there has been room all the while for interbloc cooperation when considered necessary (Sannerstedt 1992; Stenelo and Jerneck 1996; Sjölin 1993; Mattson 1996b). And since 1995, we have again witnessed a tendency to open up the two-bloc structure, in that the Social Democrats have engaged in selective parliamentary cooperation with the agrarian Center Party.

For a long time, the standard view had it that parliament was more or less powerless in relation to the government. But all that changed in the 1970s. A succession of minority governments were mainly what persuaded observers that the Riksdag had increased its power (Isberg 1982; Arter 1984; Sjölin 1991).

Up to 1994 the parliamentary term was three years; it has now been changed to four. The prime minister has the option of calling an election earlier, but the resulting parliament lasts only for the remainder of the original period; this provision has only been used once in modern times (in 1958).

The system is one of negative parliamentarism, meaning that the government and individual ministers retain their position so long as an absolute majority of all MPs do not vote against them. So far this has not happened, although individual ministers have left knowing that they would otherwise have faced a vote of no confidence (Arter 1984; Olson and Hagevi 1997).

In Finland, the change from the old four-estate assembly to the current unicameral Eduskunta occurred in 1906, in the wake of the unsuccessful revolution in Russia and the general strike in Finland. The move was radical: universal suffrage was also introduced. Finland was also the first European country to give women the vote.

The democratization of the country was linked to the fall of the tsarist empire. Following the February Revolution in Russia, the Eduskunta seized the opportunity and introduced radical changes. In the summer of 1917, the Constitutional Committee approved a regulation on parliamentary government which was then consolidated in the 1919 Constitution Act. This stated that members of the cabinet must enjoy the confidence of parliament.

The Finnish model is not one of full parliamentary democracy, since the president is given wide-ranging powers in the constitution, especially in the field of foreign policy. In its report from 1917, the constitutional drafting commission stated that the executive branch should have a fairly independent position and that this freedom of action should be based on the authority and relative independence of the president.

The president may dissolve parliament (following an initiative of the prime minister). The president also appoints the cabinet and conducts Finnish foreign policy (Anckar 1992). Governments coming into office do not need an investiture in the Eduskunta, but they cannot survive a vote of no confidence.

The first decades after independence were marked by minority governments. Seven out of the first nine governments were minority cabinets. Since the Second World War, Finland has had forty-five governments altogether, and there has been a gradual shift toward majority governments.

Governments after the 1950s have tended to be more stable and to enjoy broader parliamentary support, partly as a result of a rule (dropped in 1991) giving one-third of MPs the right to postpone the making of new laws in the Eduskunta. Since the election of 1979, governments have usually ruled for the entire parliamentary term.

For most of the post-1945 period, Finland has been dominated by center or center-left coalitions formed around the Agrarian League and its successor, the Center Party. The other main party of government has been

Table 2.1
Type of Government and Parliamentary Basis, 1945–70 and 1971–96 (%)

| | Parliamentary Basis | | | |
| | Majority | | Minority | |
Type of Government	1945–70	1971–96	1945–70	1971–96
Single party government				
Denmark	0	0	46	38
Finland	0	0	22	2
Iceland	0	0	7	1
Norway	63	0	16	80
Sweden	20	0	56	69
Coalition				
Denmark	26	9	28	53
Finland	71	95	7	3
Iceland	93	95	0	4
Norway	21	10	0	10
Sweden	24	14	0	17

Sources: European Journal of Political Research (1991–95); *Electoral Studies* (1994–96); Heidar and Berntzen (1995); Strøm (1990).

Notes: Specified time periods and total number of months: Denmark: Nov. 1945 to Dec. 1970 = 298, Jan. 1971 to Dec. 1996 = 310 (does not sum to 312 months owing to rounding errors); Finland: March 1946 to Dec. 1970 = 255, Jan. 1971 to Dec. 1996 = 298 (in the first period, Finland had 21 months with nonpartisan governments; in the second period, 10 months with nonpartisan governments—these are not included); Iceland: Feb. 1947 to Dec. 1970 = 285 (this low percentage basis due to Iceland's being without any government for several months [Strøm 1990]), Jan. 1971 to Dec. 1996 = 302 (does not sum to 312 months owing to rounding errors); Norway: Nov. 1945 to Dec. 1970 = 301, Jan. 1971 to Dec. 1996 = 312; Sweden: July 1945 to Dec. 1970 = 304, Jan. 1971 to Dec. 1996 = 310 (does not sum to 312 months owing to rounding errors).

the Social Democrats. Finnish governments have usually brought parties together across the left/right dimension, with bourgeois parties aligning with socialist parties.

The opposition in the Eduskunta has been weak for most of the post-war period. Consisting primarily of the poles of the left/right spectrum, it has suffered from a lack of coherence. The situation changed during the 1980s and 1990s, however, and the conservative National Coalition has been included in the latest cabinets. It had been in opposition from 1966 to 1987 (Anckar 1992; Wiberg 1994b).

In terms of parliamentary-executive relations, we see from table 2.1 that minority governments have predominated over the last quarter-century in the three Scandinavian countries, while majority coalitions have prevailed in Finland and Iceland. Finland has been ruled, by and large, by oversized majority coalitions, and Iceland by majority coalitions, while the Scandinavian countries have seen alternation in the 1980s and 1990s between social democratic minority governments and center-right coalitions. Denmark has also had center-left coalitions (led by the Social Democrats) during the 1990s.

ELECTING MPS

Duverger (1951/1954) argued that party systems are strongly affected by electoral systems. This electoral influence is not limited to the party system. The incentive structure within parliaments, and the operation of parliaments in general, are affected by electoral rules. Duverger's main distinction lay between majority and proportional systems. All Nordic countries use a version of proportional representation when electing their parliaments. The three Scandinavian countries use the Saint-Laguë method, while Finland and (in a certain measure) Iceland employ the d'Hondt method. The voters' ability to influence the choice of persons also varies, Finland being the exceptional case here.

The system used for parliamentary elections in Finland has remained remarkably stable since the first democratic elections in 1907. While several attempts have been made to change it, only some administrative rules have been revised.

The two hundred members of the Eduskunta are elected for a four-year term. The country is divided into fourteen multimember districts and one single-member constituency (the autonomous province of Åland). A single representative is thus chosen from Åland, while the remaining 199 seats are allocated proportionally to the fourteen multimember districts according to their population size.

Each district is a separate sub-unit in the electoral process. The parties, electoral alliances, and other groups present their lists of candidates in each district. The voters then choose between individual candidates, and the total votes for the parties' candidates are added and seats allocated to the parties according to the d'Hondt formula. Within a party, the candidates with the most personal votes get the seats.

In 1969, when the Party Law and the new Law on Parliamentary Elections came into effect, the disparity between the parties' ways of selecting candidates was radically reduced. According to the Law on Parliamentary Elections, candidates are to be selected in a secret and universal ballot from among party members living in the constituency. Primary elections are not compulsory if the number of nominated candidates does not exceed the number that the parties have the right to nominate in each constituency

(Sundberg and Gylling 1992). In practice, local party branches propose candidates while the final composition of the list is decided at a constituency party meeting (Helander 1997; Sundberg 1995, 1996; Sundberg and Gylling 1992).

Until 1982, the president was elected by an electoral college of three hundred persons. A direct voting system was employed for the first time in the 1994 elections. Voters vote directly for one candidate, and there can be two rounds of voting. If a candidate receives more than 50 percent of the votes in the first round, he or she is elected. If this does not occur, the two candidates with the highest number of votes proceed to the second round, which takes place three weeks later (Kuusela 1995; Nurmi 1990).

The sixty-three MPs in the Icelandic Althingi are elected from eight multimember districts. Fifty seats are allocated to party lists according to constituency results, using the "largest-remainder" formula. The remaining thirteen seats are then assigned, in accordance with the national result, to parties with at least one seat. (The calculation in this case is done according to the d'Hondt formula.)

A complex system for allocating these additional seats to different party-district lists is used in order to combine proportionality at the national level with the maintenance of constituency connections on the part of MPs. However, a severe regional disproportionality remains in regard to the different constituencies, as indicated by the fact that a majority of the Althingi's members are elected from six constituencies that together contain only a third of the country's voters (Hardarson 1997).

Although voters may change the order of candidates on the party lists, such changes have no impact in practice. Since 1970, primaries have become the most important method in all of the major parties for deciding the composition of candidate lists. The formal rules have varied. Only party members have been allowed to vote in the left socialist primaries (although one can join the party at the polling station), while the conservatives, the agrarians, and the Social Democrats have in practice had open elections. In some areas, it is customary to vote in several primaries in order to support local candidates! Finally, even if the results of the primaries must be confirmed by the party organization, in practice the selection of party candidates is not in the hands of the party leadership. This fact may serve to undermine the centrality of the party group in the Althingi.

In Denmark, the modified Saint-Laguë method is used to allocate 175 Folketing seats to parties within the seventeen multimember constituencies. These constituencies have two to fifteen regular seats (on average, eight). It is the national allocation quota, however, that assures a truly proportional representation of parties.[1] This system applies Hare's quota in combination with the largest-remainder method. Forty adjustment seats are used to ensure that the parties receive a share of the seats corresponding as closely as possible to their share of the national vote. Only 135 of the 175 seats (excluding the four seats in Greenland and the Faroe Islands) are allocated as regular seats within the seventeen constituencies (Elklit 1993).

Danish voters must cast their one vote either for a party or for a preferred candidate within a party. This means that voters have influence on the election of individual MPs, although the strength of the effect depends on the type of candidate list presented by the parties (see Petersson 1994: 53–58).

A study of the nomination procedures of the Danish parties concludes that individual party members play an important and decisive role in the candidate selection process (Bille 1993). This influence may be exercised through general meetings at local, constituency, or regional levels and in some parties through membership ballots.

The Swedish electoral system is strictly proportional. The distribution of seats mirrors the voters' choice of party lists. Provided a party receives more than 4 percent of the national vote, it takes part in the distribution of the thirty-nine adjustment seats. The 310 fixed district seats are first allocated in twenty-nine districts according to a modified Saint-Laguë formula, then the thirty-nine additional seats are distributed to particular parties in particular constituencies in order to achieve the highest possible degree of national proportionality.

The system of adjustment seats was introduced in 1970 in order to counter the large-party bias of the previous electoral system (Särlvik 1983; von Sydow 1991). The largest constituency (Stockholm) has thirty-six seats, the smallest (Gotland) has two; the average is twelve.

All representatives are selected from constituency lists. The parties' nomination of candidates is for the most part decentralized, and the party leadership in the constituencies controls the process. A new system was introduced at the 1998 election which gave the voters a larger say in the selection of candidates. This new system is basically the same as the candidate-preference voting system used in Denmark.

The electoral system in Norway is close to the Swedish one. The seats have been allocated since 1953 in accordance with the Saint-Laguë method, with 1.4 as the first divisor. Nineteen constituencies, each containing from four to seventeen seats, account for 157 of the 165 seats. The eight remaining seats are used to change the distribution of seats in the Storting in the direction of maximal proportionality with the national result.

The eight seats are given to candidates on the constituency lists of the parties coming closest to winning an additional seat. However, only parties with a minimum of 4 percent of the national vote may take part in this last selection.

The nomination of candidates in Norway is decentralized, and attempts on the part of the national party to influence constituency parties is considered improper and may easily backfire on the candidate in question.

The differences in electoral system are small among the Nordic countries. All are proportional represenation systems with multimember constituencies. In most cases, the peripheral districts are overrepresented in parliament (see chapter 5).

The effect of "personal" voting is stronger in Denmark, generally speaking, than in Norway and Sweden,[2] but weaker than in Finland, where the voters are asked to vote directly for persons. It is also much weaker in Denmark than in Iceland, where the major constituency parties hold primaries and the voters have a large say in the composition of constituency lists.

One major difference between the Nordic countries lies in the very different number of parliamentarians elected, ranging from sixty-three in Iceland to 349 in Sweden. (Of course, that still leaves the 0.26 million Icelanders the best represented—in terms of number of voters per MP!)

CONSTITUTIONAL POWER AND THE STRUCTURE OF PARLIAMENTS

The degree to which constitutional powers are specified in the Nordic constitutions varies a great deal. The Norwegian constitution does not give the Storting majority any right to kick out the government, but no one would seriously dispute its right to do exactly that. The postwar constitutions of Denmark and Sweden are both more explicit in regulating and shaping parliamentary power.

Still, the operation of parliaments depends on much more than constitutions and prescriptive law. It is also a question of ordinary laws, parliamentary standing orders, and traditions in a broad sense. Less tangible is the changing status and power of related institutions, organizations, and other actors. Their rise and fall obviously impinges on the role and position of parliaments; the ebb and flow of presidential power in Finland is a case in point.

The Finnish Eduskunta has several means by which to control the government. The various communiqués and reports from the government offer the plenary a chance to question and criticize government policy. Members can put forward interpellations, private initiatives, and oral and written questions. The steadily rising number of written questions shows that this channel has become an increasingly important tool for individual MPs.

Finnish governments have mostly resigned—other than in accordance with election results—on account of internal splits in the ruling coalition; only in four cases have they been forced to leave by a vote of no confidence. In eight cases, the cabinet has resigned after the Eduskunta acted contrary to its wishes (Wiberg 1994b; Anckar 1992).

The president plays a key role in appointing the cabinet. After consulting with the political parties, he nominates a negotiator. This person, who in practice is the forthcoming prime minister, is given the responsibility of conducting negotiations with the parties in order to form a cabinet. Provided an acceptable solution has been found, the president then appoints the government.

The incoming government does not face a formal vote of investiture; it does present its program in the Eduskunta. The Constitution Act states that an elected representative "shall be bound . . . to comply with the Constitution, and shall not be bound by any other regulations" (Parliament Act, section 11).

This principle of independence does not fit reality, however, for members rely heavily on their party group. In recent decades MPs' professionalism has grown, as reflected in their increasing activity (Wiberg 1994b).

The main function of the speaker is to preside over plenary meetings. Despite being a member of a party group, the speaker is expected to remain neutral in the Eduskunta's proceedings, and he/she does not have the right to vote.

The committees form the backbone of parliament; the plenary has a much less active role. Bills and other proposals introduced in parliament must be referred to a committee before a decision is taken. The final committee report contains a recommendation to the Eduskunta and a statement from the parties constituting the majority. This majority recommendation is in most cases accepted by the plenary.

Almost all MPs sit on one committee and are substitutes in another (excluding ministers). The distribution of committee places is based on the share of seats held by the different party groups. There were fourteen committees during the 1945–90 period, and fifteen later. Major changes have affected the role of the Grand Committee (which is currently the main body dealing with EU issues).

Committee work is highly specialized, with each committee given responsibility for a specific subject area by detailed provisions in the Parliament Act and the Procedures of Parliament (Wiberg and Mattila 1997).

The Eduskunta has been a highly fragmented legislature, and no single party has ever been in sole control (Wiberg and Raunio 1997). Parties are crucial actors inside the Eduskunta. They usually function as cohesive and highly disciplined units (Wiberg 1999; Sundberg 1994).

The Danish norms of government formation have actually developed gradually, over several decades (Damgaard 1992b). The present constitution, dating from 1953, stipulates that the unicameral Folketing ultimately decide on the formation and termination of governments, on the bills to be enacted, and on the budget (appropriations and taxes). It also states principles on the status of MPs. Customs and other regulations are important, too.

Formally speaking, the government may reject (veto) a bill passed by the Folketing, but that right is never used, since it would almost certainly be followed by a no-confidence motion. As far as executive-legislative relations are concerned, it is important to note that the prime minister is constitutionally empowered to dissolve parliament and to call elections at almost any time. Most Danish elections, in fact, are held before the end of the regular four-year term.

Although the basic structure, organization, and functions of the Folketing are specified in the constitution and the standing orders, such formal rules do not fully explain how the parliament actually works. In principle, MPs are independent individuals bound solely by their own conscience; in reality, they are primarily party representatives. Parties are not mentioned in the constitution, but the party groups are nevertheless the most important components of the parliamentary infrastructure.

Normally the party groups are highly disciplined collective actors with their own leadership and with their own system for the division and coordination of labor among individual group members. This means, for example, that the members of the Folketing's specialized permanent committees are basically party representatives, and as spokespersons for their party within a particular issue area, they may be quite influential within their party group. The same applies to the members of the Folketing presidium, although the chairman of the presidium (the speaker) has special powers according to the standing orders.

In the 1960s, state subsidies to the party groups were introduced, and in the 1980s secretarial assistance was provided for individual MPs. These and other resources for MPs and party groups were greatly expanded in the mid-1990s. Today the Folketing is in many ways a professionalized body.

Sweden's reformed constitution came into full effect as late as 1975. The parliamentary principles codify the procedure of negative parliamentarism, meaning that the prime minister or his ministers can carry on as long as they do not get a no-confidence majority against them (Bergman 1995). All bills are discussed and decided in parliament, but of course the government is central in preparing them.

In terms of the budgetary process, the Riksdag formerly made changes in rather detailed matters. Parliament's power to supervise the government in these areas has increased, however, during the 1994–98 period. This supervision takes place partly through the Constitutional Committee, partly through parliamentary questions from MPs (Mattson 1994).

There is also a parliamentary Audit Office (Wieslander 1994); nonetheless, overall, the control function of the Riksdag is considered weak (Rothstein et al. 1995).

Executive-parliamentary relations in Sweden are a mixture of cooperation and conflict, with a strong tradition of bargaining between the parties (Sannerstedt 1992; Stenelo and Jerneck 1996; Mattson 1996b). MPs are engaged in preparing government proposals for decision, proposing motions on an individual basis, and presenting questions to ministers. Motions are also a way of defending constituency causes; during the 1985–88 term, almost all MPs presented an individual motion (Esaiasson and Holmberg 1996). In practice, however, the most an MP can hope for in these cases is to gain support for his cause (Sjölin 1991).

The speaker has a party-political background, but exercises the office in a neutral way. The governing body of the Riksdag is the consensus-seeking Speaker's Conference. The political center of parliament as such is found in the sixteen committees, on which most MPs serve either as members or as alternates. The committees prepare the plenary votes, and in most cases the final Riksdag decision follows the proposal of the committee (Mattson and Strøm 1995). The governing party(ies) usually supplies the committee chair, while the opposition has the vice-chair (see Hagevi's chapter 10).

The parliamentary parties organize and direct the activity of their MPs, and the resources for administrative and professional assistance are channeled through party groups, not through individual MPs.

Norwegian governments do not need a positive vote of confidence to survive; they stay in power as long as a politically significant majority vote does not go against them in the Storting. Up to the mid-1970s, the accepted truth had been that parliament had lost power to the government, the bureaucracy, and the corporate channel. Since then, successive minority governments—with their concomitant political need for close cooperation with parliament—have changed all that.

On the formal level the Storting is a two-chamber assembly. For a law to be passed, it must be adopted by both chambers consecutively. In practice, though, this formal procedure does not matter, for the division in the Storting is merely an internal one, and the party composition is the same in both chambers.

Parliamentary affairs are coordinated by the Speaker's Conference, and the speaker is neutral in party-political terms. Most of the real political work of the assembly is done in the committees and the party groups. There are twelve standing committees, and all MPs are members of one (Hernes and Nergaard 1989). Financial support is given to party groups, not to individual MPs. The groups are highly disciplined, and they coordinate the political work of their members.

The Icelandic constitution (from 1944) is not very specific on the power of the major institutions.[3] But even if the constitution does not explicitly state that the government should resign if a no-confidence motion is carried in the Althingi, in practice parliamentarism has been observed since 1908–9.

The constitution gives the president the power to refuse to sign legislation, but this is not a viable option in practice either, although President Finnbogadóttir did consider so doing before she signed the law on membership in the European Economic Area in 1993. (Thousands of voters had signed a petition asking her to veto the bill. In a special statement, she declared that she was going to sign, that she did not want to alter the traditional, nonpolitical role of the president.)

On some counts, the constitution appears to give the president more power than he/she exercises in practice. In theory, MPs are bound only by their own convictions, yet parliamentary party groups are the most important units in the Althingi. Voting with one's party is clearly the norm, even though the examples of individual members' voting against their party are numerous.

Most bills passed are government bills (86 percent in the 1983–92 period), and they are scrutinized in the parliamentary groups of the governing parties before being presented to the assembly. On several occasions, bills stop at this stage or are changed on important points.

The speaker of the Althingi has the role of upholding the constitutional articles regarding the Althingi, as well as the law on parliamentary procedure.

The Althingi has twelve standing committees, and most members have to serve on more than one committee. Committee members can quite often influence individual decisions; for example, those concerning the construction of roads and harbors. MPs from a particular constituency usually decide what roads in their constituency should be surfaced each year. In many cases, they can influence both how much money is spent and (in minute detail) how the money is spent.

The party groups obtain rather large grants, and these are used mainly for the general operation of the parties, even though part of these grants is formally devoted to "specialist assistance to the parliamentary parties."

For the most part, the parliamentary groups have no specialist staff. Each group can employ one person, who may assist MPs on policy matters but usually spends most of his or her time on other things. Individual members have no assistants.

In theory, each committee has its own secretary, who can assist committee members in the gathering of material and the performance of similar tasks, but in fact there are only five committee secretaries, each assisting one to three committees.

All Nordic parliaments are without doubt "working parliaments," in that they are active in developing and formulating policies through internal procedures. The committees and the party groups are important workshops for the development of new policies (see chapters 8–10).

As far as the differences are concerned, Finnish parliamentarism diverges from the general Nordic pattern on account of its strong presidency. The Danes also deviate in view of their prime minister's prerogative to call a new election before the end of the four-year term.

Many additional small differences exist between the operations of the Nordic parliaments—some not noted in this overview are presented in table 2.2—but there are rather few eye-catching institutional differences.

PARLIAMENTS, FOREIGN POLICY, AND THE EU

The dynamism of the European Community since the adoption of the Single European Act in 1985 has no doubt been crucial in strengthening transnational and integrationist forces within western Europe. It has also triggered a debate about the "democratic deficit," that is, the limitations imposed on national democracy as decision-making increasingly takes place in Brussels. The intensity of this debate increased as the supranational aspects of the European Union and the future EU project became central in debates over the Maastricht Treaty.

The Nordic countries have opted for different ties to the EU (see chapter 14). Denmark has been a member since 1973. In 1972 Norway said no (for the first time) in a referendum. Sweden and Finland joined in 1995 after each had held a referendum the previous year. In 1994, Norwegian voters again rejected membership; Norway and Iceland settled for economic integration with the EU through the European Economic Area (EEA) agreement, which took effect in 1994. Do these different links to the EU affect parliamentary operations significantly?

The Danish Folketing has the most experience in coping with this new layer of decision-making. From the very beginning of Danish EC/EU membership (in 1973), the issue of parliamentary control has been on the political agenda. Danish (minority) governments were forced to accept restrictions on their behavior and policies in the EU.

Thus, the Market Relations Committee (now the European Affairs Committee) must give the government a mandate before a minister can commit the country in the Council of Ministers. If necessary, the government must return to the committee to receive a new mandate before commitments are made. In addition, a number of agreements have been reached among the parties in government and opposition on how to inform the European Affairs Committee (and to some extent other relevant committees of the Folketing) about initiatives and proposals from the European Commission (Arter 1995).

Comparatively speaking, the European Affairs Committee is very strong in terms of overall political control; it is a matter of debate as to whether it is capable of mastering the many technical details that are sometimes important. With a few exceptions, other committees have not so far displayed any overwhelming interest in monitoring EU affairs within their own jurisdictions.

In the Finnish Eduskunta, adjustment to EU membership (in 1995) began during the EEA phase in 1994. The preparation of EU matters is essentially based on the committee system, with the plenary in a secondary role. The Grand Committee is the main body responsible for dealing with EU issues, but the Foreign Affairs Committee handles so-called second-pillar issues (which require unanimous decisions within the EU).

The specialized standing committees are closely involved in policy formulation and play a larger role in EU politics in the Eduskunta than in the other Nordic legislatures. Foreign policy used to be the exclusive domain of the president. EU membership has changed the situation considerably. Recent amendments to the Constitution Act and the Parliament Act have extended the government's powers in the conduct of foreign policy, and this has simultaneously increased the powers of parliament (Raunio and Wiberg 1997; Wiberg and Raunio 1996).

When Sweden joined the EU, the Riksdag created a new EU council on the same basis as its ordinary standing committees. The government must consult this committee before attending EU meetings, but its advice is not formally binding. The integration of the ordinary standing committees in the process is difficult, owing to time constraints.

The Norwegian Storting did form a committee for consultations with the government on EEA issues. This was by and large to be based on the standing Foreign Affairs Committee, the members of which could be supplemented by members from the other standing committees. In the Icelandic Althingi, finally, there is no special EEA committee. Instead, these matters are dealt with in the standing committees, depending on subject.

MOST SIMILAR PARLIAMENTS?

We noted at the outset that concepts and categories rich in connotations produce a small number of similar cases, while concepts with few connotations yield many similar cases. Mezey's oft-cited sixfold classification of parliaments (1979) is not sufficiently rich in connotations to capture Nordic differences. Mezey develops his sixfold classification on the bases of two dimensions: the policy-making power of the legislature and the degree of support parliament enjoys from the elite and the public at large.

According to his three categories of power (strong, modest, little/none), most west European parliaments fall into the group of legislatures with "modest" policy influence. In the division between legislatures with "more" support and those with "less," most west European parliaments fall into the "more" category. It seems clear that all of the Nordic parliaments enjoy substantial support. They also appear to be fairly strong in policy-making terms. Opposition parties are influential vis-à-vis minority governments (Strøm 1990; Mattson and Strøm 1995), and majority governments nowadays are always coalitions consisting of two or more parties. It is never a question of one single majority party with a government wing in one place and backbenchers in another.

Mezey's schema probably is not helpful for intra-Nordic comparisons. There are problems with his measurements, and also with the fact that his six cells offer too crude a classificatory system to generate differences capable of accounting for variants of parliamentary attitudes and behavior. Within Mezey's schema, the Nordic parliaments are in fact identical systems; thus there is no variation to draw from.

More important from our perspective is the fact that Mezey does not focus on institutional differences, as we do here, but rather on power and legitimacy. His system of classification is based on effect-related variables, while we are searching for cause-related variables in this chapter.

Weaver and Rockman's "three-tier" approach has the potential of offering more nuances for capturing relevant institutional and political differences. In table 2.2, we summarize our findings on the five questions—regarding political and institutional context—put at the beginning of this chapter.

Let us begin with the party system. Traditionally, one could speak of a Nordic five-party system (Berglund and Lindström 1978). A mixed social web and a proportional electoral system have sustained multiparty systems in all five countries.

The basic cleavage underlying the party systems everywhere is the left/right cleavage (which essentially covers disagreements over the role of the state in the economy). Conservative, liberal, social democratic, and left socialist parties are seated in all of the parliaments, although in greatly varying numbers. Social democrats have been close to being the "hegemonic party" in Norway and Sweden, while conservatives have approached this position in Iceland.

We also find a urban-rural cleavage, which provides political space for the distinctive Nordic agrarian parties. The Danish situation is special here, in that the old liberal party early on became the party of the farmers. But then there is a "radical" liberal party in Denmark, not to be found in the traditional five-party formula.

Furthermore, the Christian lay movements have been the basis of small and medium-sized parties now existing in all of the parliaments (save that of Iceland); this development makes the old five-party label awkward for the Nordic party systems of today (see appendixes 2 and 3).

It would be more accurate nowadays to speak of a "six-party" system, but other parties are present as well. Since the 1970s, an electoral opening for populist anti-establishment politicians made right-wing progress parties viable in Denmark and Norway. A party of this type was also represented for a single term in the Swedish Riksdag (1991–94).

In addition, parties representing the "new politics"—such as the green parties and the Women's Alliance—have won seats in the parliaments of Finland, Sweden, and Iceland. And there are more parties still in the Nordic parliaments. The linguistic cleavage in Finland and the foreign-policy cleavages in Denmark and Iceland give added weight to the point that there are marked cross-Nordic differences in terms of the parliamentary party setting within which governments are formed and fall, party groups operate, and individual MPs act.

As regards our second area of comparison, we see that the presidential factor is operative in Finland and Iceland. Only in Finland, however, does the president play an important political role. Although his position has become weaker in the 1990s, the president can still be expected to have an impact on the way parliament operates. The strong position of the Finnish president in foreign affairs, together with his right to nominate a negotiator in the process of government formation, still makes the office important in parliamentary affairs.

Turning now to executive-legislative relations, there were at the time of the parliamentary surveys social democratic minority governments in Sweden, Norway, and Denmark (in the last case a left-center coalition). Finland had a broad "rainbow" left-right majority coalition, and Iceland had a center-left majority coalition. All of the Nordic countries have long-established parliamentary systems characterized by "negative parliamentarism," whereby the government need not leave office unless a parliamentary majority opposes it on an important issue. Nor is there any formal vote of investiture requiring a positive majority basis. The relative strength of parliament in relation to the executive has been on the increase—at least in Denmark, Sweden, and Norway in recent decades, and possibly also in Finland during the 1990s. This is partly due to the predominance of minority governments and (in Finland) the end of the Cold War.

All of the parliaments are elected for four years, and except in Norway all of the executives have the right to dissolve parliament and to call new elections. In practice, though, this is now customary only in Denmark, where the average term of parliament is two years.

Fourth, the selection and election of candidates is a rather decentralized affair in the Nordic countries. They all have multimember constituencies (with a few insignificant exceptions), ranging in number from twenty-nine in Sweden to eight in Iceland.

The electoral formula varies in technical terms, but proportional representation obtains in all five countries. The number of MPs elected varies greatly: 349 in Sweden, 200 in Finland, 175 in Denmark, 165 in Norway, 63 in Iceland. All of the countries but Finland have a national pool of seats that are allocated to the parties to improve national proportionality. In Norway and Sweden, these seats are assigned to constituency party lists. The voters in Iceland, Norway, and Sweden vote for party lists; in Finland they vote for candidates; in Denmark the parties are free to choose

Table 2.2
Institutional and Political Indicators on the Nordic Parliaments, 1994–96

	Denmark	Finland	Iceland	Norway	Sweden	UK 95	US HoR 95
Party System							
No. parties in parliaments	9	9	5	8	7	7	2
No. with min. 5% of seats	5	6	5	6	6	2	2
Regime Type							
Parliamentarism vs. presidentialism	Parliamentarism	Mixed (medium strong pres.)	Parliamentarism	Parliamentarism	Parliamentarism	Parliamentarism	Presidentialism
Parliamentary–Executive Relations							
Modal gov't type '80s and '90s	Minority coalition	Majority coalition	Majority coalition	Minority	Minority	Majority	NA (sep. of powers)
Gov't type at time of survey	SD-led minority coalition	Rainbow, SD-led, majority coalition	Conservative-led, majority coalition	SD minority coalition	SD minority coalition	Conservative majority	NA
No. parties in gov't	3	5	2	1	1	1	1
Gov't share of MPs	43	73	64	41	46	51	NA
Practice of dissolution of parliament	Yes	Rare in '80s and '90s	Happens	No	No	Yes	NA
Ministers keep place in parliament	Yes	Yes	Yes	No	No	Yes	No
Electoral System							
Electoral period (years)	4	4	4	4	4	5	2
Type of system	PR	PR	PR	PR	PR	First past the post	First past the post

	Modified Saint-Lague	D'Hondt	D'Hondt	Modified Saint-Lague	Modified Saint-Lague	Plurality single constituency	Plurality single constituency
Seat allocation formula							
Electoral threshold (%)	2	No	No	4	4	No	No
No. constituencies	17	15	8	19	28	651	435
Candidate preference voting	Medium	Strong	Small	Small	Small (since '98: medium)	Strong[a]	Strong[a]
Nomination process	Decentralized to constituency parties (and some primaries)	Decentralized to constituency parties	Primaries. Strongly decentralized	Decentralized to constituency parties	Decentralized to constituency parties	Decentralized to constituency parties (but much more to be said)	Primaries. Strongly decentralized
Parliamentary Organization							
No. of seats	175	200	68	165	349	651	435
No. of chambers	1	1	1	1 (2)	1	2	Congr: 2
Role of Speaker	Neutral	Neutral	Neutral	Neutral	Neutral	Neutral	Active
No. of standing committees	22	15	9	12	16	23	19
Power of committees	Medium	Strong	Strong	Strong	Strong	Medium	Strong
MPs seated in committees	All	Most	Most	All	Most	All if they wish	All
Position of party groups	Strong	Strong	Strong	Strong	Strong	Weak (but much more to be said)	Weak
No. of adm. & pol. assistants to MPs (and pr. MP)	158 (.89)	43 (.22)	12 (.18)	81 (.49)	148 (.42)	Very low	about 10,000 about 20

Notes: For an overview of additional institutional and political indicators (although not as relevant to our five questions), see Döring (1995). HoR = House of Representatives; NA = not applicable; SD = social democrats.

[a]This could be classified either as strong or as weak depending on whether the position of parties is emphasized or not; see Lijphart (1994).

whether to present lists or candidates (although the trend is for most parties to present party lists).[4]

The element of candidate-preference voting is present above all in Finland, and to some extent also in Denmark; but it is in Iceland that the voters—through the primaries—have the greatest say in the selection of individuals. Voters in the other countries have to choose between party lists. In all of these cases, however, prospective candidates must enter the candidate lists of their party and endorse the party platform.

In all of the countries, moreover, the process of nomination is mainly outside the control of the central party leadership. The constituency party organization generally controls the process, although the voters sometimes have a say. A few of the Danish parties hold primaries, and as mentioned above, this is a general practice in Iceland.

Turning lastly to internal organization, we may observe that today only the Norwegian parliament has elements of a two-chamber structure. In political terms, however, this division is largely unimportant. The speaker and the speaker's conference direct daily affairs in all of the parliaments, and basically in a nonpartisan manner. These are all "working parliaments" with fairly strong and specialized committees: twenty-two in Denmark (counting permanent committees with legislative functions only), sixteen in Sweden, fifteen in Finland, twelve in Norway, and nine in Iceland (Mattson and Strøm 1995:261–63).

MPs are the main parliamentary actor according to the constitutional texts in Denmark, Finland, and Iceland—they are nominally bound by their conscience alone. In reality, the position of MPs in all of the Nordic countries is roughly equal: all are bound strongly by their respective party groups. These control the politically important backrooms of every Nordic parliament. Most resources, as well as the professional assistance offered MPs, are available through the party-group secretariats. However, professional assistance in these parliaments is usually rather scarce (especially in the Icelandic Althingi).

If anything, we would expect this sweeping similarity in political and institutional context to produce a fairly high level of similarity in attitudes, opinions, and behavior in the five Nordic parliaments. On the other hand, from an institutional perspective there ought to be some potential for variation, particularly in connection with differences in size and in the ability of voters to choose candidates. Moreover, the differences in the party systems surrounding Nordic MPs could have an impact as well, given the capacity of different political forces to generate a varied set of governmental alternatives.

Finally, what can we say *at this stage* about how Nordic parliaments differ from the Westminster system and the United States Congress? Perhaps, to begin with, that one should be skeptical of any one-dimensional mapping of parliaments along a continuum stretched out between the two model systems: on the one hand the total fusion of powers, on the other their complete separation. Shaw (1979; cf. Verney 1959) places the "continental systems" in between these two extremes; Nordic parliaments are in this sense clearly "continental" and thus "in-between." This categorization clearly does little justice to Nordic parliamentarism, however, and we suspect that the price of parsimonious analysis can sometimes be too high.

Too, the multiparty nature of parliamentary politics in the three Scandinavian countries, together with the prevalence of minority governments there, differentiates the legislatures of the Nordic countries categorically both from the "mother of parliaments" and from the system in Washington. How categorically, and why, will be an underlying theme of the subsequent chapters, and one to which we shall explicitly return in the final chapter of the book (chapter 17).

NOTES

1. More precisely, proportionality among parties that either (a) survive the electoral threshold of 2 percent of the valid national vote, or (b) obtain at least one regular constituency seat, or (c) obtain the number of votes equal to the regional vote/seat ratio in two of the three electoral regions (Jutland, metropolitan Copenhagen, the Islands) into which the country is divided.

2. As noted, Sweden changed systems before the 1998 election, but this was true for the election of the MPs surveyed in 1994.

3. The constitution is formally from 1944, but in practice it was not fully implemented before 1974.

4. See above and note 2.

REPRESENTATION:
VERTICAL RELATIONS

How Members of Parliament
Define Their Task

Peter Esaiasson

There are two main ways to think about elected representatives. One is to view them as separate political actors who deliberate on their own and act independently, and who should therefore be analyzed individually. This *individualist* approach is generally associated with studies of the U.S. Congress. Another way is to view them as more or less anonymous members of a cohesive party collective, and thus best analyzed as a group. This *party-collectivist* approach tends to dominate studies of European and European-influenced parliaments.

Adherents of the collectivist perspective have doubtless good cause for their approach. Their main argument, of course, is that parliamentary systems require cohesive parties in order to function. As long as the behavior of party members in roll calls is sufficiently well-coordinated that we can predict parties' actions from their official positions, it must be reckoned less than fruitful to analyze individual members of parliament (see, e.g., Thomassen 1991; Damgaard 1994; Jensen's chapter 9 below).

However, even while the primary position of the parties is an incontestable fact, there is a well-known political circumstance that is difficult to explain on the basis of a collectivist approach—the oft-intensive internal disputes over the nomination of candidates (Gallagher and Marsh 1988). If it is a matter of so little import exactly which persons represent the party, why then are interest organizations and other political groupings so anxious that just *their* representatives shall be returned to parliament?

I shall argue in this chapter that the collectivist perspective misses critical aspects of what happens in parliament. Three things make the individualist perspective relevant even in the case of parliaments with cohesive parties. The *first* is that a parliamentary party is not just a unified actor, but an arena for debate as well. Opportunities exist, when a unified party line is in the course of emerging, for different interests to make themselves heard in the party. The *second* is that MPs generally apply a division of labor. The person or persons assigned to a particular policy area enjoy considerable opportunities for influencing party policy. The *third* is that MPs' duties allow them in practice to act in a range of capacities. One need not therefore choose between working loyally for the party and advancing a particular cause.

A more precise argument is that representatives define their task in terms of balancing different interests. Depending on how MPs see their personal task—that is, depending on the interests to which they ascribe the greatest importance—they will behave in parliament in a particular way. Members who look kindly on a particular interest are extra inclined to act on its behalf. Otherwise put, what individual members of parliament do is to champion the interests they personally consider important to champion.

This *task-definition approach* permits representatives to accommodate several interests in their view of their task. The task of an elected representative is sufficiently flexible that one who so wishes can work on behalf both of the party and of another interest.

The manner in which MPs define their task is furthermore assumed to follow definite and relatively straightforward patterns. It is in large part determined by three factors: party affiliation, group affiliation, and parliamentary position.

Party affiliation is important because there is, within every party, a predominant conception as to which interests are most important to champion. Members thus tend to see themselves as representing interests associated with their party.

Group affiliation is significant because members take their personal experiences with them into parliament. MPs tend, that is, to see themselves as representatives for the social group to which they themselves belong.

Parliamentary position is important because members in a leading position are expected by their peers to act differently from how backbenchers do. Backbenchers enjoy greater freedom of action, and so include more interests in their task definition.[1]

The task-definition approach has been assumed to apply to all types of democratically elected parliaments: to party-dominated parliaments in the style of Westminster and Continental Europe, and to the individualistic U.S. Congress as well. Thus it argues that elected representatives in all democratic political systems have something in common. If this claim is empirically supported, it would follow that a key to understanding the conduct of MPs in one important respect lies in the basic chararacteristics of representative democracies as such.

This approach has previously proved useful in analyses of Swedish national MPs (Esaiasson and Holmberg 1996:59–80) and of Swedish local representatives (Rodrigo-Blomqvist 1997; Westlund 1998). In this paper, the validity of the approach will be tested in a comparative context—the five Nordic parliamentary democracies. The Nordic parliaments offer a critical test of the least likely type. If the individually oriented task-definition approach turns out to be useful in these parliaments' party-dominated contexts, it is probably useful in most contexts.

DIFFERENCES BETWEEN SYSTEMS?

Although the task-definition approach—that is, the supposition that MPs will champion the interests they personally regard as important—is generally applicable, system characteristics may affect the precise composition of individual MPs' task definition and hence the overall distribution of champions for various interests in a particular legislative assembly. The comparative nature of this study allows for a test of the effects of specific institutional arrangements.

For this particular study, three types of institutional arrangement are relevant (cf. chapter 2 above). First: the *size of the parliamentary body*, which can be expected to have an impact on the number of interests to which members give priority. Large parliaments with many members tend to have a large number of backbenchers without formal positions of power; we may accordingly expect such parliaments to contain a large number of interest champions.

Second: the degree to which the electoral system involves the *election of individual persons*. In countries where the election of individuals is a prominent feature of the electoral system, we may expect the role of the party in MPs' task definition to be less central than in countries where the electoral system is based strictly on party lists.

Third: the type of *nominating process*. Locally dominated nominating processes can be expected to produce a higher proportion of representatives giving a high priority to local constituency interests than are produced by centralized nominating systems.

For all of these institutional arrangements, relevant variations are found in the Nordic context. As regards the size of the parliamentary body, the extremes are represented by the Swedish Riksdag (349 seats) and the

Icelandic Althingi (63 seats). Where voting systems are concerned, Finland (and to a lesser extent Denmark) allow for a personal vote, whereas the systems used in Norway and Sweden rely heavily on party lists. As regards the type of nominating process, finally, the Icelandic system is the most decentralized.

In the following, we will look for two types of pattern in the data on MPs' support for various specific interests. First, to the extent that support for specific interests is uniform across Nordic parliaments, we may conclude that existing differences in institutional arrangements are inconsequential. We can then proceed to discuss whether the pattern found is likely to be present in most parliaments or whether it is unique to the Nordic parliaments. Second, to the extent Nordic MPs vary in their support for different specific interests, we can turn to variations in the electoral system, in the nominating process, and in the size of parliament for explanations.

Good social-science research gives the data a chance to kick back. The task-definition approach can fail in several ways. Identifying relevant interests may be impracticable. Or we can fail in our attempts to measure MPs' views on the interests in question. Or MPs may refuse to accept any other interests than those of the nation as a whole, or those of their party; alternatively, they may refuse to accept anyone's judgment save their own. Or the task definitions may prove to be empty constructions, in the sense of having no behavioral consequences. Or, lastly, the task definitions may lack theoretically meaningful determinants. The analysis that follows will address each objection in turn.

IDENTIFYING RELEVANT INTERESTS

The debate over political representation has in large part concerned how different interests are weighed against each other. The debate is complicated, however, by the difficulty of separating two questions that are closely related and yet distinct: *Which* interests should MPs represent? And *how* should they decide what benefits the interest in question? (Eulau et al. 1959; Wahlke et al. 1962.)[2] The latter question has to do with weighing bounded against unbounded mandates; in practice, however, bounded mandates are linked with a particular interest, like the constituency or the party.

A further complicating factor is the fact that an important division runs between those taking the view that politics is a struggle between different specific interests and those averring that representatives owe their allegiance solely to the general public interest. There are thus two questions on which a position must be taken in the debate over interest representation: do we acknowledge the existence of legitimate specific interests, and, if we do, *what are* these legitimate specific interests?

In an oft-cited essay, Heinz Eulau and Paul Karps (1977) propose that the varying interests with which political representatives must deal can be divided into three main categories. The first consists of *territorially defined interests* (including everything from the country as a whole to individual constituencies and parts of constituencies). The second category is comprised of *functionally defined interests*—economic, religious, ethnic, and ideological. The third category includes *individually defined interests* (private citizens in need of help). To these major categories should be added, of course, the *interests of the party*.[3]

The categories proposed are related in turn to the theories of political representation that have dominated Western politics for centuries. The territorially defined interest (in the form of "one's own constituency") corresponds to *geographical representation,* which is probably the oldest theory of representation. When the first parliaments met in the Middle Ages, it was already an important task for representatives to express the viewpoints and present the problems of people living in their home district (Birch 1964; 1971; Pitkin 1967; Steed 1985).

The category of territorially defined interests is also closely related to the *liberal theory of representation.* This theory acknowledges no legitimate interest save that of the public—of "the nation as a whole," in Burke's famous formulation (Birch 1964; 1971; Pitkin 1967; Steed 1985). The view that MPs should in the first instance promote the interests of the entire country has been extremely successful, to the point now where it is difficult for a politician to argue openly against the liberal theory of representation. If we are to put the theory into practice, however, we must specify what is meant by the nation as a whole: that is, the state, the history of the nation, the majority of the citizens, or perhaps (and which accords most closely with the spirit of the theory) universal principles that can be rationally defended?

Functionally defined interests, too, have a long history, as seen in various forms of *corporative representation* (see, e.g., Christophersen 1963; 1964; Norton 1981:52–62). In many European countries, the representation of social and economic interests was institutionalized for long periods in the form of estate-based parliaments. Groups such as peasants, burghers, clergymen, and nobles were all guaranteed places in parliament. Today, the representation of social and economic group interests is topical primarily on account of the debate on the status of minorities (see, e.g., Phillips 1995).

The notion that the interests of the party should weigh heavily is a central feature of the *responsible-party model,* which is the foremost competitor today of the liberal theory of representation (see, e.g., Schattschneider 1942; Ranney 1951). If this doctrine is to function in accordance with theoretical expectation, the interests of the party must be defined as the line taken by the party leadership and/or as the content of the party platform. But for the individual representative there are other conceivable specifications as well, such as the local party organization, the party's general program, and resolutions of the party congress.

The only one of Eulau and Karp's interest categories without an independent place in the doctrinal history is the one comprised of private citizens who turn to their representative for help (what is here called *individual representation*). Assistance rendered to private persons in one's own constituency—service responsiveness, in other words—tends to loom large in analyses of political representation in Britain and the United States (see, e.g., Fenno 1978; Searing 1985; Cain et al. 1987). However, this way of specifying the concept has the consequence of leaving some of the doings of representatives outside the analysis. Swedish MPs, for instance, report having as many contacts with help-seeking persons from outside their constituency as from within it (Esaiasson and Holmberg 1996: 302). Nor is there any reason to believe that Swedish MPs are uniquely disposed to help private persons in difficulty (see, e.g., Uslaner 1985).

MEASURING REPRESENTATIVES' VIEW OF THEIR TASK

The discussion thus far shows it is possible to identify a limited number of interests toward which representatives must take a position. In addition, it points out some potential problems for the task-definition approach. If the approach is to function analytically, the representation of specific interests cannot be equated with the promotion of special interests at the expense of the general public. We must develop a neutral measurement according to which it is as acceptable for representatives to consider themselves champions of one or several specific interests as for them to reserve their sole allegiance for the core liberal interest, that of the "nation as a whole."

In accordance with our premise that the task of an elected representative is a flexible one, we propose to allow members to see themselves as champions of more than just one interest. Our measurement should also be independent of context, as well as economical (in the sense of being suitable for use in a traditional survey study).

The solution we have chosen is to ask Nordic representatives how important a number of tasks are to them personally as representatives. We asked them to rate the importance of twelve specific interests in all: that of their *party*, of their *constituency*, of *private citizens*, of seven socially and economically defined groups (*women, wage-earners, youth, pensioners, immigrants, businessmen,* and *farmers*), and of two ideologically defined groups (*Christians* and *teetotalers*).[4] These twelve interest categories do not, to be sure, cover all of the conceivable options; even so, they stand for a broad spectrum of specific interests. In the case of each item, members were asked to state whether the interest in question was "very important," "rather important," "not very important," or "not important at all."

In order to avoid the risk that a positive attitude toward a particular interest would be equated with a disposition to defend special interests, we took two measures. First, when asking MPs about their attitudes toward a given group, we asked about their attitudes toward the group as a whole and not toward an organization associated with the group in question (i.e., "women" and "wage-earners" rather than "women's organization" or "trade union"). Second, we framed the survey question in terms of "putting forward" the "interests/opinions" of the group. Identifying oneself as a champion of an interest thus entails a readiness to speak on behalf of the interest in question, to be a voice for said interest in the decision-making body. As for whether or not a representative is prepared, independently of considerations of principle, to fight for this interest in the final decision-making process—this is a question we shall not consider here.[5]

When it came to measuring members' views on the second overarching question—whether or not the liberal theory of representation is the sole legitimate one—we considered it less than meaningful to ask MPs about the importance they ascribed to representing the "interests of the whole country." We assumed a question framed in this fashion would serve mainly to evoke ritualistic concurrence and would furthermore make it hard for MPs to see themselves as defenders of any specific interest.[6] Instead, we added another option to the battery of questions: the importance of putting forward opinions one "personally consider[s] important." Strictly speaking, the question bears on the view an MP takes of independent action and of the importance of trusting to one's own judgment (i.e., it has more to do with "style" than with "focus"). Nevertheless, the question offers an opportunity for MPs who do not wish to see themselves as representatives for any specific interest to define their task in positive terms. According to our way of measuring task definitions, an exponent of Burkean principles is committed only to the defense of his/her personal views and not to the promotion of any specific interests.

Our attempt at measuring a complex viewpoint with a single closed survey question passed at least one important test of serviceability: the great majority of members taking part in the survey found it meaningful to answer the "task question." The average internal refusal rate was under 5 percent.

REPRESENTATIVES' VIEW OF THEIR TASK

For the task-definition approach to be fruitful, MPs must be prepared when defining their task to ascribe importance to more than just their Burkean "personal opinions" or the interests of their party. If members define themselves exclusively as party representatives, then it is scarcely meaningful to analyse individual behavior; the party-collectivist approach would in that case be obviously dominant. And if MPs define themselves solely as independent Burkeans, an interest-oriented analysis of this type is plainly pointless.

It proves to be the case, however, that Nordic MPs accept perfectly well the idea that an important task for them personally is to champion specific interests. Even if their party and their "personal opinions" are the two most important elements in MPs' task definition, there is substantial support for most of the identified interest groups (see table 3.1). To a considerable extent, then, Nordic MPs define their personal task in terms of the promotion of specific interests.

The view MPs take of the Burkean notion that they should put forward their personal opinions illustrates how the task of a representative is flexible, and how one and the same person can accommodate several different interests within his/her task definition. The independence principle as such enjoys considerable support in the Nordic parliaments. (On average 47 percent of MPs define themselves as "representatives of themselves.") A closer analysis shows, however, that the great majority of these "representatives of themselves" also consider it very important to champion a specific interest.[7] Thus it is considerably more common to regard the independence principle as a *complement* to the representation of specific interests than as an *alternative* to it. Nordic MPs express no opposition in principle to the basic assumptions of the task-definition approach.

Together with the interests of the party and the Burkean principle of independence, three types of interests enjoy a substantial number of champions in the Nordic parliaments: *constituencies* (25 percent of MPs on average); *private citizens seeking help* (25 percent); and women, youth and other *socioeconomically disadvantaged groups* (35 percent of MPs see themselves as champions of at least one socioeconomically disadvantaged group).

Table 3.1

Proportion of Members Who View It As Very Important to Champion Various Interests (%)

Type of Interest	All	Denmark	Finland	Iceland	Norway	Sweden	Eta²
Party representation							
Own party	52	56	9	52	68	77	.39*
Geographical representation							
Own constituency	25	18	22	24	22	39	.05*
Individual representation							
Individual voters	25	16	21	29	28	30	.03*
Group representation— underprivileged groups							
Wage earners	13	18	2	21	5	16	.05*
Women	19	10	8	33	18	25	.08*
Young people	18	12	13	33	15	16	.03*
Pensioners	9	8	3	21	4	9	.04*
Immigrants	13	10	NA	17	12	14	.04*
Any underprivileged group	35	26	18	57	34	39	.06*
Group representation— private business							
Businessmen	9	7	12	12	6	8	.02*
Farmers	7	4	6	17	0	5	.04*
Any business interest	12	7	14	21	6	10	.03*
Group representation— ideological interests							
Christians	5	6	NA	5	5	5	.00
Teetotalers	3	NA	NA	2	3	2	.00
Any ideological group	6	6	NA	5	6	5	.00
Burkean representation							
Personal views	47	58	41	76	24	34	.07*
Minimum N	751	108	119	47	146	331	

Notes: The question was worded as follows: "As a member of [the Parliament in question], how important do you personally find the following tasks to be?: 'Working with problems brought forward by individuals/voters'; 'Promoting views you personally consider important'; 'Promoting the policies of your own party'; 'Promoting the interests/views of your own region/district'; 'Promoting the interests/ views of the young'; 'Promoting the interests/views of pensioners'; 'Promoting the interests/views of wage earners'; 'Promoting the interests/views of immigrants'; 'Promoting the interests/views of businessmen'; 'Promoting the interests/views of farmers'; 'Promoting the interests/views of women'; 'Promoting the interests/views of Christians'; 'Promoting the interests/views of teetotalers.' " The following response alternatives were offered: "very important"; "fairly important"; "not very important"; "not important at all." (In the Finnish study these response alternatives were offered: "most important"; "important"; "rather unimportant"; "not very important"; "don't know.") Each eta-square value in the right-hand column is based on a one-way analysis of variance with country as the independent variable and view on an interest category as the dependent variable. The dependent variables were coded 0–3. NA = not applicable.

*$p < .05$

Business interests enjoyed less—although still sizable—support (12 percent), as did *idea-based group interests* (5 percent).

For most specific interests, country itself explains only a limited proportion of the variation in MPs' views of their task. (Only for the categories "party," "women," "personal views," and "any disadvantaged group" does country explain more than 5 percent of the variation in MPs' views.) This means there is a basis for speaking of a (partly) common Nordic pattern in the matter of MPs' task definitions. In two cases, we might argue that the similarities between countries are even more far-reaching; there is reason to believe that a similar pattern would appear in most democratically chosen parliaments and under most institutional arrangements.

The first example of a possibly universal pattern may be seen in MPs' views on *individual representation* (i.e., assistance bestowed on private citizens seeking help). The standard explanation in U.S. literature for why representatives often spend a considerable portion of their time assisting individuals is that so doing enhances their chances of re-election (e.g., Mayhew 1974).[8] This somewhat cynical explanation squares badly with our finding that a considerable proportion of members in all of the Nordic parliaments define themselves as champions of the interests of individual citizens. And it is contradicted outright by the finding that Norwegian and Swedish MPs, all of whom are chosen on party lists in multimember constituencies, are somewhat more positive toward individual representation than are Finnish and Danish MPs, who are elected on a personal basis.

It is hard to see how Norwegian and Swedish MPs can benefit electorally by helping private citizens. Hence, the inclination of Nordic MPs to regard assistance to individuals as part of their task cannot reasonably be explained by reference to electoral motives. A more reasonable explanation for this inclination is that many MPs see helping private citizens as one of their duties. For many parliamentarians, it is simply a part of the job to assist persons who seek their help; as for whether or not electoral gains then ensue—that is another matter.

The second example of a possibly universal pattern concerns MPs' views on *constituency representation*. It is common in the literature to regard the disposition to work on behalf of one's constituency as typical of representatives in single-member district systems (e.g., Cain et al. 1987) or in developing countries without strong parties (Kim et al. 1984). But this notion does not square with our finding that a substantial proportion of members in all of the Nordic parliaments define themselves as promoters of the interests of their constituency (25 percent on average). Moreover, even if Swedish members are the most inclined to give priority to the interests of their constituency, the percentage differences between the other countries are minor indeed.

The relatively strong support for constituency representation shows that old traditions live on in the Nordic parliaments, irrespective of electoral systems or cohesive national parties. The view that the geographical area from which one hails should be supported is by no means held solely by representatives in single-member district systems. This general trait among parliamentarians is scarcely surprising in view of the common history of parliaments. Most parliaments emerged historically as a means for linking localities with the central authorities of the nation-state, and this local connection seems to survive in most cases. If our purpose is to find truly divergent cases, we will probably have to seek out the small number of polities which lack any type of formal connection between representatives and specific geographical areas, or, alternatively, seek out the few polities where the nomination process is highly centralized.

As is evidenced by the eta values in the right-hand column of table 3.1, however, there are also some instances of a clear difference between countries in regard to MPs' view of their task. To what degree can these differences be attributed to differing institutional arrangements? As seen above, we would expect variations in three types of institutional arrangement in particular to influence the content of MPs' task definition: the voting system, the size of the parliamentary body, and the nominating system.

Differences in voting system should above all affect MPs' views on *party representation*. And indeed, the greatest observable difference between countries turns out to concern MPs' inclination to view themselves as representatives of their party. In Sweden and Norway, a clear majority of members define themselves as party representatives: 77 percent and 68 percent, respectively, consider representing the party a very important task. A majority of members in the Danish and Icelandic parliaments are also self-defined party representatives (56 percent and 52 percent, respectively). But among Finnish MPs it is uncommon to consider party representation a very important personal task (9 percent).

It appears that the individual-focused electoral system in Finland affects members' view of their party. By contrast, MPs in Sweden and Norway (which have highly party-dominated systems) are prepared to accept that the party comes first—that they represent the party *and* other interests. Finnish representatives, by contrast, do not ascribe such a central role to their party. Of course, the differences between the parliaments are smaller when it comes to the everyday legislative work of roll calls and negotiations; still, the divergent view of party representation in Finland underscores the fact that Finnish representatives consider their mandate less party-bound than do their Nordic colleagues.[9]

It should be pointed out that it is only in the case of a strongly individual-oriented voting system that any really important impact on MPs' views on party representation can be observed. Danish representatives, who are chosen through an electoral system with a certain individual focus, are only a bit less party-oriented than their Norwegian and Swedish counterparts, who are chosen strictly by party list. If Finland is excluded from the analysis, the difference between the countries falls dramatically (the proportion of variance explained falls to 5 percent, as compared to 39 percent when Finland is included). Thus, if we are to find powerful institutional effects on MPs' views on party representation, we must seek out extreme values in the matter of voting systems.

The nominating system—where the big difference is that between Iceland's strongly decentralized system of primary elections and the system employed by the other countries—appears to have a limited impact on MPs' task definition. The strongest effect obtains in the case of the Burkean independence principle: as expected, Icelandic MPs are substantially more disposed than are representatives in the other countries (Norway and Sweden especially) to define themselves as "representatives of themselves." In addition, the comparatively moderate views on party representation held by Icelandic members of parliament can be traced to the nominating system.[10] On the other hand, the nominating system has no observable effect on MPs' views on constituency representation. Icelandic members are actually less inclined than their Swedish colleagues to define themselves as champions of the interests of their constituency.

The size of the parliamentary body, finally, appears to have a moderate impact on the task definition of members of parliament. As expected, the sizable Swedish Riksdag contains—with its many parliamentary backbenchers—a greater number of champions of the home constituency, and of various socioeconomically disadvantaged groups besides, than do the medium-sized Danish, Finnish, and Norwegian parliaments. There is no simple linear relationship, however, between the size of the parliamentary body and the inclination of MPs to include many different interests in their task definition. Icelandic members (whose parliament is the smallest by far) are even more inclined than their Swedish colleagues to define themselves as champions of various socioeconomically defined interests.[11]

The observed differences between task definitions—in regard to party representation, the Burkean principle of independence, and the representation of socioeconomically disadvantaged groups—can thus be explained in part by the fact that the Nordic countries employ differing voting systems, use dissimilar nominating systems, and have parliaments of varying size. But other observed differences between the parliaments cannot be explained by reference to institutional arrangements. In cases like these, we will have to search for complementary explanations among more vaguely defined cultural factors.

There is at least one example in which we may reasonably explain observed differences by reference to a general cultural factor—MPs' views on the representation of women's interests. The difference between the parliaments on this point is relatively large; Danish and Finnish MPs are more skeptical toward the representation of women's interests than are Norwegian, Swedish, and Icelandic members (in statistical terms, country explains 8 percent of the variance). It is likely that these country differences reflect the great success in opinion formation which the idea of equal rights between men and women has enjoyed in recent years in Iceland, Norway, and Sweden (recall the Icelandic Women's Alliance, as well as the high proportion of women in the parliaments and governments of these countries).[12]

BEHAVIORAL CONSEQUENCES

The task-definition approach promises that MPs are prepared to turn words into actions—to act on behalf of the interests they consider important. If this approach is to make good on its promise, there must be behavioral differences between, on the one hand, members who define themselves as champions of a specific interest and, on the other, MPs who do not so regard themselves. Self-defined interest promoters should be willing to go the extra mile in support of their cause.

MPs can exploit both formal and informal channels for promoting an interest. Actions within formal channels are registered in the official parliamentary records; they take the form of questions, private member bills, floor speeches, and, last but not least, roll calls. The informal channels are more elusive, but in the judgment of many they are also more effective. They may include taking up the interest in question with influential cabinet ministers or mentioning it at meetings of the parliamentary party, or keeping actors associated with it informed, or being informed in turn by such actors.

In an earlier Swedish study, the actual doings of MPs via a series of formal and informal channels could be followed throughout an entire parliamentary term. It proved to be the case that the manner in which members defined their task at the start of their term tended to govern their behavior throughout their time in office (Esaiasson and Holmberg 1996:65–68). We do not have access here to panel data or to corresponding content analyses of parliamentary publications, but in our surveys we asked MPs about the degree to which they utilized two types of informal channel linked to specific interests: personal reminders to cabinet ministers and contacts with various organizations and agencies. We also asked about the extent to which members cooperated across party boundaries to assist specific interests. Information on the utilization of informal channels like these is relevant for testing the tenability of the task-definition approach.[13]

To measure the frequency of informal reminders to ministers, we asked MPs to state how many times during the last year they had personally contacted a cabinet minister for the purpose of putting forward the views of an interested party. We specified the same interests as in the case of the "task question," aside from the fact that we regarded it as less than meaningful to ask about contacts made on behalf of an MP's own party. For each of these interests, we offered three response alternatives: "at least once a month," "once or a few times," and "never."

The results follow a clear pattern (see table 3.2). It was more common, in all of the parliaments and for all of the specific interests, for self-defined interest promoters to contact ministers on behalf of an interested party than it was for representatives who did not so define themselves. Self-defined interest promoters were somewhat less active than other members only when it came to contacting ministers for the purpose of putting forward personal views (Finland, Iceland, and Norway) or the views of wage-earners (Iceland). It appears, then, that the task-definition approach makes good on its promise.

These results serve also to remind us that it is part of an MP's daily job to work on behalf also of such interests as he/she does *not* consider most important to champion. Large numbers of members who are not self-defined interest promoters also reported, in respect to several interest categories, that they personally contacted ministers on behalf of the interest in question. This is clearly illustrated by the fact that clear majorities among Danish, Finnish, Icelandic, and Norwegian members had conveyed the wishes of private business, as had a substantial minority of Swedish MPs, even while barely one representative in ten saw him/herself expressly as a champion of the interests of business. The task-definition approach can claim only that self-defined interest promoters are *extra* inclined to work on behalf of the interest in question.

Our second test of the behavioral consequences of MPs' task definition focuses on the frequency of informal contacts with actors associated with

Table 3.2
Proportion of Members Regularly Contacting Cabinet Ministers to Put Forward Views of Various Interests, by Task Definition (%)

Type of Interest	Denmark			Finland			Iceland			Norway			Sweden		
	Cb	O	Diff.	Cb	O	Diff.	Cb	O	Diff.	Cb	O	Diff.	Cb	O	Diff.
Geographical representation															
Own district	53	20	+33	62	59	+3	80	39	+41	47	20	+27	14	8	+6
Individual representation															
Individual voters	62	28	+34	68	38	+30	50	24	+26	25	18	+7	14	6	+8
Group representation— underprivileged groups															
Wage earners	89	50	+39	100	30	+70	56	66	−10	100	38	+62	57	36	+21
Women	73	28	+45	100	34	+66	69	25	+44	70	36	+34	48	26	+22
Pensioners	78	44	+34	100	76	+24	67	59	+8	67	29	+38	46	25	+21
Immigrants	80	36	+44	100	NI		43	26	+17	100	47	+53	41	34	+7
Group representation— private enterprises															
Businessmen	71	54	+17	86	81	+5	75	60	+15	78	69	+9	71	33	+38
Farmers	75	32	+43	100	59	+41	71	44	+27		NI		62	25	+37

Continued

Table 3.2
Continued

Type of Interest	Denmark			Finland			Iceland			Norway			Sweden		
	Ch	O	Diff.	Ch	O	Diff.	Ch	O	Diff.	Ch	O	Diff.	Ch	O	Diff.
Group representation—ideological groups															
Christians	67	12	**+55**		NI		100	13	**+87**	100	12	**+88**	40	10	**+30**
Teetotalers		NI			NI		100	10	**+90**	80	13	**+67**	34	10	**+24**
Burkean representation*															
Personal views	83	73	+10	60	68	**−8**	98	89	**−11**	60	68	**−8**	48	30	**+18**

Note: Positive figures in boldface indicate that self-defined champions of a particular interest (Ch) are more often in contact with cabinet ministers than are members who do not define themselves as champions of the interest in question (O). "Champions" (Ch) are members who reported that they view it as a "very important task" to represent the interests of the category in question (see table 3.1). The survey question on contacts with ministers was worded as follows: "During the past year, how often have you contacted cabinet ministers to discuss problems/issues of interest in your work as a politician; discuss the problems of a voter or other individual; discuss problems in particular concerning your region/constituency; put forward the views of wage earners/unions; put forward the views of business organizations; put forward the views of farmers/farmers' organizations; put forward the views of pensioners/pensioners' organizations; put forward the views of women/women's organizations; put forward the views of immigrants/immigrants' organizations; put forward the interests of Christians/religious organizations; put forward the views of teetotalers/teetotalers' organizations." The following response alternatives were offered: "at least once a month"; "occasionally"; "never." For most interest categories, table entries are percent "at least one contact during past year." However, for "geographical representation" and "individual representation," entries are percent monthly contacts. The minimum number of respondents are 3 (Icelandic champions of business interests and of farmers, respectively) and 4 (Finnish champions of pensioners and Danish champions of farming interests). NI = not included in the survey.

specific interests. Our analysis of this matter is based on a series of questions in which representatives were asked to state how many times during the last year they had been in contact with various organizations and agencies. We asked about contacts with thirteen different actors associated with the interest categories stated. Table 3.3 reviews the average contact frequency for champions of a particular interest, as compared with that for members who do not define themselves as champions of said interest.

The results in this case also match the expectations generated by the task-definition approach. In the great majority of cases, interest champions have closer contacts with actors linked to the interest in question than other representatives do. There are certain exceptions in the case of constituency representation (Finland), wage-earner representation (Iceland), and party representation (Iceland, Norway, and Sweden). But on the whole the pattern is plain. Members of parliament who look favorably on a certain interest also have closer personal contacts with that interest.

Of particular importance here is the fact that the difference between self-defined champions and other members is much smaller in the case of contacts with the MP's own party than in the case of contacts with other interest categories. Since we saw above that behavioral consequences were virtually absent in respect of MPs' views on the Burkean independence principle as well, we can draw the conclusion that these two interest categories have a special status in representatives' task definition. MPs' views on both party representation and Burkean independence tend to be pure attitudes bereft of behavioral implications. The harsh reality is that the vast majority of members consider it a practical necessity to keep within the party fold; for example, by staying in close contact with both the local and the national party organization.[14]

The third test of the validity of the task-definition approach, which we shall not present in detail, concerns the disposition of members of parliament to cooperate across party boundaries on various issues.[15] Yet again we see the pattern whereby self-defined interest promoters are more inclined than other MPs to act for the interest in question. Particularly as regards equal rights for women (representation of women's interests) and religious questions (representation of religious interests), the difference between champions and other members is substantial indeed.

PARTY AFFILIATION HAS IMPORTANCE

If we have now gathered empirical support for the proposition that MPs' task definition as such has behavioral consequences, the next step in the

Table 3.3

Proportion of Members Regularly Meeting Organizations and Government Agencies Related to Various Interest Categories, by Task Definition (means)

Type of Interest/Organization	Denmark			Finland			Iceland			Norway			Sweden		
	Cb	O	Diff.	Cb	O	Diff.	Cb	O	Diff.	Cb	O	Diff.	Cb	O	Diff.
Own district															
Local party organization	3.8	3.5	+0.3	3.1	3.2	−0.1	3.5	3.2	+0.3	3.7	3.5	+0.2	3.8	3.7	+0.1
Local state agencies	3.2	2.3	+0.9	3.0	2.9	+0.1	3.5	2.9	+0.6	2.9	2.8	+0.1	3.0	2.6	+0.4
Wage earners															
Blue-collar union (LO)	2.5	1.6	+0.9	2.5	1.6	+0.9	1.9	2.3	−0.4	3.0	2.3	+0.7	2.9	2.0	+0.9
White-collar union (TCO)	2.0	1.1	+0.9	1.5	1.1	+0.4	1.6	2.1	−0.5	1.3	1.4	−0.1	2.0	1.8	+0.2
Women															
Women's organization	2.0	0.9	+1.1		NA		1.9	0.8	+1.1	2.6	1.1	+1.5	2.4	1.5	+0.9
Pensioners															
Pensioners' organization	2.3	1.4	+0.9	2.8	2.2	+0.6	1.5	1.2	+0.3	1.7	1.1	+0.6	2.0	1.4	+0.6
Immigrants															
Immigrants' organization	1.8	1.4	+0.4		NA		0.7	0.4	+0.3	2.1	1.4	+0.7	2.0	1.4	+0.6

	O	Ch		O	Ch		O	Ch		O	Ch		O	Ch	
Businessmen															
Employers' org. (SAF)	1.7	1.7	**+0.0**	1.5	1.3	**+0.2**	1.8	1.7	**+0.1**	2.3	1.9	**+0.4**	1.7	1.5	**+0.2**
Business organization	2.1	1.9	**+0.2**			NA	2.2	1.7	**+0.5**	2.4	1.8	**+0.6**	2.0	1.8	**+0.2**
Farmers															
Farmers' organization (LRF)	2.2	1.3	**+0.9**	2.9	1.3	**+1.6**	2.4	1.4	**+1.0**			NA	2.5	1.6	**+0.9**
Christians															
Religious organization	1.8	0.7	**+1.1**			NA	1.5	0.9	**+0.6**	2.6	1.0	**+1.6**	2.0	1.0	**+1.0**
Teetotalers															
Temperance organization			NA			NA	1.0	0.7	**+0.3**	2.4	0.9	**+1.5**	2.3	1.0	**+1.3**
Own Party															
Local party organization	3.6	3.5	**+0.1**	3.4	3.2	**+0.2**	3.3	3.3	**+0.0**	3.6	3.4	**+0.2**	3.7	3.8	**−0.1**
Other local party org.	2.9	2.7	**+0.2**	2.4	2.1	**+0.3**	1.7	1.8	**−0.1**	2.7	2.3	**+0.4**	2.5	2.6	**−0.1**
Central party org.	2.9	2.7	**+0.2**	2.9	2.4	**+0.5**	2.1	2.1	**+0.0**	3.0	3.0	**+0.0**	2.7	2.6	**+0.1**

Note: Positive figures in boldface indicate that self-defined champions of a particular interest (Ch) meet more frequently with organizations and government agencies than members who do not define themselves as champions of the interest in question (O). "Champions" (Ch) are members who reported that they view it as a "very important task" to put forward the interests of the category in question (see table 3.1). The survey question on members' contacts was worded as follows: "Disregarding how the contacts were initiated, during the past year how often have you personally been in written or oral contact with the following organizations, organized groups, and state authorities?" The response alternative given were: "at least once a week" (coded 4); "once or twice per month" (coded 3); "a few times" (coded 2); "at least once" (coded 1); and "never" (coded 0). NA = data not available.

analysis is to test whether or not MPs' views of their task as representatives follow expected patterns at the individual level. According to our expectations, party affiliation is one of three main determinants of parliamentarians' view of their task. Party affiliation is significant because, within every party, there is a notion of which interests are most important to defend. Such notions may reflect crass electoral alliances with various interest groups, but they may also be rooted in visions of the good society and in ideological convictions about how a good representative behaves.

Table 3.4 presents task definitions within six dominant party families in Nordic politics (cf. von Beyme 1985). The results in the table, which as earlier pertain to self-defined interest champions, represent an average for all of the countries, and each party is assigned equal weight irrespective of size.[16] The table also includes data on the proportion of the variance in MPs' views that can be explained by party affiliation.

As expected, there are systematic differences between the party families. Party affiliation explains about as large a share of the variance in views on interest categories as does national affiliation. In the case of views on party representation, however, there is an exception: the impact of party affiliation here is weaker than that of national affiliation, which accounts for over one-third of the variance. Party affiliation thus affects members' view of their task, but no more than national affiliation is it a decisive factor in its own right.

As far as differences between the parties are concerned, representatives for leftist parties place a relatively heavy stress on party representation and, above all, on the representation of economically disadvantaged groups. Social democrats and (especially) traditional agrarians take a broad view of their task; they tend, that is, to see themselves as representatives for a greater number of specific interests than do other MPs.

MPs from right-wing parties are relatively less inclined to defend disadvantaged groups and relatively more inclined to view business interests positively. Together with agrarian members and populist MPs, moreover, right-wing representatives are most inclined to give priority to the Burkean independence principle.

It bears noting that these results represent averages and so serve partly to obscure differences within the party families. One of the clearest examples of this can be seen in the case of the agrarians: Danish agrarian MPs (Venstre) are substantially less inclined than their counterparts in Finland, Norway, and Sweden to see themselves as champions for a large number of specific interests.

Another difference has to do with the views of conservatives on party representation and on the Burkean injunction that representatives should

Table 3.4

Proportion of Members Who View It As Very Important to Champion Various Interests, by Party Family (%)

	Left Partyists	Social Democrats	Centrist Parties	Right Partyists	Agrarians	Populist Parties (only Den., Nor.)	Eta²
Own party	58	49	59	51	50	40	.01
Own district	9	25	16	30	30	0	.07*
Individual voters	13	22	20	32	26	28	.01
Weak groups	34	35	20	19	36	5	.07*
Business interests	1	7	3	17	27	18	.06*
Ideological groups (only Den., Nor., Swed.)	3	2	22	9	6	0	.09*
Personal views	41	42	39	54	50	75	.03*
N	59	295	71	136	100	14	

Notes: Table entries are average percentages with equal weight given to all parliamentary parties. Coding details of party families are given in appendix 3.

*p < .05

"represent themselves." Conservatives from Denmark, Finland, and Iceland are disposed to lay less stress on party and more on independent action than are their counterparts in Norway and Sweden. In Denmark, Finland, and Iceland, then, we find clearer traces of the critical attitude toward parties and the heavy stress on independent action usually associated with conservative members of parliament. Icelandic conservatives, finally, are unusually positive toward defending the interests of their constituency, and the interests of economically disadvantaged groups, too.

GROUP AFFILIATION HAS IMPORTANCE

Group affiliation is the second general determinant of MPs' view of their task. If we find support for the thesis that MPs are inclined to see themselves as representatives for groups to which they themselves belong, it will qualify as a theoretically important finding. Analyses of social representation commonly conclude that the effect of group affiliation on MPs' actions is a small one. If task definition proves to be an intermediary variable between MPs' group affiliation and their behavior in parliament, then the debate over the representation of social groups in parliament will undeniably seem relevant. Studies taking no account of MPs' personal view of their task would, in that case, have underestimated the importance of social-background factors.

Our reasoning here can be summarized in the following formula: not all female MPs consider it their task to represent women, but it is most often women who define their task in this fashion and it is mainly such self-defined representatives of women who work on behalf of women's interests.[17]

The earlier Swedish parliamentary study provided clear support for such a connection between group affiliation and task definition (Esaiasson and Holmberg 1996:68–70). Table 3.5 shows the results of a comparable analysis for all of the Nordic parliaments. Table entries represent the probability—both among representatives who are affiliated with the group in question and among representatives who are not—of seeing oneself as a champion of a specific interest.

In accordance with expectation, we find a clear tendency among MPs to see themselves as representatives for the group to which they themselves belong. The tendency is visible in all of the parliaments and (as shown by a more detailed analysis not here reported) within all of the party families. The relationship is not, however, equally strong for all group interests. We see the strongest tendencies toward this kind of direct group representation in the case of wage-earners, women, and youth. Farmers, too, have

Table 3.5

Members' Propensity to Define Themselves as Champions of Various Interests, By Affiliation to the Group Interest in Question (% self-defined interest champions)

Type of Interest	Denmark			Finland			Iceland			Norway			Sweden		
	A	O	Diff.	A	O	Diff.	A	O	Diff.	A	O	Diff.	A	O	Diff.
Wage earners	50	16	**+34**	14	1	**+13**		NA		23	3	**+20**	46	11	**+35**
Women	25	3	**+22**	17	4	**+13**	82	16	**+66**	44	3	**+41**	52	6	**+46**
Young people	13	10	**+3**	38	10	**+28**	50	32	**+18**	29	13	**+16**	46	12	**+34**
Pensioners	9	0	**+9**		NA			NA		22	3	**+19**	7	9	**−2**
Businessmen	25	4	**+21**	10	12	**−2**	33	10	**+23**	9	6	**+3**	6	8	**−2**
Farmers	12	3	**+9**	75	4	**+71**	33	15	**+18**	0	0	**+0**	15	5	**+10**

Note: Positive figures in boldface indicate that members who are affiliated with the group in question (A) are more likely to define themselves as champions of the interest than are members who are not affiliated with the group in question (O). Group affiliations have been defined as follows: "Wage earners" are members who were blue-collar workers when they first won a seat in parliament; "Businessmen" and "Farmers" have been defined in a corresponding way. "Young people" are defined as 34 years old or younger. "Pensioners" have been defined as 60 years old or older. The minimum number of respondents are 3 (Icelandic businessmen and farmers, respectively) and 4 (Danish wage earners, and Icelandic young people). NA = data not available.

many interest champions among affiliated MPs. By contrast, it is only in a less systematic and tangible degree that the interests of businessmen and of pensioners are championed by MPs belonging to these groups.

The results clearly demonstrate that the social experiences of MPs carry potential significance for their work in parliament. Members who belong to a given social group are generally more inclined to see themselves as champions of the group in question. This means that the nominating process of the parties stands out as of obvious interest. If persons of the "right" background end up in parliament, the interest in question will enjoy greater prospects for being heard than would otherwise have been the case (even if said interest has good relations with one or more parties).

However—and this is important to add—such direct group representation does not arise automatically for all groups and for all MPs. For this representation to be realized, MPs must identify with the group in question.

BACKBENCHERS AND MULTIVARIATE ANALYSIS

The third determinant of MPs' task definition is *parliamentary position*. We may expect "backbenchers"—publicly anonymous members and members without formal positions of power—to be more inclined than frontbenchers to include a large number of specific interests in their task definition. Backbenchers can have varying motives for defining their task so broadly; they may seek, for example, to create electoral coalitions for ensuring their re-election or they wish to do a meaningful job. The important thing in this connection is that they take another view of their task than do their more influential colleagues.

The significance of members' parliamentary position was addressed in the above analysis of the effect of institutional arrangements. Large parliaments like the Swedish Riksdag have a substantial number of backbenchers; this means, it may be assumed, that Swedish MPs as a collective regard themselves as champions of more interests than do their Nordic colleagues. We are able to observe such a tendency when comparing parliaments as collectives; whether or not such a tendency exists at the individual level remains to be studied.

The following analysis is based on testing the effect of parliamentary position simultaneously with that of other explanatory factors. Such a multivariate regression analysis allows us to ascertain the extent to which the three general determinants associated with the task-definition approach—party affiliation, group affiliation, and parliamentary position—each contribute independently to members' task definition.

In view of the focus of this study on the impact of institutional arrangements, the presence of national differences must be reckoned especially significant. If the country differences observed earlier disappear when parliamentary position, party affiliation, and social-group affiliation are controlled for, then there is reason to speak of a general Nordic pattern in respect to MPs' task definition. If, on the other hand, differences between the parliaments remain after parliamentary position (and the other factors in the model) have been controlled for, we may interpret this as indicating the existence of specifically national preconditions for members' view of their task. As discussed earlier, these differences may be the result of institutional arrangements other than parliamentary size, but they can also be caused by cultural factors.

In the following, national affiliation is represented by dummy variables for each parliament. The drawback with this standard technique is that the result can depend on the choice of baseline category. We have chosen in our case to use Norway as the reference point. We have settled on Norway because representatives in that country have proved, in a series of paired comparisons of task definitions, to diverge from their colleagues in a lesser degree than do MPs from the other Nordic countries.[18] By thus using Norway as the baseline comparison, we can get an idea of how often each country diverges from the typical Nordic pattern.

The model with individual determinants and country factors will only be tested in the case of interest categories for which it is relevant to study the consequences of group affiliation. Party representation, Burkean self-representation, and individual representation are therefore excluded from the analysis.[19] Another restriction is that our analysis is limited to Denmark, Iceland, Norway, and Sweden (we do not have information for all the variables in the case of Finland). Table 3.6 shows the results of seven multiple regression analyses in all.

The question of whether or not the basic assumptions of the task-definition approach hold up even when confronted with a multivariate analysis can be answered in the affirmative. As expected, parliamentary backbenchers tend to be extra inclined to see themselves as representatives for various specific interests (the effects are statistically significant in five of seven cases). The analyses show further that, as a rule, all three explanatory factors contribute independently to explaining members' task definition. MPs' views of their task are dependent on all three: party affiliation, group affiliation, and parliamentary position.

Table 3.6

Determinants of Members' Views on Their Personal Task As Representatives (unstandardized regression coefficients, OLS estimates)

Determinants	Constituency Representation	Type of Interest Group Representation— Underprivileged Groups			
		Women	Wage Earners	Young	Pensioners
Party affiliation					
Left party		.65*	.48*		
Soc. dem.	.34*	.54*	.69*	.35*	.22*
Agrarian	.19*	.49*	.27*	.28*	.14*
Green		.64	.56*		
Group affiliation					
Affiliated with the group	.32*	.71*	.33*	.32*	.03
Position in parliament					
Backbencher	.03	.19*	.20*	.16*	.17*
Country					
Denmark	−.13	−.25*	.08	−.20*	.02
Iceland	.04	.41*	.62*	.42*	.48*
Sweden	.19*	.10	.20*	−.01	.10
Constant	1.47*	.88*	1.04*	1.43*	1.20*
Adjusted R²	.12	.29	.19	.09	.03

Determinants	Type of Interest Group Representation— Private Business	
	Businessmen	Farmers
Party affiliation		
Agrarian	.35*	.46*
Right party	.21*	.01*
Populist	.57*	
Group affiliation		
Affiliated with the group	.07	.37*
Position in parliament		
Backbencher	.17*	.03
Country		
Denmark	−.31*	−.05
Iceland	.02	.47*
Sweden	.05	.24*
Constant	1.24*	.86*
Adjusted R²	.05	.09

Notes: All independent variables have been dichotomized. The dependent variables are coded 0–3. The number of respondents are 626. Norway has been defined as the baseline category.

*$p \leq .05$

In the matter of party affiliation, the multivariate analyses demonstrate more clearly than before that agrarian MPs are particularly inclined to define themselves as representatives for specific interests. Affiliation with a traditional agrarian party has a positive effect for *all seven* interest categories.

In addition to the generally positive attitude of agrarian MPs toward interest representation, Nordic MPs in general tend to see themselves as champions of the interests of groups with which their party has strong electoral ties (i.e., social democrats with various socioeconomically disadvantaged groups, conservatives and populists with businessmen, leftists with women, and environmentalists with women and youth).

As regards group affiliation, our analyses confirm that MPs' gender is of particular importance. On the other hand, neither an advanced age nor a background in business has any systematic impact on members' task definition.

As regards the important factor of national affiliation, the results are mixed. There is clearly no common Nordic pattern as far as overall views on interest representation are concerned. The views of Icelandic MPs in this question are too divergent. Icelandic MPs are "unwarrantedly" positive toward defending the great majority of interest groups defined.

At the same time that Iceland diverges in this question, the other countries tend to resemble one another. Swedish MPs diverge from the general Nordic pattern only in the view they take of constituency representation and the representation of agricultural interests. Danish MPs are, in a couple of cases, "unwarrantedly" negative toward the representation of social-group interests. When account is taken of the individual determinants, then, substantial similarities are evident, at least between the Danish, Norwegian, and Swedish parliaments.

CONCLUSIONS—SIMILAR YET DIFFERENT

On the most general level, the analysis indicates that the individualist perspective is fruitful even when applied to party-dominated working parliaments. The task-definition approach—which assumes that MPs are guided in their actions by their personal views about which interests are most important to champion, and which assumes that said views are determined by MPs' party affiliation, group affiliation, and parliamentary position—this approach works well for all of the Nordic parliaments. We can accordingly note the existence of a common Nordic pattern, a pattern which furthermore is probably present in most political contexts. If the task-definition approach is fruitful even when applied to the party-dominated parliaments of the Nordic countries, it is very likely applicable to the U.S. Congress, and to Westminster-style parliaments also.

When it comes to the *content* of MPs' task definition, however, the picture is more complicated. The point of departure for our analysis of why Nordic parliamentarians define their task as they do is the degree of similarity or difference between the parliaments. If MPs take a similar view of their task regardless of the parliament in which they sit, then differing institutional arrangements and politico-cultural factors cannot have any importance for task definitions. If there are differences between the parliaments, on the other hand, then institutional arrangements and/or politico-cultural factors must be part of the picture in a corresponding degree.

To what extent can we speak of similarities and differences between the Nordic parliaments? If we choose to reason strictly—and to use statistical significance as our criterion for ascertaining differences between countries—then the differences between the parliaments are large. For most of the interest categories we have studied, at least one of the parliaments diverges from the common Nordic pattern. If, however, we require as well that such differences be *substantively* significant, then the similarities between the parliaments are clear.

Looking first at the similarities between the parliaments, we find two results of general application. Irrespective of institutional arrangements and cultural conditions, elected representatives are inclined to define themselves as champions of the interests both of their constituency and of private persons who turn to them for help. There is something of general application in the role of elected representative for the people which makes MPs want to take responsibility for geographical areas to which they are linked and for individuals who seek their assistance.

A further substantive similarity between the Nordic parliaments that might be thought to apply as well to other parliaments has to do with the conditions faced by different interest groups. The interests of the constituency and of women come high on the list for MPs in all of the Nordic parliaments.

There is an important difference in principle between these two interest groups. Our analysis of members' actions shows that constituency interests are also promoted in practice by many MPs who do *not* define themselves as constituency champions.[20] Women's interests, by contrast, are promoted almost exclusively by self-defined interest champions.[21] For interest groups of the latter kind, the nominating process stands out as particularly important. It is primarily when representatives who identify with the interest in question have a seat in parliament that interest groups of this sort enjoy prospects for influencing policy.

Turning now to the differences between the Nordic parliaments, we may observe that we partly succeeded in our analyses in specifying how such differences arise. As far as institutional arrangements are concerned, the electoral system has a marked effect on MPs' views on party representation: members in party-list systems are substantially more disposed to acknowledge the dominant position of the party than are MPs in systems focused on individual candidates. Another systematic institutional effect is that produced by the size of the parliamentary body. Large parliaments like the Swedish Riksdag contain more interest champions than the medium-sized parliaments do.

Cultural factors, too, have identifiable consequences for MPs' task definition. The clearest example may be seen in the case of MPs' views on the representation of women's interests. In countries where the question of equal rights has stood high on the agenda in recent years, members are more inclined than elsewhere to define themselves as champions of the interests of women.

The main divergent case for which we have been unable to specify institutional or cultural differences is that of the Icelandic parliament, the Althingi. The views of Icelandic MPs on the representation of various interest groups are too positive to fit in with the general Nordic pattern or to be understood as the result of easily identifiable differences. On the one hand, Icelandic members' task definition resembles what we might expect to find in a clientelist system. On the other hand, the interests of the constituency—where the nominations to parliament take place—are given too low a relative priority for the Icelandic case to qualify as clientelist in the classical sense (marked as the latter is by the geographically concentrated allocation of favors). The distinctive quality of the manner in which Icelandic MPs define their task cannot be easily conceptualized.

It appears, in sum, that the view MPs take of their task is determined both by factors faced by elected representatives the world over and by institutional arrangements and cultural factors. The most we can do, as far as a more exact specification of causes is concerned, is to venture a conclusion of the refutational sort. The Nordic experience in the matter of MPs' task definition does not support the thesis that variations in institutional arrangements are of especial importance when it comes to explaining why parliaments work as they do.

NOTES

1. It should be pointed out that, in contrast to the two dominant approaches within individualistic parliamentary research—*the rational-actor approach* and *role analysis*—the task-definition approach says nothing about the *motives* underlying MPs' view of their task (cf. Mayhew 1974; Fenno 1973; Sinclair 1983; Searing 1991, 1994). This limitation at the level of principle can be turned into an advantage. By testing the degree to which task definitions are compatible with the rational goal of re-election and with notions of normatively appropriate behavior, we can gain an idea of the validity of the two approaches. Much of what representatives do can be explained by reference to an attempt on their part to maximize utility or to fulfill norms; however, certain types of behavior can hardly be understood as involving any effort either to get re-elected or to act in a normatively expected manner. For a more developed discussion, together with tentative results, see Esaiasson and Holmberg (1996).

2. The distinction is captured by the concepts "focus of representation" and "style of representation."

3. It is unclear whether Eulau and Karps have simply forgotten the party as a possible focus of representation or whether they have assigned the party instead to the category of ideologically defined functional interests. From a European perspective, and in view of the doctrinal history, it is clearly necessary to distinguish the party as a category unto itself.

4. The Danish and Finnish surveys did not ask respondents whether they were champions of "teetotalers." The Finnish survey, furthermore, did not seek to ascertain if respondents were champions of "immigrants" or "Christians." A more exact question-wording can be found in the comment to table 3.1.

5. In my view, earlier measurements of MPs' "focus of representation" have been less than successful, for three reasons: (1) the surveys have asked about organizations associated with a group rather than about the group itself, (2) they have used open-ended questions, and (3) they have used "forced-choice alternatives," which require members to describe themselves as representatives for their party or for some alternative. See Daalder and Rusk (1972); Damgaard (1982a: 15–27); Loewenberg and Kim (1978); Kim et al. (1984:84–86); Herzog et al. (1990:60–62).

6. For similar decisions, see Barnes (1977:150) and Loewenberg and Kim (1978:32).

7. Among members who judge it "very important" to put forward views they personally regard as important, between 63 percent (in Finland) and 92 percent (in Sweden) also consider the promotion of a specific interest to be part of their task as a representative.

8. For an energetic attempt to find "the electoral connection," even when the facts point the other way, see Uslaner (1985).

9. For a related analysis of representatives' views on party discipline, see Jensen's chapter 9 in this volume.

10. Icelandic MPs constitute, together with their Danish counterparts, an intermediate group between the maverick Finns and the party-loyal Norwegians and Swedes.

11. If by frontbenchers we mean the chairpersons of parliamentary committees, the proportion of backbenchers in the Nordic parliaments is as follows: in Denmark 74 percent, in Finland 88 percent, in Iceland 62 percent, in Norway 86 percent, and in Sweden 91 percent.

12. For a detailed analysis of Nordic MPs' views on the representation of women's interests, see Wängnerud's chapter 6 in this volume.

13. One limitation lies in the fact that we ask, on one and the same occasion, both about MPs' task definition and about their actual behavior. A test on the more complete Swedish data for the parliamentary period from 1985 to 1988 shows, however, that this limitation does not affect the results in any substantial way.

14. Jensen's analysis in chapter 9 is helpful for understanding why this is the case.

15. Our analysis here is based on a survey question worded as follows: "Have you actively cooperated, during the past year, with MPs from other parties in order to influence specific parliamentary decisions within one or several of the issue areas below?" The four response alternatives offered ranged from "many times" to "never." Four types of issue relevant to the analysis were included: *localization issues; other regional/local issues; religion and ethics;* and *issues bearing on equal rights for men and women.* By designing an additive index for all cross-party activities, we were also able to test for behavioral consequences of the Burkean option ("representation of personal views")—under the assumption, that is, that such "representatives of themselves" are more inclined than other members to cooperate with MPs from other parties. For a detailed presentation of these survey questions, see chapter 9 in this volume.

16. See appendix 3 for a more detailed definition of the party families. No such attempt at classification can be free of objection. For this analysis, two of our decisions are especially debatable: First, our decision to collapse the small liberal and Christian parties into the category of "Centrist Parties." Second, our classification of the Danish party Venstre as an agrarian party.

17. On the politics of presence, see Phillips (1995). For a study that shows relatively large differences between male and female representatives, see Wängnerud (1998).

18. Our conclusion here is based on paired comparisons of the five Nordic countries in respect of the ten interest categories found in all of the surveys (see table 3.1). Norwegian MPs diverge significantly from other members in 10 cases. The corresponding figures for the other countries are as follows: Denmark 13, Finland 15, Iceland 20, and Sweden 15. The maximum number of differences is 40 (five countries, ten interest categories).

19. Note that the test is not confined to interest groups where it is easy to determine whether or not an MP belongs (women, youth, pensioners, wage-

earners, farmers, and businessmen). We have delineated an affiliational aspect of *constituency representation,* too. Members from constituencies in peripheral parts of the country can be said to have particular cause to define themselves as constituency champions, as compared to members from the nation's center (with the "center" operationalized as the large metropolitan regions; see Valen, Narud, and Hardarson in this volume). Thus the multivariate analyses include, in addition to six types of group representation, constituency representation.

20. A second interest group in this particularly favored category is "businessmen."

21. Other interest groups facing similar conditions include idea-based groups such as "Christians" and "teetotalers."

4

Does Social Background Matter?

Hanne Marthe Narud and Henry Valen

Normal political processes rarely produce an elite drawn proportionately from all segments of society. The conventional view is that political leaders constitute an economic and social elite that disproportionately hails from upper-status occupations and privileged family backgrounds. Moreover, comparative evidence suggests that, relative to their incidence in the adult population as a whole, university graduates are highly overrepresented among Western legislative (and administrative) elites (Putnam 1976). Yet one of the most widely recognized theories of representative democracy holds that elected representatives should "mirror" those they represent, and not just in social, economic and demographic terms but also—and more importantly—in terms of values, beliefs, and opinions. The basic idea is that parliament should make the decisions that people themselves would have made had they themselves been able to decide. And the best guarantee for this actually happening is a national assembly that mirrors the range of social and demographic groups found in society.

Other theories of representative democracy, however, take a different view of the role of representatives. The problem at hand is often referred to as the "mandate-independent" controversy (Pitkin 1967; Thomassen 1994). According to the populist view of representative democracy described above, the representative body should constitute a society in miniature—it should contain in itself the varying interests and opinions found among the absent others. Representatives are thus instructed to act in accordance with the will and wishes of their constituents. But this raises certain questions. Legislators chosen from large populations by random sampling would be statistically representative, but would they be capable of acting collectively as effective representatives? Burke argued that some groups may be better represented through "virtual representation," that is, by being represented by people with economic and social characteristics different from their own. The "liberal theory of democracy" holds that a division of labor obtains between voters and their representatives, and that representatives should act *independently* of the views of their constituents and in accordance with their own mature judgments.

In this chapter, we shall draw attention to the social and demographic composition of Nordic legislatures and to the consequences thereof. Two questions are posed. First, to what extent are Nordic parliamentarians socially and demographically representative of their voters? And second, what is the impact of social and demographic background on the political attitudes of representatives? Before turning to the empirical analysis, we shall take a closer look at the various ways in which different types of political representation can be combined. We shall also briefly summarize previous findings on the question of social representation.

TYPES OF REPRESENTATION

Reality rarely fits any of the ideal models described above. Yet, by combining various characteristics of "persons" and "opinions" in a fourfold table, we can get several different combinations of possibilities (figure 4.1).

In the *ideal-democracy model*, representatives share both the social characteristics and the opinions of those who have elected them. They are "models in miniature" of those they represent. Policy decisions are thus made, we might say, "by people from the people for the people" (Hernes and Martinussen 1980:76). This model is similar to the so-called theory of demographic representation, which rests on the underlying premise that only firsthand experience (from one's background) is correlated with political interest and, hence, with political attitudes and behavior (see, e.g., Norris and Lovenduski 1993).

By contrast, the term *background representation* refers to a situation in which representatives are socially representative of their voters but have adopted values and opinions different from those of their constituents. The third type of model, or what Hernes and Martinussen (1980) call *advocate representation*, resembles the mandate theory of representation; it implies that those who share the opinions of a specific group are not necessarily themselves a part of that group. They represent, that is, the opinions of a group from which they deviate socially.

Finally, the *caretaker* form of representation resembles the independent theory of representation; according to this model, elected representatives

Representative of Opinions

		Yes	No
Representative of Personal Characteristics	Yes	Ideal democracy	Background representation
	No	Advocate representation	Care-taker representation

Figure 4.1 A Typology of Theories of Representation: Opinions and Persons. *Source:* Hernes and Martinusen (1980).

deviate from their voters both socially and in terms of opinion. They make decisions on behalf of the electorate, but they are not tied to the opinions of their constituents.

The framework displayed in figure 4.1 fits the analytical purpose of this chapter quite neatly. First of all, it combines the study of social representation with that of political opinions and attitudes (which is the real focus of this chapter). Second, it provides us with a typology for classifying different types of political representation in the Nordic countries. The interesting question here is which types of representation best fit the reality of the Nordic democracies. Before analyzing this question empirically, we shall present a brief overview of the study of social representation.

SOCIAL REPRESENTATION REVISITED

It should be immediately noted—as suggested in the beginning of this chapter—that reality rarely fits the "ideal" type of democracy described in figure 4.1 (in the first cell). The composition of legislatures seldom reflects that of the society from which they are drawn; parliamentarians are not at all a "mirror in miniature" of the population that voted for them. Rather, despite strong demands for the inclusion of various social and demographic groups, most elected bodies remain strikingly unrepresentative—in terms of gender, class, age, and education (Putnam 1976; Norris 1996a). The Nordic democracies are no exception to this "iron law" of social bias, for the socioeconomic status of Nordic parliamentarians is well above that of Nordic voters on average, as measured by income, occupational background, and education (Valen 1966a; 1966b; Hellevik 1969; Holmberg 1974; Eliassen and Pedersen 1978; Pedersen 1972; Damgaard 1977; 1982a;

Holmberg and Esaiasson 1988; Ruostetsaari 1993; Kristjánsson 1994; Jensen 1994; Esaiasson and Holmberg 1996; Matthews and Valen 1999).

The reason for this more or less global phenomenon may lie in *institutional* and *party-specific* factors, as well as *individual* ones (Norris and Lovenduski 1993; 1995; Norris 1996a). The effect of the *electoral system* on the representation of women, for example, is well-established. Moreover, *recruitment structures* are relevant in the sense that they constrain the choices available to the gatekeepers and, hence, the opportunities facing individual candidates. In addition, the extent to which decision-making is centralized or decentralized has an impact on the way in which lists of candidates are balanced. Finally, individual *supply* and *demand* factors must also be considered in the process of legislative recruitment (Norris and Lovenduski 1993; 1995; see also Norris 1996a).

The scope of this chapter does not allow for a detailed discussion of all the mechanisms relevant to the recruitment process. In an international perspective, however, the disparities of status between representatives and their voters in the Nordic countries cannot be considered very large. Comparative studies show the social representativeness of Nordic legislatures to be well above that of assemblies in the larger European countries, as well as above that of the U.S. Congress (Norris and Lovenduski 1995). Nevertheless, the predominant trend in the Nordic countries has been to replace farmers and blue-collar workers with career politicians (Eliassen and Pedersen 1978; Kristjánsson 1994; Esaiasson and Holmberg 1996; Matthews and Valen 1999; Narud 1997; Helander 1997; Ruostetsaari 1997). In all countries we observe a trend toward a greater professionalization of legislatures, as younger and more highly educated members—almost all of them experienced public or party officeholders—are recruited. The question to which we now turn is the social and demographic composition of Nordic parliaments in the 1990s.

THE LEGISLATURES AND THE VOTERS

The data to be used in the present chapter are taken from the general Nordleg surveys. Of relevance here are the questions providing information on representatives' background, as well as those giving information on the attitudes of representatives toward certain issues (or issue areas). In addition, we have supplemented the survey data with statistics on the demographic background of members of parliament. On the voter level, we rely on data from the surveys carried out in Iceland, Norway, Sweden, and Denmark. Since no voter data were collected for Finland, this chapter is restricted to an analysis of the other four countries.

Table 4.1 shows the social and demographic composition of the Nordic legislatures in the 1990s. Observe that information on the MP level about gender and age is based on bibliographical data, whereas information about sector, occupation, and education is taken from the questionnaires and thus is based on the respondents' self-classification. It should also be noted that the categories for occupation (on the voter level) and education (on both levels) are country-specific and so are not directly comparable from one nation to the next. In order to increase comparability, attempts have been made on the voter level to recode some of the classifications for occupation.[1]

With respect to gender, the Swedish Riksdag does "best," since more than 40 percent of its members are women. For Denmark and Norway, respectively, the figures are 33 percent and 38 percent; Iceland comes last, at 25 percent. As regards age, there is very little variation between the Nordic nations. About two-thirds of the members of the Storting, Folketing, and Riksdag fall within the middle-aged group (thirty-six to fifty-four years old), whereas three-fourths of the Icelandic representatives fall into this category. The Icelandic Althingi has strikingly few young representatives; only 3 per cent of its members were thirty-five or younger in 1996.

With respect to occupation, the table reveals that the Swedish Riksdag has recruited the highest number of blue-collar workers (16 percent), whereas the Icelandic Althingi contains no workers at all. The latter consists in a high proportion of white-collar employees; 86 percent of Althingi representatives belong to this occupational category. The Danish Folketing has the highest number of self-employed and farmers/fishermen, while only 5 percent of Swedish MPs belong to the category of self-employed. The share of representatives with a background in the primary sector is almost the same for Norway and Sweden (between 4 and 5 percent).

Turning to sector, a majority of those sitting in the Swedish Riksdag hail from the public sector. By contrast, the Danish Folketing and the Norwegian Storting have recruited more of their members from the private sector than from the public. The Icelandic Althingi has recruited about the same number from each.

In regard to education, finally, the most striking deviation lies in the large number of representatives with low education in the Storting, as compared with those in the other three legislatures (especially the Riksdag). The average share of representatives who are highly educated is significant for all four countries. The Storting has the lowest number of representatives with a mid-level education. Recall, however, that these classifications are based on country-specific categories and thus are not directly comparable.

Table 4.1
Social Representativeness of Four Nordic Parliaments (%)

Socioeconomic Group	Denmark			Iceland			Norway			Sweden		
	MPs	Voters	Diff.	MPs	Voters	Diff.	MPs	Voters	Diff.	MPs	Voters	Diff.
Gender												
Male	67	53	+14	75	50	+25	62	50	+12	59	48	+11
Female	33	47	−14	25	50	−25	38	50	−12	41	52	−11
Age group												
18–35	7	32	−25	3	35	−32	11	38	−27	8	36	−28
36–44	19	20	−1	24	26	−2	17	21	−4	14	15	−1
45–54	44	18	+26	56	18	+38	45	17	+28	44	19	+25
55+	30	29	+1	18	21	−3	27	24	+3	35	30	+5
Occupation[a]												
Blue-collar	4	38	−34	0	42	−42	10	33	−23	16	40	−24
White-collar	75	52	+23	86	48	+38	76	59	+17	75	51	+24
Self-employed	13	8	+5	7	6	+1	9	4	+5	5	7	−2
Farmer/fisher	8	2	+6	7	4	+3	5	4	+1	4	3	+1
Sector												
Public	46	NA		49	34	+15	47	39	+8	52	38	+14
Private	54	NA		51	66	−15	53	61	−8	48	62	−14
Education[b]												
Low	5	33	−28	6	34	−28	1	23	−22	11	26	−15
Middle	26	41	−15	26	46	−20	36	53	−17	16	52	−36
High	69	26	+43	68	20	+48	63	24	+39	73	23	+50

Note: NA = not available.

[a] Occupational classifications of the representatives refer to what applied when they first were elected to parliament. For purposes of this table, those MPs who defined themselves as "professional politicians" have been classified as "white-collar."

[b] Educational classifications are based on country-specific categories. For Denmark, the following definitions have been applied: "low" (*ingen erhvervsuddannelse*), "middle" (*specialarb. kurser faglærde mesterlære*), "high" (*højere uddannelse kort, højere uddannelse mellem, højere uddannelse lang, studerende*). For Iceland: "low" (compulsory), "middle" (compulsory + 1–3 years, trade/agriculture, matriculation, teacher training, nurse training), "high" (university studies with or without degree). For Norway: "low" (*barneskole, ungdomsskole*), "middle" (*gymnas 1 [yrkesskole], gymnas 2 [eksamen artium]*), "high" (*universitet 1, universitet 2, universitet 3, forsker*). For Sweden: "low" (*folkskola, yrkesskolenivå, grundskolenivå*), "middle" (*realskolenivå, gymnasienivå*), "high" (*studentnivå, universitetsnivå*). For Denmark, Iceland, and Norway, all data are from respective surveys as described in appendix 1. For Sweden, data concerning the gender and age of voters are based upon public statistics.

Turning to the level of social and demographic representativeness in the four legislatures, we find that the greatest disparities between representatives and voters have to do with education and age. The highly educated are greatly overrepresented in all four assemblies, whereas people with low and mid-level educations are underrepresented. Concerning age, the patterns are almost identical for all four countries, with the middle-aged being greatly overrepresented. The youngest part of the population—those between eighteen and thirty-five—is the most underrepresented.

Differences between representatives and voters are also evident as regards gender and sector. Women are underrepresented in all four assemblies, but most notably in Iceland. So are people working in the private sector. Public-sector employees are somewhat more overrepresented in the Riksdag and the Althingi than in the Storting. As regards occupation, blue-collar workers are greatly underrepresented in all the assemblies, and most dramatically so in Iceland. White-collar employees are overrepresented in all four parliaments, but least so in the Storting. Self-employed persons are underrepresented in the Riksdag, but slightly overrepresented in the other legislatures. Farmers are represented fairly proportionately in Norway and Sweden, whereas they are a bit overrepresented in Iceland and (especially) Denmark.

So far, and consistent with the results of previous research (see, e.g., Jensen 1994; Esaiasson and Holmberg 1996; Matthews and Valen 1999; Kristjánsson 1994), we may conclude that elected representatives in the Nordic countries do not mirror their electorates in socioeconomic and demographic terms. In respect of the typology in figure 4.1, therefore, the Nordic democracies exhibit neither the "ideal" nor the "background" type of political representation. Compared with their voters, Nordic representatives are on average much better educated, higher in occupational status, and more often middle-aged.

PARTY DIFFERENCES

The scope and character of group representation vary from one party to the next, depending on historical background, organizational affiliation, and ideology. We should expect, for instance, the proportion of blue-collar workers to be higher in socialist parties, the proportion of farmers to be higher in agrarian parties, and the proportion of white-collar employees to be higher in conservative parties. When exploring this possibility, we will use "party" as the unit of analysis and shall disregard country-specific differences. In so doing, we classify the Nordic parties into several "party families." Table 4.2 shows mass-elite differences for the four largest party categories.

Not unexpectedly, the table demonstrates that social democratic and left socialist parties are comprised of a much higher proportion of blue-collar workers than are parties of the other two types. In all parties, though, white-collar employees predominate. About 80 percent of representatives in all four party families belong to this group.

Surprisingly enough, the proportion who are farmers/fishermen is higher among conservatives than among agrarians (15 percent and 10 percent, respectively). The primary sector has but meager representation in the socialist parties, as does the group of self-employed. The latter group, in fact, is not really well-represented in any of the four party families.

Turning to gender and age, it is clear that the social democratic parties have the highest proportion of female representatives, whereas the other three party families have a female quotient of about 30 percent. The left socialist parties have by far the fewest old and young representatives: an impressive 81 percent of their MPs are middle-aged. By contrast, almost 40 percent of conservative MPs are fifty-five or older, while the share of "young" representatives comes to about 10 percent in all party families except the left socialists.

In the matter of sector, the differences between the parties follow the traditional socialist/bourgeois "bloc" pattern. The social democrats and the left socialists recruit the majority of their MPs from the public sector, whereas the opposite is true for the two nonsocialist party groupings (the conservatives and the agrarians). But the differences between the party groupings are not very big.

In respect of education, finally, interesting differences appear between the left socialists on the one hand and the social democrats on the other. The left socialist parties recruit almost 90 percent of their MPs from the highly educated, giving them an image as academic "elite" parties. The social democratic parties, on the other hand, recruit well over 40 percent of their representatives from lower or mid-level educational groups. The agrarian parties have a similar profile regarding education, while conservative MPs are predominantly highly educated. Only 1 percent of conservative representatives have low education; 16 percent report having a mid-level education.

Overall, the recruitment patterns of the parties are what we might expect from their ideology and their party platforms. In terms of education, occupation, and gender, the social democrats are more inclined than the other three party families to fit the "background" type of representation

Table 4.2
Socioeconomic Composition of Party Families in Nordic Parliaments (%)

| | Party Family | | | |
Socioeconomic Group	Left Socialists	Social Democrats	Agrarians	Conservatives
Gender				
Male	69	56	69	71
Female	31	44	31	29
Age group				
18–35	3	11	10	11
36–44	29	14	17	16
45–54	52	52	44	35
55+	16	24	30	38
Occupation				
Blue-collar	19	20	1	2
White-collar	79	78	88	81
Self-employed	0	1	1	3
Farmer/fisher	2	2	10	15
Sector				
Public	52	55	45	41
Private	48	45	55	59
Education				
Low	5	12	5	1
Middle	8	30	34	16
High	87	58	61	83

described in figure 4.1. If we recall the electoral bias of the labor vote, however, we see that social democratic MPs are hardly "mirrors in miniature" of their electorate. The question to which we now turn is the impact of social and demographic background on the political attitudes of representatives. Does background matter?

SOCIAL REPRESENTATION AND POLITICAL ATTITUDES

The "rationale" for social representation derives, we might say, from demands for "equity" and "legitimacy." The most common argument is that background and experience are important prerequisites for "representativeness" in regard to priorities, attitudes, and behavior. We disregarded the behavioral aspect and set out to test the validity of this argument in terms of the background variables listed in tables 4.1 and 4.2: gender, age, occupation, sector, and education. Do persons with higher education, for example, have attitudes on certain issues different from those of persons with lower education? Do men articulate different concerns from those of women? Do people from different sectors, age groups, and occupational groups have different policy priorities?

In order to simplify the analysis, we have divided three of the relevant criteria (education, occupation, and age) into two separate categories, with values of "low" and "high."[2] Moreover, in order to generate more robust measures, we have subjected several policy issues to a factor analysis and constructed two additive indexes based upon the items loading most strongly under two separate factors.[3]

The first index, which we have called the "left-right" index, is constructed on the basis of five items: reducing the size of the public sector, increasing taxes on high incomes, reducing income differences, privatizing health care, and reducing the influence of financial markets. The second index is based on three items that would seem to tap values of a "softer" nature: introducing a six-hour working day for all employees, prohibiting the use of private cars in town centers, and introducing women's quotas for higher positions in public administration. We have named this the "new politics" index.[4] We have recoded the values of the items so that all answers go in the same direction.[5]

In addition to devising these indexes, we have analyzed the attitudes of respondents toward four specific policy proposals: prohibiting pornography, reducing the number of refugees, allowing the manipulation of genes, and providing economic support to agricultural areas.

As a first step, we examine the bivariate relationship between group membership and political attitudes. The mean score for each group, and the differences in mean scores between the groups, are presented in table 4.3.

The table demonstrates clearly that legislators of different backgrounds hold different views on the policy questions at hand. The greatest differences arise in relation to gender and sector. On both indexes, and on three of the four items listed in the table, men and women differ to a statistically significant extent. Women are more "leftist" than men, and they are more favorable toward "new politics" (i.e., introducing a six-hour working day, prohibiting cars in the inner city, and introducing women's quotas for higher positions). Furthermore, they are much more skeptical about pornography and gene manipulation than men are, and they are less in favor of reducing the number of refugees. The same pattern is also evident for sector. That is, legislators recruited from the public sector express pretty much the same views as women, while MPs from the private sector express views similar to men's.[6]

Occupation has an impact in respect of three policy matters: left-right

Table 4.3
Policy Views of Nordic Members by Socioeconomic Group (mean scores)

Socioeconomic Group	Left-Right Index[a]	New Politics Index[b]	Pornography[c]	Reduce No. of Refugees[c]	Gene Manipulation[c]	Economic Support to Agricultural Areas[c]
Gender						
Men	16.5	7.5	3.2	3.6	2.3	2.9
Women	19.1	9.8	2.3	4.1	1.9	2.9
Diff.	**-2.6****	**-2.3****	**+0.9****	**-0.5****	**+0.4****	**0.0**
Occupation						
High	16.9	8.1	2.9	3.8	2.2	2.9
Low	21.3	9.7	2.4	3.8	2.0	2.8
Diff.	**-4.4****	**-1.6****	**+0.5****	**0.0**	**+0.2**	**+0.1**
Education						
High	17.3	8.4	2.9	3.9	2.2	2.9
Low	19.5	8.4	2.5	3.3	2.0	2.7
Diff.	**-2.2***	**+0.0**	**+0.4**	**+0.6****	**+0.2**	**+0.2**
Sector						
Public	18.4	8.9	2.7	3.9	2.1	2.9
Private	16.4	7.6	3.1	3.7	2.3	2.9
Diff.	**+2.0****	**+1.3****	**-0.4****	**+0.2***	**-0.2***	**0.0**
Age						
High (45+)	17.6	8.3	2.8	3.8	2.1	3.1
Low	17.1	8.4	3.1	4.0	2.4	2.8
Diff.	**+0.5**	**-0.1**	**-0.3***	**-0.2***	**-0.2***	**+0.3****

[a]Scale scores vary from 5 to 25.
[b]Scale scores vary from 3 to 15.
[c]Scale scores vary from 1 to 5.

*p < .05, **p < .01

issues, new politics, and pornography. There are also statistically significant differences in mean scores between MPs with "high" education and those with "low." MPs who have only completed compulsory school are more "leftist," as well as more favorable toward reducing the number of refugees, than are those with a greater formal education. Age, on the other hand, has no impact on views toward left-right issues or new politics, although a significant difference between "older" and "younger" legislators is evident in regard to the other four questions, most notably that of providing economic support to agricultural areas. None of the other groups are divided on this last question.

CROSS-COUNTRY COMPARISONS

The above analysis, which is based upon data from all four of the countries, indicates that the structural background of political representatives does indeed matter for their opinions and attitudes. As a next step, we may ask whether and how the observed patterns differ from one country to another. To shed some light on this question, we will compare mean scores for different groups within the various countries (see table 4.4).

The differences in mean scores between different groups are remarkably similar in Norway and Sweden, and these two countries come closest to reflecting the joint pattern of the four countries together. Some deviations are evident for Denmark and Iceland, particularly in respect to gender differences. Gender variations in political attitudes are most evident in the case of Icelandic MPs (perhaps because of the strong underrepresentation of women in that country), while such variations tend to be smallest in Denmark. In all countries the differences between women and men on the question of pornography are both significant and substantial.

Age is the most important factor for variations in MPs' attitudes in Denmark, whereas sector seems to be important in Sweden and to some degree also in Denmark. In Iceland and Norway, on the other hand, sector has no significant impact on variations in attitudes. Overall, the most significant variations in attitudes appear in Sweden, and the least significant in Iceland.

A MULTIVARIATE ANALYSIS

The analysis so far indicates that MPs' policy attitudes are related to their social and demographic background. However, since MPs operate within

Table 4.4
Differences in Policy Views by Socioeconomic Groups among Members of the Respective Nordic Parliaments (mean scores)

Socioeconomic Group	Left-Right Index[a]	New Politics Index[b]	Prohibit Pornography[f]	Reduce No. of Refugees[c]	Gene Manipulation[c]	Support to Agricultural Areas[c]
Denmark						
Gender	-1.9	-1.1	0.6**	-0.5	0.2	0.1
Occupation	-7.0*	-3.6*	-0.2	-0.3	0.5	0.5
Education	0.9	0.3	-0.2	1.4**	-0.4	0.5
Sector	4.1**	1.5*	0.2	0.4	-0.1	-0.1
Age	3.9**	1.4*	-0.2	0.6*	-0.4	-0.1
Iceland						
Gender	-3.5*	-3.9**	0.8*	-0.4	0.9	-0.9
Occupation[d]	—	—	—	—	—	—
Education	-3.2	-0.5	1.0	0.0	1.7**	-0.6
Sector	2.4	1.5	-0.4	-0.3	-0.4	0.6
Age	0.7	-0.2	-0.1	-0.1	-0.8*	0.1
Norway						
Gender	-2.2*	-1.9**	1.0**	-0.5**	0.3*	0.0
Occupation	-4.4**	-2.6**	-0.1	-0.6*	0.1	0.2
Education[e]	—	—	—	—	—	—
Sector	0.8	0.4	-0.5	0.0	-0.2	-0.3
Age	-0.8	-0.2	-0.1	-0.4*	-0.3	-0.6**
Sweden						
Gender	-3.5**	-2.7**	1.0**	-0.4**	0.5**	0.0
Occupation	-3.8**	-0.9	0.5**	0.1	0.2	0.1
Education	-2.7*	0.0	0.4	0.5**	0.1	0.1
Sector	1.7*	1.5**	-0.5**	0.3**	-0.2	0.1
Age	-0.6	-0.6	-0.4	-0.4**	-0.1	-0.2

[a]Scale scores vary from 5 to 25.
[b]Scale scores vary from 3 to 15.
[c]Scale scores vary from 1 to 5.
[d]No cases with the value "low" (i.e., blue-collar workers).
[e]Too few cases with "low" education for meaningful comparisons.

$* = p < .05, ** = p < .01$

Table 4.5

Social-Group Affiliation and Party Affiliation Determine Left-Right Attitudes of Nordic Members (standardized regression coefficients)

Affiliation	Bivariate	Block 1	Block 2
Social-group affiliation			
Gender	.21**	.19**	.05*
Employment sector	−.17**	−.18**	−.09**
Occupation	−.24**	−.25**	−.05*
Education	−.09*	−.09	.01
Age	.04	.04	.03
Party affiliation			
Agrarians	−.10*		−.30**
Conservatives	−.69**		−.79**
Liberals	−.13**		−.27**
Left Socialists	.30**		.08**
Populists	−.25**		−.32**
Christians	−.09*		−.20**
Greens	.11**		−.01
Adjusted R^2		.14	.76
Sig. R^2		.00	.00

Notes: The number of respondents is 510. "Left-Right Attitudes" is defined as in tables 4.3 and 4.4 above.

$^*p < .05, ^{**}p < .01$

the context of their respective parties, and since party discipline in the Nordic legislatures is high, a statistical control for party affiliation is required. One possibility we have investigated is whether the impact of structural background weakens or even disappears when party is introduced into the model. In order to examine this question, we have run a blockwise regression with the five structural variables included in block 1, and the party variables added in block 2. Observe that we do not attempt to evaluate the causal relationship between MPs' political attitudes, their party affiliation, and their social and demographic background. Our sole concern is to measure the extent to which the effect of the background variables is still significant after party is controlled for. Table 4.5 shows the results for the left-right issues included in index 1.

The second-to-last line in table 4.5 shows the amount of variance explained (R^2) when the structural variables are run separately (column 2), and also when the party variables are added to the equation (column 3).[7]

As far as the five background variables included in the first block are concerned, three of the coefficients are statistically significant: gender, sector, and occupation. The last is the most powerful, with a standardized

Table 4.6
Social-Group Affiliation and Party Affiliation
Determine New Politics Attitudes of Nordic Members
(standardized regression coefficients)

Affiliation	Bivariate	Block 1	Block 2
Social-group affiliation			
Gender	.35**	.34**	.23**
Employment sector	−.21**	−.16**	−.09**
Occupation	−.15**	−.18**	−.06*
Education	−.01	−.02	.04
Age	−.01	.04	.03
Party affiliation			
Agrarians	−.07		−.14**
Conservatives	−.55**		−.50**
Liberals	−.07		−.14**
Left Socialists	.39**		.27**
Populists	−.21**		−.22**
Christians	−.05		−.09**
Greens	.29**		.20**
Adjusted R^2		.18	.60
Sig. R^2		.00	.00

Notes: The number of respondents is 510. "New Politics Attitudes"
is defined as in tables 4.3 and 4.4 above.

*$p < .05$, **$p < .01$

beta coefficient of -.25. When party is controlled for, however, the effect of occupation is considerably reduced, but at 5 percent it remains significant. The net effects of gender and sector are also reduced when party is introduced, but they remain statistically significant. Interestingly, neither education nor age seems to matter for representatives' left-right attitudes. A separate analysis indicates, though, that the two variables are intercorrelated in a high degree. When age and education are run separately (in block 1), the coefficient for education is significant; but this is not the case when party is controlled for (in block 2).[8] Age, on the other hand, remains insignificant in both blocks. Another feature worth noting here is the enormous change in variance explained that takes place when party is included; this only confirms our previous argument about the predominant role of the party factor.

The pattern is almost the same in respect to "new politics" attitudes. Table 4.6 shows that gender, sector and occupation have significant effects in block 1, with gender as the most powerful variable (with a beta coefficient of .34). The effects of education and age are not significant at all. The effects of gender and sector are somewhat reduced after party is

Table 4.7
Social-Group Affiliation and Party Affiliation Determine Nordic Members' Attitudes toward Prohibition of All Pornography (Standardized regression coefficients)

Affiliation	Bivariate	Block 1	Block 2
Social-group affiliation			
Gender	−.34**	−.32**	−.29**
Sector	.14**	.09*	.08*
Occupation	.12**	.14**	.13**
Education	.08	.07	.06
Age	−.09	−.06	−.06
Party affiliation			
Agrarians	−.07		−.07
Conservatives	.23**		.13**
Liberals	.06		−.02
Left Socialists	.01		.03
Populists	.16**		.11**
Christians	−.09*		−.09*
Greens	−.10*		−.08*
Adjusted R²		.14	.18
Sig. R²		.00	.00

Note: The number of respondents is 510.

*$p < .05$, **$p < .01$

included, but they remain statistically significant. Again, adding party to the model increases the variance explained dramatically.

As regards the prohibition of pornography, table 4.7 shows some interesting results. On this issue, the single most important variable seems to be gender, but sector and occupation also have significant effects in the first block. After party is introduced, the effects of the three variables remain significant, albeit slightly reduced. On this question, no extensive changes in variance explained occur when party is introduced into the model.

Table 4.8 supplies information on the attitudes of respondents toward reducing the number of refugees in the Nordic countries. The bivariate correlation coefficient (Pearson's r) indicates that four of the background variables have significant effects on MPs' attitudes toward reducing the number of refugees, though only gender and education show significant effects in the first block; when party is introduced into the model, moreover, the effect of gender is strongly reduced. The net effect of education, on the other hand, remains significant (indeed it increases). When party is introduced, the variance explained substantially increases.

Table 4.8
Social-Group Affiliation and Party Affiliation Determine
Nordic Members' Attitudes toward Reducing the Number of
Refugees (standardized regression coefficients)

Affiliation	Bivariate	Block 1	Block 2
Social-group affiliation			
Gender	.19**	.17**	.08*
Sector	−.10*	−.03	.02
Occupation	.00	−.06	.04
Education	.14**	.14**	.17**
Age	−.09*	−.06	−.09
Party affiliation			
Agrarians	−.07		−.16**
Conservatives	−.43**		−.43**
Liberals	.16**		.10*
Left Socialists	.22**		.12**
Populists	−.26**		−.26**
Christians	.14**		.07
Greens	.12**		.06
Adjusted R²		.05	.34
Sig. R²		.00	.00

Note: The number of respondents is 510.

$*p < .05, **p < .01$

Finally, an analysis of representatives' attitudes toward gene manipulation and support to agricultural areas suggests that, in the case of the first item, the regression coefficients of gender and age remain significant after party is controlled for, while in the case of the second item only age has a significant effect on MPs' attitudes (details not shown).

In sum, gender differences between members of the Nordic legislatures remain significant—even after party is controlled for—on the "left-right" index, on the "new politics" index, and on the three issues of pornography, refugees, and gene manipulation.

The effects of sector and occupation also remain significant on the two indexes, as well as on the question of pornography, while the remaining two background indicators (education and age) have no significant effects on any of the indexes. Education, however, has an effect on representatives' attitudes toward refugees, and age has an effect on attitudes toward gene manipulation and economic support to agricultural areas. Occupation, finally, has a significant effect on attitudes toward pornography, but gender is by far the most important variable here, even after party is controlled for.

REPRESENTATIVES AND VOTERS

Earlier in this chapter, we demonstrated that Nordic MPs are not "representative of persons," in the sense corresponding to the first cell in figure 4. 1. On the other hand, we have seen that their social and demographic backgrounds have a significant effect on their political opinions and attitudes. We turn now to the final question where mass-elite agreement is concerned: are Nordic MPs "representative of opinions" rather than of persons? From our typology in figure 4.1, two possibilities remain: (1) MPs are "advocates" of voters' opinions; that is, they hold views similar to those of their constituents, or (2) MPs hold opinions different from those of their voters; that is, they are independent "caretakers." Sören Holmberg's analysis in chapter 7 below demonstrates that the degree of aggregate issue congruence is relatively uniform across the Nordic countries, albeit somewhat higher in little Iceland and somewhat lower in Finland (with its personal voting system). For purposes of the present chapter, we use an alternative approach, and analyze the degree of issue congruence *between* the subgroups at the two levels. In order to simplify this part of the analysis, we only consider the effect of gender, which in our previous analysis proved to be the most significant factor.

In table 4.9, distances between voters and representatives are expressed as mean score differences on several policy issues.[9] The issues correspond to those presented in table 4.3, with two important exceptions. Since some of the items included in the two indexes were not included in the voter surveys, we have replaced the "left-right" index with the self-designated left-right position of voters and representatives (on an eleven-point scale); we have also replaced the "new politics" index with two relevant items taken from that same index (i.e., "six-hour working day" and "women's quotas"). In addition, we have included information about respondents' self-placement on the European Union–scale to the table.

We have done the comparisons separately for female and for male MPs; that is, we have compared—in respect of the issue positions taken— female representatives with female voters and male representatives with male voters. Considering the gender variations observed on the level of representatives, we would expect female MPs to be closer to female than to male voters, and male MPs to be closer to male than to female voters.

Table 4.9 lends only partial support to this hypothesis. As far as average differences are concerned (as seen on the bottom row for each country), male representatives consistently represent the views of male voters better than those of female voters. The corresponding tendencies are evident for female MPs in Iceland and Sweden, but not for those in Denmark and

Table 4.9
Differences in Policy Views between Members and Voters in Four Nordic Countries by Gender

Policy Views	Denmark				Iceland				Norway				Sweden			
	Female MPs		Male MPs		Female MPs		Male MPs		Female MPs		Male MPs		Female MPs		Male MPs	
	Female Voters	Male Voters	Female Voters	Male Voters	Female Voters	Male Voters	Female Voters	Male Voters	Female Voters	Male Voters	Female Voters	Male Voters	Female Voters	Male Voters	Female Voters	Male Voters
EU scale; self-placement[a]	NI	NI	NI	NI	−0.4	−0.3	−0.6	−0.5	1.3	0.3	1.4	0.4	2.4	1.5	3.2	2.3
Left-right scale; self-placement[a]	−0.1	−0.3	+0.1	−0.1	−0.6	−1.1	−0.1	−0.6	−0.9	−1.4	−0.1	−0.6	−0.9	−0.9	0.1	0.1
Reduce public sector	−0.2	+0.1	−0.5	−0.2	+0.5	+0.8	−0.2	+0.1	0.2	0.5	−0.4	−0.1	0.0	0.5	−0.6	−0.1
Reduce defense budget	−0.1	−0.4	+0.2	−0.1	NI	NI	NI	NI	−0.4	−0.6	0.0	−0.2	−0.6	−0.6	−0.2	−0.2
Reduce income differences	−0.4	−0.6	+0.1	−0.1	+0.2	+0.0	+0.7	+0.5	−0.4	−0.5	0.1	0.0	−0.2	0.5	0.1	−0.2
Introduce 6-hour working day	+1.0	+0.4	+1.4	+0.8	−0.1	−0.9	+1.1	+0.3	0.9	0.2	1.3	0.6	0.2	0.4	1.4	0.8
Prohibit pornography	+0.5	+0.1	+1.1	+0.7	−0.1	−0.8	+1.1	+0.3	0.3	−0.6	1.3	0.4	−0.1	−1.0	0.9	0.0
Women's quotas for high positions	−0.4	−0.6	+0.1	−0.1	−1.1	−1.7	+0.7	+0.1	NI	NI	NI	NI	−0.4	−1.0	0.7	0.1
Average difference	+0.4	+0.4	+0.5	+0.3	+0.3	+0.8	+0.6	+0.3	+0.6	+0.6	+0.7	+0.3	+0.6	+0.8	+0.9	+0.5

Notes: Table entries are differences in mean scores for, on the one hand, male and female members, and, on the other hand, male and female voters. Positive values mean that the average score for members is higher than for voters; negative values mean that the average score for members is lower than for voters. NI = not included in the studies.

[a]The scale runs from 0 to 10.

Norway. On practically all items, the tendency is consistent for male representatives; for female representatives it is more blurred. A closer look at each item reveals that, in three of the countries, the views of female MPs are very similar to those of female voters in regard to pornography and the size of the public sector; in Sweden and Iceland, moreover, female MPs are much more in line with female than with male voters on the question of the six-hour working day. These results also match the findings from Sweden reported by Oskarson and Wängnerud (1995).

Taking a closer look at Sweden, we see that the most striking discrepancy in our comparative material between female MPs and voters concerns the question of EU membership. On this issue, male MPs are also out of tune with male voters, although to a slightly lesser extent. The same tendency is evident in the case of Norwegian female MPs; on the question of EU membership, they actually represent the views of male voters better than those of female voters.

Intergroup comparisons reveal a more nuanced picture. Male MPs are consistently better representatives than female MPs are for the opinions of male voters. The converse tendency is also true: female MPs represent the views of female voters better than male MPs do. The table indicates, however, that the results are issue-specific. On matters related to the public sector, the six-hour working day, and pornography, female MPs represent the views of female voters better than male MPs do, whereas the opposite tendency is visible in connection with left-right self-location and attitudes toward the reduction of income differences. Here, male MPs mirror the views of female voters better than female MPs do. On the question of women's quotas, male MPs are much better representatives for the attitudes of male voters than female MPs are. This pattern also obtains in regard to attitudes toward pornography and the public sector, except in the case of Denmark.

DISCUSSION AND CONCLUSION

Our main concern in this chapter has been to confront two types of political representation: that of persons or social groups on the one hand, and that of opinions on the other. As to the first, the conclusion is that the Nordic parliaments do not mirror the social and demographic composition of their respective populations. The major tendency is for people of middle-class background (in educational and occupational terms) to be overrepresented in parliament, while the lower strata are correspondingly underrepresented. The public sector, furthermore, is overrepresented at the expense of the private sector. As far as demographic variables are concerned, men are clearly overrepresented, as are the middle-aged.

In figure 4.1, our objective was to study possible conflicts between the "representation of persons" and the "representation of opinions." We have not been able to test this model extensively, but observe that Sören Holmberg has analyzed opinion consistency between representatives and voters in chapter 7 below. In the present chapter, we have attempted to relate background variables with representatives' political attitudes. A summary of the results may be seen in table 4.10.

The data indicate that MPs' political attitudes are indeed related to their social and demographic background. Gender differences are significantly related to five of our six attitude measures. Next follows occupation with four items, sector with three, and age with two, while education is related to just one set of attitudes (the rejection of refugees).

Continuing along the lines suggested in our model, we find that the data suggest a split between "advocate" representation and "caretaker" representation. As demonstrated in chapter 7 below, however, the degree of issue congruence between voters and representatives varies substantially from one type of attitude to another. A more thorough test of the model would require an issue-by-issue analysis in relation to each of the background variables. In the preceding pages, we have limited this part of the analysis to gender differences.

The main tendency is for male representatives to reflect the opinions of male voters better than those of female voters. Correspondingly, female representatives tend to be closest to female voters in their policy positions. There is a consistent tendency for both groups of voters to be represented better by MPs of their own gender, but this tendency is less regular for women than for men. With respect to the model presented in figure 4.1, therefore, we may argue that women (who are systematically underrepresented) are subject to "caretaker representation" in a greater degree than are men. In general, groups that are overrepresented in parliament enjoy a favorable position in the policy-making process, provided there is opinion agreement between representatives and their voters. On the other hand, groups that are underrepresented or that tend to disagree with their elected MPs are subject to caretaker representation.

Our intention in this part of the book is to compare patterns of representation in the Nordic countries. A careful inspection of the data indicates that the similarities are more striking than the differences. As a matter of fact, the general conclusions of this chapter would seem to fit each of the countries separately. Nevertheless, some differences can be observed. Patterns of recruitment are surprisingly similar in Denmark,

Table 4.10
Empirical Patterns of Representation

Socioeconomic Group	Social Representativeness	Policy Representativeness[a]					
		Left-Right	New Politics	Pornography	New Refugees	Gene Manipulation	Support to Agriculture
Gender	women under-represented	yes	yes	yes	yes	yes	no
Sector	public sector over-represented	yes	yes	yes	no	no	no
Occupation	higher status over-represented	yes	yes	yes	no	yes	no
Education	higher education over-represented	no	no	no	yes	no	no
Age	young voters under-represented	no	no	no	no	yes	yes

[a]Significant attitude differences between groups of MPs after party affiliation is controlled for.

Norway, and Sweden, while Iceland deviates to some extent. The over-representation of men and of middle-aged people is greater in Iceland than in the other three countries. The bias in favor of middle-class occupations, moreover, is strongest in Iceland. A possible explanation for this may lie in the recruitment structure; that is, the nominating system, which in Iceland allows for a personal vote to a greater extent than in the other three countries.

Overall, the similarities are greatest between Norway and Sweden, particularly in regard to the relationship between background variables and MPs' policy attitudes.

NOTES

We would like to thank Frode Berglund and Maria Oskarson for helping us out with the occupational classifications in the Norwegian and Swedish electoral data, and Bernt Aardal for providing us with critical comments.

1. In Norway, for instance, the category of "blue-collar" workers is defined much more narrowly than in the other three countries. For this reason, we have recoded the Norwegian data. We have reclassified certain occupational groups—conductors, postmen, hospital workers, caretakers, etc.—as "blue-collar." (Such employees are normally classified as "white-collar" in Norwegian surveys.) In addition, when constructing the variable for "occupation," we have excluded pensioners, students, and housewives, since no information is available in the Norwegian and Danish surveys on "former occupation," "father's occupation," or "husband's occupation" (the three classification criteria used to code the occupation of these respondent groups). See Sainsbury (1987) for a detailed discussion of the classification problems arising in connection with occupation in the Scandinavian countries.

2. Where education is concerned, we have merged respondents with high and medium education into "high," and given the value "low" to those with only compulsory school. Where age is concerned, we have merged the eighteen to thirty-five and thirty-six to forty-four groups into "low," and the forty-five to fifty-four and fifty-five plus groups into "high." Where occupation is concerned, finally, we have merged farmers and the self-employed with the group of white-collars into "high," and given blue-collars the value of "low."

3. The criteria were set for three factors with the method of maximum likelihood. The first factor, which accounted for most of the variance explained, had an eigenvalue of 5.8, whereas the second had an eigenvalue of 1.1.

4. The correlation between the two indexes is .28 (Pearson's r). The reliability measure used here is Cronbach's alpha, which varies between 0 and 1. When running the reliability test, we obtained very high scores: for the "left/right" index, Cronbach's alpha is .92; for the "new politics" index it is .75.

5. Each member's opinion on each issue was assigned a score ranging from 1 (complete agreement) to 5 (complete disagreement). The scores were averaged for each group. The average scores for the two indexes are conditioned on the number of items within each index. Hence, the scores for the first index vary between 5 and 25, whereas for the second they vary between 3 and 15. Note that, in order to get the same direction on the items, the value range on some of them has been reversed.

6. One possibility investigated is that the two variables are highly correlated, i.e., that the public sector is dominated by women and the private sector by men. The empirical evidence lends support to this assumption to a certain extent: 63 percent of female MPs come from the public sector, as against 44 percent of male MPs. It should also be observed that the results have not been weighted to adjust for the different sizes of the four legislatures; hence, the mean scores are biased by the responses of the Swedish MPs.

7. We have used Labor as our category of reference.

8. The beta value in block 1 is $-.10$, and is significant at a .05 level.

9. Each member's opinion on each issue was assigned a score ranging from 1 (complete agreement) to 5 (complete disagreement). The scores were averaged for each group. In addition, the table includes two eleven-point issues scales.

5

Geography and Political Representation

*Henry Valen, Hanne Marthe Narud,
and Ólafur Th. Hardarson*

Originally, territorial interests constituted a basic element in the concept of representation. Representatives elected from single-member constituencies were seen as spokesmen for their respective geographical areas. The extent to which representatives should commit themselves to voting in accordance with voter opinion was disputed, but it was evidently a major concern that representatives speak for the interests associated with their home base (Pitkin 1967; Christophersen 1969).

The subsequent emergence of political parties naturally affected the character of relations between voters and representatives. By articulating public opinion and virtually monopolizing the recruitment of leaders, political parties became prime actors in the process of representation. From now on, parliamentary decisions were made by the respective parties collectively, and individual members of parliament inclined toward the strict observance of party discipline.

Obviously, the character of representation has been affected by institutional reforms, in particular the introduction of proportional representation (PR) and the establishment of parliamentary government. In a system with proportional elections from multimember constituencies, voters are unable to identify any specific MP as their own representative (unless some kind of preferential-voting system is applied). Under PR, voters are represented by parties rather than by individual representatives.[1] In a similar way, a parliamentary form of government strengthens the role of parties. The maintenance of stable government quite simply requires a substantial degree of party discipline.

Since neither PR nor parliamentarism prevails in the United States, the idea of territorial representation would seem to be more relevant in regard to the presidential system of that country than in regard to the party-dominated democracies of Europe. Political parties are mainly concerned with national policies, and these tend to overshadow the interests of individual constituencies. Yet it might be argued that, indirectly, territorial conflicts play a major role even under party regimes. ·

The significance of geography is reflected in the concept of "constituency," which has survived all electoral reforms. The cry of the liberal reform movement of the nineteenth century for "one man, one vote, one value" has never been achieved. "Fair" representation has always been obstructed by distortions of a partisan or territorial nature (Taagepera and Shugart 1989). Proportionality between the preferences of voters and the composition of parliament would likely have been greatly improved by the abolition of constituencies and the instituting of elections for the whole nation. Except in the Netherlands and Israel, however, such a reform has never been attempted.[2] These two exceptions suggest, moreover, that only countries with a very small territory can afford to ignore the geographical dimension.

Several students of political representation have been concerned with the effects of territorial variations on mass-elite linkages in modern democracy (e.g., Miller and Stokes 1963; Fenno 1978; Converse and Pierce 1986). In the Nordic countries, however, scholars have not paid much attention to this question—with two notable exceptions. Peter Esaiasson (1999) has conducted a comparative analysis of the impact of geography in France, the United States, Sweden, and West Germany; while Per-Anders Roth (1996) has studied the effect of territorial variations on representation in Sweden. To the knowledge of the present authors, nobody has tried to study variations in mass-elite linkages between specified regions of given countries. In this chapter, we will present an attempt in this direction.

In so doing, we rely on basic arguments from the theory of nation-building formulated in Rokkan (1970) and in Rokkan and Urwin (1982; 1983). We submit that, when regions in the Nordic countries are arranged in a center/periphery perspective, the following thesis holds good: *on issues related to territorial conflicts, congruence between voters and representatives is likely to be higher in the periphery than in the center.*

Assuming, furthermore, that the tradition of territorial representation is related to historical, geographical, and institutional circumstances within each individual country, *we can expect a more unified pattern of representation to obtain in Denmark and Sweden than in the "new nations" of Iceland and Norway.*

Before turning to the empirical analysis, however, we must briefly discuss the role of territorial conflicts in the process of nation-building.

NATION-BUILDING

Earlier attempts at electoral analysis revealed the existence within many countries of substantial regional variations in voting patterns (Hansen 1897; Siegfried 1913; Rydenfelt 1954; Allardt 1956; Rokkan and Valen 1964).[3] Of course, a major analytical concern of the authors was whether, and to what extent, the political variations observed could be explained in terms of economic, cultural and social characteristics. And, conversely, to what extent did such variations simply reflect an unexplained geographical component?

Research on these problems gained in respectability as well as theoretical interest in the 1960s, when the concept of "nation-building" appeared on the agenda of political sociologists. Students of nation-building are concerned with the process by which the population of a given territory is transformed into a national community, in which important values, institutions, and a common identity are shared. Nation-building has been conceptualized in terms of progressive stages of political development: territorial penetration by state power; cultural standardization; participation by wider sections of the population; and, finally, redistribution and welfare policies as mechanisms of national integration (Deutsch and Foltz 1963; Bendix 1964; 1977; Eisenstadt and Rokkan 1973–74). It should be noted that these different stages of development can occur at different times and with different effects from one nation to another.

In trying to mobilize support for their policies, the dominant elites of a given nation may turn in two directions: to the lower classes or to peripheral parts of the territory. In order to study the latter, certain scholars have developed a center/periphery paradigm (Rokkan 1970; Rokkan and Urwin 1982; 1983). Center and periphery are seen as twin concepts in the study of territorial mobilization: "The center represents the seat of authority, and the periphery those geographical locations at the furthest distance from the center, but still within the territory controlled from the center" (Rokkan and Urwin 1983:2).

The definition of center and periphery may be debatable, and the border between the two types of territory may be open to dispute. The main point is that center and periphery designate a territorial dimension in which the latter constitutes the inferior pole. The periphery may differ from the center in three important domains: distance, economy, and culture. It tends, moreover, to have a sense of separate identity (Rokkan and Urwin 1983).

It has been convincingly demonstrated that center-periphery variations are reflected in the behavior of voters (Rose 1974; Rokkan and Urwin 1982). In the Nordic countries, for instance, the electoral support enjoyed by different parties varies to some extent from one region to another. An analysis of electoral turnout suggests, moreover, that the level of political activity was originally highest in the central areas, but that the differences between center and periphery have tended to decline over time (Rokkan and Valen, 1962; Rokkan and Urwin 1982). In accordance with the theory of nation-building, this tendency implies that the political parties and their leaders have been successful in mobilizing electoral participation in the periphery. It does not mean that strains between central and peripheral areas have entirely disappeared. Regional variations in electoral choice may reflect corresponding differences on the leadership level. Indeed, the analysis in chapter 3 shows that, when asked to define their task as representatives, on average 25 percent of Nordic MPs consider it very important to champion the interests of their constituency.

Our concern is how, and to what extent, constituency interests affect the relationship between voters and representatives. To what extent does issue congruence between the two levels vary from one region to another? Owing to historical circumstances, the process of nation-building is likely to have differed in character between the Nordic countries. As will be elaborated on later, some of these variations are likely to be reflected in mass-elite linkages.

Research Problems

Stein Rokkan (1970) distinguished between two types of conflict in modern society: *functional* conflicts, in which nationwide interests are involved; and *territorial* conflicts, in which regions with opposed interests confront one another. In terms of political representation, functional conflicts are expressed in the competition among political parties. The normal pattern is that each party takes a collective stand on issues related to functional conflicts, and individual MPs are expected to support the party line. However, representatives are obviously alert to specific issues of relevance to their own constituency. Consequently, as far as territorial conflicts are concerned, they are likely to display split loyalties between their party and their home district.

Type of Region

		Center	Periphery
Type of Conflict	Functional	National average	National average
	Territorial	National average	High issue-congruence

Figure 5.1 Expected Degree of Policy Congruence between Voters and Representatives by Region and Type of Conflict

As argued above, the process of nation-building starts in the center. The subsequent penetration and mobilization of peripheral parts of the territory are likely to create feelings of protest and regional identification, feelings that are directed against the center. As a result, the population of the periphery tends to be highly aware of its own territorial interests and policy issues. Consequently, the pressure on MPs to conform with constituency interests is presumably stronger in the periphery than in the center. The tendency is likely to be different in regard to functional conflicts, which are articulated in the competition among political parties. Since the character of partisan conflict tends to be uniform throughout the territory, we would not expect much variation among regions in the degree of congruence between voters and representatives on these kinds of issues. In figure 5.1, we have summarized our hypotheses in the form of a fourfold table.

We assume that the extent to which representatives express the opinion of their electorate is conditioned by the *type of policy issues* being considered, on the one hand, and the *type of pressures* to which representatives are exposed, on the other. Functional issues, which are articulated through competition among nationwide political parties, call for MPs—irrespective of regional background—to show loyalty with their party. Territorial issues, on the other hand, are less affected by partisan affiliations, since regional interests are at stake.[4] Furthermore, we would expect territorial issues to be more salient in peripheral than in central areas, and thus the pressure for voter-representative issue congruence to be greater in the former than in the latter.

Hence these hypotheses:

1. *In the case of functional issues, we would expect congruence between voters and representatives to approximate a national average for all regions.*

2. Where territorial issues are concerned, we would expect congruence between voters and representatives to be higher in peripheral than in central regions.

Our next step is to consider center-periphery variations for the Nordic countries comparatively. As indicated above, the process of nation-building is likely to have varied from one country to another, depending on historical circumstances. Most important in this regard is the fact that Denmark and Sweden have been independent states for centuries, while the other three countries can be characterized as "new nations" with a relatively short history of national independence (see chapter 2). The question is: how has this difference affected national integration in the respective countries? According to students of nation-building theory (Rokkan 1970; Rokkan and Urwin 1983), the process of integration tends to take place over a long period. Territorial penetration, cultural standardization, and economic and political integration are likely to elicit protest and resistance in outlying areas. Hence, we may expect patterns of political representation to exhibit substantial variations between center and periphery in our "new" states—that is, Iceland, Finland, and Norway. In the old nation-states of Denmark and Sweden, by contrast, integration of the national territory has been proceeding for centuries, so we would expect to find only minor territorial variations within these countries.

The particular interests of the periphery may be promoted through institutional arrangements; for example, providing for the overrepresentation of peripheral areas within the electoral system. An alternative solution would be for elected representatives from the periphery to observe a strict congruence with their constituents. Both approaches will be considered in the subsequent analysis.

When searching for center-periphery variations in the degree of issue congruence between voters and representatives, we began by confronting the notion of disciplined political parties versus regional variations in policy positions. How can political representation be analyzed in relation to these seemingly irreconcilable perspectives? Peter Esaiasson (1999) points out that two conditions must obtain for local political linkage to exist between voters and their representatives: (1) there must be geographical variations within parties in respect to policy views, and (2) these variations must be picked up by representatives tied to the relevant territorial areas.

Following this reasoning, we will look first at representatives' evaluation of their own role vis-à-vis their constituency. To what extent are their views affected by their place of residence? Next, we turn to linkages of

	Center (1)	In-between (2)	Periphery (3)
Denmark	The capital with surrounding areas	The islands	*Jutland*
Iceland	The capital with surrounding areas	Not applicable	The districts (the rest of Iceland)
Norway	The Oslofjord area	Mid-Norway	The North
Sweden	*Svealand* (South East)	*Götaland* (South West)	*Norrland* (the North)

Figure 5.2 Definitions of Regions

opinion between MPs and voters. Our task is to establish a basic test for territorially anchored variations between the two levels. A one-way analysis of variance will be applied with area of residence as the independent variable.

THE NORDIC REGIONS

Our research problem involves a focus on the contrast between central and peripheral areas within the Nordic countries. Our classification of regions should therefore reflect this dimension. At the same time, the classification must permit comparisons between the different countries, and the number of regions ought to be roughly the same in all of them. In order, moreover, to conduct a meaningful analysis, we must keep the number of territorial units low, in view of the small number of MPs in every Nordic country except Sweden. Against this background, we have decided to divide each country into three regions: center, periphery, and a middle region of mixed character (see figure 5.2). An exception has been made for Iceland, which we divide into just two regions, owing to the small size of the Althingi. Finland is left out of this analysis, since relevant data have not been collected for the Finnish electorate.

For Denmark and Sweden, the concept of a periphery is scarcely recognized. Perhaps it would be more correct to speak of two centers in these countries—regions 1 and 2. In both countries, however, region 3 is most distant from the capital. For Iceland, regions 1 and 3 seem to fit the notion of a center and a periphery quite well. The division in Norway is more complicated. The north is definitely considered the most peripheral part of the country, while the Oslofjord area makes up the center. In previous analyses, the west had also been considered a periphery, because it differs from the east with regard to cultural standardization (Rokkan and Valen 1964; Rokkan 1970). However, the peripheral character of the former region is largely limited to its rural areas, and since it includes two major urban centers, we have placed it in the middle category.

Distortion of Representation

Countries using PR tend to accept some disproportionality in geographical representation. Where party distributions are concerned, on the other hand, the degree of proportionality is relatively high (Taagepera and Shugart 1989). All of the Nordic countries use PR, but they differ to some extent in their practical arrangements; for example, the use of adjustment seats. If we inspect the degree to which representation is distorted in these countries, we may discover the extent to which institutional arrangements have been applied to promote the interests of the periphery. We have calculated the degree of proportionality (between seats and votes) for both party and territory in the last election held in each of the respective countries. In so doing, we have applied Loosemore-Hanby's index of proportionality, which is based on the percentage differences in the distribution of votes and of seats (Lijphart 1994:58).[5] The results are presented in table 5.1.

To a large extent, disproportionality by party can be explained by the votes cast for small parties falling below, or coming close to, the threshold for representation. The effect is most pronounced in Finland (where small parties jointly obtained 22.9 percent of the votes but only 16 percent of the seats) and in Norway (where small parties jointly obtained 7.2 percent of the votes but only 1.2 percent of the seats).

Except for the underrepresentation of small parties, partisan proportionality is reasonably good in the Nordic countries. Similarly, proportionality by constituency is quite good except in the case of Iceland. Prior to the use of adjustment seats, territorial distortion had been much higher in the other Nordic countries as well (Matthews and Valen 1999).

In table 5.1, adjustment seats have been included in the constituencies to which they were assigned. These tend to be large constituencies in the center of the system. The purpose of introducing adjustment seats was to improve proportionality by party; they have also improved territorial proportionality.[6] It should be noted, however, that we find considerable

Table 5.1
Distortion of Representation in the Nordic
Countries, by Party and Constituency
(Loosemore-Hanby's index values)

Country	By Party	By Constituency
Denmark	2.5	5.6
Finland	5.7	1.7
Iceland	3.1	16.9
Norway	6.4	5.7
Sweden	2.1	3.7

Note: Results pertain to the following parliamentary elections: Denmark (1994), Finland (1995), Iceland (1995), Norway (1993), and Sweden (1994).

variations from one constituency to another within a given country. The question is whether the tendency observed for selected constituencies is also valid for regions.

Table 5.2 present distortions for regions classified in a center-periphery perspective. The data indicate that overrepresentation of the periphery is far greater in Iceland than in the other three countries. Territorial distortion is negligible in Denmark and Sweden, while Norway takes a middle position.

The overrepresentation of peripheral parts of a country can conceivably stem from two sources. It may be the result of migration within the country, in which people leave their homes in remote areas and move to more central locations. Unless there is a continuous adjustment in representation consistent with the patterns of migration, territorial proportionality is bound to decline. It is indeed a cumbersome process to reduce the number of seats in certain constituencies.

But, as suggested above, the overrepresentation of outlying areas may also be the result of intended policies. It could be argued that, if they are to be adequately represented, these constituencies simply need relatively more representatives than do central areas. So argued, for instance, the Norwegian Electoral Reform Commission of 1917. Faced with a demand to increase the number of seats for the capital city, the commission stated that:

Although the commission shares the opinion that it would be desirable to allocate more seats to Kristiania [Oslo], the perception is that, as the Capital, this city has access to political and parliamentary influence which cannot be neglected. As the site of the most important newspapers in the country, of all political parties, of economic and professional organizations, and of central financial and administrative institutions, the Capital holds a special position, implying that it cannot, to the same extent as

Table 5.2
Distortion of Representation in the Nordic Countries, by Region

Region	Registered Voters	% Voters	Members	% Members	Diff.	Voters per Seat
Sweden						
Svealand	2.539.567	39.09	137	39.26	0.17	18.536
Götaland	3.035.239	46.72	161	46.13	−0.59	18.852
Norrland	921.559	14.19	51	14.61	0.42	18.059
Total	6.496.365	100	349	100		
Iceland						
Urban southwest	126.097	65.68	31	49.21	−16.47	4067
The districts	65.876	34.32	32	50.79	16.47	2058
Total	191.973	100	63	100		
Denmark						
Copenhagen area	441.700	11.07	18	10.29	−0.78	24.538
The Islands	1.709.939	42.87	73	41.71	−1.16	23.423
Jutland area	1.837.148	46.06	84	48.00	1.94	21.870
Total	3.988.787	100	175	100		
Norway						
Oslofjord area	1.318.355	40.44	62	37.58	−2.86	21.263
Middle Norway	1.585.847	48.65	81	49.09	0.44	19.578
The North	355.755	10.91	22	13.33	2.42	16.171
Total	3.259.957	100	165	100		

Notes: Results pertain to the following parliamentary elections: Denmark (1994), Finland (1995), Iceland (1995), Norway (1993), and Sweden (1994). The Loosemore-Hanby index for Sweden is 0.59; for Iceland, 16.47; for Denmark, 1.94; and for Norway, 2.86.

other constituencies, demand representation proportional to the size of its population or its electorate. (Valgkommisjonen av 1917) [The Norwegian Electoral Reform Commission of 1917])

Territorial distortion of representation has been a recognized principle in the electoral systems of the Nordic countries, especially those of Norway and Iceland. The data confirm that this distortion is still maintained in these two countries, while Denmark and Sweden come closest to territorial proportionality.

LEADERSHIP VIEWS AND REGIONAL VARIATIONS

As demonstrated in chapter 3, a substantial proportion of members in all of the Nordic parliaments define themselves as promoters of the interests of their constituency. In the present chapter, we are interested in the *effect*

Table 5.3
Members' Personal Definition of Task, by Region (mean values)

Type of Task	Center (1)	In-Between (2)	Periphery (3)	Difference (1 – 3)
Denmark				
Work with problems of individual voters	2.20	2.19	2.00	+.20
Advocate interests of own region	2.40	2.14	2.02	+.38
Advocate policies of own party	1.60	1.48	1.43	+.17
Iceland				
Work with problems of individual voters	2.50	NA	1.78	+.72**
Advocate interests of own region	2.60	NA	1.78	+.82*
Advocate policies of own party	1.74	NA	1.43	+.31
Norway				
Work with problems of individual voters	2.03	1.87	1.57	+.46**
Advocate interests of own region	2.05	1.89	1.84	+.21
Advocate policies of own party	1.34	1.36	1.31	+.03
Sweden				
Work with problems of individual voters	1.94	1.78	1.78	+.16
Advocate interests of own region	1.97	1.64	1.42	+.55**
Advocate policies of own party	1.21	1.27	1.18	+.03

Notes: Responses were coded as follows: "very important" (1); "fairly important" (2); "not very important" (3); and "not important at all" (4). Thus, the lower the mean value, the fuller the attention. NA = not applicable.

$*p < .05, **p < .01$

of regional differences on MPs' perceptions and priorities. Members were presented with a list of major tasks and asked how important each one was to them as representatives. We assume three of these tasks are relevant to our general problem: parliamentarians must (1) try to help individual voters who have contacted them, (2) champion the interests/opinions of their own constituency/region, and (3) advocate the policies of their party. In accordance with our hypotheses, we expect the first two of these items to reflect regional variations and the third to be unaffected by region. The data are presented in table 5.3.

The data accord with our expectations. In all of the countries and throughout each national territory, MPs consider it highly important to advocate the policies of their party. The pattern is different for the other two tasks: trying to help individual voters on the one hand and promoting the expressed interests of the constituency on the other. In all of the countries, representatives pay closer attention to these interests in peripheral than in central regions. Regional differences are statistically significant in Iceland for both tasks, in Norway and Sweden for just one of the tasks, and in Denmark for neither task. NB: where "advocating the interest of [one's] own region" is concerned, the difference is most pronounced in Iceland and Sweden.[7]

Similar tendencies may be observed when respondents are asked about cooperation across party lines on such questions as where to build roads, locate agencies, et cetera, as well as on other questions related to the respondent's constituency or region (see chapter 9 below). Members of parliament from the periphery are more inclined than those from the center to respond affirmatively. The differences are not very large, however, and with a few exceptions they are not statistically significant.

Nonetheless, the data suggest that representatives from peripheral parts of the territory are more alert to problems of a regional character than are representatives from central constituencies.

GEOGRAPHICAL VARIATIONS IN POLICY POSITIONS

Our next task is to consider regional variations in the pattern of differences between voters and representatives in regard to policy views. We start by considering functional issues for which we expect the response pattern to be similar in all regions (hypothesis 1). Our dependent variable is the degree of congruence between voters and representatives. Our two independent variables are region and party affiliation. As to the latter variable, we are prevented from using the fully fledged party system, since the number of representatives is very low in all of the countries except Sweden. We simply distinguish, therefore, between parties of the left and parties of the center-right.[8]

The Left/Right Dimension

As in most Western nations, the predominant ideological division determining party competition in the Nordic countries has been the socioeconomic left/right dimension (Aardal and Valen 1995; Borg and Sänkiaho 1995; Borre and Goul Andersen 1997; Gilljam and Holmberg 1995; Hardarson 1995; Narud 1996). Left/right position may be seen as a general measurement of functional issues. Table 5.4 presents the self-placement of voters and representatives along an eleven-point left/right scale.[9]

Naturally, the most notable ideological division is that between the two party blocs. Table 5.4 compares voters and representatives by region for each of the main party groups. If we compare all voters and all representatives, we find that the differences between regions are tiny in all four countries. When comparing representatives and voters for parties of the left

Table 5.4
Left-Right Ideological Self-Placement among Members and Voters, by Region (mean scores and eta values)

Region	Members			Voters		
	All	Leftist Parties	Center + Rightist Parties	All	Leftist Parties	Center + Rightist Parties
Denmark						
Center	5.0	2.8	7.8	4.8	4.0	5.9
In-between	4.8	3.5	6.8	5.3	4.6	6.2
Periphery	5.4	3.1	7.4	5.2	4.6	5.8
Eta	**.12**	**.17**	**.21**	**.09**	**.13****	**.09**
Iceland						
Center	5.0	3.8	6.9	5.7	4.7	6.6
Periphery	5.3	3.3	6.3	5.5	4.3	6.0
Eta	**.08**	**.15**	**.22**	**.06**	**.04**	**.15***
Norway						
Center	5.1	3.1	7.2	5.3	4.6	6.4
In-between	4.4	3.2	5.7	5.3	4.6	5.7
Periphery	4.4	3.5	6.1	5.5	4.8	6.3
Eta	**.15**	**.18**	**.28**	**.03**	**.04**	**.04**
Sweden						
Center	4.6	3.0	6.8	5.1	3.6	6.8
In-between	4.9	3.2	7.1	5.0	3.6	6.7
Periphery	4.2	3.2	6.5	4.3	3.3	6.4
Eta	**.11**	**.05**	**.13**	**.11****	**.06**	**.07**

Note: The scale is an 11-point scale running from 0 to 10, where 0 indicates furthest to the left and 10 furthest to the right.

$*p < .05, **p < .01$

and parties of the center-right, we find that the differences are very small in Iceland and Sweden, but more sizable in the other two countries. Regional variations are tiny on the voter level throughout the area, but greater on the representative level in the three countries in which the number of representatives is low and the sampling error correspondingly high.

A one-way analysis of variance has been applied in table 5.4. The tiny regional differences are confirmed by the eta coefficients, which measure the strength of relationships. With two minor exceptions at the voter level, the eta values are too small to reach the level of statistical significance. The major tendency in table 5.4 is consistent with our expectation that regional variations will be more or less absent where left/right position is concerned. The question is whether this tendency also applies to specific policy issues.

Table 5.5

Attitudes among Members and Voters toward Reducing Size of the Public Sector, by Region (mean scores and eta-values)

	Center (1)	In-Between (2)	Periphery (3)	Diff. (1–3)	Eta
Denmark					
Members	2.44	3.00	2.70	**.26**	.12
Voters	3.32	3.15	2.97	**.35**	.09*
Diff.	−.88	−.15	−.27		
Iceland					
Members	2.50	NA	2.04	**.46**	.21
Voters	2.16	NA	2.14	**.02**	.01
Diff.	+.34		−.10		
Norway					
Members	2.96	3.71	3.89	**.93**	.26**
Voters	3.47	3.40	3.54	**−.07**	.04
Diff.	−.51	+.31	+.35		
Sweden					
Members	3.30	3.14	3.58	**.28**	.10**
Voters	3.34	3.25	3.64	**.30**	.09*
Diff.	−.04	−.11	−.06		

Notes: Five response alternatives were coded. The lower the mean value, the more positive attitude toward reducing the size of the public sector. NA = not applicable.

*p < .05, **p < .01

Policy Issues

Eight functional issues have been included in the study of voters and representatives in the four countries.[10] All of the items are controversial in party competition, and we may assume that all are more or less related to the left/right dimension. In order to avoid fluctuations due to the small number of leadership respondents, we will limit the subsequent analysis to a comparison between voters and representatives in different regions, disregarding party affiliation.[11] Two of the eight relevant items will be discussed as examples.

Table 5.5 presents attitudes toward reducing the public sector. In Denmark and Sweden, regional variations are roughly similar for voters and for representatives, and the differences between voters and their representatives are virtually the same in all regions. In Iceland and Norway, by contrast, representatives differ substantially as between center and periphery, while voters tend to be similar in all regions. As a consequence, issue congruence between voters and representatives is higher in the periphery than

Table 5.6

Attitudes among Members and Voters toward Reducing Income Differences, by Region (mean scores and eta-values)

	Center (1)	In-Between (2)	Periphery (3)	Diff. (1-3)	Eta
Denmark					
Members	2.40	2.48	2.81	.41	.13
Voters	2.88	2.78	2.82	.06	.02
Diff.	−.48	−.30	−.01		
Iceland					
Members	1.80	NA	1.96	.16	.13
Voters	2.48	NA	2.35	.13	.04
Diff.	−.68		−.39		
Norway					
Members	2.41	1.92	1.63	78	.24*
Voters	2.30	2.19	2.31	.01	.05
Diff.	.11	−.27	−.68		
Sweden					
Members	2.22	2.19	2.00	.22	.06
Voters	2.42	2.35	2.16	.26	.06
Diff.	−.20	−.16	−.16		

Notes: Five response alternatives were coded. The lower the mean value, the more positive attitude toward reducing income differences. NA = not applicable.

$^*p < .05, ^{**}p < .01$

in the center. The call for a reduction in the public sector is an old idea of the parties at the right.

Our next example concerns the question of reducing income differences, which is a traditional demand from the left. The data are presented in table 5.6. Differences between regions are moderate for both representatives and voters in Denmark, Iceland, and Sweden. The same is true for voters in Norway, but representatives from the periphery of that country are more inclined than representatives from its center to favor reduced income differences.

Except where Norwegian representatives are concerned, the data for these two issues support the expectation that there will be no regional variations with respect to functional issues. In the case of Norway, the differences between center and periphery are consistently greater for representatives than they are for voters. The variations are statistically significant for four of the items in the case of representatives and for just two items in the case of voters. A similar pattern can be seen in Iceland, although regional variations are less distinct in that country than in Norway.

Table 5.7

Average Regional Differences among Members and Voters in Attitudes toward Eight Functional Policy Issues (average eta values)

Country	All Members	All Voters
Denmark	.10	.07
Iceland	.10	.07
Norway	.21	.05
Sweden	.08	.08

Note: The higher average eta value, the larger the regional variations.

In Sweden and Denmark, by contrast, regional variations tend to be much smaller. In addition, representatives and voters hold more similar views in these two countries than they do in Iceland and Norway.

As a final way to measure territorial variations, we may consider the average eta values based on a one-way analysis of variance for representatives as well as voters. The results are presented in table 5.7. The average eta values on the voter level are indeed low, and with three exceptions they are not statistically significant. The tendency on the MP level is less regular. In the cases of Denmark, Iceland, and Sweden, the values are low, but consistent with our previous findings; they are higher in the case of Norway.

Data for Denmark, Iceland, and Sweden support hypothesis 1, that congruence between voters and representatives over functional issues will reflect a national average in all regions. This pattern is also found among voters in Norway; representatives in that country, however, deviate from their counterparts in the other three countries. Among Norwegian MPs, we clearly find center-periphery differences in policy positions. There is therefore a gap between voters and representatives in Norway, and this gap tends to be most evident in the periphery and smallest in the center.

One might wonder whether regional variations in representatives' policy positions are reflected in corresponding variations in their perception of voters' opinions and attitudes. For each of the items we have asked representatives to indicate what they believe the voters of their own party think about the matter.[12] The analysis in chapter 7 below indicates that representatives tend to project their own attitudes on to their voters (see also Holmberg 1989). The question is whether such a tendency is evident also when regional variations are considered. If so, to what extent does such a tendency account for the deviating pattern of Norwegian representatives? Table 5.8 presents members' perceptions of the opinions of voters by region. We have restricted this part of the analysis to the two items presented in tables 5.5 and 5.6.

Table 5.8

Members' Perceptions of Voter Opinions, by Region: Proportion of Members Who Perceive That a Majority of Voters Favor the Proposal (%)

Policy Proposal	Denmark			Iceland			Norway			Sweden		
	Center	In-Between	Periphery	Center	In-Between	Periphery	Center	In-Between	Periphery	Center	In-Between	Periphery
Public sector should be reduced	44	36	48	60	NA	58	39	28	16	34	32	19
Income differences should be reduced	63	67	53	100	NA	91	71	86	95	80	81	88
No. of Respondents	9	44	54	20		23	56	70	19	123	157	50

Note: NA = not applicable.

In Denmark and Iceland, no regional differences appear concerning the item about reduction of the public sector. By contrast, MP's perceptions in Norway follow a marked regional pattern; the proportion believing the voters prefer a reduced public sector is more than twice as high in the center as in the periphery. The middle region, for its part, lies where it "should" on this matter; in between the other two regions. In Sweden, there is no difference between Svealand (center) and Götaland (middle), while the beliefs of representatives in the northern periphery tend to go in the same direction as those of their Norwegian colleagues.

The demand for income equality follows a similar pattern. In both Norway and Sweden, the periphery is perceived to be most in favor of equality. In Iceland, there is practically no difference between the regions, while in Denmark the representatives of the periphery are in fact least inclined to perceive voters' attitudes in this manner. The number of respondents is low, however, and sampling error is correspondingly high. Nevertheless, the regional pattern in representatives' perceptions is similar to that in representatives' own attitudes (as reported in tables 5.5 and 5.6). This is particularly true in the case of Norway, which is the deviating case in this analysis.

Territorial Issues

We turn now to *territorial issues* arising in connection with the opposing interests of specific regions. Where issues of this type are concerned, our hypothesis 2 is that consistency between voters and representatives will be higher in peripheral than in central regions. Moreover, we expect consistency in the periphery to be greater in Iceland and Norway than in Sweden and Denmark.

Our research design is focused on attitudes on just three issues: membership in the European Union, greater support for rural areas, and increased expenditures for the construction of roads and tunnels in outlying districts.[13] These particular issues tap long-standing controversies between central and peripheral parts of the territory over the distribution of goods and the reduction of regional inequalities in living conditions. In addition, the salience of the issue of EU membership in the Nordic countries during the 1990s had a mobilizing effect along the center-periphery dimension.

Let us begin with the second point.

The European Union Scale

The debate on EU membership in Finland, Norway, and Sweden led to relatively strong support for membership in the center and overwhelming

Table 5.9
Attitudes among Members and Voters toward EU
Membership, by Region (mean scores and eta values)

Region	All Members	All Voters	Diff.
Denmark			
Center	6.5	NA	
In-between	7.4	NA	
Periphery	6.9	NA	
Eta	**.10**		
Iceland			
Center	5.1	5.3	−.20
Periphery	3.8	4.1	−.30
Eta	**.21**	**.18****	
Norway			
Center	6.6	4.7	**1.9**
In-between	4.2	4.0	**.20**
Periphery	3.5	2.9	**.60**
Eta	**.35****	**.16****	
Sweden			
Center	6.8	5.0	**1.8**
In-between	7.6	4.9	**2.7**
Periphery	6.5	3.7	**2.8**
Eta	**.16****	**.13***	

Notes: The scale is an 11-point scale running from 0 to 10, where 0 indicates the most negative attitude toward the EU, and 10 the most favorable attitude toward the EU. Thus, the higher the mean score, the more favorable the position toward the EU. NA = not available (question not included in the survey).

$^*p < .05, {}^{**}p < .01$

opposition in peripheral regions (Jenssen et al. 1998). Typically, then, this issue has a mobilizing effect on territorial conflicts. In the case of Norway, where the question of EU membership has been raised three times since the beginning of the 1960s, this tendency has been amply illustrated (see, e.g., Rokkan and Valen 1964; Valen 1976; Bjørklund 1997). The controversial issue of EU membership is multidimensional in character. It cuts across established party lines and triggers conflicts both between and within political parties. For purposes of the present analysis, we have regarded this question as an example of a territorial issue.

Table 5.9 presents the attitudes of voters and MPs toward EU membership. NB: this issue does not have the same relevance in Denmark, which has been an EU member since 1972.

Where voters in Iceland, Norway, and Sweden are concerned, there is a substantial difference between center and periphery as regards attitudes toward EU membership. The tendency is similar on the level of representatives in Iceland and Norway. Among Danish representatives there is no such tendency. Swedish representatives display only a weak tendency of this type, with representatives from the periphery (that is, Norrland) taking a somewhat different view from representatives hailing from the other two regions.

Our main concern, however, is with consistency between representatives and voters in the respective countries, and here we find three sets of patterns. In Iceland, representatives tend to be less pro-EU than voters, but the difference between the two levels is almost identical in the two regions. In Norway, representatives are more pro-EU than voters, but the gap between the two levels is much greater in the center than in the periphery or the middle region. In Sweden, the gap between representatives and voters is greatest in the periphery. Voter attitudes in that country are consistent with the center-periphery division, while representative attitudes tend to differ very little from one region to another.

The patterns for Norway are consistent with our expectations, while the Swedish case deviates. In Norway, issue congruence is clearly evident in the periphery and in the middle region; in Sweden, by contrast, congruence is actually best in the center. We had expected the pattern for Iceland to be similar to that for Norway. The absence of such a pattern in Iceland may simply reflect the lack of debate over EU membership. Thus, the intensity of attitudes toward the EU is likely to be much lower in Iceland than in Sweden and Norway.

State Subventions to Rural Areas

Support for state subventions to rural areas is lowest in the center and highest in the periphery. As indicated in table 5.10, this tendency is consistent for all countries. Overall, the differences between representatives and voters on this issue are not very great. Observe, however, that voter-level data were not collected for Sweden. Denmark deviates in that voters and leaders are remarkably similar in all regions of that country. In Norway and Iceland, the similarity is slightly more marked in the periphery than in the center.

Construction of Roads and Tunnels

We asked both voters and representatives in Iceland and Norway about their views on the construction of roads and tunnels in outlying districts. Table 5.11 indicates that opinion congruence between voters and their

Table 5.10
Attitudes among Members and Voters toward Economic Support for Agricultural Areas, by Region (mean scores and eta values)

Region	All Members	All Voters	Diff.
Denmark			
Center	3.1	3.1	+0.0
In-between	3.0	2.6	+0.4
Periphery	2.6	2.5	+0.1
Eta	**.18**	**.13***	
Iceland			
Center	4.2	3.3	+0.9
Periphery	2.3	2.4	−0.1
Eta	**.71***	**.29***	
Norway			
Center	3.8	2.6	+1.2
In-between	2.9	2.2	+0.7
Periphery	2.6	1.8	+0.8
Eta	**.42***	**.24***	
Sweden			
Center	3.0	NA	
In-between	2.8	NA	
Periphery	1.8	NA	
Eta	**.34***		

Notes: Five response alternatives were coded. The lower the mean score, the more positive attitude toward economic support for agricultural areas. NA = not available (question not included in the survey).

*$p < .10$

Table 5.11
Attitudes among Members and Voters toward Reducing the Level of Road and Tunnel Construction in Peripheral Areas, by Region (mean scores and eta values)

Region	All Members	All Voters	Diff.
Iceland			
Center	2.9	2.5	+0.4
Periphery	1.4	1.7	+0.3
Eta	**.65***	**.28***	
Norway			
Center	3.2	2.8	+0.4
In-between	2.3	2.3	+0.0
Periphery	1.8	1.9	+0.1
Eta	**.40***	**.23***	

Notes: Five response alternatives were coded. The lower the mean score, the stronger support for construction of roads and tunnels in peripheral areas. (This question was not included in the Danish and Swedish surveys.)

*$p < .10$

representatives is remarkably high in the periphery; in Norway, it is high in the middle region as well. Representatives from the center tend to be slightly more restrictive, but representatives overall do not deviate much from their voters. In both countries, the strength of regional variations is statistically significant for both representatives and voters.

The data for our territorial issues indicate a high degree of congruence between representatives and voters, even in the center. In Iceland and Norway, congruence tends to be slightly greater in the periphery than in the center. Above all, though, the data support the hypothesis of great regional variations in the two countries.

Strong regional tendencies are also reflected in the perceptions of representatives (details not shown). Thus, when faced with a proposal to increase subventions to outlying areas, 21 percent of Icelandic representatives in the center—as compared to 62 percent in the periphery—believe their voters view this as a good idea. The corresponding figures for Norway are 40 percent and 77 percent, and for Denmark 33 percent and 56 percent.

As for representatives' perceptions of the opinions of voters regarding the EU, the center-periphery variations are clearly evident. In Norway, 57 percent in the center—compared to only 21 percent in the periphery—believe their voters prefer EU membership. In Iceland, the figures are 29 percent and 17 percent respectively, and in Sweden 67 percent and 59 percent. Although the perceptions of Swedish representatives reflect the results of the 1994 referendum, representatives from all regions have evidently projected their own pro-EU attitudes onto their electorate (see also chapters 7 and 14 below).

CONCLUSIONS

We have focused in this chapter on geographical variations in the degree of issue congruence between voters and representatives. In so doing, we have leaned upon some major arguments from nation-building theory. By arranging regions of the Nordic countries in a center-periphery perspective, we have attempted to test two hypotheses. Where functional issues connected with nationwide competition among political parties are concerned, we did not expect to find regional variations in voter-representative linkages (hypothesis 1). The data for Denmark, Iceland, and Sweden support this hypothesis. Norway is a deviating case. Although voters in that country tend to express similar attitudes throughout the territory, center-periphery variations are evident on the level of representatives. Why do Norwegian representatives deviate from the general pattern?

A possible explanation may lie in the concern for decentralization, which has a long tradition in Norwegian politics. The EU debate in the 1990s only strengthened this tradition, and the salience of the center-periphery controversy markedly increased. This highly divisive issue may have affected party competition in differing ways from one region to another.

Our second hypothesis concerns territorial issues, which relate to geographical conflicts. Our expectation is that voter-MP opinion congruence will be stronger in the periphery than in the center (hypothesis 2). There is a slight tendency in the expected direction for Iceland and Norway, but it is not large enough to be conclusive. In addition, the data demonstrate that opinion congruence between voters and representatives tend to be higher for territorial than for functional issues. Overall, the analysis indicates that regional variations on both the voter level and the MP level are strong in Iceland and Norway.

We expected to find a tendency among representatives from the periphery to be particularly alert to demands from their constituents. Our data on representatives' views of their task support this notion. MPs from peripheral areas are more inclined than their colleagues from the center to express concern for the interests of their constituency and region. In their perception of voter opinion, moreover, representatives seem to be aware of regional variations, particularly in regard to territorial issues. A correspondence thus obtains between representatives' attitudes and their perceptions of voter opinion.

We expected as well that center-periphery variations will be more pronounced in the "new" nation-states of Norway and Iceland than in the "old" nation-states of Sweden and Denmark. Our data generally support this hypothesis. In addition to the observed pattern of periphery protest over territorial issues, peripheral areas in Norway and Iceland are overrepresented in parliament through institutional arrangements. By contrast, territorial distortion in Denmark and Sweden is negligible.

Where the latter countries are concerned, our analysis suggests that the peripheral regions differ somewhat from the rest of the territory, but that the relatively small differences involved do not affect voter-representative linkages. Indeed, the results seem to run contrary to our hypothesis in the case of Sweden. A center-periphery tendency may be observed on the voter level, but no corresponding tendency is evident on the level of representatives.

The observed difference between Denmark and Sweden on the one hand and Iceland and Norway on the other, is consistent with a central assumption of nation-building theory. The process of territorial integration takes a long time. In well-integrated nation-states, the process has been going on for centuries, and protest attitudes in distant parts of the territory are rare. In "new" states, on the other hand, the center-periphery contrast constitutes an important cleavage in national politics. In order to evaluate the significance of this contrast, we shall need more information on a broad range of issues and more analysis of how these are affected by the center-periphery cleavage.

NOTES

1. Naturally, the situation varies with the number of candidates elected to parliament. For instance, in cases where a given party has only one candidate elected from a five-member constituency, the voters may regard this particular MP as "their" representative.

2. We find an interesting exception in the case of Iceland, where PR was used to elect six members (who replaced the six Royal Members) between 1916 and 1934. The whole country served as a single constituency for this purpose. The minimum age for voting in those elections was thirty-five. The majority of MPs, however, were elected by first-past-the-post.

3. These studies were based on the analysis of aggregate data for local communities.

4. Interestingly, the importance of regional ties becomes evident when MPs' roll-call behavior is analyzed. For most purposes, in Nordic parliaments, party leaders demand loyalty to the party line, but on issues reflecting strong local interests the building of local or regional alliances across party lines is normally accepted (see, e.g., Bjurulf and Glans 1976; Heidar 1995).

5. This index represents a summation of absolute percentage differences between the proportion of votes and the proportion of seats obtained by given parties divided by two. The mathematical formula is as follows: $D = \frac{1}{2} \sum |v_i - s_i|$, where v expresses the proportion of the votes of the various parties, while s expresses their proportion of the seats.

6. Iceland is an exception, because adjustment seats in that country are fixed to region: six to the outlying regions and seven to the Reykjavik area. Thus, in Iceland, adjustment seats do not reduce territorial distortion.

7. This item is significant on a higher level in Sweden than in Iceland, although the eta value is higher in the latter country. The explanation for this, of course, is that the number of observations is much higher in Sweden (for Sweden N=330, for Iceland N=43).

8. These groupings represent the traditional "blocs" in Scandinavian politics:

socialist versus nonsocialist parties in the respective countries. For purposes of this chapter, we refer to "leftist" vs. "center + rightist" parties. This distinction is made on the basis of (a) self-placement on the left/right scale, and (b) voters' placement of parties on the left/right scale. The Norwegian Center Party constitutes a deviating case. Both voters and leaders in our study have located that party to the left of Labor. This tendency corresponds to the leftist rhetoric expressed by the party in the EU debate. At the same time, the Norwegian Center Party has always considered itself part of the center, and historically it belongs to the nonsocialist camp. For this reason, and consistent with the location of agrarian parties in the other Nordic countries, we have classified the Norwegian Center Party as a party of the center and right.

9. Several authors have pointed to the risk of ambiguity arising from using actors' self-placement on the left/right scale (for one line of argument, see, e.g., Laver and Hunt 1992). The scale involves a number of interpretations and nuances, some of which may be stressed by some actors, others by others. Nevertheless, all ideological self-placements risk ambiguities of this sort. There does seem to be general agreement, however, that this dimension taps general functional conflicts between the parties in regard to the labor market.

10. The issues are as follows: "Reduce the public sector"; "Increase taxes on high incomes"; "Reduce income differences in society"; "Increase the proportion of health care run by private interests"; "Introduce six-hour working day for all gainfully employed"; "Prohibit all kinds of pornography"; "Accept fewer refugees into [country]"; "Ban private driving in inner cities." For all of these items, the respondents were offered five response alternatives: (1) very good proposal; (2) fairly good proposal; (3) neither good nor bad proposal; (4) fairly bad proposal; (5) very bad proposal.

11. The detailed results have been presented in an appendix of a research report published by the Institute for Social Research (Valen and Narud 1998).

12. The actual wording of the question was: "What do you believe *your own party's voters* think about the following proposals?" The response alternatives were: (1) Most of my party's voters think the proposal is good; (2) Most of my party's voters think the proposal is bad.

13. The question was so worded as to call for a *reduction* in allocations for this purpose. In order to make for comparable data, therefore, we have reversed the coding of this item.

6

Representing Women

Lena Wängnerud

The Nordic countries have been highlighted in recent years as an exception to the rule that politics is a man's game. Whereas the average share of members of parliament throughout the world who were women only came to 13 percent in 1998, the corresponding figure for the five Nordic countries was 37 percent. So, if we are to talk about a common Nordic model, gender equality would appear, at least at first glance, to be a pertinent aspect of parliamentary politics. All of the Nordic countries today are among the democracies with the highest number of female representatives.[1]

During the 1970s, the Nordic countries embarked on a distinct and rapid path to the representation of women. In 1965, the average proportion of MPs elected worldwide who were women was 8 percent; in the Nordic region it was 9 percent. Ten years later, in 1975, the world average was 11 percent; in the Nordic countries it was 16 percent. In 1985, the world average remained low at 12 percent, but the Nordic figure had reached 28 percent. As mentioned earlier, finally, the world average is at present 13 percent and the Nordic average 37 percent. The highest figure is found in Sweden, where more than 40 percent of MPs are women, as are fully 50 percent of members of the government.[2]

If viewed in comparative perspective, then, Nordic women may be characterized as integrated into politics.[3] A routine way of explaining this would be to highlight the electoral system. In the literature, the use of proportional representation (PR)—the current system in all of the Nordic countries—is singled out as one of the most important factors behind a high representation of women.

It is easy here, however, to fall into the trap of focusing on what is measurable rather than on what is important. I shall adopt the converse approach in this chapter. The analysis is centered on factors seldom highlighted in quantitative research on women's representation. For reasons that will become evident, I believe we must move beyond explanations focused on electoral systems if we are to understand the integration of women into politics. A strong ideological support for the idea of social representation, and an active role on the part of women themselves, are more important factors in the high level of women's representation in Nordic societies. Yet there is a trade-off here, the evidence for which requires somewhat fluid methods of measurement.

WOMEN IN PARLIAMENT: LOOKING FOR EXPLANATIONS

The main distinction made in the literature on women's representation is that between majoritarian or single-member district systems on the one hand and PR or multimember district systems on the other (Lovenduski and Norris 1993; Matland and Studlar 1996; Norris 1985; Norris 1996b; Rule 1987). In the Netherlands and Spain, for example, the electoral system is proportional, and the share of MPs who are women is large: 36 percent in the Netherlands, 25 percent in Spain. In France, by contrast, a majoritarian electoral system is in use, and only 11 percent of MPs are women.

There are shortcomings, however, in explanations that focus on the electoral system. This becomes evident if we look more closely at the Nordic case. Most telling, perhaps, is the fact that the Nordic electoral systems have not changed in any dramatic way since the 1970s. It is hard to explain changes in women's representation by reference to factors that have remained stable. If we look beyond the Nordic context, moreover, we can find contrary examples quite easily: Ireland, for instance, uses PR, but the share of female MPs in that country is still only 12 percent.

At this stage of the analysis, then, we can already conclude that electoral arrangements cannot be the *only* force behind the increasing representation of women. If we want to find out why the Nordic countries hold a unique position in this area, we must seek out alternative or supplementary explanations.

THE PASSION FOR EQUALITY

There is a widespread view that the culture of the Nordic countries is an egalitarian one. The existence of a special Nordic passion for equality, for example, has been suggested by such authors as Stephen Graubard (Graubard 1986; see also Verba et al. 1987). There is also a perception that this phenomenon is an important factor behind the political success of women in this part of the world.[4] The idea is that women benefit from a kind of egalitarian spill-over effect. Skard and Haavio-Mannila make the following point:

> During the last decade, feminists [in Nordic countries] have devoted spe-
> cial attention to politics, and on the whole, women have had relatively easy
> access to the political parties for several reasons. First, the Nordic societies
> are small and fairly homogenous, and the values of justice, equality, and
> solidarity are strong. Thus, when women as a group claimed the right to
> participate in the political decision-making process, their claim was seen
> as legitimate. (Skard and Haavio-Mannila 1986:193)

Skard and Haavio-Mannila's point is not that Nordic women have been dragged into politics. They have had to make their claim in order to obtain their reward. The point is rather that, with egalitarianism as a backbone of society, the resistance met by women was weak, or at least not as strong as in other countries.[5]

The culture argument implies the existence of significant differences between the Nordic countries and societies of a different cultural stamp. However, on the basis of a comparison between the attitudes of citizens in Sweden, Germany, and Great Britain, Svallfors (1992; 1993) denies the existence of any special Swedish attitudes toward values like equality, justice, or welfare in general. A study of gender stereotypes in Norway also reaches conclusions at odds with the culture argument (Matland 1995). Matland finds that the beliefs of citizens in Norway regarding male and female competence are no more helpful for advancing the political status of women than are the attitudes of people in the United States.

The culture argument is consistent with a system-oriented approach toward women's representation. As with electoral arrangements, it is a question of a contextual feature of society. But the culture argument has escaped serious empirical testing. This is one reason that it will form the focus of this chapter. If, however, we are to be capable of handling the cultural theme, I believe we must define culture more narrowly than in terms of the beliefs held by an entire population. The focus here will rather be on the basic values held by the political elite in the Nordic countries. It may be that persons closely connected with the political system have egalitarian values, and that this has been the important thing for legitimating women's claims for representation. Ordinary citizens do not, for example, control the recruitment of political candidates.

THE ROLE OF ACTORS

In the literature on this topic, system-oriented approaches are being called into question. Diane Sainsbury (1996:1), for example, comments as follows: "Although this scholarship is suggestive of important factors, a chief weakness of this approach is an exclusive focus on the context with no attention to agency and process." The conflict between different explanatory themes is not easy to settle. At the core of the dispute is the problem indicated by Sainsbury: system-oriented explanatory themes do not take proper account of the role of vanguards in triggering change.

On the basis of a strategy-oriented approach, for instance, Pippa Norris (1996a) stresses how critical it is that regulations actually be implemented if the number of women elected is to rise. One finding that holds good across countries is that conservative parties tend to have relatively few female representatives. Norris's explanation for this is that right-wing parties have an ideology of non-intervention. Social democratic, left, and green parties, on the other hand, are more likely to intervene in the recruitment process and to take certain actions to change the gender balance among their parliamentary representatives.

But Norris does not just note differences between right- and left-wing ideologies. She stresses that generalizations about the impact of ideology need to be qualified: after all, once strategies like positive discrimination are implemented within a political system, initially resistant parties may follow suit, owing to the competitive electoral environment (Norris 1996a). We are thus back to a system-oriented approach, inasmuch as the existence of formal or informal quotas for women (or the lack thereof) can be seen as an aspect of electoral arrangements.

SYSTEM VERSUS STRATEGY

The object of the following analysis is to find empirical evidence that may help us resolve the conflict between system- and strategy-oriented explanatory themes. We want to understand the integration of women into politics, but we do not know whether to look for contextual factors or for certain critical acts (Dahlerup 1988). What is the force behind gender equality? Should the tribute be paid to women themselves? To certain parties? To the new generation? Or is it sooner the case that the development toward equality in this area takes place more or less by itself?

At the foreground of this chapter is the question of whether common values favorable to the advancement of women can be found among the political elite in Denmark, Finland, Iceland, Norway, and Sweden.[6] In accordance with the strategy-oriented approach, we will also look at evidence regarding differences between groups of actors in the process. The analysis will consist of two steps.

First, *attitudes* on issues related to gender equality will be measured. In this way, we will be able to find out about the degree of ideological support for the idea of social representation. Second, we will look at *legislative behavior* with a bearing on gender equality. The reason for this is that there is no automatic connection between thoughts and deeds. If we are to be able to talk about the influence of critical acts, we will need more than just measurements of the attitudes of the political elite.

The variables examined in this chapter include the party affiliation, gender, age, and country background of MPs. Feminist research stresses the need for female politicians to champion the interests of women (Phillips 1995). Other scholars point to the importance of party ideology (Norris 1996a). Some contributions to the literature also suggest that the new generation will introduce new ways of looking at politics—ways more favorable to the advancement of women (Togeby 1994). The country variable is included, since one of the major tasks here is to find out whether a common Nordic model exists.

ATTITUDES ON ISSUES RELATED TO GENDER EQUALITY

The passion for equality is a concept applying more widely than to just gender relations. Should we discover, however, that Nordic MPs are indifferent to gender equality, or even nonsupportive of it, we will not be able easily to argue that egalitarian values are a factor behind the increase in women's representation.

To begin with, let us attempt to ascertain the general orientation toward gender equality prevailing among the political elite. Parliamentarians were asked to indicate, on a scale of 0 to 10, their opinion of a proposal "to work toward a society with more equality between men and women." (Zero stood for "very bad proposal;" 10, for "very good proposal.")

Only in a loose sense can this measurement be said to have anything to do with women aspiring to a political career. The next analytical step must therefore be to try to capture the extent to which MPs think that gender equality in political representation is an urgent matter. This second task is tricky. Asking whether it would be desirable to have more women in parliament would probably elicit nothing but "politically correct" answers. An attempt at capturing attitudes in a more sophisticated manner was therefore deemed necessary. Members of parliament were asked, accordingly, to evaluate various arguments in favor of increasing the number of female representatives.[7]

The question posed was as follows: "Various reasons are given for an equal distribution of women and men in parliament. How important do you consider the following arguments to be? (i) parliament should reflect the most important groups in society in its composition; (ii) women have different life experiences; (iii) working procedures and the climate of discussion will change; and (iv) there will be consequences for policies." Four response alternatives were offered for each of these arguments: "very important," "fairly important," "not very important," and "not at all important." An index was constructed on the basis of the assumption that the more arguments a person considers to be "very important," the more eager he or she is to increase women's representation. The index measures attitudes on a scale from 0 to 12, where 0 means that all arguments are considered "not at all important," and 12 means they are all considered "very important."

The findings are presented in table 6.1. This table includes the means on the two scales, as well as data on the proportion of variance explained by nationality, party affiliation, gender, and age. The party variable is divided into seven categories corresponding to the most important party families in Nordic politics.[8] The age variable is dichotomized according to whether the MPs in question were above or below forty-five years of age.[9] Nationality and gender, for their part, are straightforward categories.

If we are looking for similarities, they are most obvious between younger and older MPs. The age variable does not add anything to the variance explained where attitudes toward gender equality in society or toward women's representation in parliament are concerned (the eta-square is .00 in both cases). All of the other variables, however—nationality, party affiliation, and gender—do contribute significantly to explaining what structures opinion among Nordic parliamentarians.

Table 6.1

Members' Attitudes toward Gender Equality and Women's Representation (% and eta-square)

| | Gender Equality | | Women's Representation | | |
	Mean	Eta²	Mean	Eta²	Minimum N
Country					
Denmark	7.9	.05*	7.3	.06*	102
Finland	NI		7.8		69
Iceland	8.9		7.5		40
Norway	7.9		8.7		140
Sweden	8.8		8.8		325
Party					
Left partyists	9.5	.26*	9.1	.18*	56
Social democrats	8.8		9.0		269
Centrists	9.2		8.8		59
Right partyists	7.2		6.9		127
Agrarians	8.1		8.1		81
Greens	9.8		10.0		20
Populists	4.2		5.1		11
Gender					
Women	9.2	.10*	9.9	.23*	239
Men	7.9		7.5		387
Age					
Younger	8.6	.00	8.4	.00	160
Older	8.4		8.4		442

Notes: Attitudes toward gender equality were measured by the following survey question: "The list below contains a number of proposals with regard to what kind of society some people think we ought to work toward in the future. What is your opinion about the proposal: work toward a society with more equality between men and women?" (the list included proposals of seven different future societies; see also chapter 15 below). The table shows means on a scale running from 0 (very bad proposal) to 10 (very good proposal). Attitudes toward women's representation was measured by an index constructed from responses to the following survey question: "There are various ways to argue for an equal distribution of men and women in [the parliament in question]. How important do you consider the following arguments to be? (1) The composition of parliament should reflect the most important groups in society; (2) Women have different life experiences; (3) Working procedures and the climate of discussion will change; (4) There will be consequences for policies." The following response alternatives were offered: "very important"; "fairly important"; "not very important"; "not at all important." The table shows means on a scale running from 0 (all the arguments were considered not at all important) to 12 (all the arguments were considered very important). Cronbach alpha is 0.80 for the index. Each eta-square value is based on a one-way analysis of variance with the groups on the left-hand side in the table as independent variables, and respective scale as dependent variable. NI = question not included in the survey.

$^*p < .05$

The most striking finding in table 6.1 is that party affiliation and gender are both rather decisive factors. Where attitudes toward gender equality in society are concerned, party affiliation explains 26 percent of the variance, gender 10 percent. On attitudes toward women's representation in parliament, party affiliation explains 18 percent of the variance, gender 23 percent. The impact of nationality is also significant, but at a lower level: nationality explains 5 percent of the variance in connection with gender equality in society, and 6 percent when it comes to women's representation in parliament.

It is obvious that there are different ways of looking at issues related to gender equality. The picture seen here is not convincingly one of a common culture with shared values among the political elite. But do these findings tell us there is no common Nordic model? We should not draw that conclusion too hastily. The discussion thus far has required the culture argument to clear a rather high hurdle: that is, similarities among all categories of political leaders must be shown or the culture argument is rejected. It may be that this requirement is too stringent. Perhaps we can talk about something common even if we find differences within each of the five countries, but only modest variations across borders? We shall bear this suggestion in mind throughout the following analysis and shall address the question more fully at the end of the chapter.

QUOTAS FOR WOMEN

What makes women's representation a controversial issue is the proposal that the parties implement strategies increasing the number of women elected. The use of affirmative action—that is, quota systems of a more or less formalized character—to increase the representation of women in internal party bodies (like party boards) is fairly widespread in the Nordic countries (Dahlerup 1989; Sainsbury 1993; Skjeie 1992). As will be clear from the following analysis, there is no such agreement among Nordic MPs that quotas should be used for seats in parliament.

Table 6.2 presents two ways of capturing attitudes toward the use of gender quotas. Members of parliament have been asked their opinion on a proposal to introduce quotas for senior posts in local and central government, as well as their opinion on a proposal to introduce 40-percent quotas for each gender for seats in parliament. The table shows the number of MPs in favor of each of these proposals. Included also, as previously, is information on the proportion of variance explained by nationality, party affiliation, gender, and age.

Table 6.2
Members' Attitudes toward the Introduction of Quotas for Women

	Senior Posts in Government			40% Quotas for Each Gender to Seats in Parliament		
	% in favor	Eta²	No. of Respondents	% in favor	Eta²	No. of Respondents
Country						
Denmark	26	.03*	109	27	.16*	101
Iceland	25		44	42		43
Norway	41		143	70		146
Sweden	34		329	NI		—
Party						
Left partyists	66	.40*	56	85	.41*	33
Social democrats	48		262	78		106
Centrists	22		60	50		18
Right partyists	2		128	4		57
Agrarians	17		84	38		55
Greens	90		21	100		3
Populists	0		14	7		14
Gender						
Women	54	.16*	239	66	.05*	97
Men	22		386	42		189
Age						
Younger	41	.00	162	48	.00	86
Older	32		440	51		191

Notes: On the question about the introduction of quotas to senior posts in local and central government, the following response alternatives were offered: "very good proposal"; "fairly good proposal"; "neither good nor bad proposal"; "fairly bad proposal"; and "very bad proposal." Table entries are proportion of very or fairly good proposal. Each eta-square value is based on a one-way analysis of variance with the groups on the left-hand side in the table as independent variables and each of the proposals as dependent variables. NI = relevant question not included in the survey.

*$p < .05$

The results in table 6.2 confirm Pippa Norris's observation: party ideology means a great deal for MPs' willingness to implement quotas. When it comes to the proposal to introduce quotas for senior posts in local and central government, 40 percent of the variance is explained by party affiliation; where the proposal to introduce quotas for seats in parliament is concerned, 41 percent of the variance is explained by party affiliation. As expected, greens, leftists, and social democrats are the ones most willing to accept strategies of this kind.

It is obvious that MPs' gender and party affiliation are both important to bear in mind when discussing attitudes on gender equality, women's representation, and the use of quotas. In the final analysis, though, the impact of gender must be reckoned rather modest compared to that of party affiliation: gender explains 16 percent of the variance in connection with the proposal to use quotas in local and central government, and only 5 percent of the variance in regard to the proposal to use quotas in parliament. A preliminary conclusion would therefore be the following: even while party affiliation and gender are both significant, the former tends to be more decisive than the latter. In the next section, we shall see if this conclusion holds good in regard to legislative behavior.

LEGISLATIVE BEHAVIOR WITH A BEARING ON GENDER EQUALITY

In her classic work, *The Concept of Representation*, Hanna Pitkin (1967) argues that what really counts in politics is whether representatives act on behalf of the groups they consider important to represent. The previous sections presented indicators on what goes on in the mind of Nordic parliamentarians. We shall now look at how they behave. In order to be able to distinguish between key actors and others, we must take the analysis a step further. What we are looking for is MPs who take women's interests into account in their parliamentary work.

There is no clear-cut understanding of what qualifies as an act on behalf of women. The concept of women's interests is controversial. The first of the two indicators in the following analysis concerns contacts between MPs and women's organizations; the second has to do with MPs' efforts to influence parliamentary decisions with a bearing on gender equality. What these indicators show is whether, in the course of his or her parliamentary work, an MP recognizes women as a group in need of special attention. The underlying definition of women's interests is not far-reaching: nothing is said in the matter of standpoints or policies. The only assumption made here is that women are better served if they are recognized as a social category.

Since the data used in this chapter are based on survey studies, the following analysis relies on self-reported behavior. This should not present a problem. Ascertaining exact levels of activity is not important here. The focus, as previously, is on comparisons between categories of MPs. Table 6.3 shows the number of MPs who, in the course of the last year, were in contact with women's organizations at least once or twice a month on average. The table also shows the number of MPs who, in the course of the last

Table 6.3
Proportion of Members Acting in the Interest of Women

	Frequent Contacts		Cross-Party Initiatives		
	%	Eta²	%	Eta²	Minimum N
Country					
Denmark	10	.07*	24	.09*	93
Finland	NI		30		115
Iceland	7		41		44
Norway	14		30		134
Sweden	23		11		264
Party					
Left partyists	13	.09*	44	.08*	54
Social democrats	26		20		260
Centrists	10		28		57
Right partyists	7		14		124
Agrarians	12		20		81
Greens	40		53		19
Populists	0		0		12
Gender					
Women	41	.30*	40	.12*	219
Men	3		13		379
Age					
Younger	14	.01*	23	.00	158
Older	20		22		429

Notes: MPs' contacts with women's organizations was measured by the following survey question: "Disregarding how the contact was taken, how often have you in the past year, personally or by letter, been in touch with the organizations, groups, or authorities below?" (about 20 different organizations were listed, including women's organizations). Table entries are proportion of MPs that report having contacts "at least once a week" or "once or twice a month" (the following response alternatives were offered: "at least once a week"; "once or twice a month"; "a few times"; "occasionally"; and "never"). MPs' cross-party initiatives on issues related to gender equality were measured by the following question: "Have you in the past year cooperated actively with parliamentary members from other parties with a view to influencing specific parliamentary decisions in the following issue areas?" (six areas were mentioned including issues related to gender equality). Table entries are proportion of MPs who report themselves having cooperated "several times" or "a few times." (The following response alternatives were offered: "several times"; "a few times"; "once or twice"; and "never"). Each eta-square value is based on a one-way analysis of variance with the groups on the left-hand side in the table as independent variables and respective type of activity as dependent variables. NI = not included in the questionnaire.

*$p < .05$

year, had worked together with members of other parties in order to influence specific parliamentary decisions with a bearing on gender equality.

It is evident from the analysis in table 6.3 that legislative behavior is an area within which MPs' gender is of greater importance than their party affiliation. This is especially clear if we look at contacts between MPs and women's organizations: gender explains 30 percent of the variance; whereas party affiliation explains only 9 percent. The finding that 41 percent of female MPs are in regular contact with women's organizations, compared with just 3 percent of male MPs, is quite striking.

Another finding worthy of note in table 6.3 is that nationality turns out to be more decisive for legislative behavior than for attitudes. The impact of nationality is actually on a par with the impact of party affiliation when it comes to contacts with women's organizations (nationality explains 7 percent of the variance, party 9 percent), as well when it comes to cooperation on issues related to gender equality (nationality explains 9 percent of the variance, party 8 percent).

What is missing is a systematic pattern whereby the MPs of one country can be singled out as acting more strongly on women's behalf than the MPs of the other countries. Where contacts with women's organizations are concerned, 23 percent of Swedish MPs report having had contact at least once or twice a month, whereas only 7 percent of Icelandic MPs report a corresponding frequency of contacts. Regarding cooperation on issues related to gender equality, however, the reverse situation emerges: Icelandic MPs are found at the top, with 41 percent reporting cooperation; Swedish MPs are found at the bottom—only 11 percent report cooperation.

The analysis on legislative behavior is the only one in this chapter where MPs' age turns out to be significant: older MPs report having had more frequent contacts with women's organizations than younger MPs. But the variance explained by age is only 1 percent. It seems a safe bet to dispatch the generation hypothesis when it comes to gender equality and the parliamentary process—at least where the elite level is concerned.

The preliminary finding stated earlier was that party affiliation is a more decisive factor than gender. This finding must be revised, or at least specified: where attitudes are concerned, party affiliation is more decisive than gender (in the case of three out of four indicators); but where legislative behavior is concerned the reverse is apparently true. Before pronouncing any such conclusions to be final, we should test the results in a multivariate analysis. This shall be done. Before that, however, an analysis of the *effects* of women's representation is in order. This question is not tied altogether to the major theme of this chapter. Discussions on women's representation do become rather sterile, though, unless we take up the question of changes in policy content.

THE EFFECTS OF WOMEN'S REPRESENTATION

Tracing the effects of women's representation is a research project in itself: the task is an all-encompassing one.[10] The question is whether it is possible to judge the impact women have. How shall we proceed? One approach would be to compare democracies with a high level of women's representation to democracies with a low level. Immediately, a methodological problem presents itself. Assume, for example, that the object is to explain the differing outcomes in Sweden (where the level of women's representation is high) and in France (where it is low). How can we isolate the impact of gender from that of a host of other factors that differ between the two countries?

Another approach would be to compare one and the same country at different points in time. The same methodological problems arise here: many things doubtless differ, in addition to the number of women elected, between the one time and the other. Yet these obstacles are perhaps less disturbing. Moreover, at least this approach—one country, several time-points—has been tried in empirical research. An example is the work done in Norway by Hege Skjeie (1992), who presents systematic findings to the effect that female politicians bring different issues and priorities to the public arena than do their male counterparts. Similar evidence has been found in the United States (Thomas 1994) and in Sweden (Oskarson and Wängnerud 1995; Wängnerud 1998).

But the problem here is not entirely methodological. Feminist research must also grapple with theoretical considerations: on what grounds do we expect women to change politics? Few feminists commit themselves to essentialism or pure biologism. (Indeed, such explanations have mainly been used *against* women historically.) What is commonly put forward in current research is an explanation that can be classified as sociological: the life experiences of women differ from those of men in regard to working life, education, economic standing, access to power, and responsibility for home and children (to name just a few gender-related factors); it may be supposed, therefore, that women will develop a different way of looking at politics (Norris 1996b; Phillips 1995).

With all these theoretical and methodological notes in mind, we may still wish to consider the question about the effects of women's representation. We are heading here toward a question that is truly central to research on the workings of democracy: does it matter who our representatives are? No conclusive answer to this question is possible here; still, the data on legislative behavior considered earlier indicate that yes, it does matter who our representatives are. In what follows, we take up the experience of par-

Table 6.4
Do Women Change Politics? Proportion of Members Confirming That Their Party Has Changed Issue Position because of Increased Presence of Women in Parliament (%)

	%	Eta²	No. of Respondents
Country			
Denmark	50	.04*	98
Finland	47		115
Iceland	59		39
Norway	78		137
Sweden	60		308
Party			
Left partyists	62	.08*	60
Social democrats	74		282
Centrists	57		67
Right partyists	44		142
Agrarians	55		103
Greens	39		23
Populists	17		12
Gender			
Women	73	.04*	252
Men	53		441
Age			
Younger	58	.00	182
Older	61		486

Notes: The question was worded as follows: "In the past twenty years, the proportion of women has increased in most parties in parliament. Are there any concrete issues on which you believe the position of your party has changed because of the increased representation of women?" (Respondents were asked to indicate a yes or a no.)

*p < .05

liamentarians themselves. What is their opinion? Does the increased presence of women lead to changes in the content of policies?

The following question was asked: "In the past twenty years, the proportion of women has increased in most parties in parliament. Are there concrete issues on which you believe the position of your party has changed owing to the increased representation of women?"[11] Table 6.4 shows the number of MPs answering "yes" to that question.

One should be careful about estimating whether a high or low percentage of MPs subscribe to the idea that women change the content of policies. Table 6.4 shows, however, that in most of the categories a majority of MPs say yes, there are concrete issues on which the position of their party has changed owing to the increased representation of women. There is a correspondence between this and the previous measurement. It must be said that in comparison with earlier findings, the coefficients for variance explained (eta-square) in table 6.4 are rather small. This can be interpreted as indicative of a shared view: that is, Nordic parliamentarians agree that the gender composition of parliament matters for the political agenda.[12]

In an open-ended follow-up question, respondents were asked to indicate which issues they were thinking of. Three policy areas cropped up repeatedly in the answers: family policy was mentioned by 45 percent, gender equality by 39 percent, and social policy by 28 percent (respondents were allowed to mention more than one issue). If we are to judge from the experiences of MPs themselves, the impact of women's representation has been greatest in policy areas closely connected to the development of the Nordic welfare state.

NO NORDIC MODEL?

The main conclusion of this chapter is that the variations between male and female MPs, and between MPs of differing party affiliation, are so strong that it is hardly possible to speak of a common culture with shared values among all categories of political leaders. The passion for (gender) equality is not equally distributed among the elite: women are more passionate than men; and MPs from the right wing—conservatives and populists—are less passionate than MPs from other parties. We have noted, however, that the idea of a common Nordic model might still be saved by a finding that the cross-border variations are modest.

The last step in this chapter will be to use some techniques that may facilitate further evaluation. A multivariate regression analysis allows us to weigh the effects of nationality against those of party affiliation, gender, and age. The following analysis will include six of the indicators previously presented (all of the issues, that is to say, which have been measured in at least four countries).[13]

To do the multivariate analysis, we must choose one country as a reference point. In theory, the MPs of that country will represent what is typically Nordic. The regression test will then show how close the MPs of the other countries are to that standard. The problem here is that it is hard to define one country as being more typically Nordic than the others. All the same, a country must be selected; in line with the choice made in other chapters of this book, Norway was chosen as the baseline category. Table 6.5 shows the results of the multiple regression analysis.

Table 6.5

Determinants of Members' Position on Various Gender-Related Issues (unstandardized regression coefficients, OLS estimates)

	Attitudes		Quotas in Local/Central Government	Legislative Behavior		General Effects
	Gender Equality	Women's Representation		Contact with Women's Organization	Cooperation on Gender Equality	Perceived Changes in Party Positions
Country						
Denmark	.08	−1.18*	−.65*	−.34*	−.20	−.28*
Finland	NI	−.77*	NI	NI	.24*	−.30*
Iceland	1.31*	−.62	−.32	−.08	.29*	−.14
Sweden	.88*	.08	−.24*	.27*	−.52*	−.19*
Party	1.72*	1.88*	1.42*	.44*	.24*	.22*
Gender	1.01*	2.09*	.87*	1.11*	.70*	.16*
Age	.25	.03	.08	−.19*	−.14	−.04
Constant	6.07*	6.39*	1.58*	1.71*	1.55*	1.55*
Adjusted R²	.28	.37	.38	.38	.22	.10

Notes: Norway has been defined as the baseline category. NI = not included in the questionnaire.

Dependent variables | *Values* | *Endpoints*
Gender equality	0–10	very bad proposal—very good proposal
Women's representation	0–12	not at all important—very important (index)
Quotas	1–5	very bad proposal—very good proposal
Contact women's org.	1–5	never—at least once a week
Coop. on gender equality	1–4	never—several times
Perceived effects	1–2	no—yes

Independent variables

All the independent variables have been dichotomized. Party has been coded as affiliated with Right Partyists or Populists (0), all other parties (1). Gender: men (0), women (1). Age: older (0), younger (1). Denmark: yes (1), no (0); Finland: yes (1), no (0); Iceland: yes (1), no (0); Sweden: yes (1), no (0). Minimum number of respondents is 586. For detailed information about the variables, see tables 6.1–6.4.

$*p < .05$

The idea of a common culture with shared values is not saved by the multivariate analysis. The results in table 6.5 indicate that only one country, Iceland, may be said (possibly) to coincide with the Nordic standard. Iceland differs significantly on just two of the six issues included, whereas Denmark differs on four issues and Sweden on five. Finland—for which data were available on just three of the issues—differs significantly on every one.

What can be said, then, about the impact of nationality? The coefficients show significant values, but no neat and interpretable pattern emerges, save, perhaps, in the case of Denmark. The coefficients for Danish MPs are systematically negative. This means that, less frequently than their Nordic colleagues, Danish MPs considered it "very important" to have an equal number of men and women in parliament. In addition, they are less in favor of quotas for women, they report having had fewer contacts with women's organizations, and they are less willing to subscribe to the idea that women's representation has had an effect on the political agenda.

There are no decisive criteria for determining whether a common model exists. Yet the analysis in this chapter leaves the impression that some cross-border similarities may be found. Significant layers of the political elite in all of the Nordic countries express ideological support for the idea of social representation. It is also evident that cleavages exist within these countries. For example, female MPs stand out as a vanguard as soon as we extend the analysis beyond verbal declarations to actual legislative behavior.

CONCLUDING DISCUSSION

In the literature on women's representation, electoral arrangements have supplied the predominant explanatory theme. The core of this chapter has sought to question the impact ascribed to contextual factors in this area. In an attempt to put system-oriented approaches to the test, I have highlighted a cultural factor: namely, the presumed Nordic passion for equality. The question is whether a prevalence of egalitarian values has facilitated the political advancement of Nordic women.

The findings here should not be seen as a reason to reject the importance of the PR system or the cultural context for explaining the large number of women in Nordic parliaments. Indeed, I believe these factors have contributed to an advantageous *starting point*. A focus on such factors yields, however, a perspective that is too static to enable us to understand fully the force behind the rapid growth in the number of female representatives.

From a more dynamic point of view, what should be highlighted instead is the impact of factors like party strategies, as well as the activities of women themselves. Let us begin with the first-mentioned. The findings of this chapter indicate a reluctance within parties of the right to recognize women as a politically relevant category. In the empirical analysis, the conservatives and the populists turned out to be outliers on gender-related matters. This finding confirms the results of research in other European countries.

However, the other factor—the activities of women themselves—is seldom discussed in the literature. As mentioned before, women stand out as the most radical group in almost all of the different settings. This is especially true where behavior is concerned: female representatives report regular contact with women's organizations, for example, as well as regular parliamentary work with a bearing on gender equality. Their activities may be regarded, in comparison with those of their male colleagues, as comprehensive. I do not believe it naive to ascribe a substantial importance to these findings.

The strategy Nordic women have used to influence politics is sometimes labeled a double strategy: to work, at one and the same time, both inside and outside the parties. What needs closer study in the future is the organizing on the inside. One instance of this are the party-linked women's federations of the sort found in the Nordic countries and fairly rare elsewhere. Without a doubt, these federations have been an important recruitment base for female politicians. Recent studies have also pointed to the role that women's federations played when gender equality started to emerge as a politically recognized issue (Sainsbury 1993).

We can also start to ask whether differences exist in respect of women's activities between Denmark on the one hand and Iceland, Norway, and Sweden on the other. We saw in the empirical analysis, after all, that the coefficients for Danish MPs were systematically lower than those for MPs from the other three countries.[14] Without pushing the point too far, I would suggest that the issue of gender equality at the top political level has been less *politicized* in Denmark. In Norway in 1986, Gro Harlem Brundtland appointed an internationally recognized cabinet in which 40 percent of the ministers were women. In Iceland, the Women's Alliance entered the Althingi in 1983. In Sweden, a feminist network, known as the Support Stockings, was founded by influential women in politics, journalism, and other areas following the election of 1991, in which the proportion of female MPs had dropped from 38 to 33.5 percent. These are only a few examples, but they highlight occasions when gender equality has been placed on the political agenda in a forceful manner. Corresponding experiences are not so easy to find in the case of Denmark, which may help us understand why Denmark diverges from the other Nordic countries in this area.

It would not be correct to portray the Nordic countries as a part of the world that is glorious for women. Still, if the object is to learn how women can make their way to the top levels of politics, we might profit by a look at what has happened here during the past twenty to thirty years: that is, the number of female MPs started to grow at the same time that the welfare state expanded and gender equality became the subject of more intense debate. If we are to grasp the relationship between these factors more fully, we will need more thorough conceptualizations of the qualitative aspects of women's representation. Is it possible to mobilize women without a vision of a society in which women and men are recognized as equals? Is it possible to realize gender equality without a large number of female representatives? These questions are not easy to answer. But the data do support the argument that women have a special impact on parliamentary processes. And the guess in that case is no, it is not possible to understand the increase in women's representation without taking women's organizing into account. Nor is it possible to understand the significance of this increase without considering its impact on policy content.

Appendix

Table 6.A1

Attitudes toward Four Different Arguments for Equal Distribution of Women and Men in Parliament (% "very important argument")

	Denmark			Finland			Iceland			Norway			Sweden		
	Women	Men	Diff.	Women	Men	Diff.	Women	Men	Diff.	Women	Men	Diff.	Women	Men	Diff.
The composition of parliament should reflect the most important groups in society	66	38	+28	57	24	+33	44	52	−8	86	49	+37	73	40	+33
Women have different life experiences	30	8	+22	40	6	+34	27	16	+11	60	24	+36	74	26	+48
Working procedures and the climate of discussion will change	29	8	+21	23	4	+19	36	13	+23	31	10	+21	60	16	+44
There will be consequences for policies	24	9	+15	26	2	+24	45	13	+32	36	11	+25	50	8	+42
No. of Respondents	35	72		35	80		9	31		52	89		135	194	

Note: The wording of the question was as follows: "There are various ways to argue for an equal distribution of women and men in [the specific parliament in question]. How important do you consider the following arguments to be?" The following response alternatives were offered: "very important"; "fairly important"; "not very important"; "not at all important."

NOTES

1. Statistics from Inter-Parliamentary Union (1995) in *Women in Parliaments 1945–1995: A World Statistical Survey;* also available at <http://www.ipu.org>.

2. It is clear, though, that Iceland has lagged behind the other Nordic countries. The following table contains separate figures for Denmark, Finland, Iceland, Norway, and Sweden:

Women in Nordic Parliaments 1965–95 (%).

Year	Denmark	Finland	Iceland	Norway	Sweden	World Average
1965	9.5	14.0	1.7	8.0	11.5	8.2
1975	15.6	23.0	5.0	15.5	21.4	10.9
1985	26.3	30.5	15.0	34.4	31.5	12.1
1995	33.5	33.5	25.4	39.4	40.4	11.3
1998	37.4	33.5	25.4	36.4	42.7	12.7

Source: Inter-Parliamentary Union.

3. Saying that women in the Nordic countries are integrated into politics is not the same as saying that complete gender equality exists in these countries. From an international point of view, however, the integration of women is obvious in the Nordic countries. Moreover, many of the changes seen at the parliamentary level are also evident at local and regional levels, as well as at the level of the cabinet.

4. For a recent empirical study indicating the importance of the Nordic factor for women's representation, see Norris (1996a).

5. Many other scholars present similar arguments. Skjeie (1992) in particular bears mentioning.

6. What could be expected from the introduction above is a study focused on selection committees. The elite concept here will be understood both more widely and more narrowly: more widely in that not all members of parliaments take part in the process of selecting candidates; more narrowly in that members of selection committees are not members of parliament.

7. The question concerns arguments for an equal distribution of men and women in parliament. Since men are still in the majority, an equal distribution would mean increasing the number of women.

8. A detailed definition of the party families is provided in appendix 3. The point has been made in previous chapters that the method of classification is not free from objection: it is especially debatable to collapse liberal and Christian parties into a single category (of "centrist parties"), as well to classify the Danish Venstre as an agrarian party and the Icelandic Women's Alliance as a green party.

9. There can be no clear-cut dividing line between younger and older MPs.

The age of forty-five has been chosen in order to get a fairly large group of younger MPs: 27 percent of Nordic parliamentarians are under forty-five years of age.

10. For an analysis on the effects of gender, see also chapters 4 and 5 of this book.

11. This question was first used by Skjeie (1992).

12. Populists, greens, and conservatives are the categories with the lowest proportion of MPs perceiving effects. The pattern among green MPs is worthy of extra note, since they proved quite the opposite of right-wing parties in the earlier analysis. On the open-ended follow-up question, a great many green MPs answered that "we have always been a women's party."

13. The question on MPs' attitudes toward a 40 percent quota for women in parliament has been left out, since it was only asked in three countries.

14. It is hard to say anything about Finland here, since many of the relevant issues were left out of the Finnish questionnaire.

7

Issue Agreement

Sören Holmberg

ISSUE AGREEMENT MATTERS

The notion of some form of issue agreement between voters and their elected representatives plays a role in most theories of representative democracy (Pitkin 1967; Manin 1997). The Swedish scholar Jörgen Westerståhl has formulated the idea succinctly: "Representatives shall reflect the opinions of their voters, and the overarching goal of democracy—to implement the people's will—is to be promoted by means of this policy representation" (Westerståhl and Johansson 1981:20).

If we follow Westerståhl and define democracy as the implementation of the will of the people—and assume there is a people's will that can be implemented—the emphasis put on issue agreement is obvious. But with a different approach to democracy—for example, one in the spirit of Joseph Schumpeter's elite-oriented model, which focuses on party competition and accountability, or Leif Lewin's interactive model, which asserts the importance of maximizing participation—then issue agreement becomes less crucial (Schumpeter 1942; Lewin 1970).

Less crucial, however, does not mean nonexistent. Even in elite models like Schumpeter's or participation models like Lewin's, notions of issue agreement do play a role. Schumpeter's model assumes that interparty competition results in representativeness among the elite, while Lewin's model stresses the significance of consensus-building. Thus, issue agreement is more central in some democratic theories than in others; but it has a role to play in most theories. Consequently, the empirical study of issue agreement between elite and mass is not just an exciting exercise. It is also, and foremost, a study of one of the most important notions within the broad family of theories of representative democracy.

155

Issue agreement matters. The crucial questions are how much issue agreement there is, what explains it, and how much it matters. The purpose of the analysis presented in this chapter is to investigate the first-mentioned question: how much issue agreement is there? Since our data come from not one but five different political systems, it is only natural that we also try to say something about the second-mentioned question: what causes variation in issue congruence—that is, to what extent do degrees of issue agreement between leaders and voters differ across political systems? Are there democratic systems that are more conducive to high degrees of opinion representation than others?

HYPOTHESES

With a research design involving, in our case, five very similar Nordic political systems, we should not expect any large differences in the degree of issue agreement between members of parliament and citizens. On the contrary, given a broad enough sample of issues, the degree of issue congruence should be fairly uniform across the Nordic countries; even more so if small differences in degrees of issue agreement is a universal characteristic of most political systems no matter how they are formed constitutionally.

Since political parties rather than individual members of parliament are the principal actors in all of the Nordic countries, we shall apply a collectivist, party-centered model of representation when analyzing issue agreement. One consequence of our focus on collective party representation is that Finland becomes a potentially interesting case. The reason is that the Finnish electoral system contains, as compared with the other Nordic electoral systems, more of a personal-vote element. Thus one hypothesis would be that the more individualistic system in Finland would yield slightly less in the way of party-centered policy congruence than the system employed in the other Nordic countries. Too much money should not be placed on this hypothesis, however. Previous research on comparative issue agreement has shown the difference in degrees of policy congruence to be small to nonexistent between candidate-centered individualistic systems like the American one and party-oriented systems like those in Sweden, the Netherlands, and Germany (Holmberg 1996b; 1999).

Another rather obvious hypothesis is that the degree of issue agreement between elite and mass should be somewhat higher in a really small country like Iceland (circa 250,000 inhabitants)—here you would expect a fair proportion of members and voters to know each other and to be in personal contact—than in the medium-sized Nordic countries. The hypothesis presumes that smallness, through familiarity, brings about similarity (Dahl and Tufte 1973); but when a smallness hypothesis of this sort was tested on data relating to issue agreement between local councilmen and voters in Swedish municipalities, the results were negative. The degree of issue congruence were no higher in small-sized municipalities than in larger municipalities or in big cities (Westerståhl and Johansson 1981).

DATA

The data on which we can base our comparative analysis of issue congruence in the Nordic countries are unique and fairly extensive. They are unique in that the same set of issue questions has been administered to members of parliament and samples of eligible voters in five different countries. Furthermore, the scope of issues covered is fairly extensive; all in all, between eleven and thirteen issue questions were asked of MPs as well as of voters in the participating countries (except Finland, where only one comparative issue question is available for the analysis of issue agreement between MPs and voters). It is to our advantage, however, that the only available Finnish issue question concerns the important ideological left-right scale. Opinion formation in all of the Nordic countries is structured to a very high degree by the left-right dimension (Särlvik 1970; Holmberg 1974, 1981; Valen 1981; Aardal 1994; Aardal and Valen 1995; Pesonen et al. 1973; Hardarson 1995; Borg and Sänkiaho 1995; Borre and Andersen 1997). If we had to restrict the analysis to just one issue dimension, that dimension would be the left-right divide.

Of the eleven to thirteen questions on issues included in the Danish, Norwegian, Icelandic, and Swedish studies, eight of the issues were exactly the same: public-sector size, taxes on high incomes, income differences, privately run health care, six-hour working day, ban on pornography, restrictions on immigration, and ban on inner-city driving. Two issue questions were asked of MPs and voters in Denmark, Norway, and Iceland but not in Sweden: ban on interference with hereditary dispositions of humans and animals, and priority to rural areas. Another two issues were included in the Danish, Icelandic, and Swedish studies but not in Norway: power of financial markets and gender-based affirmative action when recruiting higher civil servants. Finally, Iceland does not have any defense forces, hence a question on defense costs was included in the Danish, Norwegian, and Swedish studies but not in the Icelandic surveys.

Three different measures of policy agreement will be used (Esaiasson and Holmberg 1996): The *means difference measure* shows the divergence between MPs' and voters' opinions when all issue items have been scaled between 1 and 5, with 3 as a middle alternative and with don't-know answers excluded. The means difference measure can vary between 0.0 (perfect congruence) and 4.0 (maximum difference). The *percentage difference measure* is calculated as half the summed difference between members' and voters' answers to dichotomized issue questions, after don't-know answers and middle-of-the-road answers (3's) have been excluded. Zero (0) stands for perfect agreement and 100 for maximum policy difference. The third measure acknowledges the fact that democratic decision-making should be based on majority support; it indicates the *proportion of issues characterized by differing majority positions* among members and voters. When deciding what the majority position is, we looked at the dichotomized issue results. As with the previous measures, zero (0) stands for perfect congruence while 100 indicates maximum difference.

NORDIC SIMILARITY

An overview of our issue-agreement measurements country by country, and broken down by issue and party, is given in the appendix to this chapter. A first striking impression from the results is the extent of similarity across the Nordic countries. No matter how we measure issue agreement, the degree of congruence between MPs and voters is about the same in Denmark, Norway, Iceland, and Sweden.

If we look more in detail, however, it is evident that the results give some support to our second hypothesis—the degree of issue congruence is somewhat higher in Iceland than in the other Nordic countries, especially if we compare the results for the entire parliament with the results for all eligible voters. This conclusion is further strengthened if we look at the results, analyzed by Narud and Valen in chapter 15, on members' and voters' ideological attitudes toward the future development of society. These results indicate, too, that elite-mass congruence is higher in Iceland than in Norway and Sweden. It is apparent in our case that smallness is associated with likeness.

POOR SHOWING AMONG PARTIES ON THE RIGHT

A second striking result is revealed if we look at intraparty degrees of issue agreement (see table 7.1). It is obvious that, across all four Nordic countries, parties on the right—conservative parties and progressive parties—

exhibit the lowest average degrees of issue congruence between MPs and voters. By contrast, parties on the far left tend—across all four countries—to exhibit degrees of issue agreement that are among the highest.

If we rank Nordic parties with respect to the degree of issue agreement between MPs and voters (according to the percentage difference measure in table 7.1), the highest nine are: Left Socialists (Norway), Social Democrats (Iceland), Greens (Sweden), Agrarians (Iceland), Left Party (Sweden), Social Democrats (Sweden), Left Socialists (Denmark), Christian Democrats (Norway), and Left Socialists (Iceland). Similarly, starting from the bottom, the lowest nine would be: Progress Party (Denmark), Progress Party (Norway), Conservatives (Norway), Conservatives (Denmark), Women's Alliance (Iceland), Liberals (Denmark), Conservatives (Sweden), Agrarians/Venstre (Denmark), and Conservatives (Iceland).

One explanation for the poor showing of the right-wing parties could be that our sample of issues is somehow biased, containing an undue number of odd issues, but that is not a very plausible argument. After all, if we look at which specific issues reveal the lowest degrees of issue congruence among conservative and progress parties, they do not turn out to be in any way marginal or odd. On the contrary, in most cases they tend to be salient and much discussed left-right issues. If we stick to the eight exactly comparable issues, the issues in Denmark with the worst congruence results for the Conservatives and Progress Party were, respectively, privately run health care and taxes on high incomes. In Norway, the comparable issue for both Conservatives and the Progress Party was taxes on high incomes. In Iceland and Sweden, as in Norway, conservatives exhibited their lowest issue agreement on the issue of taxes on high incomes.

The reason for the poor congruence was the same in all cases. Compared to their representatives, a higher proportion of conservative and progress voters wanted tax increases for people with high incomes, and a lower percentage wanted privately run health care. Expressed in ideological terms, conservative and progress members tended to be positioned clearly to the right of their voters.

If we look more closely at the results for the Swedish Conservatives, for whom we have time-series data going back to the 1960s, it is clear that this is a rather new phenomenon. In the 1960s, Conservative MPs in Sweden were somewhat to the left of their voters on average, and the degree of issue agreement among Conservatives was higher than among any of the other Swedish parties (Holmberg 1974). In the 1990s, Swedish Conservatives exhibit, like their counterparts in the other Nordic countries, comparatively low figures of issue agreement, and they tend to be situated to the right of their voters (Holmberg 1996b).

Table 7.1

Within-Party Issue Agreement between Nordic Members and Voters on Eight Comparable Issues

	Average Difference between Mean Issue Positions	Average Difference between Dichotomized Percentage Distributions	Number of Issues Where Parliament Members and Voters Have Different Majorities
Denmark			
Party			
Left socialists	0.7	19	0
Social democrats	0.7	29	2
Liberals (Rad. Venstre)	0.9	35	3
Agrarians (Venstre)	0.9	31	0
Conservatives	1.0	36	3
Progress party (FrP)	1.3	43	4
Average 6 parties	0.9	32	2
All	0.4	13	4
Norway			
Party			
Left socialists	0.5	12	0
Labor	0.7	25	2
Christian democrats	0.5	21	0
Agrarians (Senter)	0.5	23	1
Conservatives	0.9	37	3
Progress party (FrP)	1.4	41	2
Average 6 parties	0.8	27	1
All	0.4	15	3

Iceland

Party			
Left socialists (PA)	0.6	21	2
Social democrats (SDP + PM)	0.5	13	0
Greens/Women's Alliance (WA)	0.8	36	2
Agrarians (PP)	0.4	16	0
Conservatives (IP)	0.9	30	1
Average 5 parties	0.6	23	1
All	0.4	9	1

Sweden

Party			
Left party	0.7	16	1
Greens	0.5	14	0
Social democrats	0.5	17	2
Agrarians	0.4	22	4
Liberals	0.7	27	3
Christian democrats	0.5	24	2
Conservatives	1.0	31	2
Average 7 parties	0.6	22	2
All	0.4	14	2

Note: The issue questions were formulated in the same way in the four countries for the MP studies as well as for the voter surveys. The eight issues comprise the first eight issues in tables 7.A1–7.A4 (excluding defense spending). The three different measures of policy congruence are constructed as follows: The *means difference measure* shows the divergence between members' and voters' opinions when all issue items have been scaled between 1 and 5, with 3 as a middle alternative, but excluding don't knows. The measure can vary between 0.0 (perfect congruence) and 4.0 (maximum difference). The *percentage difference measure* is calculated as half the summed difference between members' and voters' answers to dichotomized issue questions after don't knows and persons without clear issue positions (3's) were excluded. Zero (0) stands for perfect congruence and 100 for maximum policy difference. The third measure, *number of issues displaying different majority positions* among members and voters, is based on the results from the analysis of dichotomized items. As in the previous measure, zero (0) stands for perfect congruence, but 8 indicates maximum policy difference.

In political terms, most observers of Nordic politics would agree that what has happened in the meantime is that conservative parties have become more ideological and focused on a neo-liberal market message that they try to impress on voters. Many of the other parties—such as, in the Swedish case, most notably the Social Democrats and the Left Party—have become more pragmatic and have moved toward the political center; as a consequence, they have improved their issue agreement (Holmberg 1997).

To be fair, there were of course issues where the right-wing parties exhibited high levels of congruence between members and voters. For example, the issue with the best agreement between MPs and voters for the progress parties of Denmark and Norway was the immigration issue. Incidently, the immigration issue was also the issue with the highest level of elite-mass congruence among Swedish Conservatives.

REPRESENTATIONAL PROCESSES AT WORK

If we look at the agreement figures from an issue perspective instead of a party perspective, we can clearly rule out one plausible and readily available explanation for the rather strong similarity in degrees of opinion congruence across the Nordic countries. That explanation is that people from the Nordic countries—across all borders and political systems—basically think in the same way and have the same political opinions. Consequently, degrees of issue agreement will be similar across borders, not because of representational processes, but because Nordic MPs will have similar views across borders and Nordic voters will have similar views across borders. A cursory look at the graphs in figure 7.1 reveals that this argument is clearly wrong. It should be observed that the results presented are relevant for the comparison of all members with all eligible voters; no party breakdowns are featured.

On most issues, Nordic MPs as well as voters held rather different opinions across borders. For example, there is only one issue where the maximum percentage spread between the country results is less than fifteen points among MPs or voters; that issue is the six-hour working day. On many issues, country differences were surprisingly large. The most dramatic examples are the issue of the size of the public sector, where Icelandic MPs and voters are much more inclined to reduce than are their counterparts in the rest of Scandinavia, and the issue of banning pornography, which Danish members and voters are much less in favor of than their counterparts outside Denmark. Clearly, representational processes creating agreement between MPs and voters must have been at work in these cases. A common Nordic outlook does not exist and so cannot be adduced as an explanation for the rather similar congruence results across countries.

LOW AGREEMENT ON THE IMMIGRATION ISSUE

The graphs in figure 7.1 also demonstrate that, among our eight issue cases, there are only two where the degree of issue agreement between all MPs and all eligible voters is clearly below average in most, if not all, Nordic countries. These two issues are immigration and the six-hour working day. In the case of immigration, MPs tend to be more positive, while voters want to accept fewer refugees. The Swedish results are the most extreme, with only 17 percent of MPs expressing the opinion that fewer refugees should be accepted, as compared to 70 percent of all eligible voters (yielding a large difference score of 53). On the issue of the six-hour working day, voters in all of the Nordic countries tend to be more in favor than members, most notably so in Denmark and Norway.

LEFT-RIGHT ISSUES BETTER THAN AVERAGE

The other six issues indicate fairly high levels of issue agreement in most Nordic countries. Look, for example, at the results of the four left-right issues—the size of the public sector, taxes on high incomes, income differences, and privately run health care. Across the four countries, issue agreement on these issues tends to be better than average, with only two minor exceptions (Denmark and Sweden on taxes on high incomes) and one major exception (Norway on privately run health care).

The fact that left-right issues tend to exhibit above-average levels of issue agreement is no surprise. It has been noted before, and it follows from a rather obvious hypothesis that opinion congruence between members and voters should be highest on salient and politicized issues at the center of political discourse—a description that fits left-right issues well in all of the Nordic countries (Esaiasson and Holmberg 1996).

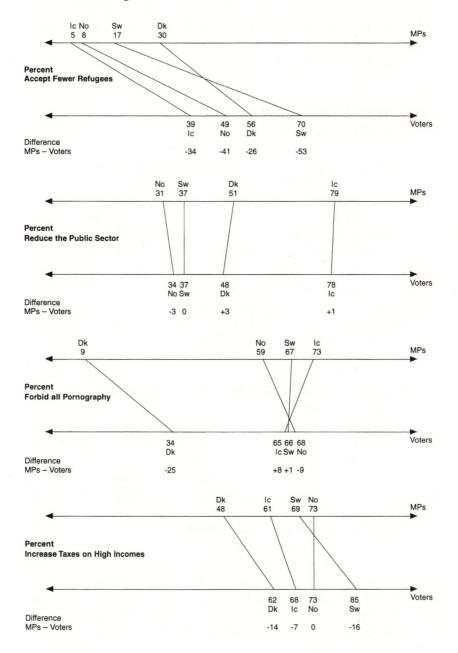

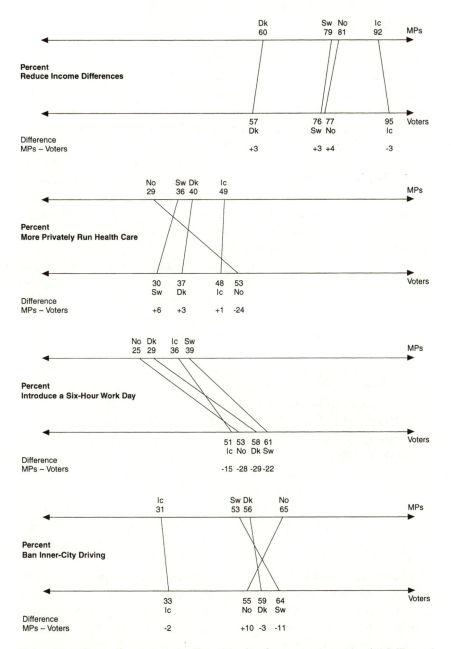

Figure 7.1 Issue Agreement in Four Nordic Countries between All MPs and Eligible Voters on Eight Comparable Issues (%). The results show percent MPs and voters supporting the various policy proposals. Ic = Iceland; No = Norway; Sw = Sweden; and Dk = Denmark.

A PARADOX

If we look more closely at how a high degree of opinion congruence is built up at the level of the entire parliament and the entire electorate, an interesting paradox becomes apparent. It turns out that high policy agreement between all MPs and all voters can come about not only when the parties reflect the views of their voters but also when parties do not reflect the opinions of their voters. The first case is rather obvious. High degrees of intraparty congruence across most parties produce a high congruence between the entire parliament and the electorate. The second case is less self-evident: high levels of agreement between the entire parliament and the entire electorate can come about even if all parties exhibit low degrees of intraparty opinion congruence, provided that opinions tend to be more (or less) polarized among MPs.

A well-known example with a clear relevance in many political systems, including the Nordic ones, may be seen when socialist members are positioned to the left of their voters at the same time that nonsocialist MPs are located to the right of theirs. The outcome could then very well be a parliament that fairly accurately reflects the main focus of the views of all voters.

Let us take a hypothetical example: Imagine a party system with two equally sized parties where parliamentarians have totally different and polarized views on an issue—100 percent of the MPs of party A are in favor while 100 percent of the MPs of party B are against. Moreover, the degree of intraparty congruence is rather bad, since voter opinion in both parties is split down the middle—50 percent of party A's and of party B's voters are in favor, 50 percent are against. Were we to compare the entire parliament in this example with all of the voters, we would discover that a perfect issue agreement obtained. Half the MPs and half the voters would be in favor; half the MPs and half the voters would be against. Thus, polarized parties characterized by a low degree of intraparty congruence can produce a high level of parliamentary representativeness.

If we return to table 7.1 and look at the average intraparty figures for the degree of issue agreement across the Nordic countries, it is apparent that the results for the Danish and Norwegian parties are slightly lower than those for the Swedish and Icelandic parties. On average, Swedish and Icelandic parties exhibit a somewhat higher issue congruence between MPs and voters than do Norwegian and especially Danish parties. In the case of Sweden versus Denmark and Norway, however, the slightly lower degree of congruence among Danish and Norwegian parties has not resulted in a lower degree of total opinion representativeness for the Folketing or Storting as compared to the Riksdag. As shown previously, the degree of opinion agreement between all MPs and all voters is about the same in Denmark, Norway, and Sweden. Behind this seeming paradox lies the fact that, for some issues (like the size of the public sector), Danish and Norwegian MPs exhibited more polarized opinions than did their voters, producing a poor intraparty congruence that was evened out at the level of the Folketing and the Storting.

THE FINNISH CASE

The less than perfect correlation between intraparty results and results on the parliamentary level is clearly illustrated in figures 7.2 and 7.3. The analysis is based on the subjective self-placement of members and voters on the left-right scale. Since the left-right measurements were also administered in Finland, the results give us the added opportunity of addressing our first hypothesis; that is, that collective issue congruence will be less in Finland—with its person-oriented electoral system—than in the other Nordic countries.

Looking at the results on the parliamentary level, it is clear that the degree of congruence is less in Finland than in the other Nordic countries. Finnish MPs, on average, place themselves (46) further left than do their voters (56), as do MPs in most countries, including the other Nordic ones (Converse and Pierce 1986; Barnes 1977; Thomassen 1976; Dalton 1985). However, the difference between where members and voters place themselves is somewhat larger in Finland (10 units) than in the other four Nordic countries (between 1 and 7 units).

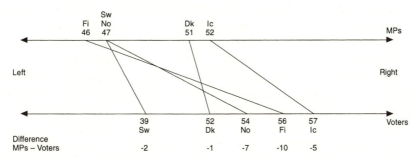

Figure 7.2 Average Left-Right Self-Placement among All MPs and All Eligible Voters in the Five Nordic Countries (means). The results are multiplied by a factor of 10 on an 11-point scale running from 0 (far left) to 10 (far right). Fi = Finland; SW = Sweden; No = Norway; Dk = Denmark; Ic = Iceland.

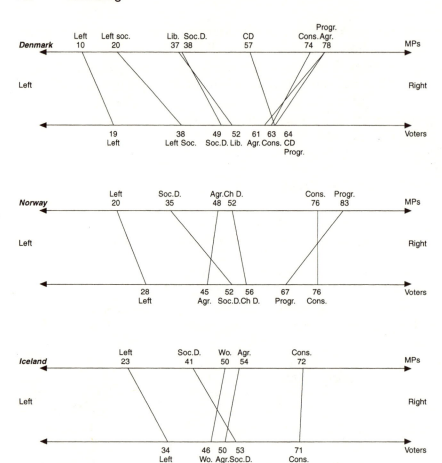

A glance at figure 7.3 and the results on intraparty congruence reveals why the Finnish outcome on the parliamentary level was somewhat worse than in the other Nordic countries. It turns out that the Finnish intraparty results (7) are on average about the same as those in Norway (8), Iceland (6), and Sweden (6), and noticeably better than those in Denmark (13). But in contrast to the situation in the other countries, MPs from all Finnish parties tended to place themselves further left than their respective voters did, creating a pattern of left-leaning elite parties. In the other four countries, MPs on the ideological left and ideological right tended to locate themselves to the left and to the right of their voters, respectively, forming a polarized elite pattern.

A polarized elite pattern, like that in Denmark, tends to yield better issue-agreement results on the parliamentary level than does a pattern, like that in Finland, in which all or most elite parties tend to lean in the same

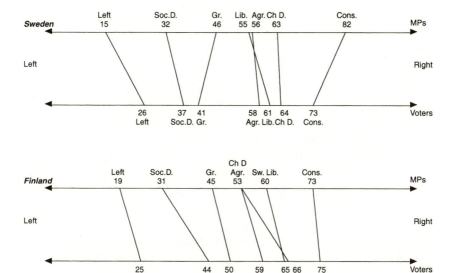

Figure 7.3 Average Left-Right Self-Placement among All MPs and Party Voters in the Five Nordic Countries (means). The results are multiplied by a factor of 10 on an 11-point scale running from 0 (far left) to 10 (far right). The means for all respondents were: Denmark, MPs 51, voters 52; Norway, MPs 47, voters 54; Iceland, MPs 52, voters 57; Sweden, MPs 47, voters 49; Finland, MPs 46, voters 56. Left = Left Socialists; Soc.D. = Social Democrats; Gr. = Greens; Lib. = Liberals; Agr. = Agrarians; Ch.D. = Christian Democrats; Cons. = Conservatives; CD = Center Democrats; Progr. = Right Populists; Wo. = Women's Alliance; Sw.Lib. = Swedish Liberals.

direction. In the first case, the main focus—the *Schwerpunkt* of the MP distribution as well as of the voter distribution—tends to end up toward the middle, while MPs' opinions tend in the second case to be shifted to the left or to the right of voter opinions.

NOT BETTER THAN WESTMINSTER OR CONGRESS

Although our data base is fairly limited, the outcome of our analysis has been a reasonable one, as well as supportive in the main of our hypotheses. As expected, degrees of aggregate issue congruence between members of parliament and eligible voters turned out to be relatively similar across the Nordic countries. The small differences we did find were in accordance with our hypotheses, with a somewhat higher level of issue agreement in little Iceland and a somewhat lower one in Finland, with its personal-vote system. Also as expected, the degree of issue congruence tended to be highest for politicized left-right issues—issues that have dominated Nordic politics for a long time.

Less expected was the finding that parties on the right—the conservatives and the progress parties—exhibited lower levels of issue congruence than did parties in the middle or on the left. A speculative explanation—with some support from the Swedish case, for which we have time-series data going back to the 1960s—is that conservative parties in the 1980s and 1990s have become more ideological and more neo-liberal, as well as keener on forming opinions, while many of the other parties have become more pragmatic and moved toward the political center, thus improving their issue agreement with the voters.

We may conclude, then, that it is politics—not the structure of the political system—that explains the difference in degrees of issue agreement between parties of the left and the right in the Nordic countries in the 1990s. The political system matters, but so apparently does politics.

More generally, considering the results from an issue perspective, it is clear that representational processes producing congruence between elected representatives and voters must have been at work on many issues. On most issues, the opinions of both MPs and voters varied rather considerably across borders in the Nordic countries. No common Nordic outlook, accordingly, can explain the similar congruence results across countries. The representative process does work. Issue agreement is created, at least to a degree.

Whether that degree should be assessed as high or low in the Nordic case is a difficult question to answer. Available research does not point to higher congruence levels in the Nordic countries than in such nations as France, Germany, the Netherlands or the United States. Issue agreement seems to be something of an universal characteristic that does not vary too much across different political systems. And that universal characteristic should probably not be viewed as signaling any high level of congruence since, if we compare our empirical levels of issue agreement with what a purely random model would yield—that is, if parliamentarians were chosen by lot—the random selection method would most often outperform the representative process.

In view of these results, the cautious conclusion would perhaps be that the level of issue agreement produced by the Nordic alternative is no higher than that produced by Westminister or Congress. On the other hand, our findings may suggest that there are no major differences in terms of issue agreement across most any democratic political systems.

Appendix

Table 7.A1
Issue Agreement between Members of the Danish Folketing and Eligible Voters in 1995

Issue	Left			Social Democrats			Liberals			Agrarians (Venstre)			Conservatives			Progress			All		
	MPs	Voters	Diff.	MPs	Voters	Diff.	MPs	Voters	Diff.	MPs	Voters	Diff.	MPs	Voters	Diff.	MPs	Voters	Diff.	MPs	Voters	Diff.
Reduce the public sector	10	32	22	6	32	26	100	28	72	100	73	27	100	53	47	100	68	32	51	48	3
Reduce defense spending	100	78	22	92	64	28	80	62	18	0	42	42	5	34	29	100	38	62	62	56	6
Increase taxes on high incomes	100	82	18	91	75	16	25	54	29	0	45	45	6	51	45	0	63	63	48	62	14
Reduce income differences	100	84	16	100	70	30	100	59	41	0	41	41	0	30	30	0	33	33	60	57	3
More privately run health care	10	20	10	0	30	30	0	29	29	100	58	42	94	41	53	100	48	52	40	37	3
Introduce a six-hour work day	100	79	21	31	72	41	25	57	32	0	33	33	8	43	35	0	50	50	29	58	29
Forbid all pornography	0	28	28	10	30	20	0	18	18	13	34	21	16	29	13	0	40	40	9	34	25
Accept fewer refugees	10	28	18	20	58	38	0	36	36	60	66	6	86	72	14	100	91	9	30	56	26
Ban inner-city driving	100	80	20	94	66	28	80	58	22	13	47	34	5	53	48	0	67	67	56	59	3
Reduce political influence of financial markets	100	69	31	92	60	32	67	44	23	8	53	45	11	55	44	0	75	75	62	62	0

Policy proposal	1 (M / V / D)	2 (M / V / D)	3 (M / V / D)	4 (M / V / D)	5 (M / V / D)	6 (M / V / D)	7 (M / V / D)
Introduce gender-based affirmative action when recruiting higher civil servants	**88** / 34 / 54	**61** / 29 / 32	20 / 24 / 4	0 / 20 / 20	5 / 24 / 19	0 / 10 / 10	30 / 25 / 5
Forbid interference with hereditary dispositions of humans and animals	100 / 75 / 25	65 / 60 / 5	100 / 82 / 18	50 / 62 / 12	79 / 57 / 22	50 / 62 / 12	72 / 64 / 8
Give higher priority to rural areas	83 / 77 / 6	76 / 70 / 6	67 / 55 / 12	77 / 72 / 5	**45** / **62** / 17	**25** / **65** / 40	67 / 67 / 0
Average 13 issues	22	26	27	29	32	42	8
Proportion of issues where the Folketing members and voters have different majorities	23	31	8	46	31	8	9

Notes: Respondents were asked to indicate to what extent they thought the policy proposals were good or bad. All response alternatives have been dichotomized. Persons without explicit opinions (don't knows and middle alternative answers "neither good nor bad") were excluded from the percentage calculations. The degree of policy agreement is measured by a simple percentage difference measure running from 0 (perfect agreement) to 100 (perfect disagreement).

Table 7.A2
Issue Agreement between Members of the Norwegian Storting and Eligible Voters in 1996

Issue	Left			Labor			Christian Democrats			Agrarians (Senter)			Conservatives			Progress			All		
	MPs	Voters	Diff.	MPs	Voters	Diff.	MPs	Voters	Diff.	MPs	Voters	Diff.	MPs	Voters	Diff.	MPs	Voters	Diff.	MPs	Voters	Diff.
Reduce the public sector	0	9	9	0	25	25	71	49	22	0	19	19	100	64	36	100	50	50	31	34	3
Reduce defense spending	100	81	19	89	49	40	75	44	31	37	33	4	8	34	26	0	47	47	59	46	13
Increase taxes on high incomes	92	92	0	96	76	20	88	76	12	100	80	20	0	51	51	0	66	66	73	73	0
Reduce income differences	92	94	2	98	80	18	100	76	24	96	83	13	13	60	47	0	63	63	81	77	4
More privately run health care	0	17	17	0	42	42	50	64	14	10	42	32	100	84	16	100	78	22	29	53	24
Introduce a six-hour work day	100	83	17	25	57	32	22	44	22	42	50	8	0	37	37	0	50	50	25	53	28
Forbid all pornography	83	77	6	66	70	4	75	85	10	85	75	10	16	60	44	20	47	27	59	68	9
Accept fewer refugees	0	15	15	4	47	43	0	43	43	0	59	59	11	50	39	100	85	15	8	49	41
Ban inner-city driving	100	73	27	77	59	18	75	53	22	83	64	19	14	40	26	0	35	35	65	55	10
Reduce political influence of financial markets	100	—	—	88	—	—	33	—	—	96	—	—	18	—	—	0	—	—	73	—	—

Introduce gender-based affirmative action when recruiting higher civil servants	100	—	74	—	—	43	—	—	47	6	—	0	—	53	—	3
Forbid interference with hereditary dispositions of humans and animals	100	95	85	77	8	90	85	5	96	84	82	14	68	18	84	81
Give higher priority to rural areas	70	**73**	**40**	**73**	33	80	89	9	80	93	**63**	**0**	**76**	76	**40**	36
Average 11 issues		11		26			19	19			36			43		16
Proportion of issues where Storting members and voters have different majorities	0		27			0			9		36		27		36	

Note: See notes to table 7.A1.

Table 7.A3

Issue Agreement between Members of the Icelandic Althingi and Eligible Voters in 1996

Issue	Left			Social Democrats			Women's Alliance			Agrarians			Conservatives			All		
	MPs	Vo	Diff.	MPs	Vo	Diff.	MPs	Vo	Diff.	MPs	Vo	Diff.	MPs	Vo	Diff.	MPs	Vo	Diff.
Reduce the public sector	25	63	38	83	74	9	0	74	74	100	78	22	100	89	11	79	78	1
Reduce defense spending	—	—	—	—	—	—	—	—	—	—	—	—	—	—	—	—	—	—
Increase taxes on high incomes	100	86	14	98	68	10	100	79	21	75	76	1	0	56	56	61	68	7
Reduce income differences	100	99	1	100	98	2	100	100	0	89	96	7	71	92	21	92	95	3
More privately run health care	0	27	27	33	45	12	0	37	37	33	41	8	100	63	37	49	48	1
Introduce a six-hour work day	67	62	5	67	54	13	100	64	36	33	49	16	0	45	45	36	51	15
Forbid all pornography	60	73	13	67	60	7	100	70	30	86	72	14	67	61	6	73	65	8
Accept fewer refugees	0	31	31	0	38	38	0	22	22	14	44	30	8	45	37	5	39	34
Ban inner-city driving	83	46	37	50	39	11	100	36	64	11	39	28	0	24	24	31	33	2
Reduce political influence of financial markets	86	92	6	100	90	10	100	87	13	83	90	7	43	75	32	80	84	4

Introduce gender-based affirmative action when recruiting higher civil servants	**60**	**33**	27	50	31	19	**100**	**49**	51	13	31	18	0	28	28	30	31	1
Forbid interference with hereditary dispositions of humans and animals	100	69	31	63	51	12	67	52	15	67	60	7	50	52	2	66	57	9
Give higher priority to rural areas	**33**	**59**	26	14	40	26	0	46	46	63	66	3	**60**	**45**	15	**41**	**51**	10
Average 12 Issues			21			14			34			13		26				8
Proportion of issues where Althingi members and voters have different majorities		33			0		25	25			0		25				17	

Note: See notes to table 7.A1.

Table 7.A4
Issue Agreement between Members of the Swedish Riksdag and Eligible Voters in 1994

Issue	Left			Greens			Social Democrats			Center			Liberals			Christian Democrats			Conservatives			All		
	MPs	Vo	Diff.	MPs	Vo	Diff.	MPs	Vo	Diff.	MPs	Vo	Diff.	MPs	Vo	Diff.	MPs	Vo	Diff.	MPs	Vo	Diff.	MPs	Vo	Diff.
Reduce the public sector	0	14	14	0	18	18	3	16	13	69	40	29	64	62	2	89	61	28	100	77	23	37	37	0
Reduce defense spending	100	91	9	100	92	8	99	77	22	83	63	20	100	78	22	92	70	22	8	45	37	82	71	11
Increase taxes on high incomes	100	97	3	81	92	11	97	96	1	95	91	4	27	75	48	44	67	23	2	51	49	69	85	16
Reduce income differences	100	96	4	94	78	16	98	88	10	94	79	15	50	59	9	71	51	20	2	47	45	79	76	3
More privately run health care	0	5	5	0	19	19	1	15	14	63	29	34	90	47	43	88	50	38	100	67	33	36	30	6
Introduce a six-hour work day	100	85	15	100	75	25	49	74	25	41	58	17	14	47	33	13	38	25	0	34	34	39	61	22
Forbid all pornography	83	57	26	75	68	7	78	71	7	76	78	2	50	55	5	79	80	1	32	55	23	67	66	1
Accept fewer refugees	0	51	51	0	40	40	9	75	66	6	74	68	0	43	43	0	56	56	74	78	4	17	70	53
Ban inner-city driving	90	77	13	94	86	8	66	68	2	80	77	3	27	59	32	50	49	1	5	44	39	53	64	11
Reduce political influence of financial markets	100	88	12	100	93	7	97	87	10	95	85	10	80	58	22	50	71	21	6	53	47	82	79	3

Issue	Values
Introduce gender-based affirmative action when recruiting higher civil servants	82, 55, 27, 100, 57, 43, 65, 50, 15, 22, 46, 24, 30, 32, 2, 23, 33, 10, 0, 25, 25, 44, 42, 2
Avoid interference with hereditary dispositions of humans and animals	88, —, —, 100, —, —, 85, —, —, 96, —, 83, —, —, 93, —, 59, —, —, 83, —
Give higher priority to rural areas	100, —, —, 100, —, —, 53, —, —, 100, —, 50, —, —, 44, —, 40, —, —, 61, —
Average 11 Issues	16, 0, 14, 18, 17, 36, 21, 27, 24, 18, 22, 33, 12
Proportion of issues where Riksdag members and voters have different majorities	9, 0, 18, 27, 18, 36, 27, 24, 27, 18, 27, 18

Note: See notes to table 7.A1.

PARLIAMENTARY AFFAIRS: INTERNAL RELATIONS

8

Parliamentary Party Groups

Knut Heidar

In representative democracies, "parliamentary democracy" and "party government" are two sides of the same coin. According to Richard Katz, the degree of "party governmentness" depends on the extent to which "all major governmental decisions" are made by people "chosen in elections conducted along party lines, or by individuals appointed by and responsible to such people"; and policies are "decided within the governing party" or "by negotiations among parties when there is a coalition" (Katz 1986:42–43). Parliamentary democracy means that no government can carry on governing if a majority in the freely elected parliament actively seeks its departure. The degree of executive stability and power reflects the government's measure of parliamentary support, and it is closely connected with the organization and coherence of both supporters and adversaries. This is why King's 1976 article—in which he broke with the old two-body institutional analysis and introduced the various modes of executive-legislative relations—was so important (see chapter 1).

It may be expected that, in multiparty parliamentary systems, the practice of negotiating and sustaining coalition governments will grant the parties a pivotal position as brokers in parliament. Daalder and Rusk argue, for example, that Dutch parties must "at all times be prepared to adjust their activities toward other parties," and that this need for "constant coalition-building . . . demands wide discretion of parliamentary parties vis-à-vis extra-parliamentary party organs" (1972:168). Although this diagnosis is from the early 1970s, it would not require much revision today (Gladdish 1990:107).

The question is whether the argument can be extended to other multiparty systems, such as the Nordic ones. Traditionally, party groups in Nordic parliaments have been considered strong (Damgaard 1992d). Recent studies of party groups in four of the Nordic parliaments all present those groups as the major and dominant parliamentary actor[1] (Bille 2000; Hagevi 2000; Heidar 1995; Wiberg 2000). Nor are there any indications that the position of party groups in the Icelandic Althingi is different (Hardarson 1997). The main hypothesis of this chapter is that multiparty systems and frequent coalition governments (see chapter 2) have nurtured strong party groups in all five countries.

To understand parliamentary democracies, we must understand how parties operate within parliament. In this chapter, our empirical focus will be on the organization and power of parliamentary party groups: how decisions are taken, what decision-makers consider important, and who "really" decides within parliamentary party groups (PPG). Analyzing power is inevitably a work of Sisyphus, however. If, therefore, we are to have any comparative benchmarks for analysis, we need to spell out the ideal-types underlying the inquiry. The following four types of PPG power structure clearly do not exhaust the alternatives, but they would seem the most likely candidates.

First, internal power may be dispersed equally among members of the party group, indicating an *MP-directed group*. In this type of PPG, power rests with the individual representatives, but each member of parliament is only one of many equals participating legitimately in the decision-making process. An alternative and elitist type is the *parliamentary leader-directed group*, in which the leader(s) formally or informally controls group decisions. These two types are characterized by a weak and by a strong organizational hierarchy, respectively.

But power may not be internal at all, since external actors may be able to control the group. According to the broad (and old-socialist) conception of party democracy, decision-making is the prerogative of the extra-parliamentary party organization (EPO); thus we have the *EPO-directed group*. This type, in which the external party organization is in charge, may take two different forms: either the central party organs issue orders or the PPG is told what to do by the constituency parties.

The fourth type of power structure existent in PPGs emerges when the party is in government and group decisions are dictated by ministers. This is the *government-directed group*. In this type of PPG, the party line is finalized in ministerial discussions or in negotiations between coalition partners at government level.

Two main questions are central to this chapter: how strong are the Nordic PPGs, and what characterizes their mode of decision-making? We would expect the groups to be strong, but we have no clear expectations about their decision-making mode, aside from the presumption that we will find mixed and not pure types. In discussing these questions, we shall analyze three PPG relationships by analogy with the general book approach (see chapter 1).

In the first part, we discuss how internal party-group relations are organized. In the second, we turn to the two external relationships: we ask how PPGs relate to their EPOs and to the government, respectively.

Before going into these relationships, however, we shall briefly consider the general historical background to the rise of PPGs, as well as the position of parties in the main alternatives discussed in this book: Westminster and Congress.

HISTORICAL BACKGROUND AND THE SPECIAL CASES OF WESTMINSTER AND CONGRESS

The historical origins of parties lie within parliaments, but the extended franchise added weight to the development of stable and disciplined party groups. As suffrage broadened, factions within parliaments organized extra-parliamentary support in order to mobilize their voters. In Britain, the Reform Act of 1867 was crucial: Members of parliament concluded—hungry as they were for re-election—that they needed to mobilize their voters by joining in concerted action (though parties) with like-minded politicians. In one sense, the move backfired for the individual MP. Since parties made election promises during campaigns, these needed to be carried out, making a cohesive party group of MPs necessary. This in turn restricted the political freedom of MPs (Norton 1991:317). In the two-party Westminster system, cohesive parties paved the way for governments elected by voters and no longer by MPs. Although governments were still elected *in* parliament, the "party linkage" produced governments dependent on electoral majorities.[2]

With organized political parties inside as well as outside parliament, the phrase "representing the people" took on a new meaning. According to advocates of the "free mandate," party linkage destroyed the virtues of parliament. It reduced the deliberating representatives of the people to "lobby fodder" driven into the voting chambers by party whips; no longer were MPs motivated by personal convictions based on experience, reading, and debate. Around the turn of the century, Moisei Ostrogorski claimed that organized parties based outside parliament lead to the degeneration of public debate, for "equality of rights cannot make up for the natural inequality of brains and character" (Ostrogoski 1902, vol. 2:640). The "decline of parliament" literature, clearly, had its predecessors.

Later party watchers have argued, however, that organized parties in fact created the necessary institutional framework for an operative mass democracy. Parties organized political alternatives for mass electorates in ways that made decision-makers accountable: "Modern democracy is unthinkable save in terms of parties" (Schattschneider 1942:1).

Today, analysts generally place parties in a more positive light than did Ostrogoski. Some stress how parties stabilize parliaments and legislatures by providing structural constraints to the otherwise limitless opportunities for instability produced by a stream of voting decisions (Cox and McCubbins 1993). Others focus on policy outcome, arguing that internal structures like parliamentary parties (and committees) enable MPs "to identify both the multiple interests of the represented and the general interest—at least to the extent that deliberation among the best informed leaders of government can determine it" (Loewenberg 1995:742). In conjunction with the information-trading taking place among MPs, parties counteract *distributive politics* (in which "everyone appears to win but the collectivity is ill served") and so-called "pork barrel" legislation (Loewenberg 1995).

Parliamentary parties in Britain are generally considered strong, since MPs in that country by and large control the policies of their party. Extraparliamentary party organizations (EPOs) play only a minor role, or none at all, in policy formation. The PPGs, however, are a weak instrument for individual MPs, since group decisions do not determine how MPs vote. MPs are more dependent on their local constituency organization than on their whip for securing re-election (Norton 1999). More importantly, however, the whip is not primarily an instrument of the party group, but rather of the party leadership. The front bench, and the leader particularly, has traditionally been very powerful in both parties, a fact that has served to counteract the rise of a strong group structure. As a result, British PPGs are extremely hierarchical organizations; otherwise put, they are "leadership-directed groups."

In the United States, with its separation of powers, the situation is very different. Thanks to seniority rights, feeble EPOs, and the nature of the electoral system, the parties in Congress are comparatively weak.

THE INTERNAL ORGANIZATION OF PARTY GROUPS

When Brady and Bullock reviewed the literature on party groups more than ten years ago, they referred to an "inside model" that describes the "key structural and behavior variables characterizing parties and factions within legislatures" (1985:137–41). These key internal variables include stability, membership, range of activities, organizational attributes, goals, and size. Among *organizational attributes,* Brady and Bullock considered the "distribution of tasks and power" to be "an important aspect of a party's organization in the legislature" (1985:139). Task distribution has to do with the division of labor within the group, while power distribution deals with the degree of centralization in decision-making.

In this section, we present the basic organizational structures of Nordic PPGs, focusing on "tasks and power." The aim is to uncover, from the standpoint of internal relationships, the general importance of PPGs in Nordic parliaments, as well as to describe their mode of decision-making.

We divide our empirical discussion into two parts: First, we discuss the formal organization of PPGs, and the question of organizational hierarchy in particular. Second, we explore how MPs perceive group power. Here our discussion is based on the "participant evaluations" found in the parliamentary surveys (see chapter 1).

We introduce two explanatory variables to account for differences between the five parliaments: first, the institutional setting of the different party families; and second, the ideological factor represented by them. We shall also examine, in a more rudimentary fashion, some explanations focusing on group size and relation to the government.

Organizational Context and Hierarchies

In constitutional terms, parties are not a prominent part of Nordic parliaments. In fact, they are barely mentioned, and some of the constitutions are even "antiparty" in their letter. For example, the Danish and Finnish constitutions state that MPs shall be guided, respectively, only by their personal convictions and by the Constitution. In practice, however, no one would take this seriously today, and party groups enjoy official recognition in all of the Nordic parliaments in terms of office space, financial contributions and *de facto* control over parliamentary work.

The Standing Orders of the Norwegian Storting give detailed procedural guidelines for most parliamentary activities, from committee memberships to the sequence of party speakers in public debates. The intent is to give each party the power and public visibility justified by its share of MPs. Thus the "rights" on the statute book are mainly those of groups, not of individual MPs. This reflects the party-driven character of the Storting. In both Norway and Sweden, moreover, the money offered for political and administrative secretarial aid is given to the groups, not to individual MPs.

Formal membership in PPGs is restricted, with insignificant exceptions, to the MPs elected on party lists (see chapter 2). The groups vary in organizational structure and political coherence, but their common aim is to coordinate and plan group activity, with an eye to presenting and promoting the party's electoral program in parliament with maximum effectiveness. An elected group board prepares important issues for debate at group meetings and decides the less important matters itself. Most groups meet once a week when parliament is in session; the Danish groups meet daily. Some large party groups also have a small steering committee, which, aided by the chief political secretaries, plans group activities. The parties have whips, but these are not nearly as important as at Westminster. In systems with alternates,[3] strong group coherence, and internalized discipline, whips do not carry much political weight. Their job is mainly to keep track of representatives and to check pairing arrangements.

Policy decisions are prepared, in general, by the party's committee faction working in close cooperation with the group board and the political secretaries. Later, the formal decision (and on controversial issues the real decision) is taken at the group meeting. The group meeting lays down *the* party position in parliament, and dissent from the official party line is infrequent (see chapter 9). In the Danish Folketing, dissent dropped from 13 percent in 1970 to 7 percent in 1980 (Bille 2000). Dissent mainly crops up on issues of conscience or on important constituency matters. Public dissent must be cleared with the group meeting in advance.

The group secretariats vary in size. In 1997, the parties in the Finnish Eduskunta had forty-three political and administrative secretaries on their payroll (0.22 per MP), a level of assistance just above that in the Icelandic Althingi, which had twelve such secretaries (0.18 per MP). The corresponding figures for Sweden are 148 (0.42), for Norway eighty-one (0.49), and for Denmark 158 (0.89).

This is not always the only group aid available, however, since work in the party groups and in the central party offices (EPOs) is often closely coordinated. The internal organization of Danish groups is summed up in the formula "specialization, segmentation, and professionalization." This is to a great extent true in the other Nordic parliaments as well (Bille 2000). For obvious reasons, the size of the PPG has a large impact on the *degree* to which it is true.

In Denmark, Iceland, and Norway, roughly one MP in four holds a board position.[4] Only 14 percent of Swedish MPs serve on boards, a fact easily explained by the fact that the Riksdag, with 349 members, is the largest Nordic parliament by far. The Riksdag contains no more parties than the other Nordic parliaments do, and it has no more board positions

Table 8.1

Membership of the Board of Parliamentary Party Group, by Centrality of Position in the Party Organization, among Nordic MPs (%)

| | Position in Central Party Organization | | |
	Very Central	Fairly Central	Not Particularly Central
Board Member			
Yes	40	34	15
No	60	66	85
Total	100	100	100
No. of respondents	65	155	536

Note: Finland is excluded owing to lack of data. Party centrality is measured by an additive index where "central party office now" counts 2 and "previous central party office" counts 1; ministerial experience counts 2, central office in a party auxiliary organization 1; and more than two terms in parliament counts 1. A "no answer" on one or more of these variables is given a 0 score. "Very central" is defined as scores of 4 or more points; "fairly central" as 2 to 3; and "not particularly central" as 0 to 1.

to fill. This size effect is also reflected in the fact that the share of board members rises from one in ten in large groups to about one in three in small ones.

Board positions are important if the groups themselves are important, and in that case one would expect central MPs to seek a board position. Table 8.1 reports the board composition in terms of "party centrality" for all of the Nordic countries apart from Finland (for which we lack data). We have constructed a composite variable of MPs' political importance or "party centrality" on the basis of ministerial experience, parliamentary tenure, and the holding of office in the central party organization or an auxiliary party organization (for women, youth, etc.).

The table shows that MPs who have accumulated but few of these positional qualifications—and who consequently score low on the index of party centrality—also score lower than average on board positions. The share with a board position increases from 15 percent to 40 percent as we move from MPs with low centrality to those with high. In one sense this is trivial: important party politicians get elected to the board. But it is only trivial if we assume board positions are important and provide a basis for exercising power. This is a clear indication of hierarchy within the PPGs: some MPs are "more equal than others."

PERCEPTIONS OF POWER—
INTERNAL AND EXTERNAL

In the survey, we asked MPs to evaluate the importance of several factors in influencing the internal decision-making processes of their respective party groups.[5] In general, we would expect MPs to report egalitarian experiences and to stress the importance of the external party. Tables 8.2 and 8.3 present the "very important" answers according to country and party family.

The backing of "a strong intraparty opinion" (labeled "party support" in the tables) is clearly crucial. On average, 45 percent of MPs in the five Nordic parliaments consider it "very important" for internal group decisions. This is almost twice the proportion giving the "very important" rating to the second most influential factor (the support of "a strong electoral opinion"). We are obviously not talking about the U.S. Congress here. In addition, a Nordic average of 25 percent think it very important to succeed in debates at group meetings, and about one in six (17 percent) say it is very important to have "personal contact" with the party leadership.

The importance attributed to "party support" in intragroup decision-making is striking. This reflects the historic transition to *party* representation (at the expense of the individual MP) in the age of mass politics. It also reflects the high degree of legitimacy ascribed in group debates to a strong intraparty opinion (the "EPO opinion"). As in the case of internalized norms of party cohesion, this is a sign that MPs very much consider themselves representatives of their party (cf. Esaiasson, chapter 3). It also points clearly to a strong impact on the part of the external party organization; that is, it indicates an EPO-directed group.

Internal group debates are also important: being successful in debates at group meetings is very important to 25 percent of MPs. Representatives no doubt believe there is a process inside the parliamentary party group through which individual MPs can influence group decisions; in other words, they believe the group to be MP-directed.

Contact with the party leadership (described by 17 percent as very important) is also largely an internal PPG affair (although indicating a degree of top-down hierarchy rather than egalitarianism). Elements of leadership direction are clearly present in group decision-making, but it is also quite clear we are not reporting from the precincts of Westminster.

An average of 22 percent, finally, describe strong electoral support as very important. This may be taken, if anything, as evidence of a *vox populi* approach to group decisions. The old notion that the voters should be represented somehow is not extinct.

Table 8.2

Members' Perceptions of the Influence of Various Factors on Decision-Making in Parliamentary Party Groups, by Country (% "very important factor")

	Denmark	Finland	Iceland	Norway	Sweden	Average	Eta^2
Party support	27	33	52	49	62	45	.06*
Succeed in debate	41	21	23	25	17	25	.05*
Electoral support	19	20	19	21	31	22	.02*
Party leadership contacts	7	28	21	11	17	17	.05*
Mass media contacts	13	17	14	12	11	13	.04*
Support from orgs./authorities	10	10	14	9	7	10	.01
Contacts in other parties	12	8	7	3	3	7	.08*
Support from experts	4	9	5	2	7	5	.03*
Minimum N	103	86	42	139	313		

Notes: The question was worded as follows: "According to your experience: How important are the following factors when it comes to influencing decisions in your parliamentary party group?" The following response alternatives were offered: "very important"; "fairly important"; "not particularly important"; "not at all important." Nine missing cases from Finland are not included in the percentage base. Each eta-square value is based on a one-way analysis of variance with country as the independent variable.

*p < .05.

Table 8.3

Members' Perceptions of Influence of Various Factors on Decision-Making in Parliamentary Party Groups, by Party Family (% "very important factor")

	Left Parties	Social Dems.	Parties of the Center	Conservatives	Agrarians	Greens	Populists	Average	Eta²
Party support	29	54	46	52	48	68	23	46	.03*
Succeed in debate	22	19	27	28	27	17	31	24	.02
Electoral support	26	28	15	18	29	28	15	23	.03*
Party leadership contacts	10	15	16	25	17	4	8	14	.05*
Mass media contacts	10	13	12	11	15	4	15	11	.02*
Support from orgs./authorities	10	11	6	6	12	4	0	7	.07*
Contacts in other parties	7	2	7	7	11	0	8	6	.04*
Support from experts	5	5	7	5	7	9	0	5	.01
Minimum N	58	284	65	136	101	22	13		

Notes: Nine missing cases from Finland are not included in the percentage base. Each eta-square value is based on a one-way analysis of variance with party family as the independent variable.

*p < .05.

There are major differences among Nordic parliamentarians in how they perceive group decision-making. There are no pure types to be found anywhere, of course—only a range of mixes. The power of party opinion is a case in point. Of Swedish MPs, 62 percent believe it to be very important, indicating a stronger tendency toward EPO-directed groups in the Riksdag than in the other Nordic parliaments. More than half the MPs in Iceland and in Norway report the same experience, while the party-opinion factor is substantially weaker in Denmark and Finland (with "very important" scores of around 30 percent).

The belief in deliberative politics is stronger in the Danish Folketing than in the other parliaments: 41 percent of its members state that success in debates at group meetings is very important. Together with the low score on the importance of leadership contacts (7 percent), this indicates a more egalitarian, MP-directed structure of group decision-making in the Folketing.

The Danes also pay less attention to their party organization: a comparative few—27 percent—ascribe great weight to support from party opinion.

In Finland, personal contact with the party leadership is almost as important for the outcome of party-group decisions as is support from party opinion. This may signal a more elite-centered, personalized type of politics in Finnish party groups (which may in turn be an effect of the electoral rules and the presidential system).

There is no common perception among Nordic parliamentarians of how decisions are made within party groups. In terms of decision-making types, the results are mixed; all of the mixes, however, indicate the presence of strong party groups, and no mix resembles anything we would expect to find at Westminster or in Congress. Swedish parliamentarians (followed in part by their colleagues in Iceland and Norway) lean toward the EPO-directed group type, the Danes are more MP-directed, and the Finns have a tendency to be more leadership-directed than the others.

In table 8.3, the grassroots and party-activist profile of the greens is borne out: 68 percent of the (admittedly few) green MPs emphasize the importance of party opinion. Social democrats are also very attentive—as might be expected in view of their historical legacy—to the voice of the party organization. They lean toward the EPO-directed group type.

The two party families that do not pay much attention to the party are the populists and the left parties, with 23 percent and 29 percent respectively.

The conservatives, the agrarians, and the parties of the center give high scores to party opinion. Oddly, the conservative parties—traditionally strong supporters of the old parliamentary virtues—actually give their highest impact scores to the opinions of the party organization. On the other hand, conservative MPs pay the most attention to contact with the party leadership and to success in debates, indicating (at one and the same time) both leadership direction and an MP-centered process.

One critical question is whether these figures merely reflect verbal embellishment and wishful thinking, or whether instead they point to real political experiences usually hidden to the outside observer. Do we have, in other words, any behavioral data to substantiate our findings?

If we look at Nordic parliamentarians as a group, rather than at the average score of the individual parliaments, we see that succeeding in debates at group meetings is "very important" to 23 percent and "fairly important" to 56 percent. We might expect this to have behavioral consequences. According to the reports of MPs themselves, about one-third "almost always" take part in debates (see table 8.4). Less than half say they never or only occasionally address group meetings. Members of parliament do have rather crowded schedules, and meetings and engagements have to be squeezed in between numerous obligations. It is difficult to imagine parliamentary norms tolerating empty talk at closed party meetings. Some of the Norwegian parties, in fact, have group statutes which state explicitly that said meetings are not to last longer than two hours. When it is reported that one-third almost always participate in these debates, this must be considered a high figure; it is definitely a contrast to the low level of turnout, and frequently ritual performance, found at public parliamentary debates.

The figures in table 8.4 make clear that the higher MPs rate the importance of group debates, the more often they actually take part in them— indicating that behavior follows (as expected) from the importance attributed to group debates.

It also turns out that frequency of debate participation is closely connected with group size. In small party groups, 65 percent "almost always" speak at meetings, while 31 percent in mid-sized groups and only 5 percent in large groups address group meetings as often (figures not shown).

Nordic MPs abide by group decisions. If group debates are important to these decisions, and the latter are not dictated by the leadership, the EPO, or government ministers, then we would expect not only that debates at group meetings would be taken very seriously by rank-and-file MPs, but also that prominent MPs would address party meetings more often than backbenchers would. To qualify as an important decision-making forum, such meetings must not only offer backbenchers a chance to relieve their frustrations; they must also make the party elite feel obliged to try to control their political home ground. In table 8.5, we see that this is indeed the case. Of the MPs classified as centrally placed in terms of

Table 8.4

Nordic Members' Participation in Parliamentary Party Group Debates according to How Important Group Debate Is Perceived To Be (%)

	Very Important	Fairly Important	Not Particularly/ Not At All	All
Almost always	37	29	25	30
Often	23	23	22	23
Occasionally/never	40	48	53	47
Total	100	100	100	100
No. of respondents	162	385	147	694

Note: Participation in group debates was measured by the following survey question: "About how often do you voice your opinion at an ordinary meeting of the parliamentary party group?"

Table 8.5

Members' Participation in Parliamentary Party Group Debates by Centrality of Position in Party Organization (%)

	Very Central	Fairly Central	Not Particularly Central	All
Almost always	53	41	23	29
Often	36	26	18	21
Occasionally/never	11	33	59	50
Total	100	100	100	100
No. of respondents	45	126	445	616

Note: Party centrality is measured as in table 8.1.

position and experience, 53 percent take part in group debates almost always, while only 23 percent of more peripheral members do so. If we combine the "almost always" and the "often" answers, the contrast is 89 to 41 percent.

If we look at the absolute totals, however, we see there is no reason to conclude such debates are *dominated* by the most centrally placed party MPs: 90 percent here means a total of 21 highly central MPs; 41 percent means 344 rank-and-file MPs!

EXTERNAL RELATIONSHIPS: CENTRAL EPOS, CONSTITUENCY PARTIES, AND GOVERNMENT MINISTERS

Parliamentary party groups operate at the intersection of the state and civil society. Constitutionally speaking, the duty of MPs is to represent their *constituency,* but their job perceptions are a mixed bag. They regard it as their task to present their personal views, to promote the interests of groups with whom they are affiliated, to advance their parliamentary status, and—not least—to represent their *party* (see Esaiasson, chapter 3). In order to promote the interests of constituencies, groups, and parties, parliamentarians must stay in touch with their "clients." The level of contact may indicate what impact different actors have on decision-makers.

Of course, contacts alone never prove influence (just as "no contact" does not in principle exclude it). What is more, the data on contacts that we present in the first part of this section do not indicate the direction of influence. Contacts are opportunities; they indicate *potential* influence. To supplement these data, we also present MPs' evaluations of the power that different groups have on parliamentary decisions. Again: perceived power is not actual power; even so, contacts and power perceptions ought—taken together—to provide some fairly good indications of actual power.

The perception-of-power question deals mostly with internal groups, so we will use it to supplement our earlier analysis about organizational hierarchies and internal group power. The reason for presenting these data here is that they include the rating of external actors like government ministers and the leader of the central EPO.

Patterns of Contact

The survey data do not describe the contact pattern for party groups as such; rather, they let us know who it is that individual MPs—in whatever capacity—are talking to. Nevertheless, aggregate scores according to party indicate whether the party groups have varying profiles of interaction. We shall concentrate on relations to the central party organization, the constituency party, and cabinet ministers.

Table 8.6 shows that close to one MP in four has contact with the central party organization at least once a week. It is the task of the central EPO bodies to sum up the politics of the national party organization and to channel the "views of the party" into parliament. As we have seen, MPs themselves rate party opinion a very influential factor in the shaping of group decisions (see tables 8.2 and 8.3). Obviously, therefore, EPO contacts are of great factual and strategic interest. Twenty-three percent of MPs report contacts with central party authorities at least once a week. More than half have such contacts once a month, while a meager 2 percent report never having such contact (this last figure is not in the table).

When looking at the five parliaments separately, we see that the Norwegians keep weekly contacts in the highest proportion. This suggests a

Table 8.6

Members' Self-Reported Personal Contacts with Extra-Parliamentary Party Organizations (EPOs), Own Constituency Party, and Cabinet Ministers (% "weekly contacts")

	Denmark	Finland	Iceland	Norway	Sweden	Average	Eta^2
Central EPOs	26	24	5	37	22	23	.05*
Own constituency party	62	42	47	60	77	57	.10*
Cabinet ministers	63	66	58	44	27	51	.14*
Minimum N	103	117	43	141	320		

Notes: Members' personal contacts were measured by the following survey question: "This question deals with your contacts as a politician with different organizations, groups, and public authorities during the last year. Regardless of who initiated the contact, how often have you, *during the last year*, been in contact—written or oral—with the organizations, groups, or public authorities mentioned below?" Five response alternatives were offered: "at least once a week"; "once or twice a month"; "a few times"; "occasionally"; "never." Out of a total of twenty-three items, three are reported here: "central party authorities outside of parliament"; "local/regional party authorities in your own constituency"; and "cabinet ministers." Each eta-square value is based on a one-way analysis of variance with country as the independent variable.

*$p < .05$.

higher degree of central EPO direction in Norway. The Swedes do not report weekly contacts in so high a proportion (although they do rate this factor above all other contacts in table 8.2). In Iceland, on the other hand, very few parliamentarians keep much in touch with party headquarters.

The constituency parties articulate primarily regional party politics, but they also represent the voters who elect (and possibly re-elect) members of parliament. The voter linkage in the three Scandinavian countries is indirect, in that local party organizations handle the nominations (see chapter 2). Individual candidates figure more prominently in Finland—at least formally—since they are elected, yet nominations are party-controlled in Finland, too. In Iceland, primaries reduce the dependence of MPs on the party organization. We may presume that frequent constituency contacts reinforce the role of MPs in the party groups, since such contacts offer MPs an alternative source of legitimacy to that conferred either by the central party organization or by the parliamentary leadership.

The message of table 8.6 is that the individual MP is much closer, by and large, to the constituency party than to central party headquarters. A cross-national average of 57 percent of MPs keep weekly contacts with their constituency party; by contrast, only 23 percent keep weekly contacts with the central EPO. Sweden is at the top with 76 percent of MPs reporting weekly contacts with their constituency party, indicating that the strong emphasis on party opinion in that country may refer to opinion within the constituency party. Finland and Iceland are both low in constituency contacts, with 42 and 47 percent respectively—a not unexpected result, in view of the more personalized electoral arrangements in the two countries. The low rate of constituency contacts may also have something to do with a greater dependence on elite networks in Icelandic (and possibly also Finnish) politics (Kristinsson 1996).

The Norwegian figure of 59 percent, although above average, is surprisingly low given the traditional analysis of the territorial dimension as extraordinary important in Norwegian politics (Valen and Rokkan 1974). The center-periphery cleavage actually produces a stronger stream of constituency contacts in Denmark and, especially, Sweden.

Nordic MPs have slightly less contact with cabinet ministers than with their constituency parties (51 percent report weekly contacts with the former). This figure is higher, however, than the proportion reporting frequent contacts with central EPOs. The fact that every other MP actually makes contact with a minister at least once a week is a strong indicator of a close and integrated executive-legislative relationship in the Nordic countries. This is clearly parliamentarism, not "separation of powers" (of the sort one finds in the U.S. Congress).

At the same time, the fairly high proportion of MPs keeping weekly contacts with the central party organization (23 percent on average) reminds us that the Nordic mode is not very similar to what might be expected in the Westminster model of parliamentarism.

Finnish MPs have the broadest stream of ministerial contacts, with 66 percent in weekly touch. This is a much larger proportion than keep contact with either the party organization or the constituency party; again, this hints at a more elitist type of parliamentary politics in Finland. But the Danes also score high on minister contact. Another explanation might be that both Finnish and Danish ministers are allowed to continue to serve as MPs while in government. In addition, these countries have had the highest frequency of coalition governments in recent years (together with Iceland, which also scores high). (See chapter 2.)

The Swedes are, in this respect, at the opposite end of the scale, with just 27 percent in weekly contact with ministers.

There are clear differences in this regard between MPs in governing parties and those in opposition; this may be taken as indicative of an intraparty mode of executive-legislative relations. For obvious reasons, it is easier for MPs in governing parties to establish contacts with ministers on a regular basis (59 percent have weekly contacts) than it is for opposition MPs to do the same (28 percent). It is nonetheless striking that as many as every fourth MP from the opposition parties has weekly contact with ministers in accordance, that is, with the nonparty mode of executive-legislative relations. It may well be that these figures reflect a system of negotiations, power-sharing, power-integration—whatever the term one prefers—which makes Nordic parliamentarism clearly different from from that of Westminster.

If, finally, we turn to the different party families (this table is not presented), we find that the social democrats score high on frequency of government contacts (which is scarcely surprising, since they were in government in every Nordic country except Iceland at the time of the survey). But ministers also talk to the left parties (in Finland, where they are in government) and to the conservatives (in Finland and Iceland, where they are in government). Only the greens and the populists do not have particularly "hot lines" to the executive power: they score a mere 14 percent on weekly contacts.

Several conclusions are in order here. Beneath the general Nordic picture, the contact pattern of MPs divides the five parliaments into two groups. In Sweden and Norway, constituency contacts have pride of place, while Finnish, Danish, and Icelandic parliamentarians give the top priority to keeping contacts with ministers. The Danes, it must be said, actually fall somewhere in between: they also pay a lot of attention to their constituency parties. The differences may in part reflect the different position of individual candidates in the nomination process. We may expect that, in Finland and Iceland, this will produce looser connections between constituency parties and MPs.

Another important finding is that the potential for government-directed groups is higher in Finland, Denmark, and Iceland than in Sweden and Norway, though the strong belief in the importance of internal group debates in Denmark makes it unlikely that government direction will gain much ground there.

We can also conclude that the central party organization, although important, is not the center of attention for Nordic MPs. In terms of daily politics, constituency parties and ministers are much more important. The high score for constituency contacts cannot, however, be taken as a sign of constituency-directed groups. The wishes of constituency parties seldom add up to a cohesive political force; we may conclude, therefore, that the figures indicate the likelihood of MP-directed groups, particularly in Sweden. It bears recalling here that internal party opinion is rated a very important influence on group decisions by Swedish MPs. Obviously, it is party opinion as found in the constituency parties and not in central EPOs that we are talking about.

Perceptions of Parliamentary Power

In the surveys, MPs were asked to rate a whole range of parliamentary actors in terms of influence on parliamentary decisions.[6] The questions did not specify policy area or type of decision, but were intended to map how MPs evaluate *general* influence on decision-making processes. They rated the degree of influence on a scale ranging from 0 (specified as "very little influence") to 10 ("very great influence").

The figures presented in table 8.7 are averages times 10; thus the possible scores vary between 0 and 100. The ratings summarize, by country, MPs' own evaluations of parliamentary power. The question is phrased so as to focus on actors and structures in general, and not on an MP's own party group or parliamentary leader in particular. The figures in themselves mean little, but we would expect clear differences in perceptions to indicate actual differences in power as collectively experienced by MPs.

Table 8.7 shows that the most powerful actors, according to Nordic MPs, are the cabinet ministers: they receive a score of eighty-five points. The party in various incarnations—the external party leader, the party group, and the parliamentary leader—is rated next. Here the EPO leader is given the edge over the PPG leader, but it is important to remember that these are often the same person.

Table 8.7

Members' Perceptions of the Actual Influence of Various Groups and Bodies on Decision-Making in Parliament, by Country (average perceived influence)

	Denmark	Finland	Iceland	Norway	Sweden	Average	Eta^2
Government ministers	83	91	90	78	82	85	.07*
Party leaders	77	79	79	73	76	77	.01
Party groups	77	74	71	83	74	76	.04*
Group board	NI	NI	NI	70	NI	70	.00
Parl. party leadership	72	76	64	74	65	70	.07*
Committees	57	66	68	75	76	68	.10*
Individual MPs	52	46	50	47	38	47	.07*
Group secretaries	37	NI	20	40	52	37	.14*
Minimum N	97	115	40	130	253		

Notes: Members were asked to rank the influence of each group and body on a scale reaching from 0 (very little influence) to 10 (very influential). The average perceived influence has been transformed to values between 0 and 100. The Swedish data are from a survey done in 1988 (see Esaiasson and Holmberg 1996:219–21). Nine missing cases from Finland not included in the base. Each eta-square value is based on a one-way analysis of variance with country as the independent variable. NI = item not included in the survey.

*$p < .05$.

At the low end of the power scale is the individual MP: he/she gets a mere forty-seven points on average. This is the lowest average apart from that given to the party-group secretaries (thirty-seven points). The scores given to secretaries vary from thirty-eight points for Sweden[7] to fifty-two for Denmark; however, we must control for the fact that an individual MP is just one person, while a PPG consists of many. Yet it is doubtful that this alone can explain MPs' low self-evaluation. The conclusion seems warranted that, in all of the Nordic parliaments, MPs think *party groups* play a vital role in parliamentary decision-making. General power and influence in Nordic parliaments is primarily exercised through party groups. One is clearly well-placed, however, to influence both the group and other relevant structures if one happens to be a cabinet minister or a party leader (in an EPO or a PPG).

The highest rating for the power of cabinet ministers is given by Finnish MPs (with a score of ninety-one points), and the lowest by members of the Norwegian Storting (with 78).

Only in a single case are ministers not rated the most powerful actors. Norwegian parliamentarians consider the influence of the party groups to be higher, with eighty-three points. This is in line with the fairly recent (for Norway) assertive role for parliament, which reflects a situation characterized by minority governments, an absence of stable supporting party(ies), and no clear government alternative.

It bears noting that the other two minority-government countries—Sweden and Denmark—also give ministers below-average ratings.

If we consider party leaders and party groups jointly, we find they take a second- or third-place position on the power scale everywhere but in Norway. In Finland, party leaders in both the PPGs and the EPOs are rated ahead of the groups as such. Only the Finlanders rate parliamentary leaders ahead of the groups. An egalitarian group culture seems more dominant in the Norwegian parliament: the group score exceeds that of the parliamentary leader by nine points, and that of the external party leader by ten. The group leader is most important to parliamentary decision-making in Finland, less so in Iceland and Sweden.

In all of the parliaments save the Swedish one, finally, groups are considered more powerful than committees. Swedish and Icelandic MPs give groups and committees about the same rating, while in Denmark the difference is as much as twenty points.

Is the structure of parliamentary power perceived differently according to party background and institutional position? Does party family, group size, or party power affect MPs' perceptions of power? Table 8.8 indicates that the power of party groups and ministers is considered high within all

Table 8.8

Members' Perceptions of Actual Influence of Various Groups and Bodies on Decision-Making in Parliament, by Party Family (average perceived influence)

	Left Parties	Social Dems.	Parties of the Center	Conservatives	Agrarians	Greens	Populists	Average	Eta²
Government ministers	84	83	84	82	84	84	87	84	.00
Party groups	74	78	75	76	76	73	81	76	.01
Party leaders	63	79	78	77	76	66	79	74	.06*
Committees	63	72	72	72	72	69	55	68	.02*
Parl. party leadership	62	72	67	72	69	57	73	67	.04*
Group board	75	68	73	78	64	NA	73	62	.06
Individual MPs	46	47	40	43	43	36	43	43	.02
Group secretaries	37	41	52	49	41	38	29	41	.04*
Minimum N	41	216	55	106	89	12	10		

Notes: Members were asked to rank the influence of each group and body on a scale reaching from 0 (very little influence) to 10 (very influential). The average perceived influence has been transformed to values between 0 and 100. The Swedish data are from a survey done in 1988 (see Esaiasson and Holmberg 1996:219–21). Nine missing cases from Finland not included in the base. Each eta-square value is based on a one-way analysis of variance with party family as the independent variable. NA = no information available.

*$p < .05$.

party families. Similarly, there is not much difference in the rating accorded the power of individual MPs (except in the case of the greens, who are apparently more disillusioned than the others).

The importance of party leaders is rated variously. The social democrats, the conservatives, and the populists find both the leader of the group and the external party leader to be rather important. It should again be noted, however, that the parliamentary leader is identical with the EPO leader in most of these parties. It is clear (from material not presented here) that neither the size of the party group nor the distinction between government and opposition adds much variation to the perception of parliamentary power.

These "expert judgments" tell us, first of all, that we must indeed analyze party groups if we are to understand the operation of Nordic parliaments. PPGs certainly do have power; in fact, save in the case of Sweden, they are *the* most important actor inside parliament.

In addition, these power perceptions tell us that parliamentarism is a relationship with two sides. It obviously grants parliament, and particularly the established party group(s), a central role. But parliamentarism also *balances* party power, in that government ministers are *the* most influential actors in determining the policies of the group (only Norwegian parliamentarians rate the group as such higher than the ministers). Since these ministers make their presence felt within the party group of the governing party(ies), the possibility of a "government-directed" group finds support.

One slightly odd feature is the fact that MPs from party families that are never in government—like the populists and the greens—opt for minister power in the same measure as do MPs from government parties. This may be due to their role as "participant observers" of what goes on inside the governing parties. Here again, Finnish and Icelandic MPs stand out as more hierarchical than the others (particularly their Norwegian colleagues).

THE POSITION OF PARTY GROUPS IN THE NORDIC PARLIAMENTS

Early on, the Nordic countries developed strong parties whose parliamentary members acted cohesively to promote party interests. In this chapter, we have discussed the importance and character of intragroup decision-making. The grip of the groups over MPs' voting is no doubt very solid (see chapter 9). In organizational terms, the "tasks and power" of party groups turn out to be substantial. The groups are stable organizations with a fairly high level of organizational complexity. They are strongly integrated into the institution of parliament through the Standing Orders, which give them a high level of control over parliamentary resources and work schedules. The individual MP may be highly praised in constitutional texts, but the party group rules in practice.

Stability, voting discipline, group organization, resources, and parliamentary rights all point toward a high disciplinary potential on the part of the PPGs, which is precisely why MPs fight hard to influence group decisions *before* they are locked in. Representatives strongly believe that intragroup decisions depend on *their* activities and arguments. Several of the best arguments, however, are not (entirely) of their own making, inasmuch as prevailing opinion in the party organization and in the electorate is thought to be highly influential.

Formal organizational structures still indicate a fairly high level of group autonomy vis-à-vis external actors like the central party organization. Exceptions must be made here for the party's own semi-external ministers and for the leader of the party organization—all are entitled to participate in group meetings. (In Denmark, Finland, and Iceland, ministers remain proper members if they were MPs at the outset.)

The question is what "real life" looks like inside the organizational structures. MPs' evaluations of parliamentary decision-making support the view that party groups are the real centers of power in Nordic parliaments. We have seen that, in the judgement of MPs themselves, the power of groups is inferior only to that of cabinet ministers and (just barely) that of the party leader. The parliamentary committees—another structural candidate for internal power—are perceived as more powerful than the party groups only in the Swedish Riksdag (and again only barely).

The power of the groups is supported by other evidence, too. Group leaders are important decision-makers. Members of parliament identify internal group debates as very important, and they try in practice to make an impact at the meetings. The finding that PPGs are centers of power comes as no surprise, since earlier studies of Nordic parliaments based on historical material have reached the same conclusion (Stavang 1964; Worre 1970).

A comprehensive description of Nordic parliamentary groups would not just point to the fact that they more or less determine the way parliamentarians behave in public; it would emphasize as well that group strength relies on complex intragroup processes in which MPs—notwithstanding their modest estimate of their power as individuals—figure prominently.

If forced to chose one of our four decision-making types, we would have to say that the *MP-directed party group* is the basis of the Nordic model. Nordic representative democracies are clearly characterized by "party government"; policies are "decided within the governing party" or "by negotiations among parties when there is a coalition" (Katz 1986). We would also add: by negotiations between parties in parliament when the government does not have a majority.

But the Nordic model is not absolutely a clear-cut case of MP-directed groups. Government ministers are the most powerful actors in deciding group policies when the party is in power (although they are not, it seems, able to issue dictates). This suggests a strong dose of *government direct-edness* in group operations. The central party organization makes its impact felt, but when MPs assess the relative power of different groups and structures, they place the external party leadership well behind ministers.

Still, they know the advantage of having a strong internal party opinion on their side. Frequent contact with the constituency party provides MPs with an individual platform, suggesting that EPO direction is more a question of keeping in line with the constituency party than it is one of keeping in line with the central organs of the external party organization.

How does this compare to what we know about the U.S. Congress and the Westminster system? In table 8.9, we sum up the four relationships of party groups in an attempt to furnish a basis for classifying legislatures in terms of the dominant mode of party-group decision-making.

According to this rough guide of how party groups operate in the United States, the United Kingdom, and the Nordic countries, the differences are fairly clear. The main message is that the Nordic systems are different from the two dominant models in terms of parliamentary discourse.

The U.S. Congress is weak on party-group organization, strong on the power of individual representatives, and strong on local voter ties. The mode of party-group decision-making would have to be considered MP-directed, although party groups do not exist in the European sense. This is a system based on the MP-constituency relationship, but it lacks the discipline induced by the strong organizational ties found in Nordic party groups.

The Westminster party-group system is leadership-directed, and it makes little difference whether the leadership is in government or just on the front benches.

In the Nordic parliaments, party groups are at the center of parliamentary decision-making, and party leaders, ministers, EPOs, and individual MPs all have to make their impact in the group arena. These groups constitute, in general, more open arenas for decision-making than their American and British counterparts: they make up an *arena*, in contrast

Table 8.9
**Dimensions of Structural Party Power within the U.S. Congress,
Westminster, and Nordic Parliaments**

Relationships	U.S. Congress	Westminster	Nordic
Internal			
Organization	weak	weak	strong
Discipline	weak	strong	strong
Hierarchy	weak/medium	extremely strong	medium
EPO			
To national party	weak	medium	strong/medium
Constituency			
To local party	weak	strong	strong
To local voters	strong	strong/medium	medium/weak
Government			
To ministers	weak	strong	strong

to the situation in the United States, and they are more *open* than their counterparts in the United Kingdom.

Do some Nordic parliaments house stronger, less leadership-directed party groups than others? The data are somewhat ambiguous, but we would venture the thesis that Denmark, Norway, and Sweden are on the stronger side, while Finland and Iceland contain groups that are slightly weaker and also more hierarchical.

The Finnish Eduskunta and the Icelandic Althingi look slightly more like Westminster. Contact patterns indicate that the constituency party is most important for Swedish MPs. Norwegian representatives put the influence of party groups ahead of that of ministers.

Danish MPs rate group power higher than do their Swedish counterparts, and they describe a very lively internal PPG decision-making process in which individual MPs count for more than in other Nordic parliaments. More than other Nordic MPs, moreover, the Danes mention contacts with other parliamentary parties as important for winning internal group debates.

The importance of a favorable party opinion for winning PPG decisions is just as great in Iceland as in Norway, but the Icelanders and also the Finns indicate that personal leadership contacts are rather important.

In sum, we find that the Danish Folketing is probably the most interesting place to be posted as a journalist if one is reporting from the parliamentary arena. There are no pure types to be found, certainly, but the Danish party groups show the strongest indications of MP direction.

The Nordic parliaments fall into three broad groups. The Danish Folketing is the most MP-directed. The Swedish Riksdag and the Norwegian Storting are not much weaker in terms of their groups' MP-directedness; however, the impact of individual MPs in these bodies is smaller, and the impact of parliamentary committees is greater. The mode of group decision-making in the Finnish Eduskunta and in the Icelandic Althingi, finally, exhibits a stronger element of leadership direction.

The deviating party families in this picture are comprised of new parties operating outside the traditional network of power—that is, the populists and the greens. The traditional parties are fairly similar on most counts, save for the low importance placed by leftist MPs on internal party opinion and the relatively high importance placed by conservative MPs on leadership contacts.

Explaining Party-Group Strength

Even if they display varying mixtures of decision-making modes, the PPGs are no doubt very important actors in all of the Nordic parliaments. How can we explain this strong impact? In table 2.1 in chapter 2, it was shown that coalitions and/or minority governments have become more common in all five countries over the course of the last twenty-five years. According to a recent study of the Swedish parliament, the difference between majority and minority governments is one of degree only: "All governments get through most of their proposals, and all governments find their proposals modified now and then in the parliamentary process" (Sannerstedt and Sjölin 1994:98).[8]

The key to explaining the strength of party groups within Nordic parliaments seems to be that these are multiparty parliamentary legislatures without a dominant party. This means the Nordic parliaments are in a high degree negotiating parliaments. More than one party has to agree on how to define the situation, and what to do about it, if a working parliament and an effective government are to be secured (Stenelo and Jerneck 1996; Sannerstedt 1992). In the process, party programs have to be compromised, and the group is the most appropriate party assembly for deciding operative party priorities.

Party policy in parliament is mostly decided on the basis of the party's contract with the voters—that is, by the party program—but current party opinion and constituency sentiments also figure prominently, together with a judgment of what will yield voter support in the long run and what can be done within the sitting parliament. Only PPG members are in a position to decide while taking all of these elements into account.

At the level of the parties, ideology has not emerged as central in explaining group decision-making. Size, or perhaps more to the point, parliamentary position, to some extent has. Moreover, new and more peripheral party groups evidently operate along somewhat different lines from old and well-integrated ones.

Furthermore, the indications that party groups are weaker in Finland and Iceland than in the three Scandinavian countries support the argument that a strong presidency and a personal element in the electoral process affect the power of parliamentary party groups. Institutional factors do leave a mark. Since the overall differences are small, however, and since Finland and Iceland differ somewhat from the others in terms of party system and political culture, it would be unwarranted to conclude that the institutional perspective has won the day. Rather, the essential impetus for the Nordic interparty, group mode of parliamentarism would seem to lie in the negotiations and coordination necessary for coherent government to emerge within multiparty parliaments without a dominant party, and without large ideological or party-political differences.

NOTES

The computer work to produce the tables for this chapter has been done by Jonny Arnesen. In writing this chapter, I have benefited from discussions at the Nordic project conferences. I would also like in particular to acknowledge the suggestions and comments of my co-editor Peter Esaiasson and those of Jo Saglie at the University of Oslo.

1. These studies are all based on general organizational and historical materials; see Heidar and Koole (2000).

2. More precisely, in the case of the United Kingdom: an electoral plurality in a majority of the constituencies.

3. In Norway and Sweden, government ministers recruited from parliament have alternates, too.

4. According to the survey material.

5. The question could be understood as probing both MPs' accumulated experience and their strategy for influencing future decisions. To experienced politicians, however, the two would probably be identical, since past experience provides the basis for planning the next battle.

6. These questions were included in the 1988 Swedish survey but not in the 1994 one. The 1988 data are included in the following analysis; see Esaiasson and Holmberg (1990). There is no obvious reason why the Swedish responses should have changed substantially in the years from 1988 to 1994.

7. Even less than the figure for the committee secretaries, which is not reported here.

8. My translation.

9

Party Cohesion

Torben K. Jensen

Modern representative government has developed, in practice, into party government. The idea of *responsible party government* is a well-established norm in representative democracies, including the Nordic countries. But the extent to which political parties are able to influence parliamentary and governmental decisions *depends very much on their cohesion.* Party cohesion is a crucial precondition for party government. By virtue of their functional and normative significance, therefore, party coherence and party discipline are among the most important informal parliamentary norms.

Parties in parliamentary systems around the world show a high degree of cohesion and discipline when it comes to voting in parliament (Ozbudun 1970; Collier 1985). Yet this likeness may cover important differences, such as that between majority democracies (the Westminster model) and other types of parliamentary system.

Examining indices of voting discipline is not enough, for at least two reasons. First, if we seek an in-depth understanding of party cohesion and party discipline, we cannot be satisfied with an *outcome approach;* that is, measuring the extent to which group members vote along similar lines in parliament. We must apply a *process approach* as well. If we restrict ourselves to the former approach, parliamentary parties will seem to be unitary actors. If we apply the latter perspective as well, and focus on what takes place within parliamentary parties before decisions are made, the picture that emerges is a much more differentiated one: parliamentary parties will appear to be much more open to a variety of actors, considerations, and interests.

Second, it is common in the literature to distinguish between party cohesion and party discipline.[1] Cohesion is associated with a certain consensus in values and attitudes, while discipline is related to compulsion. In the Nordic parliaments, party loyalty has much more to do with consensus than with compulsion; it is more appropriate, consequently, to speak of *party coherence* than of party discipline (though the element of discipline is not absent altogether). We expect parliamentary groups to organize and to work in highly various ways, depending on how unity is established within each individual group.

The aim of this chapter, then, is to analyze the strength and character of party discipline in the Nordic parliamentary systems and in the process to provide a better understanding of how, in practice, cohesive parliamentary parties in multiparty systems work.

THEORETICAL CONSIDERATIONS OF PARTY COHESION AND PARTY DISCIPLINE

Structural and Institutional Explanations and Nordic Expectations

In a comparative study from 1970, Ergun Ozbudun analyzed the impact of what he termed certain *structural factors* on party discipline (that is, voting behavior in parliamentary parties) in Western democratic political systems. The main conclusion of his classical study is that constitutional factors in particular are crucial. "*Parliamentary government* is a sufficiently strong factor to produce cohesive legislative parties, provided that it operates in a two-party or moderate multiparty government" (Ozbudun 1970:363). The reason for this is that parliamentary government, by turning a great many roll calls into a question of confidence in the government, provides an entirely rational incentive for party cohesion—an incentive sustained by the efforts of parties and individual members of parliament to maximize their own influence. This influence does not exist under a system characterized by the separation of powers. To reiterate, as Ozbudun spells out, the incentive obtains not only for the parliamentary party as a whole but also for the individual legislator: "A legislator who has contributed to the fall of his party's government also loses his share in the obvious benefits of executive power for his party," and "his own electoral fortunes would be likely to suffer with his party's if the party shows itself so uncohesive as to fail to maintain its leadership in office" (1970:356).

The second most important factor making for increased party cohesion, according to Ozbudun, is political culture—in the form of the predominant operative ideals of representation. If the *collectivist theory of rep-*

resentation—which attaches great importance to party government and functional representation, and thus presumes that representatives emphasize their own party, social class, and group in their job definition—is the prevalent one, then party cohesion tends to increase. To the extent, however, that a liberal or radical theory of representation is present, party cohesion tends to decrease (Ozbudun 1970:363–66).

Furthermore, Ozbudun finds that social conditions—such as a high degree of class polarization—have a slight tendency to increase party coherence, and that working-class parties tend to be more cohesive than middle-class parties. Finally, parties based on mass membership, as well as parties concerned with the integration of their members into a wide range of party activities, tend to be more cohesive than other types of parties.

Some scholars have suggested other, *institutional* explanations in addition to Ozbudun's structural ones. Bjørn Erik Rasch argues that we should expect the *electoral system* to influence parliamentary party cohesion. His first argument is that a low district magnitude—that is, a low number of seats per district—will have a negative effect on party discipline. For with decreasing district magnitude, the home district becomes more and more clearly defined to the representative, and a need to cultivate the district is likely to emerge. The second argument has to do with voters' impact on candidate selection: to the extent voters are invited to choose individual candidates, the result may be to undermine parliamentary party cohesion. If voters are offered party lists, on the other hand, someone has to arrange the placement of candidates on this list; to the extent this is done under central control, representatives have an incentive to cultivate the party leadership (Rasch 1995:7–8).

Another institutional explanation is that offered by Palle Svensson (1982). In every Nordic welfare state, the scope of government has expanded. This has involved an increase in the number and complexity of bills proposed and passed, and the number of parliamentary resolutions, interpellations, and questions has grown substantially too (see Damgaard 1977 and 1992b; Gudmundsson 1997). This *heavier workload* has resulted in a number of structural adjustments in parliaments—first and foremost the establishment of *specialized and permanent committees*. Such committees allow for the simultaneous consideration of many different items, and they make possible a division of labor whereby issues are handled by those members of the parties with special knowledge of, experience with, or interest in the matter at hand (Damgaard 1977; H. Jensen 1995).

As Palle Svensson argues: "The increased workload combined with the division of labor and specialization among members of Parliament has made it impossible for each member to follow every legislative issue closely. . . . They must rely on party experts and have more or less been forced to a low information strategy of decision-making and to take cues from their colleagues. In sum, they follow the party line, unless special circumstances make deviant behavior both possible and desirable" (1982: 21).

The above-mentioned increase in parliamentary activity, and the related increase in MPs' workload, have also been fueled by an *increase in the level of parliamentary conflict* (Damgaard 1992d; Wiberg 1994b). Parliamentary activity has increased on account of changes in the party system, with a greater number of parties, less loyal voters, changes in the electoral system conferring greater importance on personal voting, and a more person- and conflict-oriented media coverage of the political debate. The consequences have been twofold: On the one hand, these changes have contributed to the increase in the workload and so to the division of labor and the resulting strict party discipline. On the other hand, they have increased the need of individual MPs for attention and for a personal profile, thus causing new tensions between the individual and the group. The MPs are caught in a *dilemma between attention-seeking behavior and party loyalty.*

There are quite a few structural and institutional reasons, then, why we should generally expect a high level of party cohesion in Nordic parliamentary party groups: (1) four of the Nordic countries have a parliamentary form of government; (2) the operative idea of representation among Nordic parliamentarians is distinctly collectivist (see Esaiasson's analysis in chapter 3 above); (3) the party systems have traditionally mirrored social class divisions; and (4) the Nordic party systems are still marked by strong social democratic parties. In addition, (5) the electoral system is based on multimember constituencies; and finally, (6) over time we should expect more party unity in all parties because of the increased workload in parliament.

If we were to make a qualified guess about differences between the Nordic countries, we would expect party cohesion to be somewhat lower in Finland, because its form of government is semi-presidential (or semi-parliamentarian), its MPs adhere in a lesser degree to a collectivist theory of representation, and its electoral system means that only personal votes—and not the placement of candidates on party lists—decide who is elected and who is not.

Different Elements in Party Discipline, and Different Reasons for It

So far we have discussed and operationalized party discipline as a matter of MPs' voting with their own group in roll calls. But party discipline is a more complex phenomenon than voting behavior and should rather be conceived of as a set of norms that group members follow "in given situations" in order to "work together for the group's goals in one and the same way" (to paraphrase Ozbudun's definition quoted in note 1).

On the basis of interviews with members of the Danish parliament, Torben Worre was able to chart at least four elements of party discipline in Danish parliamentary parties: (1) group members were expected to keep the content of internal party discussions to themselves; (2) group members were under an obligation to participate in parliamentary roll calls at their party's request; (3) individual members of the group were expected not to take political initiatives without authorization from their party; and—last but not least—(4) group members were expected to stick to the party line in parliamentary votes (Worre 1970:169–70).

Other scholars, too, have analyzed party discipline on the assumption of a range of norms. In his analysis of breaches of party discipline in the British House of Commons, for example, Edward Crowe used research questions from a study in which individual MPs were asked to rank breaches of party discipline of seven different kinds.[2] Crowe's analysis shows that two kinds of breach are considered the most serious: those highly visible to the public and those likely to threaten the government (or protect it, if viewed from an opposition standpoint). Furthermore, Crowe's study shows there is no difference, when it comes to how the various elements in party discipline are assessed, between frontbenchers and backbenchers, Conservatives and Labourites, and newcomers and more senior MPs. Crowe therefore concludes these crucial parliamentarian norms on party discipline are widespread and approved, and that an effective socialization takes place, partly in the form of anticipated socialization: already before their first election, prospective MPs know and accept these rules of the game (Crowe 1983:917).

In another study, the same author discusses in more detail the reasons given by individual MPs for respecting the norms of party discipline (Crowe 1986). Crowe distinguishes here between three different types of reason, which are said to correspond to different social forces.

First, parliamentary party members may be loyal to their group because of *positive or negative incentives*. Members may, among other things, entertain the hope of future promotion in the group or fear potential criticism from constituency associations. Group members may thus comply for *fear of sanctions*.

Second, members may stay loyal on grounds of *duty*, in which case MPs are consciously aware of the expectations associated with their role; they may not agree with their leaders on the issue in question, but they recognize the importance and utility of party loyalty. This kind of loyalty is based on an explicit process of exchange, in which individual preferences are traded off against the organizational goal of greater unity. The social force at work here is *identification with one's role* as representative.

Third, group loyalty can be rooted in *agreement with the leaders*. In such a case, group members basically agree with the party leader's position, and have a genuine feeling of loyalty toward him/her. The social force in this case is *internalization* of attitudes, norms, and models. This analysis was also based on survey data.[3] Crowe asked members of the House of Commons to rank their reasons for dismissing the idea of cross-voting. The main conclusion seems to be that MPs' conformity on this point is a voluntary process. Mechanisms of power and compliance are seldom necessary to secure group loyalty (Crowe 1986:167).[4]

Motives for Accepting Party Discipline

In this study, we have not asked MPs to specify their reasons for voting with their party. But we can get an indication of their motives for staying loyal if we look both at their attitudes toward party discipline and their attitudes toward the power of the chairman of their parliamentary party group. In practice, the chairman organizes decision-making processes and coordinating efforts in the parliamentary party. Furthermore, he/she is the one who chairs group meetings and draws the conclusions when it comes to the position of the parliamentary party on various policy issues. In many ways, then, the chairman personifies power and leadership in the group.

If a group member ascribes great legitimacy to his/her chairman and at the same time is satisfied with the current level of party discipline (or would even welcome a tightening), then we would regard him/her as someone who tends to define the situation as one in which *the power is legitimate and used rightly in discipline questions*. We would expect this MP to belong to the category of those who have internalized the norms of party discipline.

If a member ascribes great legitimacy to his/her chairman but wants less discipline, we would say that he/she tends to see the situation as one in which *the power is legitimate but used wrongly in discipline matters*. Here the situation is more ambiguous; it calls for clarification and argument. The member may reason as follows: "I do not agree with the way my chairman exercises authority, but all things considered—my opportunities and interests, the voters' expectations of me as a representative, et cetera—I will be loyal to my party." These calculations indicate role identification.

Similar calculations may be found when a member ascribes little legitimacy to his/her chairman but wants more discipline. In that case he/she

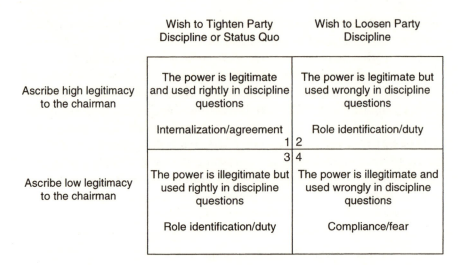

	Wish to Tighten Party Discipline or Status Quo	Wish to Loosen Party Discipline
Ascribe high legitimacy to the chairman	The power is legitimate and used rightly in discipline questions Internalization/agreement 1	The power is legitimate but used wrongly in discipline questions Role identification/duty 2
Ascribe low legitimacy to the chairman	3 The power is illegitimate but used rightly in discipline questions Role identification/duty	4 The power is illegitimate and used wrongly in discipline questions Compliance/fear

Figure 9.1 A Typology of Motives for Party Loyalty

defines the situation as one in which *the power is illegitimate but used rightly in discipline questions*. In this case as well, the ambiguity of the situation calls for argument and the pondering of pros and cons. Here, too, party loyalty is a result of role identification.

Finally, we can identify a type of member who ascribes little legitimacy to his/her chairman and also wants party discipline to be loosened, but who nevertheless votes with the party as a general rule. Such a member is likely to define the situation as one in which *the power is illegitimate and used wrongly in discipline questions*. The loyalty of such an MP to the party—when it comes to voting—probably reflects a fear of sanctions. Figure 9.1 illustrates the different motives.

In the Nordic parliamentary multiparty systems (which are sometimes labeled consensus systems), we would expect a high proportion of MPs to have internalized the norms of loyalty. We will now move from theory to description and explanation. We shall address the following questions: To what extent do Nordic parties behave as unitary actors in parliament? What are the attitudes of MPs toward different norms of party discipline? What are these attitudes based on? How, finally, can the similarities and differences be explained?

PARTY DISCIPLINE IN NORDIC PARLIAMENTS: PATTERNS AND EXPLANATIONS

IntraParty Agreement in Nordic Parliaments—Rice's Index

New data about roll-call behavior in Nordic parliamentary parties confirm our theoretical expectation of high party cohesion. From table 9.1, it appears that voting discipline in all of the parties in four of the Nordic countries is very high. In Denmark, the average score on the Rice index for all parties is 99.9, in Norway 97.5, in Iceland 96.9, in Sweden 96.6, and in Finland 88.6.[5]

To a remarkable extent, parties in the Nordic parliaments behave as unitary actors, and party voting is no less dominant than it had been decades ago. In all Nordic parties (save the Norwegian and Finnish left parties), the degree of party cohesion has increased.

It is notable as well that there is very little variation on this point between the different parliamentary parties. Various hypotheses about differences have been put forward in the literature: for example, that working-class parties will exhibit greater cohesion, since they traditionally emphasize cohesion and solidarity; that conservatives will show greater cohesion than liberals, because they generally put more stress on discipline; that small parliamentary parties will show greater cohesion than large ones; that fringe parties will maintain stricter discipline than other parties, since they are far from power and decision-making, and also because they supposedly exhibit a marked homogeneity of attitudes and preferences; and that government parties will show more cohesion than opposition parties. None of these hypotheses appears to be supported by the present data.

The results are consistent, then, with the expectations raised by the institutional explanatory factors suggested. The high level of party cohesion is explained by parliamentary government, a collectivist notion of representation, an electoral system with multimember constituencies, and party dominance over the choice of candidates. The increase in party cohesion is probably due to the heavier workload in all of the parliaments. Support for this explanation may be found in a detailed study of developments in parliamentary activities and voting behavior in Danish parliamentary parties from 1953 to 1995 (Skjæveland 1997).

Social forces that have blurred cleavages in society at large, and made the electorate more volatile and less loyal to parties, have apparently not affected the party loyalty of MPs. Alternatively, these factors have been counterbalanced by changes in MPs' conditions of work. That Finland, as

Table 9.1
Intraparty Agreement in the Nordic Parliaments: Rice's Index of Party Cohesion

	Green	Left Parties	Social Democrats	Parties of the Center	Conservatives	Agrarians	Populists
DENMARK							
		The Unitary List / Socialist People's Party	Social Democrats	Radical Liberal Party / Center Democrats	Conservatives	Liberals	Progressive Party
1971–79		— / 99.8	99.8	99.5 / 99.6	99.8	99.9	99.5
1994/95		100 / 100	99.9	100 / 100	100	99.7	99.9
FINLAND							
	The Green League	Left-Wing Alliance	Social Democrats	Swedish Peoples Party / Christian League	National Coalition	Center Party	
1951–54		94.9	81.7	81.3 /	85.5	86.2	
1995/96	88.5	85.3	84.9	90.7 / 91.5	90.1	89.4	
ICELAND							
	Women's Alliance	People's Alliance	People's Mov. / Social Dems.		Independence Party	Progressive Party	
1995/96	98.1	91.6	96.9 / 96.6		99.1	99.3	

NORWAY

	Socialist Left Party	Labor Party	Christian People's Party	Conservatives	Center Party	Progressive Party
1979/80	98.9	98.2	93.4	96.8	96.9	—
1993/94	98.3	99.2	97.4	98.1	98.1	94.1

SWEDEN

	Ecology Party	Left Party	Social Democrats	People's Party	Christian Democrats	Moderate Unity Party	Center Party
1969	—	96	92	80	—	82	86
1994/95	96	96	100	96	96	96	96

Notes: Rice's index of party cohesion is obtained by dividing the number of votes cast by the majority of each party on a roll call by the total number of party members who voted and converting the percentage obtained to a scale from 0 to 100 (by subtracting 50 from the percentage and multiplying by 2, the starting point being the assumption that a fifty-fifty split in a party signifies zero cohesion). Information about the Danish case are from Svensson (1982) and Skjæveland (1997). The Danish figures are based on voting behavior at the third reading of governmental and private bills passed in the period. Information about the Finnish case are from Nyholm and Hagfors (1968) and from data collected by Niko Mellanen for this study. The figures from 1995–96 are based on voting behavior on eighty-three final divisions after the third reading of bills passed in this session. Information about the Icelandic case are from a data collection organized by Ólafur Hardarson. Included are laws after third reading in the 1995–96 term. The figures are based on 122 final divisions. Information about the Norwegian case are from Rasch (1995). The Norwegian figures are based on data that include all roll calls taken by electronic voting device of the Storting, which means that unanimous or nearly unanimous votes are excluded from the data set. Two hundred and eighty-five roll calls in 1979–80 and 1,178 in 1993–93 are included. Information about the Swedish case are from Holmberg (1974) and Wetterqvist (1996). The figures are based on 406 final divisions in 1969 and 637 in 1994–95.

expected, turns out to be a deviant case can be explained by these very same factors. Yet our explanations—both for the generally high level of cohesion and for some of the differences observed between the countries—can be refined by including actor-based factors.

Attitudes toward Different Components of Party Coherence and of Party Discipline

In the survey, Nordic MPs were asked about their attitudes both toward party cohesion and party discipline in general, and toward the different components of these phenomena. It appears from table 9.2 that, taken together, a huge majority of Nordic parliamentarians (72 percent) are satisfied with the extent of party discipline within their respective parliamentary parties. And a majority of those who are dissatisfied wish to *tighten* party discipline. Just 9 percent would like to see discipline loosened. Since actual voting discipline is very strong, these results indicate a very great acceptance of party discipline as such. Thus, we plainly see a very strong institutional norm in operation here.

Although the similarities among the five countries are striking, there are differences too. Only two-thirds of Icelandic parliamentarians are satisfied. About one-third seek greater discipline. A little more than one-fifth of the Finnish representatives—a significantly higher proportion than among their Nordic colleagues—seem to want less discipline. These results indicate that some of the differences in attitudes might be due to differences in the political systems of the five countries.

Table 9.2 indicates as well how MPs from the different party families look upon actual party discipline. Most dissatisfied are MPs from the populist parties. Less than half are content with things as they are, while the rest seek greater discipline. This is easily explained. The fact is that, during the period under review, both the Norwegian and Danish progress parties experienced a vigorous internal power struggle, which shortly afterward led to a split within both parties.

Among the left parties, only two-thirds are satisfied with the present state of things. Here the dissatisfied are divided into two groups of equal size: one seeking more discipline, the other less. The same is true of the conservatives. Among social democrats, about one-third think discipline needs tightening.

The most contented MPs seem to be those hailing from agrarian parties and parties of the center, as well as from the few greens. When we run a control for third variables, however, country turns out to be the most important factor. It appears, accordingly, that MPs from all of the parties in Iceland have a relatively stronger desire for increased discipline. The

Table 9.2
Members' Attitudes toward Party Discipline, by Country, Party Family, and Seniority (%)

	Should Be Stronger than Today	*Good As It Is Today*	*Should Be Looser than Today*	*Total*	N
Average	19	72	9	100	728
Country					
Denmark	17	73	10	99	108
Finland	8	72	20	101	114
Iceland	32	66	2	100	44
Norway	26	70	4	100	143
Sweden	12	78	10	100	327
Party families					
Green	11	87	2	100	24
Left parties	19	65	17	100	66
Social democrats	30	64	7	100	299
Parties of the center	6	83	11	100	71
Conservatives	15	70	15	101	148
Agrarians	10	84	6	100	107
Populists	42	46	13	101	13
Seniority					
0–4 years of seniority	15	73	12	100	347
More than 4 years	22	71	7	100	388

Notes: The question was worded as follows: "Generally speaking, what is your opinion about party cohesion and party discipline in your party?" The following response alternatives were offered: "should be much stronger than today"; "should be somewhat stronger than today"; "good as it is today"; "should be somewhat looser than today"; "should be much looser than today." Data are weighted so each country counts equally.

In the Finnish study the question was worded as follows: "What is your opinion about party cohesion in your party and about so-called party discipline?" Finnish respondents were then asked to give their opinion about "cohesion" and "discipline" separately. Not surprisingly, Finnish MPs want more cohesion and less discipline. Forty-eight percent would like to have stronger cohesion, 50 percent find it good as it is today, while 3 percent ask for less cohesion. The figures for their opinion about "discipline" are shown in the table.

Obviously, "cohesion" and "discipline" have different connotations to different MPs, but there is a theoretical point in asking them about both at once. In doing that, we ask MPs to balance advantages and disadvantages, all things considered, about joint action. Since it costs MPs nothing to wish more cohesion, it is their opinion about discipline that has been used in the analyses.

same is true for Norway, except in the case of the middle parties. In Finland, MPs from most of the parties want to loosen discipline.

To understand the complexity of parliamentary practice, we might most appropriately view party discipline as *a range of norms*. When, moreover, we ask members about their attitude toward the different components of

Table 9.3
Members' Attitudes toward Various Elements in Party Discipline, by Country (%)

	Denmark	Iceland	Norway	Sweden	All	Finland	
"Sticking to party line in votes"							
Tighten	5	7	15	4	7	Difficult to say	21
Status quo	88	91	79	86	85	Agree	10
Loosen	7	2	7	10	8	Disagree	69
Total	100	100	100	100	100		100
"Not taking political initiatives without party authorization"							
Tighten	11	19	19	6	11	Difficult to say	4
Status quo	80	79	69	75	75	Agree	2
Loosen	9	2	12	19	14	Disagree	94
Total	100	100	100	100	100		100
"Not talking to outsiders about internal party discussions"							
Tighten	28	57	42	33	36	Difficult to say	18
Status quo	67	43	56	63	61	Agree	63
Loosen	6	0	2	5	4	Disagree	20
Total	101	100	100	101	101		100
Minimum *N*	108	43	143	328	622		117

Notes: The question was worded as follows: "What is your opinion about party cohesion and party discipline in your party when it comes to the following norms for parliamentary work? (1) secrecy concerning internal party discussions; (2) not taking political initiatives without party authorization; (3) sticking to the party line in votes." The following response alternatives were offered: "should be much stronger than today"; "should be somewhat stronger than today"; "good as it is today"; "should be somewhat looser than today"; "should be much looser than today." In the Finnish study the question was worded as follows: "What is your opinion about the following norms of party cohesion/party discipline? (1) Secrecy concerning internal party discussions; (2) Not initiating political motions without party authorization; (3) Sticking to the party line in votes." The following response alternatives were offered: "same opinion"; "difficult to say"; "other opinion."

party discipline, their answers show considerable variation. From table 9.3 we can see that the vast majority (85 percent) of parliamentarians are satisfied with the current norm of sticking to the party line in votes. The same applies to the norm of not taking political initiatives without authorization from the party (75 percent). However, a substantially smaller share (61 percent) are satisfied with the principle of secrecy regarding internal party discussions.

When it come to the rule of *sticking to the party line in votes*, the strongest wish for greater discipline is found in Norway. Here about 20 percent of MPs from the two largest parties, the Labor Party and the Conservatives, call for more discipline. Given the actual level of voting cohesion (see above), it would seem strange at first sight that so many members of these two parties seek greater discipline. We shall return to this later on.

Only in eight out of forty parties do we find a substantial share of members calling for less discipline.

If we look at the norm of *secrecy regarding internal party discussions*, we find a widespread desire to tighten discipline. This desire is apparently felt least in Denmark and Sweden, most in Iceland and Norway.

Finally, as regards the rule of *not taking political initiatives without authorization from the party*, we once again find the Norwegian parliamentarians among the hard-liners, together with their Icelandic colleagues. In both countries, about one-fifth of MPs call for more discipline.

Two conclusions may thus be drawn. First, if we add those accepting the status quo to those recommending greater discipline, we are confirmed in our impression that there is very strong support for the above-mentioned institutional norms in all of the Nordic countries, apart from Finland. In Finland, only 10 percent of MPs say they agree with the norm of voting with one's party, while just 2 percent agree with the norm of not taking political initiatives without party authorization. This is a surprisingly massive refusal. It must be interpreted as indicating a strong wish to loosen party discipline.[6]

Second, the act of voting does not seem to be the problem. It is during the processes prior to the actual roll call—when issues are debated, initiatives taken, et cetera—that the rules of party discipline are really put to the test. Perhaps we should take these answers as evidence of the conflict MPs feel between the need to attract attention as a candidate and the need for party loyalty.

Different Motives for Loyalty to Parliamentary Parties

In the survey, members were asked to indicate on an eleven-point scale how much power various institutions and actors in parliament—including the chairman of their parliamentary party—*have today*, and how much power they *should have*. Notwithstanding some variations, chairmen are perceived as rather powerful by members of all parties in all of the countries. On a scale measuring *actual* influence from 0 (very little) to 100 (very great), Nordic MPs give their chairman 70 points on average. On a scale measuring how much power their chairman *should* have, however, MPs give their chairman just 66 points. These aggregate results hide the fact, however, that as many as 74 percent of parliamentarians would actually be willing to confer a little *more* power on their chairman, while just 26 percent think their chairman has too much power (see figure 9.2). Chairmen of the parliamentary parties are thus ascribed great legitimacy by three-fourths of MPs and little legitimacy by the remaining fourth.[7]

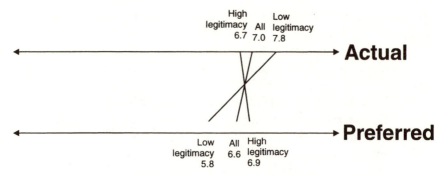

Figure 9.2 Members' Attitudes toward the Actual Level of Influence and Preferred Level of Influence of Their Respective Party Chairman by the Degree of Legitimacy They Ascribe to the Chairman (mean position). Swedish MPs are not included in this analysis because the relevant question was asked in the 1988 survey only (see Esaiasson and Holmberg 1996). The number of respondents are 571 (all); 423 (high legitimacy); and 148 (low legitimacy).

How parliamentarians in the five countries assess the legitimacy of their chairmen may be seen in table 9.4 (the marginal distribution under "Overall Total"). The lowest level of confidence in the chairman is found in Finland, where only 66 percent of MPs would accept giving the chairman of their parliamentary party more power than he/she currently has. This share is about three-fourths in Iceland, Norway, and Sweden (77 percent, 75 percent and 73 percent, respectively). The highest level of legitimacy is found in Denmark, where four-fifths of parliamentarians (82 percent) ascribe great legitimacy to their leaders.

The point of departure for the following line of reasoning is that we in the Nordic parliamentary parties have an extremely strong party discipline, as measured by voting behavior. This means most MPs follow their parliamentary party most of the time. But they do it for a range of reasons.

Table 9.4 shows the distribution of MPs in the five countries according to motives given for party loyalty. In Denmark, Iceland, and Norway, about three-fourths of parliamentarians seem somehow to have internalized the norms of party discipline (73 percent, 74 percent, and 72 percent, respectively). Nearly 25 percent have a more calculating attitude; that is, they respect the discipline mainly from a sense of duty.

Matters are otherwise in Finland and Sweden. In Finland, as many as 13 percent of representatives both distrust their leader and wish to see looser discipline; while 28 percent show loyalty on grounds of duty (21 percent plus 7 percent). Observe how the different motives are operationalized in the note to table 9.4. Only 59 percent seem to have internalized

Table 9.4

Motives for Party Loyalty: Proportion of Nordic Members Loyal to Their Party because of Internalization, Role Identification, and Compliance, Respectively

	Attitude toward Party Discipline														
	Denmark			Finland			Iceland			Norway			Sweden		
Degree of Legitimacy Ascribed to Parliamentary Party Leader	Tighten/ Status Quo	Loosen	Overall Total	Tighten/ Status Quo	Loosen	Overall Total	Tighten/ Status Quo	Loosen	Overall Total	Tighten/ Status Quo	Loosen	Overall Total	Tighten/ Status Quo	Loosen	Overall Total
High legitimacy	73	9	82	59	7	66	74	3	77	72	3	75	67	6	73
Low legitimacy	**17**	1	18	**21**	13	34	**23**	0	23	**23**	2	25	**22**	5	
Row total	89	11	100	80	20	100	97	3	100	95	5	100	89	11	100
No. of respondents			85			106			39			127			332

Note: The table should be read as follows. Cell I shows proportion of "internalization motives." Cell II shows proportion of "compliance motive." "Internalization motives" are thus operationalized as the combination of ascribing high legitimacy to the leader plus a wish for stronger party discipline, or plus a wish to keep the status quo. "Identification motives" (duty) are operationalized as the combination of either ascribing low legitimacy to the leader plus a wish to tighten party discipline or to keep status quo or ascribing high legitimacy to the leader plus a wish to loosen party discipline. Compliance motives (fear) are operationalized as ascribing low legitimacy to the leader plus a wish for looser party discipline. The index of legitimacy builds upon responses to survey questions on the internal influence over decision-making in parliaments (see, e.g., chapter 8 above). Attitudes toward party discipline are measured as in table 9.2 above. This particular analysis draws upon responses to two specific items: (1) "How much power *should* the chairman of the parliamentary party ideally have, when it comes to decisions in the parliament?"; and (2) "How much power is she actually perceived to have, when it comes to decisions in the parliament?" Responses to the first question were subtracted from responses given to the second question. Thus, positive values means that the chairman be given even more power in the parliamentary decision-making process, which we interpret as ascribing high legitimacy to the chairman. Negative values means that the chairman is considered to have too much power, which is interpreted as ascribing low legitimacy to the chairman. Since not all relevant questions were not included in the survey, the data for the Swedish case are from the 1988 parliamentary survey.

the norms.[8] The attitudes of Finnish MPs toward their party thus appear to be much more instrumental.

Sweden ends up between Finland and the other Nordic countries. Here two-thirds of MPs have internalized the norms. The fact that the Swedish parliamentary parties are much bigger than the rest may explain why a higher proportion of MPs in that country have some reservations about their leaders and about norms of discipline; for such MPs, following the party is more a question of duty. The more pronouncedly instrumental attitude in Sweden and (especially) Finland may help to explain the lower level of party cohesion in these two countries.

The results indicate, on the one hand, that party discipline in the Nordic parliamentary parties has more to do with coherence than with compliance, and, on the other, that there are cross-national differences. They also confirm the impression that the Finnish party system in particular is under pressure. It is not just one's attitudes, and the motives behind them, which are likely to influence one's behavior. The manner in which said attitudes have been generated—in *the socialization process*—is critical as well. Taken strictly, our data do not tell us much about how MPs' attitudes and motives develop over time, although table 9.5 may be said to contain some evidence for such processes.

The results tell us that the proportion who have internalized the norms of party discipline is much higher among those who have been MPs for four years or more than among those who have arrived in parliament recently. On the other hand, a far greater share of the newcomers are loyal because of a sense of duty. This pattern is very distinct in the Icelandic case, but it is also clear in Norway and Finland. In Denmark, a very high proportion of both groups have internalized the norms.

If we interpret these data dynamically—which they, strictly speaking, do not allow—we can see that some kind of socialization takes place during the first years in parliament. The high level of party loyalty is not a matter of course; it is not achieved automatically and without tension. The share of newcomers who find it difficult to accept the norms of party discipline right away may help to explain differences between the countries. There is, for example, less socialization work to do in Danish parties than in Norwegian ones, while the latter have an easier task than those in Iceland.

But this shift in motives for loyalty, which seems to take place during the first period in parliament, also helps to explain why so many party members—even in parties coming close to complete unity in voting, such as the social democrats and conservatives in Norway—call for greater voting discipline. The reason could very well be that representatives in a par-

Table 9.5

Motives for Party Loyalty: Seniority and Proportion of Members Loyal to Their Party because of Internalization, Duty, and Fear (Compliance), Respectively (%)

	Denmark		Finland		Iceland		Norway		Sweden	
	Country and Seniority (years in parliament)									
	0–4	4–	0–4	4–	0–4	4–	0–4	4–	0–4	4–
Internalization	70	74	50	68	46	89	60	84	65	70
Duty	30	24	34	22	54	12	37	16	29	28
Compliance	0	2	16	11	0	0	3	0	6	3
Total	100	100	100	101	100	101	100	100	100	101
N	27	58	50	56	13	26	60	67	94	115

Notes: "Internalization motives" are operationalized as the combination of ascribing high legitimacy to the leader plus a wish for stronger party discipline or plus a wish to keep the status quo. "Identification motives" (duty) are operationalized as the combination of either ascribing low legitimacy to the leader plus a wish to tighten party discipline (or plus a wish to keep the status quo) or ascribing high legitimacy to the leader plus a wish to loosen party discipline. Compliance motives (fear) are operationalized as ascribing low legitimacy to the leader plus a wish for looser party discipline. Since all the relevant questions were not asked in 1994, data about Sweden are from the 1988 parliamentary survey.

liamentary party are faced with dilemmas and with friction—difficulties that newcomers must first learn to deal with and to accept. Socialization and internalization are by no means automatic processes. To be reinforced, norms must be mentioned and brought up for discussion.

COOPERATION ACROSS PARTY LINES

The analysis so far—which has been based on the outcome approach—has contributed to an image of the Nordic parliamentary parties as unitary actors. But this monolithic image needs considerable qualification. Or as Kopecky and Nijzink (1995:11) put it: "Analysts only looking at the final product of the parliamentary work, particularly those who do roll-call analysis, tend to overlook that a number of steps precedes final decisions. During these steps, many interests, not always partisan in character, influence and shape the final product. When in the end of the process MPs almost always vote along party lines, it does not necessarily mean that individual MPs have had no non-party or cross-party influence whatsoever." We focus below on some of these activities that take place before the final vote.

It is clear that, if the Nordic representative political systems—characterized as they are by many parties (between six and ten), few majority governments (and these formed as a rule by coalitions), and many minority governments (sometimes even formed by minority coalitions)—are to be capable of producing political solutions and decisions, there must be a great many contacts and negotiations across party lines. These contacts can be established in a range of ways; they can vary by policy field; and they can be more centralized or less.

In the survey, MPs were asked how often they had actively cooperated with MPs from other parties with a view to influencing specific parliamentary decisions in different areas during the last year. The extent and patterns of these contacts across party lines are interesting, both because they may contribute to our understanding of the decision-making process in general (including various policy networks) and because behavior, norms, and rules may supplement and differentiate the picture of party discipline painted above.

Cooperation a Rather Common Phenomenon

From table 9.6 we learn that cooperation across party lines is a rather common phenomenon. Roughly speaking—and forgetting Sweden for the

Table 9.6
Proportion of Members Who Have Cooperated across Party Lines during Past Year (%)

| | | | Type of Issue | | | |
	Localization issues	Other Regional/ Local Issues	Issues Related to Religion/ Ethics	Issues Related to Gender Equality	EU-Related Issues	Environmental issues	Minimum N
All	51	64	23	27	49	50	649
Country							
Denmark	47	65	35	24	47	63	92
Finland	81	92	27	30	72	64	115
Iceland	47	59	23	41	34	52	43
Norway	64	72	23	30	58	49	134
Sweden	18	32	8	11	32	19	263
Party family							
Green	17	28	36	75	62	86	19
Left parties	50	53	27	47	62	69	54
Social democrats	46	59	14	28	40	45	257
Parties of the center	50	68	62	34	71	56	64
Conservatives	60	71	26	17	55	42	132
Agrarians	59	78	17	18	46	53	99
Populists	44	75	19	0	38	38	12
Parliamentary position							
Government parties	51	64	16	25	39	46	314
Opposition parties	51	62	30	29	57	50	323

Continued

Table 9.6
Continued

	Type of Issue						
	Localization issues	Other Regional/ Local Issues	Issues Related to Religion/ Ethics	Issues Related to Gender Equality	EU-Related Issues	Environmental issues	Minimum N
Focus of representation							
Region/constituency	59	72	23	26	47	51	519
Other focus	27	36	21	29	53	48	121
Seniority in parliament							
0–4 years	47	65	22	24	43	43	287
5–8 years	56	64	28	33	55	58	145
9– years	52	64	19	28	50	52	215
Gender							
Men	54	64	21	16	49	48	426
Women	44	62	28	52	44	54	212

Notes: The question was worded as follows: "Have you in the past year cooperated actively with members of parliament from other parties with a view to influencing specific parliamentarian decisions in the following areas?" The following response alternatives were offered: "several times"; "a few times"; "once or twice"; "never." Data are weighted so that each country counts equally.

moment—more than half the Danish and Icelandic MPs, more than two-thirds of Norwegian MPs, and more than four-fifths of Finnish MPs have actively cooperated across party lines during the last year on localization and other local and regional issues (with the figure rising as high as 92 percent in the case of Finland). More than half the MPs have cooperated on issues related to the European Union and to environmental regulation. And between a fourth and a third of MPs have cooperated on religious, ethical, and gender-related issues.

The second thing we learn from table 9.6 is that the level of cooperation also *depends on policy area*. The third thing is that there are *considerable differences between the Nordic countries*. Most striking is the very low level of reported cooperation in all policy areas in the Swedish parliament. The level is highest in Finland, followed by Norway, Denmark, and Iceland.

It seems reasonable to start by seeking an institutional explanation for the substantial differences between the countries. The Swedish combination of a relatively large representative body (349 seats) and, by Nordic standards, relatively few parties (seven) results in comparatively large parliamentary parties. In a setting of this sort, greater numbers of MPs will be occupied with discussions, coordination, coalition-building, and internal analysis within their own parties. At the other end of the scale, we find Finland—with 200 seats, ten parties, and a majority coalition government based on five parties. Everyday politics in such a structural setting necessarily involves a lot of activity across party lines.

Localization and regional/local issues concern such matters as the placement of governmental institutions, military barracks, and highways; the regulation and subvention of industry and trade of importance to a region; and the administration of governmental block grants. Typically, local interest in these issues is easy to define and therefore rather easy to represent. Local interests may conflict with general interests and party goals, but more often than not, issues of the former sort can be characterized as "low politics," in which representatives enjoy greater freedom of action.

Cooperation across party lines in the furtherance of local and regional interests is most widespread in Finland and Norway. This may both indicate and be caused by a relatively sharper cleavage between center and periphery. In the Finnish case, however, it probably also mirrors the weak role assigned to the party in MPs' job definitions.

Further analysis shows that the agrarians are the most active among the parliamentary parties. These parties are often characterized as "district" or "rural" parties, because they have attended historically to the interests of the villages and outlying districts. But it is worth noting that all parties participate in this way of handling interests by means of contacts across party lines. A close analysis of the Danish case shows that the old parties with a widely ramified organizational structure most often cooperate over local interests.

In *policy areas related to religion, ethics, and gender,* it is not always obvious there is a specific party dimension to the conflict. In rare cases, the parliamentary parties decide to suspend party discipline on such issues. The intensity of cooperation is less in these areas, which may to some degree reflect the fact that such issues were not on the political agenda in the year in question. What we see here, however, is a different pattern of participation from that seen in connection with local/regional issues. It is most especially the parties of the left, the small parties of the center, and the green parties which are active here.

Issues related *to the EU and to environmental protection and regulation* have been placed high on the political agenda of the Nordic countries. In contrast to their counterparts in most other nations, Nordic MPs often characterize issues of this sort as "high politics." All of the parties, with the exception of the social democrats and the populists, have cooperated rather intensively across party lines on EU issues.

More detailed analysis also reveals that the *focus of representation* partly explains the extent to which MPs engage in localization and regional issues; furthermore, it makes clear that *gender* in fact—or of course—makes a difference in contact behavior and coalition-building efforts across party lines where gender equality issues are concerned. *Seniority* is also of importance. Cooperating across party lines requires resources in the form of contacts and connections with other MPs. This explains why MPs serving their second term are more active than freshmen. But the results also indicate that, after several years in parliament, involvement in this form of coalition-making declines. The reason for this might be that, concurrently with growing seniority, other bases of power and influence within parliament appear (Jensen 1998).

CONCLUSION: PARTY COHESION AS A COMPLEX OF NORMS IN A COMPLEX PROCESS

In all parties in all of the Nordic countries, only a minuscule share of all individual votes cast on parliamentary roll calls break with the party position. In Denmark the average score on the Rice index for all parties together is 99.9, in Norway 97.5, in Iceland 96.9, in Sweden 96.6, and in Finland 88.6. Measured this way, party cohesion is very strong everywhere; it has even increased in recent years. The Nordic parliamentary parties may be close to the world record when it comes to following the party line in parliamentary votes.

Three *institutional/structural factors*—the form of government, the electoral system, and the workload—seem crucial for explaining the high level of intraparty coherence in the Nordic parliaments, as well as for explaining why Finland to some extent proves a deviant case.

First, all of the Nordic countries—except Finland, which has a semi-presidential system—have *parliamentary governments*. Because the ability of a party to gain and keep power in a parliamentary system depends very much on its ability to act as a unit, this form of government provides very strong rational incentives for party cohesion. These incentives are weaker in a semi-presidential system.

Second, the *electoral systems* in the Nordic countries—founded as they are on proportional representation, multimember constituencies, and party lists of various kinds—result in a need for MPs to "cultivate" their party. In some Nordic countries, however, minor reforms and party decisions have increased the importance of personal voting, thus strengthening the impact of voters on candidate selection. These changes in the electoral system increase individual MPs' need for attention and for a personal profile, again giving them reason to break with the party line under certain circumstances. In this area, too, Finland has gone the furthest.

Third, if we are to explain the increased coherence over time in all five of the parliaments, we must consider a dynamic factor. The *increase in MPs' workload*—as a result of the substantial increase in parliamentary activities caused by the expanded scope of government and by the sharpening of parliamentary conflict—has resulted in specialization and a division of labor among MPs. This development has made it impossible for individual members to follow each and every legislative issue closely. They are forced to rely on party experts. As a general rule, therefore, MPs follow the party line unless special circumstances make breaking with the party line possible and desirable.

It is difficult to imagine, however, that the Nordic level of party cohesion could be achieved without a supportive normative system among MPs. And this is what we find. A belief in the party as the main focus of representation is strong in all parties across the ideological spectrum in every Nordic country (with some reservations in the case of Finland). Direct support for the overall norm of party cohesion among MPs is—again with the exception of Finland—massive throughout the Nordic region. Most MPs in Denmark, Norway, and Iceland, furthermore, appear to have internalized the norms rather than followed them due to fear or a sense of duty; by contrast, MPs in Sweden and especially Finland have a more instrumental relation to the norms. In most countries, finally, the norm of party cohesion is to some extent anticipated among newcomers in parliament; this tendency is most pronounced in Denmark, least in Iceland.

The institutional arrangements behind the high level of party cohesion are thus supported by strong institutional norms. Generally speaking, the extremely high party cohesion in Nordic parliamentary parties is voluntary and consensual. Thus we may speak more properly of party cohesion than of party discipline. As for the connotations still clinging to the concept of party cohesion—group pressure, compulsion, acting against the promptings of one's conscience, et cetera—these seem quite groundless. Among the range of norms constituting party cohesion, it is the norm of secrecy in respect to internal party discussions that occasions the greatest problems and the most dissatisfaction among parliamentarians. On this point, a substantial proportion of MPs recommend greater discipline.

Although no one denies the final vote is important (as the outcome approach emphasizes), it is also true that, from another standpoint (the process approach), the final vote takes place "when everything is over and done with."[9] The existence of high party cohesion does not forbid or prevent contacts and cooperation across party lines. As we have seen, there is extensive cooperation and coalition-building within various policy areas. The norms of party cohesion regulate this traffic—they do not stop it—and they might even facilitate cooperation, inasmuch as they provide norms for how far individual MPs may go when exchanging information and taking political initiatives. In view, then, of the level and patterns of cooperation across party lines, we must qualify the picture of parliamentary parties as unitary actors.

We find the same qualification when we turn to the internal life of the parliamentary parties and focus not on norms of party cohesion but rather on strategies for influencing the decisions of the group (see Knut Heidar's analysis of these strategies in chapter 8 above). Here as well, the focus is on the processes prior to the one in which the final decisions are made. There is reason to believe that what counts as a good argument for the individual MP depends on more than mere rhetoric. If, for example, an MP seeking to persuade his/her fellow group members makes reference to the organizations affected by the policies under consideration, this MP will probably spend more time on these organizations, and be more accessible and amenable to the receipt of advice. The same is true for party activists, journalists, experts, and other MPs. By analyzing strategies of influence, therefore, as by analyzing cooperation across party lines, we get an idea of what can—and actually does—penetrate the parliamentary parties.

If we are to understand party cohesion in the Nordic parliamentarian systems, we must understand parliamentary parties as unitary actors, and we must also—*at the same time*—qualify this image. Such an approach complements the conclusion reached by Peter Esaiasson—see chapter 3 above—that while party is dominant in MPs' job definition, members view themselves as representatives both of their party and of various other interests.

Such is the distinctive brew of Nordic parliaments: strong internalized norms, widespread voluntary support, very high internal party cohesion, the coexistence of many parties, and the existence of a great many more or less informal contacts across party lines at all levels and in all policy areas. The Nordic parliaments are working parliaments in which the *interparty mode* exists side by side with the *cross-party mode*.

NOTES

I would like to thank Lena Wängnerud for providing me with data from the 1988 Swedish survey; and Ólafur Th. Hardarson and Niko Mellanen for their efficient work in collecting, respectively, the Icelandic and Finnish roll-call data. Asbjørn Skjæveland too should be thanked for providing the Danish roll-call data and for offering critical comments. Last but not least, I would like to thank Knut Heidar and Peter Esaiasson for their constructive comments.

1. Ozbudun, for example, defines *party cohesion* as "the extent to which, in a given situation, group members can be observed to work together for the group's goals in one and the same way," and *party discipline* as "cohesion of such character that followers regularly accept and act upon the commands of the leader or leaders . . . and availability to the leader of ways and means of inducing recalcitrant members to accept and act upon his commands" (Ozbudun 1970:305).

2. The seven elements (ranked here by MPs according to seriousness) were: (1) cross-voting; (2) abstaining from voting; (3) writing critical letters and articles in the press; (4) making critical speeches outside the House; (5) making critical speeches in Parliament; (6) signing a critical Early Day Motion; and (7) privately expressing dissent to whips. The research question was worded as follows: "Political commentators sometimes disagree about the seriousness of different breaches of party discipline. Could you write the number '1' alongside the act which you personally consider the most serious, '2' beside the next most serious, and so on down to number 7 for the least serious?" The research questions were taken from a larger study directed by Donald Searing. The MPs were interviewed in 1971 and 1972.

3. MPs were asked to rank the reasons that best explain why they refrain from cross-voting. The (rearranged) list is as follows: [compliance] (1) potential criticism from constituency association, (2) hope of future promotion, (3) fear of withdrawal of the whip, (4) potential patronage; [identification] (5) cross-voting not

in line with best traditions, (6) recognizing the need for party unity, (7) recognizing that MPs are elected on party manifesto; [internalization] (8) basic agreement with party leaders' position, (9) feeling of loyalty to party leaders.

4. For two reasons, the way in which the survey questions are worded is problematic: (1) Crowe runs the risk of putting words in the MP's mouth and to some extent eliciting political correct answers, on account of his emphasis on "basic agreement" and "feeling loyal." In my view, therefore, Crowe may overestimate the internalization factor and underestimate the duty and compliance element. (2) Crowe wants to measure internalization. But one could argue that internalized norms are *motives* of a latent and unconscious nature that can hardly be captured by a battery of clearly defined *reasons*.

5. To compare with other parliaments: the Rice index is not usually used to measure party cohesion in the U.S. Congress. Party cohesion in that body is so weak that it is common first to calculate the share of divisions in which the party structure is identifiable at all. This is done by *the party unity vote index,* which is a measure of recorded votes that split the parties, with a majority of voting Democrats opposing a majority of voting Republicans. For the divisions where the party structure is identifiable, a *party unity support index*—which measures the percentage of party unity votes on which members voted 'yea' or 'nay' in agreement with a majority of their party—is calculated. In 1995, the party unity vote index was 68.8 percent for the Senate and 73.2 percent for the House. The average score in 1995 for each party in both houses of Congress on the party unity support index was 91 percent for the Republicans and 80 percent for the Democrats (*Congressional Quarterly* 1996). In the European Parliament from 1989 to 1994, the Rice index varied between 64.5 and 93.8, with an average for all the parties of 86. In the Swiss parliament from 1991 to 1994, the Rice index varied between 68.3 and 89.2, with 86 as the average.

6. As can be seen from the table, the Finnish questions are worded differently: they refer to absolute norms, not to the situation in the respective parties. The response alternatives are also different. The respondents are allowed to agree, to disagree, or to decline to answer. Confronted with this rather categorical wording of the norms, a large number of Finnish parliamentarians disagree.

7. Some might argue that the survey question is so worded as to make respondents think of the chairman as an institution, instead of having their own particular chairman in mind when answering the question. On the other hand, parliamentary parties in the same country are seen to differ considerably in their perception of how much power their chairmen actually have. These differences are very hard to explain if we do not assume that the answers mirror group members' experiences with and attitudes toward the chairman of their own parliamentary party group. At any rate, this is what is suggested in the following analysis.

8. This pattern applies to all the Finnish parties except the Greens. The level of internalization is especially low in the case of the Social Democratic Party, the National Coalition, and the Left-Wing Alliance.

9. As one member of the Danish parliament put it in an interview (Jensen 1993).

10

Nordic Light on Committee Assignments

Magnus Hagevi

WHO CONTROLS COMMITTEES?

Sweden has just lost the war against Russia. The Swedish parliament—the Riksdag—reacts by deposing the king as absolute ruler. The provisional government hastily draws up a new constitution, and expects the Riksdag to adopt it without protest. These events, which take place in 1809, lead to the formation of the oldest parliamentary committee still in use in the Nordic countries. The government's plans for a quick adoption of the new constitution awaken vigorous protests from members of the Riksdag, who form the Constitution Committee in order to produce a new Instrument of Government. Within a couple of weeks, the new committee has made substantial revisions in the original proposal (Wieslander 1994: 11–12).[1]

If committees are an important factor in the parliamentary power structure, it is important to know who controls their power. Is this control in the hands of the members of parliament who sit on the committees or is it in the hands of the party group leaders who assign MPs to these committees? The objective of this chapter is to investigate whether MPs' committee preferences are accommodated independently of their loyalty to the party group leadership or whether committee assignments are controlled by party group leaders instead.

Of course, the main actors in the Nordic parliaments, as well as in the Nordic electorates, are the parties (Westerståhl 1993:99–108; Esaiasson and Holmberg 1996:49–58; for party groups, see chapter 8 in this volume). Party cohesion in Nordic parliaments is generally very high (see chapter 9). Members of committees are considered to behave as party representatives (Sannerstedt 1992:95–6; H. Jensen 1995:123).[2] It is common for negotiations between parties to be conducted by committee members during the committee stage (Sannerstedt 1992; Mattson 1996b).

Nevertheless, the committee system is the core of internal party group specialization in all of the Nordic parliaments. Such specialization means that MPs holding a position on a standing committee gain recognition as party spokespersons within a particular policy area. As such, they can affect their party's standpoint in that area, especially if they serve as committee chairman (Isberg 1984:25–29; Arter 1984:201–2; Larsson 1986:61–62; Sannerstedt 1992:67; Jensen 1993:122–23).

During the preparation of a government bill in some parliaments—such as the Swedish Riksdag—the responsible minister takes care to obtain the consent and strategic advice of representatives of the governing party on the relevant committee, particularly the chairman (Sannerstedt 1992:59–81; Sundström 1994; Hagevi 1996). It is important to bear such committee clearance in mind when attempting to assess the importance of different committees (Shaw 1979:384–85).

COMMITTEE ASSIGNMENTS AND THE PARTY LEADERSHIP

Committee assignments are a potential source of conflict among MPs. As a result, party cohesion may be put in jeopardy. The division of labor generated by the committee system creates resources that are allocated among members, and members are motivated to obtain these resources. Some resources are limited, so that demand exceeds supply. This leads to competition between members of the parliamentary party (Hagevi 1994:180–81). The allocation of limited resources and the desire for party cohesion create a need to manage these competing goals; this is usually considered a task for the party group leadership in parliament (Anckar 1972; Hernes 1977:296–97; Cox and McCubbins 1993:90–99; Damgaard 1995:308–9). We shall assume, accordingly, that the party group leadership handles committee assignments.

The motives and actions of the party group leadership are important constraints on the ability of individual members to achieve their own goals. The actions of the party leadership are not restricted, however, to imposing constraints on the activities of individual MPs. Through their leaders, parties are important actors pursuing their own goals (Molin 1965; Sjöblom 1968). The fulfillment of these goals can be affected by the behavior of members on committees (Anckar 1972). Party leaders have an interest, consequently, in controlling committee assignments.

In his seminal study of committees in the U.S. Congress, Richard Fenno (1973) concluded that congressmen have three basic goals when serving on a committee: making good policy, securing re-election, and acquiring influence within Congress. Members are likely to seek, in Fenno's view, to achieve every one of these goals; but the priority assigned to the different goals, and the intensity with which they are desired, will vary in a manner unique to each individual member. He certified as well that committees differ from one another, and he tried to prove that members conduct committee business in such a way as to satisfy their distinctive goals.[3]

Party leaders seem to have many of the same goals that Fenno claims individual members do. Gunnar Sjöblom (1968:73–87) identifies four basic party goals: program realization, vote maximization, maximization of parliamentary influence, and party cohesion. Program realization—or making good policy, in Fenno's terms—relates to the ideological systems of the parties; it is assumed to be the major determinant of the actions of party leaders. Vote maximization recalls Fenno's claim regarding individual members' interest in re-election. Party leaders also seek parliamentary influence, much as Fenno suggested that individual members do.

Party cohesion is the only party goal clearly absent from Fenno's list of basic member goals. Party cohesion consists in the support of members for those actions of the party leadership that are taken in the name of the party. For Fenno, of course, party cohesion was not an issue, since he was concerned only with individual members.

Actually, party cohesion is the sole party goal that can constrain the purposive behavior of members in seeking their own fortune. Without it, party group leaders would not be interested in engaging members' loyalty on behalf of other party goals. When we say, then, that party leaders have party cohesion as a goal, we are saying that they want the actions and attitudes of individual party members to support all of the goals of the party.

As specialists, committee members have a responsibility for formulating policy as well as for conducting negotiations with other party representatives within the policy areas covered by their committee. This is one reason that party leaders regard the loyalty of committee members as important. Otherwise party cohesion may suffer, and the prospects for realizing the party program may diminish.

On account of the resources attached to committee assignments, the task of choosing members generates power for party leaders (Hernes 1977: 296). They can use committee assignments as a component in a reward system. To obtain party cohesion, party leaders can reward party loyalty by granting assignments on preferred committees.[4]

This one-sided view of the relation between leaders and individual members fails to recognize, however, that party group leaders are vulnerable and cannot act just as they please. They can be deposed, after all. Moreover, even when a rebellion against the party leadership fails, the resulting dissension does not promote party cohesion. Members also sometimes leave their parliamentary party group and become independents (Abram and Cooper 1968; Hagevi 1997; Olson and Hagevi 1998). This, too, runs counter to the goal of party cohesion.

The ability of both individual members and party group leaders to achieve their goals depends on how much they are constrained when they pursue their goals. Two contrary images may be distinguished here: party group leaders may be seen as Leviathan or as marionettes. As Leviathan, they are unconstrained and can act as they wish. Individual members are merely "lovely voting brutes" (Tingsten 1966:215). As marionettes, on the other hand, party group leaders are constrained by detailed norms governing their behavior, while individual members are not dependent on their group leaders. Because of the structure of these norms, individual members are able to pursue their own goals and to select their own committee assignment (so-called self-selection). As self-selection increases, moreover, the more decisive are individual members' goals for the committee assignment process.

Norms

We are interested here in norms governing the relation between party group leaders and individual members over committee assignments. Norms are informal rules of parliamentary conduct that generate stable patterns of action and widely shared standards of desirable behavior (Wahlke et al. 1962:141–42; Hedlund 1985:337; Hinckley 1988:105). They may be followed strictly, but they may also serve as general guidelines. Both ordinary members and party group leaders must show allegiance to them. Disobedient members may not get the assignment they desire; self-willed leaders can cause disturbances and undermine cohesion in the party group.

One of the most fundamental norms is *committee-preference accommodation*. This norm dictates that party group leaders try to accommodate the committee preferences of all members. The drawback of preference accommodation is that it does not discriminate among members seeking an assignment on committees where the demand for committee seats exceeds the supply.

The most famous parliamentary norm is probably that of *seniority*. In Nordic parliaments, seniority is dictated by the number of sessions for which a member has served. According to this principle, MPs with higher seniority have priority over MPs with lower seniority when it comes to choosing committee assignments.

Both the norm of seniority and that of committee-preference accommodation limit the ability of party group leaders to assign members as they please. If the principle of seniority is implemented without exception, individual members can choose any committee they prefer and then just wait in line until they receive the assignment. All individual members, however disloyal they may be toward the party group leadership, will sooner or later receive their preferred committee assignment if they stay in office long enough.

To what extent can self-selection be obtained if party group leaders obey the principle of seniority in the main, yet make some exceptions at the same time? This question has been answered in two different ways. Investigating the U.S. House of Representatives, Polsby, Gallaher, and Rundquist (1969:790) stressed that the principle of seniority must be followed absolutely: "When seniority operates as a partial influence . . . political influence flows to those empowered to vary the applications of the diverse criteria of choice—normally party leaders. When seniority is sovereign and inviolate, power is decentralized to those accordingly protected."

Irwin Gertzog (1976:705) has challenged this view. He suggests that the influence of party group leaders over the committee assignments of individual members are as great as the prospects enjoyed by individual members for self-selection are small (cf. Cox and McCubbins 1993:53). If we develop Gertzog's idea further, we see that even a restricted use of the principle of seniority can still hamper the influence of party group leaders. The more violations of the principle of seniority are tolerated by members, the more freedom of choice belongs to party group leaders. But if the ability of party group leaders to violate the principle of seniority is small, their influence over individual members will be correspondingly small.

It would be surprising, in view of the goal of party cohesion, if we found a fully effective principle of seniority operating in a parliament dominated by highly cohesive parties. Moreover, we will probably find that the principle of seniority is implemented less strictly in parties where decision-making is strongly concentrated in the hands of the party group leadership than in party groups marked by more decentralized decision-making.

COMMITTEE ASSIGNMENTS IN
A NORDIC PERSPECTIVE

The attention to parliamentary committee assignments derives mainly
from the American Congress, a legislative system that has been labeled
committee (or subcommittee) government (Hall and Evans 1990; cf. Cox
and McCubbins 1993:60–82). Although committee systems are less significant elsewhere, examinations of committee assignments outside the
United States are not totally absent.[5]

Of course, committee-preference accommodation has been noted in
the U.S. House of Representatives. It is believed to be the primary goal
when the Democratic Party allocates committee assignments among its
House members (Rohde and Shepsle 1973:898–99; Gertzog 1976:704–8;
Shepsle 1978:237; Bullock 1985:800). The importance attached to obtaining a preferred committee placement has also attracted attention in
research on Scandinavian parliamentary assignments. Members of the
Norwegian Storting and the Swedish Riksdag tend inevitably to get their
requested committee assignment. Swedish party group leaders say they try
to satisfy the committee preferences of members first of all (Hellevik
1969:155–56; Hagevi 1993:28–29; 1998).

In the U.S. Congress, the *principle of seniority* is still important when
committee chairmanships are assigned, but it is said to be less crucial when
members are placed on the various committees (Rohde and Shepsle
1973:899; Cox and McCubbins 1993; cf. Goodwin 1970:86–88; cf. Matthews 1960:151–53; Sinclair 1989:76–77). At the end of the 1960s, hardly
any uncompensated violations of seniority took place (Polsby et al. 1969:
791–96). Since the famous rebellion of 1975, violations of the seniority
principle have increased somewhat, together with the importance of the
party caucus (Hinckley 1976; Cox and McCubbins 1993). Although seniority violations are relatively rare, the mere threat and possibility of being disregarded, despite one's high seniority, has made members aspiring
to a committee chairmanship more supportive of party policy (Crook and
Hibbing 1985:224–26; Cox and McCubbins 1993:49–55).

Most scholars agree on the importance of parliamentary seniority
when members are assigned to committees in the Nordic parliaments
(Hellevik 1969:157; Anckar 1972:7, 12–18; Stjernquist 1966:323). Yet reports on the strength of seniority norms are rare (Björnberg 1946:194–96;
Hagevi 1994:192–95; 1997:168–74). Despite the diminished importance
of seniority norms, about 85 percent of committee assignments in the
Swedish Riksdag in 1994 were assigned in accordance with seniority. To
some extent, moreover, committee chairmanships in the Norwegian Stort-

ing and the Swedish Riksdag are assigned in accordance with parliamentary seniority. But seniority rank is often violated (Olsen 1983:59; Hagevi 1997:174–78).[6]

Party loyalty is the core of party cohesion. Nordic MPs are very party-loyal in their public behavior. According to Erik Damgaard, the committee behavior of MPs "is definitely constrained by parties." The individual preferences of members "can be strengthened by relevant expertise, seniority and a good record of party loyalty. . . . While trying to further the assumed basic aims, the parliamentarian is aware of the goals, routine actions, and possible reactions of the party group and its leadership. . . . The party group and especially the leadership has a large say in assigning committee positions and . . . may also reward or punish individual MPs according to their performance in the light of the party aims" (Damgaard 1995:321–22).

STANDING COMMITTEES, THE NORDIC WAY

How interesting are committees in Nordic parliaments? As between the American system of power-sharing and the British Westminster model, the Nordic parliaments are sometimes portrayed as exemplars of the latter—as operating in accordance with the responsible party model and the British-style parliamentary system (Brusewitz 1929:326–30; Bellquist 1959:38–39; 1993:155, 206–7; von Sydow 1995:90). Little ought therefore to be settled in parliament; the assumption is that most matters are in reality decided elsewhere (in the government, the party leadership, etc.). In fact, there should be no room for division by committees where parties are cohesive actors (Thomassen 1988:13; Katz and Mair 1992:2–5; Esaiasson and Holmberg 1996:3–5, 11–13).

Malcolm Shaw, however, divides the parliamentary category into two: Westminster and the Continental system. He argues that the Westminster model presupposes that political executives operate within the legislature and lead it. The Continental model, by contrast, presupposes a range of "'parallel' executive-legislative relationships" that tend to fall at various points between the American system and the British (Shaw 1979:399; cf. Bellquist 1959:38–39).

Strong committees are important; weak ones are not. By committee importance, we mean the ability of committees to influence the outputs of the legislature (Shaw 1979:384). Strong legislative committees are commonly considered to thrive in what Shaw terms Continental parliamentary systems; they are also thought to thrive in the absence of a single majority party (Shaw 1979:398–404). A combination of strong committees and cohesive parliamentary party groups gives the opposition the option of taking part in policy-making without assuming government responsibility. Majority voting coalitions are often formed by negotiations between committee members acting as party representatives (Sannerstedt 1992; Sjölin 1993). According to Kaare Strøm, choosing to be such a *responsible opposition* is sometimes more advantageous than embarking on an electorally risky participation in government. This alters Shaw's causal hypothesis. Strøm identifies strong committees as a reason that minority governments are common in the Nordic countries (Strøm 1986; 1990:42–44, 70–73, 108–13).

In the Nordic parliaments, two types of committee system have been in effect. According to the principle of functional committees, some committees deal with income (taxes), others with expenses, and still others with lawmaking. By contrast, in a committee system based on subject matter, almost every committee deals with all of these functions, for responsibilities are instead allocated among committees in accordance with their subject matter.

Beginning in the 1970s, committee systems in the Nordic region have developed from diverse conditions into a rather standardized form, albeit one that may not be distinctively Nordic. The present arrangement is based on standing committees that are specialized according to subject matter. Yet divergent traits exist. The committee system in the Finnish Eduskunta is the one that follows the subject-matter principle most loosely. Finland retains some important remnants of the old principle of functional committees. The subject-matter–based committee system has been in use longest in the Norwegian Storting and for the briefest time in the Danish Folketing. Nevertheless, the tradition of important committees is strong not only in the Storting but also in the Riksdag, the Eduskunta, and the Icelandic Althingi. Only the Folketing has a history of weak committees in the style of Westminster.

Table 10.1 lists twenty committee characteristics and prerogatives. It is not unusual to associate the institutional characteristics of a committee system with whether it is strong or weak, since these characteristics affect a committee system's strength. Committee importance is usually correlated with committee independence and freedom to act. The greater the freedom, the stronger the committee. If a committee chooses its own chairman, this is a sign of independence. If it can treat bills more or less as it wishes, this is a sign of freedom. Table 10.1 will not be discussed in detail here, but the degree to which committee characteristics promote committee strength is indicated by the numbers in parentheses. Commit-

Table 10.1

Institutional Characteristics of Committees in the Nordic Parliaments

	Danish Folketing	Finnish Eduskunta	Icelandic Althingi	Norwegian Storting	Swedish Riksdag
Number of standing committees	24[a] (4)	12 (3)	13[b] (3)	12 (3)	16 (3)
Size of committees (mean number of members)	17 (3)	17 (3)	9 (4)	14 (3)	17 (3)
Do committees correlate with government ministers?	yes, roughly (3)	yes roughly (3)	yes, roughly (3)	yes, roughly (3)	yes, roughly (3)
Are committees organized according to subject matter?	yes (4)	yes, mostly (3)	yes (4)	yes (4)	yes (4)
Do committee delib. take place before or after plenary stage?	after (1)	before (4)	after (1)	before (4)	before (4)
Are the committee preparations compulsory?	no (1)	yes (4)	yes, according to praxis (3)	no (1)	yes (4)
Are committee reports on all bills compulsory?	no (4)	yes (1)	no (4)	no (4)	yes (1)
Are regular committee meetings open or closed?	closed, except to ministers (3)	closed, except to ministers (3)	closed (4)	closed (4)	closed (4)
Can committees divide or merge bills?	no (1)	yes (4)	yes (4)	yes (4)	yes (4)
Can committees change bills or make amendments of similar value?	yes (4)	yes (4)	yes (4)	yes (4)	yes (4)
Do committees tend to use the right to make changes in bills?	yes (4)	yes (4)	yes (4)	yes (4)	yes (4)
Can committees initiate bills?	no (1)	no, except 2 committees (2)	yes (4)	no (1)	yes (4)
Can the chamber recall bills after they are sent to committee?	no (4)	yes, according to praxis (2)	no, not according to praxis (3)	yes (1)	no (4)

Continued

Table 10.1
Continued

	Danish Folketing	Finnish Eduskunta	Icelandic Althingi	Norwegian Storting	Swedish Riksdag
Are members forbidden to serve on more than one committee?	no (1)	no (1)	no (1)	yes (4)	no, only informally (2)
Do committees choose their own committee chairman and vice-chairman?	no (1)	no, only formally (2)	no, only formally (2)	no, only formally (2)	no, only formally (2)
Are committee chairmen allocated to parties by majority or proportionally?	proportionally (4)	proportionally (4)	by majority, except 3 comms. (2)	proportionally (4)	proportionally (4)
Can committees call people to hearings?	yes, ministers (3)	no, only invite (2)	no, only invite (2)	no, only invite (2)	no, only invite (2)
Can committee hearings be open?	yes (4)	yes (4)	no (1)	yes (4)	yes (4)
Can committee order documents to be scrutinized?	yes (4)	no, only gov. documents (2)	yes (4)	yes (4)	no, only state documents (2)
Are dissenting opinions attached to ordinary committee reports?	yes (4)	yes (4)	yes (4)	yes (4)	yes (4)
Mean of committee importance	2.9	3.0	3.1	3.2	3.3

Notes: Points presented in parentheses indicate, on a scale reaching from 1 (weak) to 4 (strong), whether the characteristics promote strong or weak committees. Scale of strong or weak committee characteristic is constructed as follows: 1—results in weak committees with no exceptions; 2—results in weak committees with some exceptions; 3—results in strong committees with some exceptions; 4—results in strong committees with no exception. Information about relevant laws and praxis of parliamentary conduct was helpfully supplied by Erik Damgaard (the Danish Folketing), Tapio Raunio (the Finnish Eduskunta), Thorsteinn Magnusson (the Icelandic Althingi), and Knut Heidar (the Norwegian Storting). Cf. Mattson and Strøm (1995:261–91).

[a] Of the Danish Folketing committees, two do not perform legislative functions.

[b] Of the Icelandic Althingi committees, one does not perform legislative functions.

tee characteristics are rated on a scale ranging from 1 (clearly promotes committee weakness) to 4 (clearly promotes committee strength).

David Arter (1984:169) argues that, if there are many specialized committees, each of which corresponds to a government ministry, the committees will tend to be strong; this is because such an arrangement encourages members to specialize and endows them with expertise. He claims as well that committee strength is promoted if meetings are closed and the number of committee members is limited: this on account of the confidential environment thereby created, wherein committee members can conduct negotiations and reach compromises. Shaw (1979:412–18) is more doubtful as to the importance of committee size but tends to agree with Arter. Committee importance is also promoted if committee preparation is compulsory and if the chamber cannot recall bills from committees. When committees are not required to report all bills to the chamber, it becomes possible to kill bills in committee; that is, committees can stop the further treatment of bills. The only Nordic committee system with this feature is found in the Althingi.

With these institutional characteristics in mind, we can rank the Nordic parliaments roughly in accordance with the importance of their committees. Committees are most important in the Riksdag, then (in descending order) in the Storting, the Althingi, and the Eduskunta. The institutional characteristics of the committee system in the Folketing suggest that committees are weaker in that body than in any other Nordic parliament.[7]

COMMITTEE POWER VERSUS PARTY-LEADERSHIP POWER

As already mentioned, more power for party group leaders is believed to mean less power for committees. Individual MPs are the actors in the clash between centralized decision-making by the party group leadership and decentralized decision-making in committees. It is important, if we are to understand the committee assignment process and the relevance of party loyalty, that we know how members of parliament perceive the power of committees and of party leaders. Do perceptions of the one affect perceptions of the other?

We asked Nordic parliamentarians to estimate the power of committees and of party leaders using an eleven-point scale ranging from 0 (very little influence) to 10 (very influential).[8] If members report relatively high power scores for committees, they will also—according to the hypothesis stated—report relatively low scores for party leaders. And vice versa.

Table 10.2

Members' Perceptions of the Actual Influence of Standing Committees and Parliamentary Party Leaders on Decision Making in Their Respective Parliament (average perceived influence)

Parliament	Committee	Party Leaders	Difference
Swedish Riksdag	76	76	00
Norwegian Storting	75	73	+02
Icelandic Althingi	68	79	−11
Finnish Eduskunta	66	80	−14
Danish Folketing	57	77	−20

Notes: Members were asked to rank the influence of committees and party leadership (along with six other bodies) on a scale reaching from 0 (very little influence) to 10 (very influential). The average perceived influence has been transformed to values between 0 and 100. The lowest number of respondents for each parliament is as follows: the Norwegian Storting (130), the Swedish Riksdag (265), the Icelandic Althingi (40), the Finnish Eduskunta (116), the Danish Folketing (97). The Swedish data are from a survey done in 1988.

Table 10.2 shows that, in parliaments where committees are perceived as relatively powerful, party leaders are perceived as somewhat less powerful. Nevertheless, it appears that the variations found among Nordic parliaments concern the power of committees more than that of party leaders. It may be of interest here, moreover, to compare tables 10.1 and 10.2. As seen in table 10.2, members subjectively rank the influence of committees in the same order that the institutional importance of committees is ranked in table 10.1. Indeed, according to Norwegian and Swedish MPs, the influence of committees is equal to that of party leaders.

Where perceived power is concerned, the contrast between the parliaments is greater with respect to committees than with respect to party leaders. The difference between the highest and lowest mean scores is +19 for committees and +07 for party leaders. We can use the difference between the mean power scores of committees and of party leaders in order to rank the parliaments according to relative influence of committees and of party leaders: the figure for the Storting is +02, for the Riksdag 00, for the Althingi −11, for the Eduskunta −14, and for the Folketing −20. This indicates that committees play a more important role in the distribution of power in the Storting and the Riksdag than in the other Nordic parliaments.

If committees are powerful, it may be interesting to see how they are perceived by MPs, as well as how heavy the competition for committee seats is. We shall, accordingly, focus on the structure of the Nordic committee systems, as well as on the committee preferences of members.

COMMITTEE OPPORTUNITY STRUCTURE

The collective committee preferences of MPs indicate the committee seats for which competition is heavy. There are both positive and negative preferences for committees. A committee preference is positive if it refers to a committee on which a member wishes to serve, negative if it refers to a committee on which a member does not wish to serve. If MPs hold similar committee preferences, the competition for attractive committee assignments is higher than if their preferences are distributed more evenly among the committees. It is difficult to receive a committee assignment on a highly preferred committee (that is, a committee that gathers many positive and few negative committee preferences). It is quite easy, by contrast, to land an assignment on a nonpreferred committee (that is, a committee that gathers many negative and few positive committee preferences). This is why the sum of the members' committee preferences is called the committee opportunity structure (Rohde and Shepsle 1973: 892–93).

We measured positive committee preferences by putting the following question to Nordic parliamentarians: "Given a free choice, of which parliamentary committee would you most like to be a member?" We measured negative committee preferences by asking: "Of which parliamentary committee are you *least* interested in becoming a member?" From this, we obtained the opportunity structures of the committee systems in the Nordic parliaments. They are pictured in table 10.3.[9]

Committees that gather many negative preferences tend also to gather few positive ones, which is scarcely surprising. Among the sixty-five Nordic standing committees examined in all, however, the correlation is weaker than might be suspected ($r = -0.28$). It also varies between the parliaments. It is strong in the Storting ($r = -0.58$) and the Riksdag ($r = -0.58$) but weaker in the Althingi ($r = -0.36$), and it is especially weak in the Folketing ($r = -0.20$). One reason for this is that the number of committees provoking both few positive feelings and few negative ones is relatively high in the Folketing and the Althingi.

In all of the Nordic parliaments, the committees that handle foreign affairs and financial and budgetary tasks are highly preferred. The Danish Foreign Affairs Committee is the exception; in the Folketing, the European Affairs Committee is most preferred (20 percent). Among Danish MPs, moreover, the Justice Committee is preferred to an extent unusual in Nordic politics (12 percent). It would appear that the socioeconomic structure of the different countries finds expression in the preferences of

Table 10.3
Members' Positive and Negative Committee Preferences (%)

Danish Folketing Committees	Positive	Negative	Icelandic Althingi Committees	Positive	Negative
European Affairs	20	1	Economic and Trade	32	3
Justice	12	1	Budget	21	9
Finance	12	0	Foreign Affairs	16	0
Environment and Regional Planning	9	0	Fisheries	11	0
Agriculture and Fisheries	8	9	Health and Social Security	8	9
Labor Market	6	0	Transport and Communication	5	3
Social Affairs	6	2	Education	3	0
Political Economy	5	0	Industry	3	3
Education	5	0	Environment	3	6
Taxation	3	15	Credentials	0	0
Foreign Affairs	2	2	Social Affairs	0	19
Cultural Affairs	2	1	General	0	19
Health	2	1	Agriculture	0	28
Energy	2	0			
Labor Force	2	0			
Science	2	0			
Standing Orders	0	0			
Transport and Communication	0	1			
Defense	0	2			
Municipal Affairs	0	2			
Credentials	0	2			
Housing	0	5			

	Positive	Negative
Immigration	0	5
Church	0	49
Total	102	99
No. of Respondents	38	32

Swedish Riksdag Committees	Positive	Negative
Finance	15	1
Industry and Trade	11	1
Foreign Affairs	10	1
Health and Welfare	8	2
Agriculture	8	10
Labor Market	7	0
Education	7	1
Transport and Communication	7	2
Cultural Affairs	5	8
Taxation	4	3
Social Insurance	4	5
Justice	4	6
Constitution	4	7
Defense	4	8
Housing	2	9
Civil Law	1	36
Total	101	100
No. of Respondents	308	289

Norwegian Storting Committees	Positive	Negative
Finance	17	2
Industry and Trade	16	0
Foreign Affairs	14	0
Energy and Environment	10	1
Social	10	6
Transport and Communication	9	3
Church and Education	6	5
Family and Culture	5	8
Defense	5	20
Justice	4	10
Municipal Affairs	3	2
Control and Constitution	2	43
Total	101	100
No. of Respondents	133	131

Notes: Respondents were asked the following two questions: "Given a free choice, of which standing committee would you most like to be a member?" (positive committee preference); "Of which standing committee are you *least* interested in becoming a member?" (negative committee preference).

MPs. This is especially clear in the case of the Riksdag and the Althingi: 11 percent of MPs in the former prefer the Industry and Trade Committee; 11 percent of MPs in the latter prefer the Fisheries Committee.

In contrast to the most preferred committees, the least preferred committees are more heterogeneous in terms of their jurisdiction. Yet, within each parliament, members tend to agree on which committee is least to be preferred. The least-preferred Nordic committee is the Danish Church Committee, followed by the Norwegian Control and Constitution Committee (which scrutinizes the government). Negative preferences for the former come to 46 percent, and for the latter 44 percent. The Swedish Civil Law Committee—the only Riksdag committee with no budgetary tasks—is rejected by 36 percent of members. In the Althingi, the Agriculture Committee is least preferred by 28 percent of members; however, both the General Committee (which handles matters not falling within the jurisdiction of the other committees) and the Social Affairs Committee collect as many as 19 percent of the negative committee preferences.

Supply of Committee Seats

Nordic parliaments exhibit considerable variation in their supply of committee seats. In the Riksdag, the ratio between the number of parliamentary members and the number of committee seats (the committee seat ratio) is as low as 0.78. In the Storting, the committee seat ratio is 1.00, which means that every MP is guaranteed a committee seat. Even higher committee seat ratios are found in the other Nordic parliaments: 1.25 in the Eduskunta, 1.92 in the Althingi, and 2.27 in the Folketing. A high committee seat ratio makes it possible to accommodate more of the committee preferences of members.

Another important institutional factor affecting committee-preference accommodation is committee size. The manipulation of committee size is often considered a result of pressure on the party group leadership to accommodate the committee preferences of members (Westefield 1974: 1595; Eulau 1985:196–202). Only in the Riksdag and the Folketing is every committee of equal size. The variation in the size of committees in the other Nordic parliaments is not random. Committees preferred by many MPs tend to be larger than average. This is most obvious in the Norwegian committee system, where the correlation between committee preferences and committee size is strong ($r = 0.90$). This tendency is also found, however, in the Althingi ($r = 0.41$).

We may conclude that MPs compete for favorable assignments. We know as well that Nordic representatives connect committees with power.

Table 10.4
Committee Preference Accommodation in Nordic Parliaments (%)

	Accommodated Committee Preferences			
Parliament	Yes	No	Total	N
Danish Folketing	71	29	100	66
Icelandic Althingi	63	37	100	38
Norwegian Storting	59	41	100	133
Swedish Riksdag	49	51	100	308

If committees are associated with influence, it becomes reasonable to ask whether individual members can obtain committee seats independently of their loyalty toward their party group leadership, or whether instead they are totally controlled by the latter. Our next question is therefore: to what extent are committee assignments controlled by party group leaders?

COMMITTEE-PREFERENCE ACCOMMODATION

In what way do party leaders accommodate the committee preferences of members? The answer in part reveals the extent to which MPs' own preferences affect their committee assignments. If committee-preference accommodation is important, this is an indication that MPs select themselves in a high degree. If committee preferences are unimportant, this suggests that party group leaders assign members as they please and that party loyalty is an important criterion for committee assignments. Table 10.4 shows the degree to which the committee preferences of Nordic MPs are accommodated.[10] It reports the percentage of MPs who are full members of their most preferred committee; that is, the committee-preference accommodation rate.

Usually, more than half the committee preferences of Nordic MPs are accommodated. According to table 10.4, the committee-preference accommodation rate co-varies with the committee seat ratio. The highest committee-preference accommodation rate—71 percent—is found in the parliament with the highest committee seat ratio, the Folketing. By contrast, only 49 percent of committee preferences are accommodated in the Riksdag, which also is the parliament with the lowest committee seat ratio.

Not all Riksdag members have a full committee membership. If we disregard the committee structure and consider only the full committee members of the Riksdag, the percent of accommodated committee members is higher—indeed, on a level similar to that in the other Nordic parliaments:

61 percent. It appears that the committee opportunity structure is less crucial to preference accommodation than is the committee seat ratio. There is no correlation between committee opportunity structure and preference accommodation. However, the effect of the committee seat ratio on committee preference accommodation is not negligible.

Most of the committee preferences of Nordic committee members are accommodated. This supports the proposition that individual MPs themselves select their committee assignments. Yet this is not enough. How are they assigned?

THE PRINCIPLE OF SENIORITY

The proposition that individual members select themselves is supported if the principle of seniority is used to assign members to committees. The principle of seniority also makes it difficult for party group leaders to reward party loyalty among individual members. When the principle of seniority is mentioned in connection with Nordic parliaments, it refers to parliamentary seniority—that is, to the total number of sessions a member of parliament has attended. If seniority is important during the committee assignment process, the wishes of more senior members ought to be accommodated more frequently than those of freshman or junior members are. Large differences in the rate at which the committee preferences of freshman, junior, senior, and veteran MPs are accommodated mean that the principle of seniority is relatively important. The committee accommodation rate according to seniority is shown in table 10.5.

Table 10.5 shows important variation among Nordic parliaments in the significance of seniority. Only in the Riksdag and the Folketing is seniority obviously important: it is clear that, as time goes by, the committee preferences of Riksdag and Folketing members are accommodated to a considerable extent.[11] In the Norwegian parliament, by contrast, the impact of seniority is quite modest, while in the Althingi it is altogether absent.

According to the theory presented above, this accommodation of seniors in the Riksdag and the Folketing ought to have two effects. First, the leaders of the parliamentary parties in Sweden and Denmark ought to enjoy less control and room for maneuver than their counterparts in the other Nordic countries. Second, the party group leadership in the Riksdag and the Folketing should control freshman and junior members more than they do veterans and senior members; in the other Nordic parliaments, meanwhile, this tendency ought to be weaker or absent altogether.

Table 10.5
Seniority and Committee Preference Accommodation in Nordic Parliaments (% accommodated committee preferences)

Seniority	Danish Folketing	Icelandic Althingi	Norwegian Storting	Swedish Riksdag
9– (high)	88	62	69	73
5–8 (middle)	77	73	57	57
0–4 (low)	65	57	56	32
Difference	+23	+5	+13	+41

Party Loyalty

The only party goal that can be distinguished from the goals of individual members is party cohesion (see above). Party group leaders ought to have an incentive to promote what they regard as party-loyal members. It would appear that the goal of party cohesion conflicts with the principle of seniority. When the latter norm is fully operative, members of parliament are promoted irrespective of their party loyalty or opinions.

According to the principle of seniority, self-selection is more a concern for members with long parliamentary experience—so-called parliamentary veterans—than for newly elected members (meaning parliamentary freshmen as well as junior members with not more than four sessions of experience). This means that party group leaders are freer to act in accordance with their wishes when assigning newly elected members to committees than when assigning parliamentary veterans. If they want to promote party loyalty, and if seniority is important, their prospects are better among freshmen and junior members. Therefore, if party group leaders try to promote party loyalty, this ought to be more visible among newly elected members than among veterans. If the principle of seniority is strong, party group leaders have less room for maneuver. They cannot do as they wish; they cannot reward party loyalty among parliamentary veterans without constraint.

The kind of party loyalty in which we are interested concerns the extent to which individual members are loyal toward their leaders. One possibly helpful way of operationalizing such party loyalty is to measure the opinion distance between individual members and party group leaders (Hagevi 1995:95–106, 138–42). The concept of opinion distance is used to describe the degree to which political opinion within a party is uniform (Valen 1990:17; Oscarsson 1994:142–4). If party loyalty is important, party group leaders will wish committee members to hold opinions resembling their own.

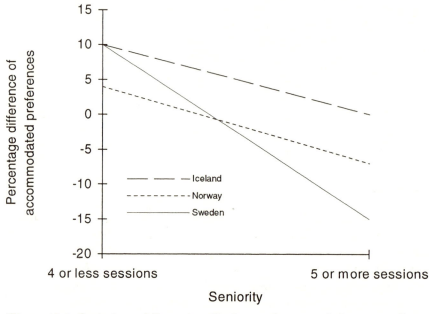

Figure 10.1 Seniority and Committee Preference Accommodation among Super-loyalists and Party Mavericks (% of superloyalists minus % of mavericks who are serving on their preferred committee). Members' committee preferences were measured as in table 10.3. Other coding details are in the appendix to this chapter.

Members of parliament were asked their opinion of the parties within their own parliament. Members whose opinions resemble those of their party group leaders are considered party-loyal. Three categories may be distinguished: superloyalists, loyalists, and mavericks (Davidson 1969: 143–62; see appendix for coding details).

The empirical test of the hypothesis is as follows. If the principle of seniority is important, the committee preferences of freshman and junior members who are superloyalist ought to be accommodated more frequently than the committee preferences of their maverick counterparts. Among veterans, party loyalty should not matter. This pattern should manifest itself most clearly in the Riksdag, since the principle of seniority is strongest in that body. Conversely, we would expect the effect of seniority on the importance of party loyalty to be weakest in the Althingi. Figure 10.1 shows the difference in committee preference accommodation between superloyalists and mavericks in three of the Nordic parliaments.[12]

Attempts on the part of party group leaders to promote party loyalty with the help of committee assignments are most constrained by seniority in the Riksdag and second most constrained in the Storting. In the three parliaments here considered, however, party leaders place a greater stress on party loyalty when assigning newly elected members to committees than when assigning their more senior colleagues. When newly elected members are assigned, the principle of seniority does not afford them the same protection. This means that party group leaders not only have the opportunity to demand party loyalty from newly elected members; they also try to enforce it. Among newly elected members, superloyalists find their committee preferences accommodated more often than do their maverick colleagues. Still, the pattern of seniority protection is strongest in the Riksdag, as predicted. In fact, the committee preferences of Swedish veteran mavericks are accommodated more often than are those of veteran Swedish superloyalists.

CONCLUSIONS

Where standing committees in the Nordic parliaments are concerned, parliamentary institutions are important. Nordic parliamentarians tend to get their preferred committee assignment. To a considerable extent, in fact, some of them choose their own committee assignment. An important reason for this is the principle of seniority. This principle is strongest in the Riksdag, but it has at least some importance in the committee assignment process in all of the Nordic parliaments except the Althingi. The principle of seniority is especially helpful for parliamentary veterans. When it is operative, they tend to get their preferred committee assignment irrespective of the degree to which they are loyal toward their leaders. However, party group leaders enjoy better prospects for promoting party-loyal attitudes when assigning newly elected members to committees. Party group leaders take this opportunity, moreover; indeed, they actually promote loyal MPs among newly elected members in a higher proportion than among parliamentary veterans.

The stronger the principle of seniority, the more constrained are party group leaders when assigning committee seats. This pattern is clearest where the principle of seniority is relatively strong, as in the Riksdag, and less clear where it is weaker, as in the Althingi. We may conclude that, even if the principle of seniority is not absolute, it still matters. This is, after all, a question of degree. The emphasis on reward and punishment in earlier studies of committee assignments would appear to be overdone. The results show that the committee assignment process in democracies with a parliamentary system need not be entirely controlled by party leaders. A committee assignment can therefore be a position of influence for individual members and not just a reward for party loyalists.

These results highlight an oft-neglected part of the representative process in parliamentary systems: the individual parliamentarian. If individuals are able to attain a valuable and powerful committee assignment without caving in to the leaders of their party group, then the decision-making process within parliamentary party groups might be more decentralized than is usually appreciated.

Where standing committees in the Nordic parliaments are concerned, parliamentary institutions are important. The standing committees—especially in the Riksdag and the Storting—distance the Nordic assemblies from the Westminster ideal, demonstrating that they belong to a Continental tradition that is closer to the congressional system of the United States.

APPENDIX

The party loyalty index consists of a set of questions asked in Nordleg questionnaires: *"Where would you personally locate the different political parties on the following scale?"* An eleven-point scale is presented to the members. It ranges from −5 ("dislike strongly") to +5 (*like strongly*). The 0-position is marked with *"neither like nor dislike."* The respondent got the opportunity to indicate where on this scale he or she perceived each parliamentary party. These answers are called the *party opinions*. The party-loyalty index consists of party opinions on the current parties in the parliament of the individual member.

The party-loyalty index is the summarized distance between the private members' party opinions and the party opinions of the party group leadership (the steering committee). The party opinion of the party group leadership is calculated by summarizing the party opinions of all party group leadership members and then calculating the mean. The next step is to obtain the party opinion distance between private members and the mean of the party group leadership. The absolute difference between the private members' party opinion on a particular party and the mean party opinion of the party group leadership on the same party is calculated. The same procedure is repeated regarding all party opinions on every party. The absolute differences are summarized for each private member, which is the party loyalty score for that member.

The 25 percent of members most similar to the party group leadership (those with the smallest deviation from the party group leadership) are called superloyalists. The 25 percent of members most dissimilar from the party group leadership (those with the largest deviation from the party group leadership) are called mavericks. The 50 percent between these groups are called loyalists.

NOTES

1. Perhaps the most famous innovation of the newly formed Constitution Committee was the creation of the Parliamentary Ombudsman. The results of the Swedish-Russian war affected parliamentary history in two other Nordic countries as well. Russia seized Finland from Sweden, and the Tsar granted Finland a parliament of its own. After the losses in the east, the new Swedish king campaigned in the west, invading Denmark and abolishing that country's union with Norway. Norway was then forced into a new union with Sweden, but only after its own parliament—the Storting—had been established.

2. Of 105 committee reports in the Swedish Riksdag during 1971–88, only 4 percent featured breaks with party cohesion (Sjölin 1993:96.)

3. For applications of Fenno, see Perkins (1980); Smith and Deering (1983; 1984:83–124); Bullock (1976; 1985:794–99); and for discussion, see Smith (1986).

4. For discussion and investigation of the reward theory in the United States, see Master (1961:351, 356); Rohde and Shepsle (1973:900–904); Francis (1985: 243–44); and Cox and McCubbins (1993). For the European discussion, see Damgaard (1995:318–21). For Norway, see Hellevik (1969:123); and Hernes (1973:23–25; 1977:295–97). For Sweden, see Stjernquist (1966:322–23); Gahrton (1983:262–80); Isberg (1984:24–27, 33); Hagevi (1995; 1998:187–214).

5. On the Norwegian Storting, the following studies deal with committee assignments: Hellevik (1969); Hernes (1971; 1973; 1977); Skard (1980:132–50); Sandberg (1992); Skjeie (1992:123–33). Stjernquist (1966); Gustafsson and Carlsson (1968); Andersson (1984); Hagevi (1993; 1994; 1997; 1998). Wängnerud (1997) and Olson and Hagevi (1998) report on assignments to committees in the Swedish Riksdag. Studies on committee assignments in the Danish Folketing have been done by Damgaard (1977; 1979; 1982a; 1995); Refsgaard (1990:108–16); and H. Jensen (1995:59–64). Anckar (1972) and Magnusson (1987) have done studies on committee assignments in the Finnish Eduskunta and the Icelandic Althingi, respectively.

6. Committee seniority is the ranking of members by party according to their consecutive service on the committee in question (Hinckley 1971:4; cf. Goodwin 1970:94). It has little importance in the Nordic parliaments (Olsen 1983:59–60; Hagevi 1994:186–88). In the Swedish Riksdag, it is more common that members of the presidency are recruited from outside the committee than from among committee members.

7. Although the Danish committee system would seem to be of the weaker sort, some of its units may be regarded as fairly strong, e.g., the Market Relations Committee (cf. chapter 14 in this volume).

8. The question reads as follows (see also chapters 8 and 9 in this volume): "Using the scale below, please state your view of the following two aspects of influence—on the part of the groups and bodies given below—over decision-making in parliament: a) their actual influence, b) the influence you would consider appropriate." The data from the Swedish Riksdag have been reported by Esaiasson and Holmberg (1996:215–35).

9. Could the responses of members be rationalizations after the fact, i.e., do some members report their committee assignment as their preferred one, even if it really was not at the outset? Do members tend to abandon their committee preferences if they are not met? To test this, we need panel data. Fortunately, the question of committee preferences was put to Swedish Riksdag members in 1985, 1988, and 1994. The results show that members tend to be persistent; they do not change their committee preferences readily (Hagevi 1998). This indicates that most members actually state their preferred committee and do not offer rationalizations after the fact.

10. Data on committee preferences are not available for the Finnish Eduskunta.

11. It should be noted that while the principle of seniority is strong, it is not absolute. During the period in question, it was commonly the case that somewhat over 15 percent of Riksdag committee seats were assigned in violation of seniority (Hagevi 1997).

12. Data on party loyalty are not available for the Danish Folketing and the Finnish Eduskunta.

DEALING WITH OTHER INSTITUTIONS: HORIZONTAL RELATIONS

11

Parliament and Government

Erik Damgaard

The comparative literature on legislatures and legislative systems contains a considerable number of typologies and classifications designed to highlight important similarities and differences among national parliaments in their native political settings (e.g., Blondel 1973; Polsby 1975; Loewenberg and Patterson 1979; Mezey 1979; Norton 1990a). Such classifications often aim at measuring the political strength, power, or influence of parliaments, usually by focusing on the relationship between parliament and government in policy-making terms. The basic question asked, albeit formulated in different ways, seems to be: "How strong is the legislature in relation to the executive?"

There has been a tendency, in the field of legislative studies, to regard the U.S. Congress as the only "real" legislature, compared with which European parliaments possess only modest influence (see Mezey 1979; Mann 1986). In Mezey's terms, European parliaments are not really "active" but only "reactive" (since they essentially react to whatever the executive proposes), and their policy-making power is modest. Philip Norton (1990b), who surveyed the development of seven parliaments in western Europe as described by various country experts, concluded that the parliaments of Britain, France, Italy, Germany, Ireland, the Netherlands, and Sweden were still "reactive." He claimed further that they had not declined over the past two decades. He might as well have concluded that a few of the parliaments in question had actually gained influence over the past two decades.

With the not always very solid evidence available, it can sometimes be quite hard to place individual parliaments in the classifications proposed (Damgaard 1992c). Such difficulties may ultimately be due to an inappropriate conceptualization of executive-legislative relations. There is

265

certainly still a tendency to conceive of "the" parliament as a unitary actor versus "the" executive or government.

The purpose of this chapter is to look closely into some ways of conceptualizing the relationship between parliaments and governments which may prove promising, and to present some empirical evidence from parliamentary surveys of the Nordic countries.

The following section reviews recent attempts at conceptualizing executive-legislative relations, and subsequent sections present new evidence on the relationship between governments and parliaments in the Nordic countries. Such an effort is long overdue in research on parliaments in democratic multiparty systems based on proportional representation and cabinet responsibility. The U.S. and British systems of democratic governance are not appropriate as general models in this field of academic studies.

MODES OF EXECUTIVE-LEGISLATIVE RELATIONS

Some twenty years ago, Anthony King published what turned out to be a seminal lead article in the very first issue of the *Legislative Studies Quarterly* (King 1976). King argued that it is usually highly misleading to speak of "executive-legislative relations" *tout court,* and that a number of quite distinct relationships under that heading must be analytically separated and empirically investigated. We must "think behind" the "Montesquieu formula" to understand the realities of modern parliamentary politics, he argued. King looked mainly at Britain, but France and (West) Germany also figured in his analysis.

To understand British politics, one must, according to King, distinguish between at least three quite distinct patterns of interaction, or "modes of executive-legislative relations," to wit: (1) the "intraparty" mode, (2) the "opposition" mode, and (3) the "nonparty" or "Private Members" mode. The first relates to conflicts within parties (such as between government ministers and backbenchers, or even between different groupings in the extraparliamentary party). The second refers to conflicts between the government and opposition parties, and the third to conflicts between the government and backbenchers from the governing party and opposition parties. King found that, in British politics, the intraparty mode was the most important of the three, although the opposition mode was important also: "If the intra-party mode can be likened to a marriage (however stormy at times), the opposition mode resembles a war-game" (1976:18).

King found that the intraparty mode was the most important one in France as well, whereas a fourth "inter-party" mode was crucial in Germany, because bargaining among political parties in that country determined which parties would combine to form a government. In addition, a fifth "cross-party mode," operating within fairly important and specialized parliamentary committees with jurisdiction over certain policy areas, was quite significant in the Federal Republic, at any rate, as compared with the situation in Britain and France.

King's article is still worth reading, for several reasons. First, because it forcefully argues that the dualism between government and parliament had come to an end with the development of mass parties and parliamentary systems in twentieth-century western Europe (this notwithstanding the fact that political and academic writings on parliamentary politics continued to assume this dualism). Second, and no less significantly, the article indicates a more adequate way of looking at the relationship between members of parliament in government and MPs outside of government. It is further to be noted that, according to King, the British situation is less complex than, for example, that of Germany. Finally, it is worth mentioning that King ends his article by emphasizing that "the present paper has considered neither a political system in which minority governments are the norm, nor a system with a true separation-of-powers constitution" (1976:32). Aside from the slightly veiled reference to the United States, this quotation indicates that political realities in other countries might be even more complex than those described in King's article. This is certainly the case in some Nordic systems in which minority governments are frequently formed.

Quite a few scholars in western Europe have drawn inspiration from King's analysis. Thus, Thomas Saalfeld (1990) uses the four modes that King found relevant to Germany (interparty, intraparty, opposition, cross-party) to organize his analysis of the role of the German Bundestag in the postwar period. He finds that the intraparty and interparty modes have placed the most important restrictions on the activities of German governments, whereas the cross-party mode is only of secondary importance.

In an article dealing with parliamentary politics in the Netherlands, Rudy Andeweg (1992) concludes that King's classification must be modified. Like King, Andeweg speaks of nonparty, intraparty, and cross-party modes. But Andeweg subsumes King's opposition mode within a more general interparty mode, which thus consists of two "sub-modes": the opposition mode, "in which ministers and MPs of the governing majority confront opposition MPs," and the "intra-coalition mode," in which "ministers and MPs of one governing party interact with ministers and MPs of another governing party." The latter pattern reflects the circumstance that the Netherlands is invariably governed by two or more parties (1992:163).

The historical development of parliamentary politics in the Netherlands since 1848 has consisted, according to Andeweg, of a progression from the nonparty through the intraparty to the interparty mode (with the last-mentioned having been dominant since the 1960s). Andeweg also maintains, however, that a cross-party mode exists in connection with the rather strong specialized committees of the Dutch parliament. He claims, in fact, that all five modes are still relevant in the Netherlands. He suggests that the Dutch parliament be regarded as a "gear box" that can shift modes according to the issues and interests at hand.

Wolfgang C. Müller (1993) notes a certain difference between King and Andeweg in their understanding of the modes of executive-legislative relations: "In establishing the relative importance of the modes, King takes the angle from the government: the relationship that is most important for the government's survival is the most important one. In contrast, Andeweg takes the angle from the political system: the most conflictual relationship is the most important one" (490). Müller is probably right, but both procedures may of course serve sensible purposes.

In an analysis of the Austrian case, Müller prefers to treat the relationship within the government bloc under one heading, and to use the term "intra-government mode" for these relations, which include interactions between ministers and MPs of the government party or parties. Since Müller also mentions the nonparty, opposition, and cross-party modes, this decision implies that the intragovernment mode encompasses intraparty relations and such interparty interactions as involve only government parties.

Although, according to Müller, some examples of the nonparty and cross-party modes may be found in postwar Austria, the intragovernment and opposition modes are certainly the most important ones. Müller also notes a peculiar form of opposition, known as "Bereichsopposition," which arises when a coalition forms the government: thus, members of one government party may criticize ministers from another government party, although all are supposed to display governmental solidarity.

In a comparative perspective, it is interesting that the opposition mode is generally found to be more important in Austria—especially under the distinctive type of minority government that prevailed in that country from 1970 to 1971—than in the countries studied by King and Andeweg. As mentioned above, King did not consider such governments, and in the

Dutch case Andeweg could simply note: "By definition, the opposition is a minority and therefore powerless except for the rare occasions when a wedge can be driven between the governing parties" (1992:168).

Rudy Andeweg and Lia Nijzink (1995) have given further thought to the conceptualization of executive-legislative relations. They repeat King's message on the need to look beyond "the two-body image." They claim that three modes, rather than the five originally suggested by King, are necessary and sufficient for analyzing the parliamentary systems of western Europe. The three modes basically correspond to those defined by Andeweg in his 1992 article (cf. also Kopecký and Nijzink 1995), except that the intraparty mode appears to have disappeared as a distinct category (or perhaps it is included in the intracoalition mode?). In any case, the three main patterns of interaction are each illustrated by an appropriate image of parliament:

1. "The" parliament as an "institution" versus "the" government (that is, the nonparty mode corresponding to the two-body image).
2. Parliament as an "arena" for struggle (and presumably cooperation?) between political parties (that is, the interparty mode, including an intracoalition mode and an opposition mode).
3. Parliament as a "marketplace" for competition among various special interests (that is, the cross-party mode).

To obtain evidence for the three patterns of interaction, Andeweg and Nijzink have collected information on institutional norms and practices in eighteen west European countries. They conclude that the three modes coexist in the parliament/government complex, and they speculate a bit (1995:174–75) about reasons for this coexistence. Parliamentary specialization could be one of the explanations, they think: some MPs may act primarily as party representatives, others may in the main represent social interests, and still others may behave as "true" parliamentarians (according to the classic two-body image) with ministers as their main opponents. Another explanation could be that MPs shift from one mode to another according to the issues and problems at stake. On highly controversial issues, therefore, MPs can be expected to operate within the interparty mode. If legislative oversight is crucial, or if parliament as an institution is involved, MPs may shift to the nonparty mode. If, finally, policy-oriented, technocratic, or regional issues are on the agenda, the cross-party mode may be preferred by most MPs.

More recently, Andeweg has argued that the three modes incorporate distinct representational roles at the individual level:

in the non-party mode, the MP sees his role as a 'parliamentarian,' feels loyalty to the institution of parliament, representing 'the' people . . .; in the inter-party mode, the MP sees himself as a 'partisan,' loyal to his political party and its programme, representing his party's voters . . .; and in the cross-party mode, an MP defines his role as an 'advocate,' representing a particular regional or sectoral (but non-partisan) interest. (1997:116)

To a certain extent, these roles correspond to the backbench roles identified (more inductively) by Donald Searing (1994), in his study of the British House of Commons. At least according to Andeweg (1997), the "advocate" is strikingly similar to Searing's "policy advocate," and the "parliamentarian" is just as close to Searing's "parliament man." Otherwise the two typologies differ somewhat, presumably owing to the different approaches selected by the two authors.

The purpose of the following sections is to investigate, against the background of the above review, the various modes characterizing relations between parliament and government in the Nordic countries. To what extent does a focus on such modes enhance our understanding of how Nordic parliamentary systems actually work?

A mode of executive-legislative relations is defined as a distinct pattern of interaction—one involving cooperation as well as conflict—among MPs and government ministers. We shall look at parliament as institution (the nonparty mode), intraparty relations, the cross-party mode (the marketplace image), and the interparty mode (the arena image). We know that parties play an important role in executive-legislative relations in the Nordic countries, but we would like to know how and to what extent. The nonparty and cross-party modes are not based on parties at all; the intra- and interparty modes are both party-based, but in different ways.

Figure 11.1 may help to clarify the relevant distinctions. In the following four sections, we shall explore the relevance of each of the four modes, by means of the information and indicators available.

PARLIAMENT VERSUS GOVERNMENT (THE NONPARTY MODE)

One would not expect the nonparty mode to be very significant, since the traditional two-body image ignores the role played by modern political parties. Yet one should not completely rule it out. King (1976:20) concluded that it was "the least important mode" at Westminster. Andeweg (1997) found that Dutch MPs still considered the role of "parliamentar-

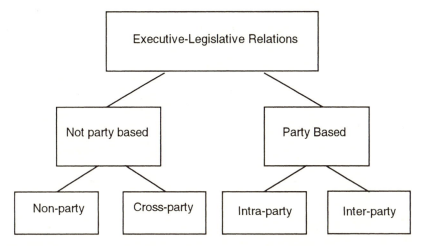

Figure 11.1 Four Modes of Executive-Legislative Relations

ian" the most appropriate one. The two-body image may not account for much of current Nordic "Realpolitik," but it remains a powerful symbol in political discourse nonetheless. Its historical roots lie in the early democratic development of the nineteenth century (cf. chapter 2), as well as in the theory of representative government. Even today, it is often used to buttress arguments to the benefit of "parliament" or of some of the parties represented in it (cf. Svensson 1996). Parties simply do not enjoy the same level of support or legitimacy as does parliament and democracy. Peter Esaiasson and Sören Holmberg (1996:233) conclude that, in Sweden, competition between the institutions of parliament and government is less visible than competition between parties, yet it remains an important factor to take into account.

Several questions in the Nordleg questionnaire contain the two-body terms of "parliament" and "government." It seems these questions at least make sense to MPs, although their answers may to some extent reflect wishful thinking. Thus, as shown in table 11.1, an overwhelming majority of MPs in all of the Nordic countries think their parliament should perform several important functions: these include, on the one hand, making the crucial decisions for the development of society at large, as well as taking the initiative on issues neglected by the government; and, on the other, scrutinizing the work of the government and its ministers, as well as serving as the central forum for political debate. Whether or not these tasks are actually performed is quite another matter, of course, but on the whole, MPs in both governing and opposition parties agree that they

Table 11.1

Members' View of the Importance of Parliamentary Tasks by Parliamentary Position of Party (% "very important" and "rather important")

Parliamentary Task	Denmark	Finland	Iceland	Norway	Sweden
Make crucial decisions					
Government party	100	100	100	100	99
Oppposition party	98	100	95	100	98
Take initiatives					
Government party	83	71	75	79	95
Opposition party	88	68	100	94	91
Control government					
Government party	92	98	100	79	86
Opposition party	98	91	95	95	96
Debating forum					
Government party	90	89	92	97	95
Opposoition party	87	100	74	95	93
Minimum N	48/59	79/31	24/19	61/85	155/176

Notes: The question was worded as follows: "How important do you personally consider the following tasks of parliament to be: to make the crucial decisions on large-scale societal developments; to take initiatives on issues that the government neglects; to oversee the work of the government and its ministers; to be the central forum for political debate?" The following response alternatives were offered: "very important"; "rather important"; "neither important nor unimportant"; "not very important"; "not at all important."

are very important or rather important. Finnish MPs, however, appear somewhat less likely than their Nordic colleagues to stress parliamentary initiative.

Nordic MPs also generally agree that their respective parliament and government are quite powerful, as compared to a number of other collective actors (cf. Hardarson, chapter 12). But when they are forced to choose in two-body image terms, they report that governments are more influential than parliaments and that it ought to be the other way round.

Interestingly, these general views are again held by members of both governing and opposition parties. Nor are there any major differences between MPs from the various party families, although there are some quite significant national variations. Finnish and Icelandic MPs, accordingly, report the power of the government to be far greater than that of the parliament. The only possible explanation for this difference lies in the fact that Finland and Iceland are usually ruled by majority coalition governments, whereas the dominant pattern in the other three Nordic countries is minority rule (cf. table 2.1, which shows majority rule occurring 95 percent of the time since 1971 in Finland and Iceland, and only 9–14 percent of the time in the other three countries). This finding clearly demonstrates that institutional practices do matter with respect to the working of representative democracy, even in cases where the party systems are fairly similar. In all of the Nordic countries, a government can be formed without a positive majority vote in parliament, since cabinet formation is based on "negative parliamentarism" (cf. Bergman 1995, and the contributions to Müller and Strøm 1997). But evidently the outcomes are different in practise.

Minority-government systems were not considered by Anthony King and others, but they clearly make a difference. One might even argue that they imply an element of the nonparty mode, inasmuch as minority governments do not control parliament at all, but are instead highly vulnerable and dependent on whatever certain opposition parties decide to do. The Swedish Liberal government of 1978–79, which faced four opposition parties, controlled just 11 percent of the seats in the Riksdag; and the Liberal Danish government of 1973–75, which faced nine opposition parties, commanded only 12 percent of the seats in the Folketing. These examples are admittedly extreme, but Danish (minority) governments between 1982 and 1993 were also defeated numerous times by parliamentary majorities in legislative voting (cf. Damgaard 1992b). Hilmar Rommetvedt (1997:100–103) reports on a similar development in Norway since the early 1980s.

Even during other minority-rule periods, however, and under majority governance as well, examples of the nonparty mode can be found in matters where the prestige or dignity of parliament is at stake (and MPs exhibit what Donald Matthews [1960:101–2] called "institutional patriotism"). Ministers, for example, must respect the rules and informal norms of parliamentary proceedings if they are to avoid being sanctioned (Damgaard 1987). Henrik Jensen (1995:31–33) shows that Danish cases can be found in which MPs from all parties publicly criticize a government minister, such cases are extremely rare.

It sometimes happens, finally, that MPs from both government and opposition parties are allowed a "free vote" in parliament. Although party discipline is the norm here, there are certain rare cases—with moral or religious aspects, typically—in which Nordic parliaments (and most other parliaments too, presumably) behave in accordance with the two-body image. In sum, the traditional image of the parliament confronting the government still has some symbolic power, but it is not, save in certain rare instances, an adequate rendering of parliamentary reality in the Nordic countries.

INTRAPARTY RELATIONS

Anthony King emphasized the intraparty mode because he was concerned with the need of governments to know that they could rely on the support of their own backbenchers. Such a concern is probably universal in parliamentary systems. Party discipline, cohesion, solidarity, loyalty—whatever the chosen expression—is needed to make the system work. This applies whether the government consists of a single party or of a coalition, and whether it commands a majority or only a minority.

As several legislative voting studies over the past three decades have shown, party discipline is indeed very high in the Nordic parliaments. This finds confirmation in Torben K. Jensen's analysis in chapter 9. Jensen adds that Nordic MPs are generally quite satisfied with the existing high levels of party cohesion. Those desiring change in this area want more discipline rather than less (Finnish MPs excepted). It is furthermore less than surprising, perhaps, that MPs from government parties in particular tend to think MPs should not say too much in public about internal party discussions.

In chapter 8, moreover, Knut Heidar shows that parliamentary party groups are very important in Nordic politics. He demonstrates as well that MPs generally consider parliamentary parties to be second only to governments in terms of influence on parliamentary decisions. Norwegian MPs even consider the parties to be more powerful than the government. Furthermore, although Peter Esaiasson emphasizes (in chapter 3) the various interests that MPs can promote in policy-making, he also finds that party looms largest—except possibly in Finland—in the representational self-conception of parliamentarians. In chapter 10, finally, Magnus Hagevi shows the party leadership is generally as influential as the committees are—even more influential, in fact.

The overall message from these findings is that MPs do not just accept the role of parties in directing parliamentary work; they also value it. How is it, then, that party discipline is voluntary and not forced on MPs? Broadly speaking, there are at least two good explanations. One is that MPs live in a party world to which they have been socialized. They share the basic ideology, goals, and interests of their party. According to such a cultural or sociological interpretation, MPs know that they, as individuals, are only members of a larger enterprise, not its directors. They take part in parliamentary politics, but they do not claim to be Burkean trustees (although they may pay lip service to liberal theories of representation). They know that party governments are needed for political solutions to society's problems.

The other explanation is just as persuasive. One may assume that MPs

Table 11.2

Members' Self-Reported Personal Contacts with Government Ministers by Parliamentary Position of Party (%)

Frequency	Denmark	Finland	Iceland	Norway	Sweden
Government party					
At least weekly	89	80	92	87	24
Once or twice a month	9	11	8	12	38
Opposition party					
At least weekly	40	34	16	13	29
Once or twice a month	47	41	42	63	33
No. of respondents	42/57	79/32	24/19	60/82	152/170

Notes: The question was worded as follows: "Disregarding how the contact were initiated, during the past year, how often have you personally been in written or oral contact with the following organizations, organized groups, and state authorities?" "Government ministers" were included as one of about twenty items. The following response alternatives were given: "at least once a week"; "once or twice a month"; "a few times"; "occasionally"; "never."

behave as rational individuals. As such, they pursue their own personal goals in a party setting that constrains their behavior. MPs want not just to be re-elected (cf. Mayhew 1974), but also to advance within the party hierarchy. They strive to occupy leading positions in parliament and government. Parties as collective actors, moreover, usually seek government office and/or policy influence (Laver and Schofield 1991). The fulfillment of both sets of goals requires, in a parliamentary system of government, a rather high level of party discipline and loyalty (Damgaard 1995).

The daily work of Nordic parliaments reflects the importance of parties in many ways, apart from cohesion in legislative voting. Government ministers, for example, cannot function effectively unless they retain a good relationship with their parliamentary party. Whether ministers are members of parliament or not, they participate as prominent actors in regular party group meetings (cf. Heidar, chapter 8). Heidar (tables 8.2 and 8.3) also shows that party support is far more important than are party leadership contacts, as far as influence on decisions in the party group is concerned. Nordic parliamentary parties are probably more egalitarian than their counterparts in Westminster, but the Finnish and Icelandic parties seem somewhat closer to the centralized party group model than the Danish, Norwegian, and Swedish parties (cf. also tables 8.7 and 8.8).

Most Nordic MPs have regular contacts with government ministers, as shown in table 11.2. In four of the countries, 80 percent to 92 percent of governing-party MPs report at least weekly contacts with ministers. Opposition members, by contrast, have much less frequent contacts with ministers.

Sweden is an exception here. In that country, MPs from both governing and opposition parties report that their contacts with ministers are fairly infrequent. The difference may be due to the relatively high ratio of MPs to ministers in Sweden. From the perspective of a government minister, that is, one might argue that the number of contacts with members is roughly the same in all five countries. However, the change of government in Sweden immediately prior to the implementation of the parliamentary survey may also play a role in explaining the cross-national variation.

Finally, it should be noted that, after all, most opposition MPs report weekly or monthly contacts with ministers. These patterns of contact likely reflect the importance of interparty relations in the Nordic multiparty systems; they might also, however, represent cross-party contacts, and they are neatly consistent with earlier findings on parliamentarian contacts in Norway (Hernes and Nergaard 1989) and Denmark (Damgaard 1982a).

PARLIAMENT AS MARKETPLACE
(THE CROSS-PARTY MODE)

While Nordic MPs report that they represent primarily their parties, much evidence shows that they are also able to represent other interests that are narrower or more specialized. In chapter 5, Valen, Narud, and Hardarson show that geographical or territorial conflicts play a role even in the small Nordic party regimes, with their proportional electoral systems. Peripheral areas are somewhat overrepresented, particularly in Norway and Iceland. But even without such overrepresentation, it is likely that geographical or constituency interests lead to cross-party cooperation for the protection and promotion of such interests. More generally, as Peter Esaiasson shows in chapter 3, individual MPs define their job to some extent in terms of representation. Party affiliation is important, of course, but group membership and parliamentary position affect the behavior of MPs, too.

It is significant, in the present context, that many Nordic MPs regard it as very important to represent their constituency (and also various social groups), in addition to their party and their own policy views—and that they act accordingly. For example, one-fourth of all Nordic MPs consider the representation of constituency interests to be very important; these MPs are more likely than their fellows, moreover, to contact ministers in an effort to promote local interests.

Lena Wängnerud's findings in chapter 6 on the representation of women are also quite interesting in a cross-party perspective. She finds that female MPs "stand out as a vanguard as soon as we extend the analysis beyond verbal declarations to actual legislative behavior." Furthermore, female MPs are more active than male MPs in promoting the interests of women, as measured by contacts with women's organizations and by cooperative efforts with MPs from other parties on issues related to gender equality. This is highly significant, considering that most MPs believe that the increased representation of women in parliament has changed the position of their parties on specific issues.

To a considerable extent, the cross-party mode centers on parliamentary committees, as King originally suggested in the case of Germany; he did not, by contrast, find that mode in Great Britain or France. Magnus Hagevi notes in chapter 10 that the committee system is the core feature of internal group specialization; he concludes that a committee assignment can be a "position of influence for the private member" and not just a reward for the party loyalist. He finds that Nordic MPs tend to get their preferred committee assignment, although the principle of seniority is also of some importance (except in the Icelandic Althingi).

Unfortunately, Hagevi's data cannot show how committees and their members actually work in terms of the cross-party and interparty modes. Pertinent questions would be whether the committees are "mini-parliaments" in which party representatives work to promote party interests, or whether they instead constitute groups of specialized MPs engaged in genuine cross-party dealings with the minister in question. Presumably both models are relevant, depending on the issue at hand, as Andeweg (1992) suggests in the Dutch case. He finds the cross-party mode to be quite important in budgetary matters (in which sector specialists from various parties compete with similar specialists in other areas).

Torben K. Jensen's analysis (in chapter 9) documents that the cross-party mode of cooperation is common in several areas of Nordic public policy. Nordic parliamentarians cooperate with MPs from other parties quite frequently in their efforts to influence specific legislative decisions, at least in regard to the environment, gender, European Union affairs, morality and religion, and local and regional issues. This kind of cooperation presumably is bound to involve the responsible ministers one way or another. It is noteworthy that hardly any differences between opposition- and government-party MPs appear in the reported patterns of cooperation across party lines.

There is no doubt that the Nordic committee structures are important for the competent and specialized conduct of parliamentary work. Even after "the rise of the policy advocate" in Westminster and the introduction of seventeen select committees covering all government departments (Norton 1997), British MPs are still less likely than Nordic MPs to display cross-party behavior, although they certainly represent constituency interests.

Formally speaking, the Nordic committees are collective actors in the processing of legislative items. But when forced to rank the relative importance in parliamentary decision-making of party groups/party leaders and committees/committee leaders, Nordic MPs generally choose party over committee (Heidar, chapter 8). (Swedish MPs report a tie, however.) The greatest difference in perceived power is found in Denmark, but the differences on the whole are not dramatic, indicating that parliamentary committees are considered, when all is said and done, to be important. On some issues, as Torben K. Jensen shows, committees can be decisive, for party spokespersons—who are always committee members in the relevant area—are sometimes able to convince their party colleagues that the group as a whole should make a certain decision.

PARLIAMENT AS ARENA (THE INTERPARTY MODE)

The idea that the Nordic parliaments and governments should be regarded as arenas for cooperation and conflict among political parties, rather than as collective actors in their own right, is obvious (cf. Anckar 1990). This is also the approach chosen by Henrik Jensen (1995) in his analysis of Danish parliamentary committees. He argues convincingly that these committees are best understood as arenas—even if, as indicated above, they may in rare cases behave as unitary actors, and may even serve at times as fora for cross-party efforts. Similarly, Ingvar Mattson concludes, in a comparative analysis of committees in Sweden and Denmark, that the role of such committees must be evaluated "within the framework of party dominance in the parliaments" (Mattson 1996a:137).

The basic idea of the arena mode of executive-legislative relations is that the game in Nordic politics is not between government and parliament, but between different cohesive parties in parliament and government. Members of parliament are organized in political parties, of which at least one occupies government office, while two (or more likely several) are in opposition (Damgaard 1992c). Competition among political parties for government power is the most important game in town. Yet some of the parties may prefer to stay out of the game, since they believe they can influence parliamentary decisions anyway; they may be disposed so to calculate particularly when they know (or can ensure) that no majority government will be formed (Strøm 1986; 1990).

Interparty bargaining is crucial in all of the Nordic countries for the work of parliament and government. Swedish scholars even speak of "bargaining democracy" (as distinct from Westminster-style "voting democracy"), thus highlighting the broad importance of interparty negotiations (cf. such recent works as Stenelo and Jerneck 1996; Mattson 1996b; Lewin 1996; Sannerstedt 1992; Sjölin 1993). Yet a focus on parties is also found in the literature on the other Nordic countries (e.g., Rommetvedt 1991; Jansson 1992; Magnusson 1987; Damgaard 1992d).

Should we conclude, then, that a unique Nordic arena model of executive-legislative relations exists, which perhaps we can call interparty bargaining? It is clear that the Nordic systems differ from the single-party majoritarian Westminster system. They also plainly differ from the U.S. presidential model, with its comparatively weak parties. Executive-legislative relations in the Nordic countries do exhibit, however, cross-national variations that must be taken into account.

Anders Sannerstedt (1996:52–54) has proposed a distinction among European multiparty parliamentary systems that might prove useful in this context: Is the government based on a majority coalition (as in, e.g., Germany, the Netherlands, and usually Austria)? Or is it founded on a minority? In Denmark, Norway, and Sweden, minority governments have been the rule, which requires almost constant bargaining among governing and opposition parties in parliamentary decision-making. Icelandic and Finnish governments, by contrast, have been based on majority coalitions that are able to rely, to a greater extent, on their own votes in policy-making. Interparty bargaining does take place in Iceland and Finland, certainly, but negotiations can be restricted in a higher degree to the governing parties themselves; in Denmark, Norway, and Sweden, they are bound to include opposition parties, too.

In Müller's and Andeweg's terms, respectively, we could thus emphasize the importance of the "intra-government" or "intra-coalition" mode in Iceland and Finland. Similarly, we might say that the "opposition" mode is more important in Denmark, Norway, and Sweden. Thus, while we cannot speak of a common Nordic model of interparty relations, we can at any rate discern a Scandinavian model, including Denmark, Norway, and Sweden. Finland and Iceland are much closer to a continental interparty model. These patterns fit well with Heidar's tentative conclusion in chapter 8 that parliamentary party groups in Denmark, Norway, and Sweden are somewhat stronger than their counterparts in Finland and Iceland.

CONCLUSIONS

The analysis in this chapter demonstrates that all four modes of executive-legislative relations are relevant in the Nordic countries. Some modes, however, are clearly more important than others. An explanation of parliamentary politics in terms of the interparty arena mode seems best suited, on the whole, to describing the hard political realities. As mentioned above, this mode prevails in two different variants: the one in Scandinavia and the other in Finland and Iceland. The interparty mode is also in general the most visible one, inasmuch as it is controversies among the parties that really influences the headlines in daily political reporting.

But other modes also exist—in more subtle ways, perhaps, and without much publicity. Thus, the Nordic parliaments in rare cases work according to the two-body or nonparty model (as do many other parliaments, presumably). Furthermore, the intraparty mode is definitely important for all governing parties in the Nordic countries and elsewhere.

It appears, moreover, that parliamentary parties in the three Scandinavian countries are more egalitarian than those in Finland and Iceland (or Britain for that matter), where majority governments usually rule. Finally, the cross-party or marketplace mode is probably more common than is usually assumed, particularly in Norway and Sweden (with their rather influential committees) and possibly also in Denmark (where contacts with other parties may be important for influencing party group decisions).

12

Might and Right:
Views of Power in Society

Ólafur Th. Hardarson

Power has always been of major interest to students of politics. Aristotle classified political systems according to the distribution of power. Machiavelli discussed the manipulative face of power—and offered advice on its use (and abuse). Power became a central concept of scholarly political science in the twentieth century. Some optimistic scholars even believed that the power concept could become the discipline's equivalent of the concept of price in economics.

While power is obviously important in politics, it is a difficult concept. The definition and measurement of power have been extensively discussed in the scholarly literature. These discussions clearly show how complex and multifaceted a phenomenon power is (see, e.g., Bachrach and Baratz 1962; 1963; Lukes 1974; Petersson 1987; Polsby 1963). Attempts to measure power have been based on widely different approaches. In their famous study of power relations in New Haven, Dahl and his associates used the decision-making approach: only those taking part in the decision-making process were considered to have power (Dahl 1961). The reputational approach was used in various community studies in the United States in the middle of the twentieth century: a group of people were simply asked who had the power (Hunter 1953; Polsby 1963). A positional approach analyzes political positions; it examines, for example, if power is concentrated in such a way that the same individuals occupy influential positions in many fields (Grímsson 1976). An approach based on resources tends to equate the possession of great political or economic resources with the possession of great power.

While many studies of power consist of conceptual and theoretical discussions rather than empirical research, studies of the latter kind have also been carried out. The most ambitious of such studies in recent years are probably the large government-sponsored research projects on power in society carried out in Norway and Sweden during the 1970s and 1980s (see, e.g., Hernes 1975; Petersson 1991b).

POWER RELATIONS AND MODERN DEMOCRATIC SOCIETY: A FEW MODELS

There is an abundance of models of modern democratic society: pluralist, elitist, corporatist, bureaucratic, socialist, postmodern, to name but a few. These different models of democratic societies are to a large extent based on different conceptions of power relations between different elements or actors in the political system or society as a whole. We do not intend to carry out a systematic analysis of such models here—or a rigid test of their hypotheses. For our purposes, it is enough simply to sketch roughly the main features of the different models and to examine what actors would be considered most influential in these models.

According to the classical theories of representative democracy—which are largely reflected in most west European constitutions—ultimate power rests with the people or electorate, which elects representatives to the legislature, to which in turn the cabinet is usually responsible. In modern democracies, both legislature and executive are usually structured by political parties, which also serve as a link between the electorate and the representative institutions. Thus a modern version of classical theory about representative democracy theory would perhaps tell us to expect power to rest with the electorate and its representatives: the parliament, the cabinet, and the political parties. We may refer to this model as the *textbook model*.

Many scholars have argued that this ideal of democratic theory is not a realistic description of power relations in modern democratic society; they have, however, reached differing conclusions on the implications for democracy. Elitists have argued that democracy is in fact impossible, on account of the limited power of the ordinary voter or party member (Michels 1968). Pluralists, on the other hand, have maintained that the essence of democracy consists in the electorate's power to throw out the government in elections, rather than in any ability to influence daily decisions or policies (see e.g., Sartori 1965; Schumpeter 1942). According to this *liberal model of representative democracy*, the power of the electorate can be viewed as rather limited, if compared for instance to that of the cabinet or parliament.

The *decline of parliaments thesis* tells us that the cabinet (and perhaps the parties) has become the major actor in modern democracy, while the legislature has been reduced to a rubber stamp. A *corporatist model* emphasizes the cooperation between the government and the large labor market associations; according to this model, we would expect the cabinet, the employers' associations, and the trade unions to be most influential.

An extreme version of a *bureaucratic model* can be seen in the popular BBC television production *Yes, Minister,* in which the political masters are really at the mercy of the all-powerful civil servants. While few scholars would subscribe to such a simple view, an emphasis on the impact of bureaucrats is quite common in the scholarly literature as well as in public debate. According to another simple view, the *mass media* (or fourth estate) has become the most powerful actor in society in the information age.

A Marxist model of power relations claims that the so-called political masters are not really powerful at all (to say nothing of those who elected them): real power rests with the capitalists. The Marxist view would lead us to expect private business, financial markets, and employers' organizations to be most powerful.

Economic globalization and the increasing integration of the European Union have given rise to what we might call the *superstate model:* the view that no decisions of any importance are taken by political actors in nation-states any more—power has been transferred to the international financial markets and the bureaucrats and politicians in Brussels.

Finally, a classical *elitist model* would have us believe that society is run by a cohesive power elite, while a *pluralist model* would maintain that society is run by many (and competing) elites. The former view would lead us to expect one actor (or one cohesive group of actors) to dominate; the latter view, by contrast, says such a concentration of power is not to be expected.[1]

NORDIC PARLIAMENTARIANS' VIEW OF POWER: DESIGN OF THE STUDY

In our elite surveys, we asked parliamentarians in the five Nordic countries to use a 0–10 scale to measure how much influence several actors actually have in their society today and how much influence these same actors should have. The following eleven actors were included in all five questionnaires: the electorate, the parliament, the political parties, the cabinet, civil servants, the mass media, the major associations of trade unions and of employers, financial markets, private business, and the European

Union. For our presentation here, we have transformed the scale in such a way that each of the eleven actors can obtain from 0 to 100 power points.[2]

The method used here can be described as a variant of the reputational method;[3] it has been used previously in Swedish interview studies of the Riksdag and the electorate (Holmberg and Esaiasson 1988; Esaiasson and Holmberg 1996; Holmberg 1996a).[4] We would not claim that the results necessarily represent any "real" distribution of power in society—even though one might assume that members of parliament are rather well-suited in general for assessing the power of various institutions. What is of interest here is simply the power perceptions that parliamentarians have, as well as the normative assessment they make of how power relations ideally should be in their society. Is there a common Nordic perception of prevailing power relations, or does the assessment of MPs vary greatly by country? If such a Nordic model exists, what does it look like? Does it reflect one of the earlier-discussed models of society better than the others? Is there, furthermore, a common Nordic model of the ideal power structure? If so, does it greatly differ from reality as parliamentarians see it? We will try to answer these questions in this chapter. We shall also explore whether the political parties hold differing views of the power structure. Are the differences in this area perhaps greater, for example, between socialist and conservative MPs than they are between MPs in the different countries?

MIGHT: WHO HAS THE POWER?

First, we will examine whether a common Nordic model of power relations exists. In table 12.1, we see the power points (means) given to the various actors by Nordic parliamentarians as a whole and also by members from individual countries. We also show the ranking order of the actors, as well as the squared etas for each actor, showing explained variance by country.

The first thing to note in table 12.1 is that parliamentarians perceive the influence of the various actors as a continuum, rather than as a dichotomy where one actor or group of actors is perceived to have great power and the rest to have little. The power points given to individual actors range from 55 to 84 for Nordic MPs as a whole.[5] In the individual countries, all actors receive a score over 50, except for private business in Iceland (46). Only in eight cases in the five countries is the difference between two actors in the ranking order greater than five points, and only in one case does it exceed ten points. Essentially, then, there are no large gaps in the

Table 12.1

Members' Perceptions of the Actual Power of Eleven Actors, by Country (average power points, ranking order, and eta-square)

	All Nordic		Denmark		Finland		Iceland		Norway		Sweden		Eta²
Cabinet	84	(1)	84	(1)	87	(1)	85	(1)	81	(1)	83	(1)	.04
Mass media	77	(2)	81	(2)	80	(3)	71	(2)	76	(2)	79	(2)	.06
Parliament	72	(3)	77	(3)	69	(8)	69	(4)	73	(3)	74	(4)	.03
Financial markets	69	(4)	67	(4)	80	(2)	54	(9)	63	(7)	79	(3)	.24
Trade unions	68	(5)	65	(7)	77	(4)	59	(8)	72	(4)	65	(6)	.12
Political parties	67	(6)	67	(5)	71	(7)	66	(6)	63	(6)	67	(5)	.03
Employers' orgs.	65	(7)	61	(10)	72	(5)	68	(5)	63	(5)	63	(8)	.06
Civil servants	64	(8)	62	(9)	72	(6)	70	(3)	50	(11)	65	(7)	.18
Electorate	60	(9)	62	(8)	58	(11)	61	(7)	60	(8)	60	(10)	.00
European Union	59	(10)	65	(6)	68	(9)	52	(10)	54	(9)	56	(11)	.10
Private Business	55	(11)	56	(11)	58	(10)	46	(11)	52	(10)	61	(9)	.08
Minimum N	662		94		114		41		129		277		

Notes: For wordings of question, see note 2 to this chapter. The results have been transformed into figures running from 0 to 100. Ranking order in parentheses. In case of ties, ranking is decided by decimal places. Data are weighted by size of parliament.

power ranking of the actors. We can say that all actors are considered to have considerable power, even if some have more power than others.

Second, we can observe a general Nordic agreement among MPs concerning the power structure. While there are some differences in power points given to individual actors in the five countries, and the ranking order of actors also varies, in general these differences are not great. The low squared etas indicate that only a small portion of the variance in power scores for each actor can be accounted for by country differences. The major exceptions to this are financial markets ($eta^2 = .24$) and civil servants ($eta^2 = .18$).[6]

Nordic representatives clearly consider *the cabinet* to be most powerful. The cabinet comes out on top in all five countries (81–87 power points). The lead is greatest in Iceland, where the cabinet receives fourteen points more than its nearest competitor.

The mass media comes second in the overall ranking (71–81 power points in the individual countries). This is perhaps not surprising. Politicians have increasingly had to operate in an independent—and often hostile—media market, a market which has become more competitive in recent years in the Nordic countries, especially with the emergence of commercial television stations. Nevertheless, it is highly interesting to find that Nordic MPs consider only cabinet ministers to be more powerful than journalists.

Parliament occupies third place (72 power points) when the views of Nordic parliamentarians as a whole are considered. In the individual countries, parliament occupies third or fourth place, except in the case of Finland, where the Eduskunta is eighth in the ranking; it should be noted, however, that the power points given by the Finns leave parliament only three points behind fifth place. For all MPs taken together, the influence of parliament is twelve points below that of the cabinet. However, in the two countries where majority coalitions are the rule—Iceland and Finland—the cabinet is perceived as much stronger vis-à-vis parliament (by sixteen to eighteen points) than in the countries where minority governments are common—Denmark, Norway, and Sweden (seven to nine points stronger).

Financial markets occupy second to fourth place in Finland, Sweden, and Denmark, while they come seventh in Norway and ninth in Iceland. Clear differences in power points given can also be observed here ($eta^2 = .24$): Financial markets are considered more powerful in Sweden and Finland (79–80 power points) than in Norway and Denmark (63–67 points) and especially Iceland (54 points). This may be related to the great difficulties Sweden and Finland have experienced with their financial markets in the 1990s. The financial market in Iceland is still in its infancy, so the low power ranking there is not surprising.

Trade unions occupy fifth place overall, scoring 59 to 77 points; they take fourth to eighth place in the individual countries. Trade unions are considered strongest in Finland and Norway, and weakest in Iceland.

Political parties take sixth place in the overall power ranking, one point below trade unions. The parties rank fifth to seventh in the individual countries (63–71 power points).

Employers' organizations come seventh in the overall ranking, scoring 65 points, or three points below the trade unions. So while the powers of the large labor market organizations are considered roughly equal, trade unions are seen to have the edge slightly in Sweden, Denmark, and Finland (two to five points) and more markedly so in Norway (nine points). In Iceland, however, trade unions score nine points lower than the employers' organization.

Civil servants come in eighth in the overall ranking, scoring 64 points. Here we have considerable differences between individual countries ($eta^2 = .18$). Civil servants rank third in Iceland, with 70 points, and take sixth place in Finland with 72. In Sweden and Denmark, civil servants occupy seventh and ninth place with a score of 65 and 62, respectively. In Norway, on the other hand, civil servants occupy—somewhat surprisingly—the eleventh and last place, scoring only 50 power points. It is also somewhat surprising that Icelandic MPs consider the power of the civil service to be so great, since the Icelandic bureaucracy is small and rather weak, while Icelandic parliamentarians have enjoyed an unusually broad scope for maneuver in the executive and the administration (Kristinsson 1996).

The electorate comes ninth in the overall power ranking. Members of parliament in the individual countries are in good agreement on voter power, giving the electorate 58–62 power points. The electorate's ranking ranges from seventh to eleventh place.

The *European Union* occupies tenth place (59 points) in the overall ranking. It ranks ninth to eleventh in all of the countries except Denmark, the long-standing member of the EU, where it comes sixth. The Danes and the Finns give the EU more points (65–68) than do the others (52–56).

Private business comes in eleventh and last place (55 points); it is the actor considered to have the least power by Nordic parliamentarians overall. Private business takes eleventh place in Denmark and Iceland, tenth place in Finland and Norway, and ninth place in Sweden.

While some differences remain among the countries, we can say that a common Nordic power structure does exist in the minds of Nordic parliamentarians. This structure clearly resembles a pluralist model rather than an elitist one; since the power ranking forms a continuum, no one group of actors can be said to form a clear group of power-holders. Of course, an elitist could maintain that the four most powerful actors, say, constitute the power elite, but it is difficult to see cabinet ministers, media moguls, parliamentarians, and actors on the financial markets as a single cohesive elite.

The power structure as perceived by Nordic MPs does not really fall neatly into any of the other simple models sketched at the beginning of this chapter. While the great perceived power of parliaments and cabinets is in accordance with the textbook model of democracy, the electorate's lack of power is not. In this respect, the perceived Nordic power structure seems closer to the liberal model of representative democracy. At odds with both of these models, however, is the fact that legislatures and executives are also seen as competing for influence with several actors not mentioned in any of the constitutions, notably the mass media and (in some cases) the financial markets.

Members of parliament certainly do not see the legislature as a rubber stamp. While cabinet ministers are perceived as the most powerful, parliaments are also seen as among the most influential institutions in society. The decline-of-parliament thesis does not get much support here—at least not in any strong version.

While parliamentarians clearly think that the labor market organizations—the trade unions and the employers' associations—do have considerable power, their perceived power structure can hardly be termed corporatist in the sense of claiming that these actors—along with cabinet ministers—run the show. While civil servants are considered influential, they are not seen as more powerful than their political masters in parliament and cabinet. And both the Marxist model and the superstate model are obviously very different from the Nordic model of the prevailing power structure, when we consider the views of Nordic parliamentarians as a whole.

The overall power structure as perceived by Nordic MPs can perhaps be described in the following way: The power structure is pluralistic, with many different actors wielding considerable influence. While the cabinet is still the most powerful institution in society, and the legislature among the most influential, these traditional actors must compete for influence with a highly influential mass media and with financial markets as well. The labor market organizations still have considerable power, about equal to that of the political parties. Civil servants do matter, but in no way dominate. While the electorate, the European Union, and private business are at the bottom of the list, they are nevertheless considered to have substantial power.

RIGHT: WHO SHOULD HAVE THE POWER?

Not only did the Nordic MPs assess the actual power of various actors, they also indicated how much power they thought these actors should have. Table 12.2 shows the amount of power each of the eleven actors should have, according to Nordic MPs taken both as a whole and by individual country. A very clear image of the desired power structure emerges.

The power structure preferred by parliamentarians is very different from the actual power structure as they see it.[7] While they saw the actual power structure as a continuum, their ideal power structure is really a dichotomy. Parliamentarians want four actors to have great power, and they want the other seven to have much less.

Parliament, the electorate, the cabinet, and the political parties should have great power, according to Nordic MPs. In all five countries, these four actors receive more than 70 power points, with one exception: the Finns give the political parties only 66 points—which is eleven points more, however, than they give to the next actor.

Not unexpectedly, perhaps, MPs think that parliaments should be on top in this powerful political stratum—the legislatures receive 84–92 power points and come out ahead in all five countries. The cabinet (76–84 points) and the electorate (72–83 points) come second, followed by the political parties (66–76 points).

The preferred power of the other seven actors is much less: 46–53 power points if we consider Nordic parliamentarians as a whole. The picture does not change much if we look at individual countries. Out of thirty-five national entries in table 12.2 (five countries times seven actors), 29 or 83 percent receive power points ranging from 43 to 53. Only trade unions in Norway (59 points) and civil servants in Finland (55) have higher points, while four entries are below 40: Norwegian and Icelandic parliamentarians think 38 power points are enough for the European Union, while private business in Iceland and civil servants in Norway come last, with 37 points.

There is thus a clear gap between those who should have great power (generally 70–90 power points) and those who should have less (generally 43–53 points). In all five of the countries, the political parties occupy fourth place in the power ranking, and in all cases the gap to the fifth

Table 12.2
Members' Assessments of Preferred Power of Eleven Actors, by Country (average power points and eta-square)

	All Nordic	Denmark	Finland	Iceland	Norway	Sweden	Eta^2
Parliament	88	88	92	84	87	89	.05
Cabinet	80	80	82	78	76	84	.04
Electorate	79	80	80	72	79	83	.06
Political parties	71	74	66	72	71	76	.04
Trade unions	53	48	52	51	59	53	.04
Employers' orgs.	48	45	52	49	51	45	.03
Mass media.	47	47	51	49	43	43	.03
Private business	46	49	49	37	49	48	.06
Financial markets	46	47	52	44	44	44	.03
Civil servants	46	44	55	48	37	46	.11
European Union	46	53	52	38	38	47	.09
Minimum N	643	89	112	39	124	274	

Notes: For wordings of question, see note 2. The results have been transformed into figures running from 0 to 100. Data are weighted by size of parliament.

actor is large: 21–23 power points for Denmark, Iceland, and Sweden, and 11–12 points for Finland and Norway.

Not only do parliamentarians in all five countries wish the four traditional political actors to have much greater power than the other seven, there is also great agreement among the five nations about how much power each actor should ideally have, as indicated by the low squared etas in table 12.2.[8] The major exceptions concern civil servants and the European Union. Representatives in Denmark, Sweden, and Iceland agree that the proper influence of civil servants amounts to 44–48 power points, while the Finns would like to give them more power (55 points) and the Norwegians less (37 points). Not unexpectedly, MPs in member states of the European Union are prepared to give more power to the EU than are their colleagues in Iceland and Norway, which are not members.

The power structure preferred by MPs is easily recognized from classical theories of representative democracy—and indeed most written constitutions. It is very close to the textbook model. The actors given formal responsibility for the legislative and executive functions in the nation-state should have the most power, along with the electorate that parliament and cabinet represent. The political parties—which provide the organizational links between the three constitutional actors—are also welcome to the house of power, although the welcome is a somewhat reluctant one.

Other actors—interest organizations, financial markets, private business, bureaucrats, the mass media, and the EU—should only have modest (and roughly equal) power. Their role would be clearly limited in the ideal power game of Nordic parliamentarians. Perhaps we can say that their proper place is thought to be in the lobby.

IF MIGHT IS TO BE RIGHT, WHAT HAS TO CHANGE?

While we did not ask MPs directly what changes in the power structure they wanted to see, we can obtain a measure of desired change by comparing their perceptions of power and their preferred power. Table 12.3 both shows to what extent parliamentarians agreed on a *direction of change*, as seen in the percentages desiring an increase, a decrease, or no change in the power of individual actors; and on the *amount of desired change*, as indicated by the mean difference between preferred and perceived power points, both for the Nordic region and for individual countries. While there are some interesting differences in desired change among

Table 12.3
Members on Who Should Have More or Less Power in Respective Country (differences between preferred power and actual power)

	All Nordic Members			Mean Change in Power Points by Country						
	More Power (%)	No Change (%)	Less Power (%)	All Nordic	Denmark	Finland	Iceland	Norway	Sweden	Eta²
Electorate	69	28	3	+19	+18	+23	+11	+19	+23	.05
Parliament	71	28	1	+16	+11	+24	+14	+14	+15	.08
Political parties	39	48	13	+4	+7	−5	+6	+7	+9	.11
Cabinet	15	46	39	−4	−4	−6	−8	−5	+1	.05
Private business	20	29	51	−8	−7	−9	−8	−3	−14	.02
European Union	10	44	46	−14	−12	−16	−15	−16	−9	.01
Trade unions	14	26	60	−15	−17	−24	−8	−13	−13	.06
Employers' orgs.	4	24	72	−17	−16	−20	−20	−13	−18	.02
Civil servants	3	24	73	−18	−18	−17	−22	−12	−19	.03
Financial markets	6	23	71	−23	−20	−28	−10	−19	−35	.13
Mass media	1	10	89	−31	−33	−29	−22	−34	−36	.06
Minimum N				633	88	112	39	122	267	

Notes: For wordings of question, see note 2. Data are weighted by size of parliament.

parliamentarians from the five countries, in general the country differences are not large, as can be seen from the squared etas.[9]

We saw before that Nordic MPs desire a power structure strongly influenced by political actors: parliament, cabinet, electorate, and political parties. Sixty-nine percent want to increase the power of the democratic actor perceived to be weakest—the electorate. On average, they recommend an increase of 19 power points for the voters. Seventy-one percent of MPs also want to increase the influence of the legislature, on average by 16 points, thus putting parliament on top in the power structure. Small changes are thought necessary for the already powerful cabinets, and the same goes for political parties.

Nordic parliamentarians would like to see a decrease in the power of all other actors. They want to reduce the power of the media most dramatically—89 percent think media power should be reduced, on average by 31 power points.[10] Financial markets come second on the target list: 71 percent want less power for the markets—an average decrease of 23 points.

There is also a clear majority (60 percent to 73 percent) for a reduction of 15 to 18 points in the power of trade unions, employers' organizations and civil servants. The two actors perceived as having the least power— the EU and private business—also receive the smallest cuts: 13 and 8 power points respectively. Around half of Nordic MPs would like to see a reduction in the power of these two actors.

PARTY FAMILIES: DIFFERENT PERCEPTIONS OF THE POWER STRUCTURE?

We have seen that a common Nordic view of the power structure exists, in the sense that country differences are not large when we consider Nordic parliamentarians as a whole. This picture may nevertheless hide considerable differences between groups in the individual countries. There is especially cause to believe that party affiliation or ideology may be related to perceptions of the actual power structure, as well as of the desired one. And this is indeed the case. Clear differences emerge when we look at individual parties.

We cannot present a comparison of all thirty-six Nordic political parties represented in our data; instead, we have grouped the parties into seven party families: left socialists, green parties, social democrats, centrist parties, agrarian parties, conservatives, and right-wing populist parties.[11] While parties within each family tend to express rather similar views on the power structure, there are nevertheless some differences. The overall results for the party families cannot, therefore, be applied to individual parties automatically.

Table 12.4 presents the perceived power structure of the seven party families, much as table 12.1 does for the countries. The squared etas show that members of different party families agree on the power of some actors and disagree on the power of others. Disagreement is greatest concerning the power of trade unions, private business, financial markets, and the European Union. This disagreement is clearly related to the ideological left-right dimension in the first three cases.

If we look at table 12.4—and if we examine the correlations between the perceived power structures of individual party families—two basic models emerge. The first model is that of the left socialist and green parties. The second model is the common Nordic model, to which the other party families are close—although there are important differences between the social democrats and the nonsocialist parties.[12]

The left socialists and the greens have a very similar perception of the power structure ($r = .83$). Their model of the power structure clearly deviates from the common Nordic model ($r = .57$ and $.31$), and it differs from the perceived power structure of both the social democrats ($r = .60$ and $.28$) and the other party families ($r = .02$ to $.46$).

In the left socialist/green power structure, the most powerful actors are the financial markets (74–86 power points), the cabinet (80–81), the mass media (73–77), the EU (68–80), employers' organizations (72–75), and private business (67 points). Parliament and the political parties are seen as less powerful (62–66 points), while the trade unions (54–62) and especially the electorate (45–51) have the least power. This model thus deviates from the common model in that financial markets, employers' organizations, private business, and the EU are seen to have greater power, while trade unions, parliament, the electorate, and the political parties have less. In short: in line with the Marxist model, the left socialists and the greens believe that the capitalists are more influential than the common Nordic model suggests, and that the traditional democratic actors are less influential than the average Nordic representative believes. The model of the European superstate also gets some support here, especially among the greens.

The common Nordic power structure is largely reflected in the perceived power structure of social democrats ($r = .94$), agrarian parties ($r = .93$), centrist and conservative parties ($r = .92$), and, to somewhat lesser extent, the populist parties ($r = .86$). The power structures of individual party families, on the other hand, deviate in differing ways from the common model, thus becoming more distinct from each other.

Table 12.4

Members' Perceptions of the Actual Power of Eleven Actors, by Party Family (average power points, ranking power, and eta-square)

	All Nordic		Left Socs.		Greens		Soc. Dems.		Centrists		Agrarians		Conservatives		Populists		Eta²
Cabinet	84	(1)	81	(1)	80	(3)	86	(1)	83	(1)	83	(1)	83	(1)	80	(1)	.02
Mass media	78	(2)	77	(2)	73	(5)	78	(2)	79	(2)	77	(2)	78	(2)	78	(2)	.00
Parliament	72	(3)	66	(7)	62	(10)	77	(3)	74	(4)	71	(4)	72	(3)	62	(5)	.06
Financial markets	69	(4)	74	(3)	86	(1)	74	(4)	69	(5)	68	(5)	58	(9)	58	(8)	.11
Trade unions	68	(5)	54	(10)	62	(9)	64	(7)	77	(3)	75	(3)	70	(4)	73	(3)	.14
Political parties	67	(6)	61	(9)	64	(8)	69	(5)	66	(6)	66	(7)	66	(6)	69	(4)	.03
Employers' orgs.	65	(7)	72	(4)	75	(4)	65	(6)	62	(8)	68	(6)	60	(7)	60	(7)	.06
Civil servants	64	(8)	63	(8)	70	(6)	61	(9)	58	(10)	66	(8)	68	(5)	61	(6)	.03
Electorate	60	(9)	51	(11)	45	(11)	64	(8)	63	(7)	62	(10)	59	(8)	42	(11)	.06
European Union	59	(10)	68	(5)	80	(2)	59	(10)	58	(9)	66	(9)	49	(10)	54	(9)	.11
Private business	55	(11)	67	(6)	67	(7)	58	(11)	55	(11)	53	(11)	44	(11)	49	(10)	.14
Minimum N	652		59		20		265		61		101		128		13		

Notes: For wordings of question, see note 2. The results have been transformed into figures running from 0 to 100. Ranking order in parentheses. In case of ties, ranking is decided by decimal places. Data are weighted by size of parliament. Power points given to the mass media here by all members come to 78, as compared to 77 in table 12.1—for reasons explained in notes to table 12.6.

It is interesting that the perceived power structure of the social democrats is closer to the centrist parties (r = .86), the conservative parties (r = .79), the agrarian parties (r = .78), and even the populists (r = .67) than to the left socialists (r = .60) and the greens (r = .28). The social-democratic deviations from the common Nordic model consist mainly in that they think trade unions have somewhat less power (four power points), and that parliament, financial markets, voters and private business have slightly more (three to five points).

The deviations of the nonsocialist parties from the common model tend to go in the opposite direction. They all see the trade unions as the third or fourth most powerful actor in society, as compared with the social-democratic view of trade unions as occupying seventh place. Private business and financial markets, on the other hand, are viewed as less powerful, especially by conservatives and populists.

The perceived power structure of the centrist parties, agrarian parties, and conservative parties is very similar (r = .86 to .90). The largest deviation—by far—concerns the power of the EU, which is perceived as seventeen points greater among agrarians than among conservatives.

The populist power structure is much closer to that of the other three nonsocialist party families (r = .80 to .86) than to that of the social democrats (r = .67)—or, of course, than to those of the greens and left socialists (r = .36 and .46). The populists mainly deviate from the other nonsocialists (as well as the social democrats) in perceiving parliament and the electorate as having much less power. In this they resemble the left socialists and greens.

PARTY FAMILIES: PREFERRED POWER

The desired power structure of six of the party families resembles the preferred Nordic power structure very closely (r = .93 to .99; see table 12.5). The preferred populist power structure diverges more (r = .79), and since there are two clear gaps in the populists' power ranking, their power structure is in fact quite distinct: the populists want parliament and the electorate to have great power (81–83 power points); political parties, the cabinet, financial markets, and private business to have clearly less but still a lot (56–67 points); and the remaining five actors to have very little power (32–36 points). The preferred populist power structure is closer to that of the other nonsocialist parties (r = .83 to .84) than to that of the left socialists, the greens or the social democrats (r = .63 to .75).

In general, there are great similarities between the preferred power

Table 12.5
Members' Assessments of Preferred Power of Eleven Actors, by Party Family (average power points and eta-square)

	All Nordic	Left Socs.	Greens	Soc. Dems.	Centrists	Agrarians	Conservatives	Populists	Eta^2
Parliament	88	88	89	89	90	87	87	81	.02
Cabinet	80	72	81	85	82	78	80	61	.14
Electorate	79	78	82	81	82	79	74	83	.03
Political parties	72	70	64	75	67	73	68	67	.04
Trade unions	53	59	49	61	45	46	46	34	.21
Employers' orgs.	48	45	45	52	45	45	48	36	.04
Financial markets	46	31	34	48	49	46	51	64	.11
Mass media	46	51	43	46	50	46	45	35	.02
Private business	46	36	41	47	46	46	50	56	.06
Civil servants	46	47	40	47	45	48	46	32	.02
European Union	46	30	33	54	43	40	48	34	.14
Minimum N	633	58	19	255	60	97	127	13	

Notes: For wordings of question, see note 2. Data are weighted by size of parliament. Power points and ranking by all members differ slightly here from those in table 12.2, for reasons explained in notes to table 12.6.

structures of the other six party families (r = .89 to .98), with the partial exception of the left socialists and the conservatives (r = .84).[13] More importantly, all these party families adhere to the dichotomy of the common Nordic model of a desired power structure: they want parliament, the electorate, the cabinet, and the political parties to be much more powerful than other actors. These four democratic actors generally receive 70 to 90 power points. The gap from the fourth most powerful actor (in all cases the parties) to the fifth ranges from eleven to twenty-five power points.

In these six party families, the seven remaining actors are generally given 43–54 power points, a pattern that clearly repeats, in thirty-two out of forty-two cases (76 percent), that found for the countries in table 12.2. The centrist parties and the conservatives put all seven actors in this range. Two marks are above the range: the left socialists and the social democrats want somewhat greater power for the trade unions (59–61 power points). Eight marks are below the range: seven of them are given by the left socialists or the greens, who both want very little power for the EU (30–33 points), financial markets (31–34 points), or private business (36–41 points). In addition, only 40 power points are given to the EU by the agrarians and to civil servants by the greens.

While all party families except the populists thus agree that the four democratic actors—parliament, the cabinet, the electorate, and the parties—should have great power, while all the others should have much less, some disagreements on the ideal power structure can be discerned. In general, however, there is a good agreement among the party families on how much power should be given to three of the four democratic actors deserving to be powerful. All party families except the populists put parliament on top (87–90 power points), and all agree that the electorate should have great power (74–83 points). All party families except the populists also agree that the political parties should be the least powerful of the four democratic actors (64–75 points).

There is more disagreement on the preferred power of the cabinet (eta^2 = .14).[14] The populists stand out in that they only want to give the cabinet 61 power points, some twenty points below parliament and the electorate. The left socialists also want the cabinet to have less power (72 points) than do the other party families, while the social democrats are most in favor of strong cabinet power (85 points). Other party families come in between (78–82 points).

While the party families generally agree that the other seven actors should have less power than the four democratic ones, a considerable disagreement on the preferred power of some of these actors remains, especially the trade unions (eta^2 = .21), the EU (eta^2 = .14), the financial markets (eta² = .11), and private business (eta² = .06). These disagreements clearly reflect ideological differences.

The left socialists and the social democrats are most friendly toward the trade unions, giving them 59–61 power points. The unions take fifth place in their preferred power ranking, seven to eight points above the sixth actor. The left socialists and the social democrats are ready to give the trade unions ten to twelve more power points than are the greens, thirteen to sixteen more power points than are the centrist parties, the agrarian parties, and the conservatives, and fully twenty-five to twenty-seven more points than are the populists.

The party families also disagree on how much power the EU should have. As expected, these differences do not follow the left-right continuum. The conservatives and the social democrats are ready to give the EU greater power (48–54 power points) than are the agrarians and the centrist parties (40–43 points) and especially the left socialists, the greens, and the populists (30–34 points).

Divisions on the preferred power of financial markets and private business, on the other hand, clearly follow the left-right continuum. The difference is mainly between the left socialists and the greens on the one hand (who give just 31–34 power points to the financial markets) and the populists on the other (64 points). The other party families—including the social democrats—fall between these two extremes (46–51 power points). The pattern is repeated for private business, albeit in a weaker form.

All party families except the populists agree on the preferred power of employers' organizations, civil servants, and the mass media (40–52 power points). In all cases, the populists want these actors to have less power (32–36 points). It is noteworthy that the social democrats are the most generous toward the employers' organizations, giving them 52 power points.

PARTY FAMILIES: WHAT SHOULD CHANGE?

We saw before that, if the views of Nordic parliamentarians as a whole are considered, similar changes in the power structure are generally desired in all five Nordic countries. Table 12.6 shows that, while the party families agree on many changes in the power structure, there are also considerable differences.

The first column in table 12.6 shows the changes desired in the power structure by Nordic parliamentarians as a whole. The changes sought by

Table 12.6

Members on Who Should Have More or Less Power, by Party Family (average difference between preferred power and actual power)

	All Nordic	Left Socs.	Greens	Soc. Dems.	Centrists	Agrarians	Conservatives	Populists	Eta²
Electorate	+19	+27	+37	+18	+20	+17	+15	+41	.07
Parliament	+16	+22	+26	+13	+17	+16	+15	+19	.04
Political parties	+5	+8	0	+6	+2	+7	+2	−2	.03
Cabinet	−4	−9	+2	−2	−1	−5	−4	−19	.07
Private business	−9	−30	−25	−11	−8	−7	+6	+7	.25
European Union	−13	−37	−48	−4	−14	−26	−1	−17	.29
Trade unions	−15	+5	−14	−3	−33	−29	−24	−39	.35
Employers' orgs.	−17	−27	−30	−13	−17	−23	−13	−23	.09
Civil servants	−18	−17	−30	−15	−12	−18	−22	−30	.05
Financial markets	−23	−43	−52	−27	−20	−22	−7	+6	.24
Mass media	−31	−26	−30	−31	−29	−32	−33	−43	.02
Average Change	15	23	27	13	16	18	13	22	
Minimum N	623	56	19	249	60	97	125	13	

Notes: For wordings of question, see note 2. Data are weighted by size of parliament. For some items, results for all members in table 12.6 differ slightly from those in table 12.3, because the Icelandic Women's Alliance was not included in the party families, and because information about party affiliation was not available for nine Finnish MPs.

individual party families reflect this Nordic model to varying degrees. The changes wanted by agrarians, social democrats, and centrist parties are closest to the model (r = .93 to .95), followed by the changes desired by the greens (r = .89), the conservatives (r = .86), the left socialists (r = .83), and the populists (r = .79).

The left socialists and the greens want almost identical changes in the power structure (r = .95). There is also substantial agreement among the centrist parties, agrarian parties, conservatives and populists on the changes desired (r = .83 to .96). The social-democratic vision of change lies nearer that held by the left socialists, the greens, the agrarians, and the centrist parties (r = .80 to .84) than that held by the conservatives (r = .75) and especially the populists (r = .61). There is a special affinity between the left socialists and the agrarians (r = .86), while the greens are closer to both the centrist parties and the agrarians (r = .80 and .76) than the left socialists are to the centrist parties (r = .67). Furthest apart are the conservatives and the populists on the one hand and the greens (r = .57) and the left socialists (r = .44) on the other.

A large part of the changes desired are common to all the party families. They all want to increase the power of the electorate and parliament greatly. Since the left socialists, the greens, and the populists consider the actual power of these actors to be less than the other party families do, they also think that a greater increase in their power is needed (especially in the case of the voters).

All party families also agree that little in the way of changes is needed as far as the power of the cabinet and the political parties is concerned (except that the populists seek a considerable reduction in cabinet power). They also agree that the power of civil servants and the employers' organizations should be reduced; the greens and the populists, however, see a greater need to cut civil servants' power than do others, while the greens, the left socialists, the agrarians, and the populists would like to see a greater reduction in the power of employers' organizations than would the social democrats and the conservatives. And all party families most certainly agree that a great reduction in the power of the mass media is needed.

On the other hand, the party families do strongly disagree on power changes in regard to four actors: the trade unions (eta^2 = .35), the EU (eta^2 = .29), private business (eta^2 = .25), and the financial markets (eta^2 = .24). While similar differences could be observed in both the perceived and the preferred power structures of the party families, they become much clearer when we look at desired change. This is mainly because party ideology influences both perceptions of power and preferences regarding it: those who deserve little power are seen to have a lot of it. For instance, the nonsocialist parties think that the trade unions deserve much less power (34–46 points) than do the left socialists and the social democrats (59–61 points). By contrast, the nonsocialists consider the actual power of the trade unions much greater (70–77 points) than do the left socialists (54 points) and the social democrats (64 points).[15]

The patterns of desired change conform to the left-right continuum, except where the power of the EU is concerned. The nonsocialist parties want to see a great reduction in trade-union power (by 24 to 39 points), while the greens favor a much smaller reduction (14 points), and the left socialists and the social democrats see little need for change. Thus we have here a traditional socialist/nonsocialist division.

All parties except the populists want a reduction in the power of financial markets. The amount of desired change, on the other hand, varies. The conservatives seek only a minor reduction (of 7 points), while the centrist parties, the agrarian parties, and the social democrats think a greater power cut is needed (of 20 to 27 points). The left socialists and the greens clearly see the power of financial markets as a major threat: they want to reduce their power by fully 43–52 power points.

The greens and the left socialists also see a need for a great reduction in the power of private business (of 25–30 power points), while the social democrats favor only a minor reduction (of 11 points), and the other parties see little need for change.

The left socialists and the greens think the EU is much too powerful; they want a major reduction in EU power (by 37–48 power points). The agrarian parties also favor a greater reduction of EU power (by 26 points) than do the centrist parties and the populists (14–17 points), while the conservatives and the social democrats see little need for change.

It is clearly the left socialists, the greens, and the populists who are most dissatisfied with the power structure in general. In table 12.6 we see that, on average, these party families desire the biggest changes (by 22–27 power points).[16] Other party families are more content with the power structure, especially the social democrats and the conservatives, who advocate on average a modest change of 13 power points.

Another way to measure the dissatisfaction of the party families with the power structure is to examine the correspondence between their perceived and their preferred power structure. For three of the party families, the preferred power structure tends to be the direct opposite of the perceived power structure. This is most clearly the case with the greens (r = −.55), but also the left socialists (r = −.32) and the populists (r = −.31). The preferred power structure of the other party families is positively correlated with their perceived power structure. This is the case for the social democrats (r = .47), the centrist parties (r = .42), the conservative parties (r = .37), and the agrarian parties (r = .20). Thus the established parties are much more content with the power structure than are the left socialists and the new protest parties, who really want to stand the present power structure—as they see it—on its head.

CONCLUSIONS

Is there a common view among Nordic parliamentarians on what the power structure looks like, how the power structure should ideally be, and what changes are therefore necessary? The answer is both yes and no. If we look at Nordic MPs according to country (but undifferentiated by party), the similarities are much greater than the differences. If, on the other hand, we analyze the views of the different party families, we discover important ideological differences within the Nordic countries.

The views of the average Nordic parliamentarian on the actual power structure do not fit neatly into any of our simple models except a general pluralist one: there is no cohesive power elite—the power structure is seen as a continuum in which all eleven actors wield considerable power (albeit in varying amounts). In this Nordic version of pluralist democracy, the cabinet is seen as most powerful, followed by the media and by parliament. While financial markets, trade unions, political parties, employers' organizations, and civil servants are seen as somewhat less powerful, they nevertheless have more power than the electorate, the European Union, and private business.

According to this Nordic version, democracy in the Nordic countries gives a lot more power to representatives than to those represented—thus clearly diverging from the textbook model of democracy. Cabinet and parliament are seen as much more powerful than the electorate. The power of the political parties—the traditional meeting place of elite and grassroots activists—is seen to lie in between.

Several actors who are not given power in the constitutions are seen to exercise great power. Of these, the mass media is considered the most powerful. Market forces play an important role, especially in the form of financial markets, which interestingly enough are considered much more powerful than private business.

The organized interests in the labor market—the trade unions and the employers' organizations—are considered to possess roughly equal power. They occupy a middle position in the power hierarchy, just above the civil servants. Clearly, society is thought to be dominated neither by organized interests nor by bureaucrats.

Despite the fact that an increasing share of legislation in all the Nordic countries stems from Brussels, the average Nordic parliamentarian does not see the European Union as powerful in comparison with national power-holders. Power is still perceived to remain largely within the boundaries of the nation-state. The model of the European superstate does not get much support here.

The ideal power structure is very different from the actual one. Nordic parliamentarians want to put their constitutions into practice. In their ideal world, the purely political or democratic actors dominate in accordance with classical democratic theory and the textbook model: parliament, the cabinet, the electorate, and the political parties have great power, while the power of all the other actors is much more limited.

The changes needed to realize this ideal are twofold: increased power for some of the democratic actors, less power for all the other actors.

On the democratic front, a great increase in the power of the electorate is obviously called for if the ideal is to be achieved. But Nordic MPs also want to increase the power of the already strong parliament—putting the legislature on top in the power hierarchy. The present power of cabinet ministers and political parties, on the other hand, is considered to be about right.

The power of all other actors should be reduced, according to the average Nordic parliamentarian. The two actors considered most powerful—the mass media and the financial markets—are the primary targets.

While the similarities between countries allow us to speak of a common Nordic view of the overall power structure, some interesting differences between the countries remain. Some of these differences can be tentatively explained by differences in institutional setting: for example, the small perceived power of the new and underdeveloped financial market in Iceland and the perception of MPs in Finland and Iceland—where majority governments are the rule—that the power of their cabinet exceeds that of the legislature in a particularly high degree. Other differences may be more difficult to explain: for example, why Swedish and especially Finnish parliamentarians are more discontent with the power structure as they see it than are MPs in the other three countries.

If we compare party families instead of countries, greater differences emerge. Ideological differences within the countries influence the view of power, as clearly seen in table 12.6.

The most important deviation from the Nordic model of pluralist democracy is found among the left socialists and the greens, who hold a remarkably similar view of the power structure. Their perceived power structure is a continuum, like that of the other party families; it has some Marxist overtones, however, and it gives some support to the model of the European superstate. In sum, the left socialists and the greens perceive the capitalists—financial markets, employers' organizations, private business and the EU—as more powerful than do the other party families. The greens and the left socialists believe, moreover, that parliament, the political parties, the trade unions, and the electorate have less power than the average Nordic parliamentarian believes they have.

The perceived power structures of the other party families are much closer to the Nordic model. There are important differences, however, between the social democrats and the nonsocialist parties. The nonsocialists consider the trade unions to be much more powerful than do the social democrats. The social democrats think that financial markets and private business are more influential than do the nonsocialists, especially the conservatives and the populists.

The ideal power structure of all party families except the populists is close to the textbook model: the four democratic actors should have great power and all the other actors should have much less. The party families nevertheless disagree on how little power should be given to some of these other actors.

Since ideological considerations tend to influence both perceived power and preferred power, we obtain the clearest view of the differences between the party families by looking at the changes they desire in the power structure. Strong disagreement is confined to four actors: the trade unions, the European Union, financial markets, and private business.

The nonsocialist parties call for a great reduction in trade-union power, while the left socialists and the social democrats do not see much need for change.

The greens and the left socialists want a great reduction in the power of the EU. This view is to some extent shared by the centrist parties, the populists, and especially the agrarians, but not by the social democrats and the conservatives.

The greens and the left socialists also see a need to greatly reduce the power of financial markets and private business. Their view of financial markets is partly shared by the social democrats, the agrarian parties, and the centrists, and even to a slight extent by the conservatives. However, the social democrats, the centrists, and the agrarian parties favor only a modest reduction in the power of private business, while the conservatives and the populists would like to see a slight increase in private business power.

There is much more agreement among the party families on the changes desired in the power of other actors. All party families want to increase the power of the electorate and of parliament. All think that the powers of the cabinet and the political parties are about right, except for the populists, who want to reduce cabinet power. All party families agree that the power of employers' organizations and of civil servants should be reduced. And all party families most certainly agree that media power has grown out of all decent proportions!

While the similarities in the overall views of power held by the five "average parliamentarians" in the Nordic countries justify speaking of a common Nordic model, one should of course bear in mind that the average parliamentarian does not exist: within each of the five countries, important ideological differences remain, which find expression in the more divergent views of the party families (as we have seen). Two aspects of these differences are of greatest interest.

First, the overall view of power held by the left socialists and the greens is quite different from that held by the nonsocialist parties. While the social democrats deviate from both camps, they seem clearly to be closer to the nonsocialists. These differences are readily understandable in terms of the importance of the left-right spectrum in Nordic politics (given that we classify the greens as on the left).

Second, we can discern a difference between "pro-system" and "anti-system" parties. The parties usually excluded from government—the left socialists,[17] the greens, and the right-wing populists—are extremely discontent with the power structure as they see it, while parties regularly taking part in government coalitions are much more content, especially the social democrats, the centrist parties, and the conservatives.

The Nordic parliaments are by no means rubber stamps, according to the parliamentarians. The average representative in all five countries considers the legislature to be quite powerful, with the partial exception of Finnish MPs and of MPs from "anti-system" parties. How does this compare with other systems?

Since we lack similar measurements from other systems, we cannot really answer this question. We can observe that the U.S. Congress is generally considered one of the most powerful legislatures in the world, while the parliament at Westminster is often judged one of the weakest. From this standpoint, the power of Nordic parliaments probably resembles that of Congress more than that of Westminster—if we take the estimates of Nordic parliamentarians at face value. Nevertheless, an increase in the power of the legislature is called for by the average parliamentarians in all five countries and in all seven party families. They want to be second to none.

NOTES

1. Different variants of the elitist model are possible, of course, depending on what actor or actors are seen to constitute the power elite. Similarly, different variants of the pluralist model are possible, depending on differences in the power ranking of individual actors. A pluralist model does not necessarily imply that all actors have equal power.

2. This transformation from a 0–10 into a 0–100 scale is simply made to omit decimal places in our presentation. The question was as follows: "Using the scale below, could you say how much influence the listed organizations/groups *do have* and how much influence they *ought to have* in today's (name of country) society?" The scale run from "0" (very little influence) to "10" (very influential). The following items were included:(main blue-collar union in country); (main employers' organization in country); private enterprise; press, radio, and TV; voters (electorate as a group); (name of parliament in country); the government; officials in central and local government (civil servants); the political parties; the financial markets; the European Union (EU).

3. Our method clearly differs, however, from that of, e.g., Hunter (1953), who asked a panel of fourteen judges to rank the power of individuals. We ask, by contrast, about the power of institutions/groups, and the answers represent the views of a clearly defined group—Nordic parliamentarians.

4. The question format is designed by Sören Holmberg. In 1985, Swedish parliamentarians were asked to estimate both the actual and the preferred power of eight actors on a 0–10 scale (Holmberg and Esaiasson 1988). Damgaard (1983) reports a Danish study in which voters, parliamentarians, employees of organizations, and civil servants were asked to rank the actual power of five actors, resulting in a differently constructed 0–8 point scale.

5. The range for the whole is thus twenty-nine power points. The range for individual countries is from twenty-seven to thirty-one points, except for Iceland, which shows a larger range of thirty-nine power points.

6. We can also examine the agreement on the power structures in table 12.1 by calculating Pearson's r between the columns. The common Nordic perceived power structure (column 1 in table 12.1) is most strongly correlated with the Danish (r = .93), Norwegian, and Swedish (for both, r = .90) power structures, while its correlations with the Finnish (r = .85) and Icelandic (r = .83) power structures are a bit weaker, but still very high.

If we compare the perceived power structures of individual Nordic countries, the strongest correlations are between Denmark and Norway (r = .86), Denmark and Sweden (r = .84), Sweden and Norway (r = .78), Finland and Sweden (r = .78), and Denmark and Iceland (r = .73). Other correlations are between r = .61 and r = .70.

7. The correlation between the perceived and the preferred power structure for Nordic MPs as a whole is r = .38. The correspondence between the perceived and the preferred power structure is greater in Iceland (r = .64), Norway (r = .51), and Denmark (r = .45) than in Sweden (r = .22) and especially Finland (r = −.03).

8. The correlations between the preferred power structures in individual countries and the preferred Nordic power structure (column 1 in table 12.2) are very high (r = .97 to .99), as are the correlations between individual countries (r = .91 to .99).

9. The change desired by Nordic parliamentarians as a whole (column 1 in table 12.3) is strongly correlated with the desired change in individual countries (r = .92 for Iceland, and r = .97 to .99 for the other countries). Correlations for desired change in individual countries are also very high (r = .85 to .98).

10. Only two out of 659 parliamentarians wanted an increase (by one unit) in media power!

11. We have excluded the Icelandic Women's Alliance from this analysis, as it does not fit within any party family. In some respects, the Women's Alliance resembles the greens, but their views on the power structure differ radically from those of the greens. The remaining thirty-five parties are classified according to the coding of party families presented in appendix 3.

12. By nonsocialist parties we mean the traditional nonsocialists (the centrist parties, agrarian parties, and conservatives) as well as the populists. We are not claiming the greens are socialists, but they have little in common either with the traditional nonsocialists or with the populists, at least where their views on the power structure are concerned.

13. While five of the six party families are very close indeed on their preferred ranking (r = .95 to .98), the left socialists tend to diverge a bit more from the other five. Their correlation with the conservatives is .84, with the centrist parties .89, with the social democrats .90, with the agrarians .92, and with the greens .95.

14. If the populists are excluded, eta^2 = .10. If the left socialists are also excluded, eta^2 = .05.

15. The same trend can be discerned for the other three ideologically controversial actors. The left socialists and the greens consider the EU much more powerful (68–80 power points) than do the conservatives and the social democrats (49–59 points). The left socialists and the greens, on the other hand, think the EU only deserves 30–33 power points, compared to the 48–54 points given to the EU by the conservatives and the social democrats. The left socialists and the greens see financial markets (74–86 points) and private business (67 points) as much more powerful than do the conservatives and the populists (58 points for financial markets and 44–49 points for private business). Conversely, the left socialists and the greens think that financial markets (31–34 points) and private

business (36–41 points) should have much less power than do the conservatives and the populists (50–64 points).

16. If we look only at the four ideologically most controversial actors, the left socialists and the greens want an even bigger change (on average 34–35 points). This is not the case for the other party families. The average changes desired for the four ideologically controversial actors by the social democrats (11 points), the centrist parties (19 points), the agrarian parties (21 points), and the conservatives (10 points) are quite similar to the average changes desired for all actors. The average changes desired by the populists are smaller for the four ideologically controversial actors (17 points) than for all eleven actors (22 points).

17. The left socialist party in Iceland—the People's Alliance—is an exception, inasmuch as it has taken part in three government coalitions in the last twenty years. The Icelandic left socialists are also more content with the power structure ($r = .23$) than are left socialists in the other countries ($r = -.19$ to $-.72$ for individual parties).

DEALING WITH THE OUTSIDE WORLD: EXTERNAL RELATIONS

13

International Networking

Martin Brothén

A characteristic tendency of the postwar period has been the increased internationalization of economic and political life. But internationalization is no new phenomenon in economic and political life; what is new is its sharp acceleration. The economic and political realities of traditional nation-states have been influenced in a sweeping manner by the increase, in well-nigh all policy areas, of mutual dependence and international cooperation between states. The terms of politics are set to an increasing extent by conditions prevailing abroad. Such matters as trade, currency, environmental protection, and international crime-fighting are thought nowadays to be global and cross-border in character. National decisions must take account of international pressures and agreements. Developments abroad have rapid consequences in one's own country. Internationalization thus represents a challenge to the Western democracies, on account of the denser international contacts and weakened national power of decision it entails. Robert Dahl, for one, expects internationalization to result in a shift of the locus of modern democracy from decision-making on a national level to decision-making on a global and international level (1989). Other political scientists have agreed with the assessment that internationalization and globalization represent a challenge to Western democracies (Held 1991; 1995; 1999).

Internationalization and growing international dependence also have a decisive importance for national parliaments (see, for example, Goldmann 1993:93). Nation-building and democratic strivings have historically gone hand in hand. The idea of popular rule through representative and indirect democracy is associated with institutions of a widely ranging character, such as parliament, government, parties, and interest organizations. These institutions have in common their close connection to the nation-state.

The tasks of parliaments have been defined by the needs of the nation-state. But studies in Western democracies have shown that an increased number of tasks in national parliaments are characterized by an international orientation (Jerneck et al. 1988; Jerneck 1990). It has been feared that, with increasing internationalization, national parliaments will lose power and influence. Political and economic developments have thus posed new challenges to parliaments where organization and working procedures are concerned.

For individual members of parliament, too, increased internationalization demands change. The penetration of internationalization and of institutional change is closely related to individual members of the institution in question (Polsby 1968; Sinclair 1989). Parliamentarians have found it difficult to assert themselves in an internationalized and partly new and unaccustomed environment. With internationalization, political and economic decisions are increasingly transferred to the borderland between domestic and foreign policy. Foreign policy has traditionally been the domain of specialists, and of experienced or otherwise exclusive MPs. Internationalization can therefore mean—which is of particular interest from the standpoint of democratic theory—an increasing elitization among parliamentarians, inasmuch as it is primarily MPs with extensive education, good foreign-language skills, and a broad network of international contacts who enjoy prospects for influence in an internationalized environment (Aberbach et al. 1981; Dahl 1989; Sjöblom 1989; Hibbing 1991).

It bears mentioning as well that foreign policy has been seen among voters as an exclusive area and thus scarcely as decisive for how they place their vote in national parliamentary elections (see, e.g., Almond 1960; Rosenau 1961; Converse 1964; Bjereld and Demker 1995).[1] Only seldom have foreign policy and international cooperation been issues in electoral campaigns in Western democracies (Petersson 1982; Goldmann et al. 1986; Gilljam and Holmberg 1993). The common assumption is that the main goals of members of parliament are to make good public policy, to seek influence within the house, and to get re-elected (Fenno 1973). In view of the weak standing in elections and among voters of foreign policy and international questions, MPs working with international and foreign-policy matters have met with difficulty in their re-election bids. International work has had a low merit rating and has scarcely supplied a suitable foundation on which to base one's re-election. MPs involved in international work therefore find themselves in a dilemma. Re-election is a precondition for making good public policy, gaining political influence in parliament, and working further with international questions; at the same time, however, internationally oriented members are penalized by a low merit rating. One may plausibly conclude that, as a result of international-ization, a greater number of MPs will be faced with this dilemma in the future.

It follows, from the definition of internationalization itself, that a study of the internationalization of national parliaments and individual MPs ought to examine MPs' extra-national contacts. The concept of interna-tionalization refers to "processes that manifest themselves in the growth of various kinds of networks of communication, exchange and organization across state borders" (Underdal 1984:4; Hansson and Stenelo 1990:7; cf. Ds 1993:44). Goldmann (1993:84) also argues that internationalization involves an increase in transnational relations across state borders. Some German scholars have stressed that more intensive international contacts among parliamentarians are needed if the challenges of internationaliza-tion are to be met (Kaiser 1971). Sannerstedt and Jerneck (1994:13) write that internationalization and increased dependence on the outside world in a series of policy areas have led to "a sharp expansion in international and transnational contacts on all levels." In recent years, interest in the internationalization of political parties and their contact networks has in-creased (see, e.g., Heidar and Svåsand 1997). Jerneck has used the concept of "Party Diplomacy" in a number of studies to illuminate how interna-tional networks are created through international organizations and party federations (see, among others, Jerneck 1987; 1990; 1997).

The purpose of this study, therefore, is to investigate how increased internationalization will affect and alter the internationally oriented con-tacts and networks developed by individual MPs. Our knowledge about such contacts and networks is limited, as is our knowledge more generally about the manner in which networks and contacts are structured within power elites. As a result of internationalization, efforts at studying the structure of these political networks and contacts must satisfy some new demands; in particular, greater attention must be paid to the territorial and geographical aspect of networks of political power (see, e.g., Petersson 1989:30–32; Petersson et al. 1996:75; cf. Knoke 1990).

One of the foremost dilemmas facing our modern and international-ized democracies is how to combine the international aspects of decision-making with the national aspects, without having to renounce the prin-ciples of popular rule through representative and indirect democracy that have won broad acceptance in Western societies. The question is also whether internationalization can proceed without producing a powerful process of elitization at the same time.

The Nordic countries comprise, in many respects, a geographical area within which the conditions for solving this dilemma may be assumed to be especially good. A widespread Nordism and internationalism, together with far-reaching efforts to achieve equality in political and economic life, have been characteristic of the Nordic societies. Indeed, some scholars speak of a "Nordic model," thus emphasizing similarities among the countries of the region. The Nordic countries have similar welfare systems, for instance. In addition, they bear a mutual likeness in their tradition of popular movements, their spirit of consensus, and their culture of pragmatic decision-making (Heckscher 1984; Esping-Andersen 1990; Petersson 1995:22; see also chapter 2 in this volume).

Petersson claims that three main factors can be detected behind the strong Nordic sense of community: identity, integration, and internationalization. Where integration is concerned, Petersson adduces both formal and informal aspects of contact between the Nordic countries.[2] Petersson indicates that this Nordic orientation has had its strongest support in Iceland. The common cultural and historical background has made close cooperation natural in many areas—economic, political, and cultural. Linguistic affinity has also served to further cooperation among the Nordic countries. Where political matters are concerned, it would appear that the similar structure of the party system in the different Nordic nations has promoted cooperation (Petersson 1991a:148).

Regarding the contacts of MPs in general, we may venture the following hypotheses: First, in line with the findings of previous research, we would expect MPs in general to maintain few cross-border contacts. Second, we would expect MPs to be much better placed to establish such contacts if they have the "right" traits. The "right traits" are often "elite traits," like being highly educated, possessing good foreign-language skills, and having a background as a higher civil servant (see, e.g., Aberbach et al. 1981; NOU 1982; Petersson 1989; Esaiasson and Holmberg 1996; Petersson et al. 1997).

In a geographical region like that formed by the Nordic countries—with their similar culture, history, and political environment—the two general hypotheses may be somewhat rewritten. Thus we would expect Nordic MPs to have more contacts with actors from the other Nordic countries than with actors from outside the Nordic region. We would also expect elite factors to be less important when Nordic MPs establish contacts with actors from the other Nordic countries than when they establish such contacts with non-Nordic actors.

If parliamentarians anywhere have extensive international contacts, and if elite factors anywhere are relatively unimportant for the establishment of such contacts, it is probably in the Nordic region. It should be possible, therefore, to test the general hypotheses using the Nordic region as a critical case of the most likely type (Eckstein 1975).

We would expect the similarity of culture, history, and political environment across the Nordic countries to have the effect of furthering contacts in that region. Therefore, we should find a substantial number of Nordic MPs keeping regular contacts with actors from the other Nordic countries. Furthermore, individual-level factors like education, economic standing, and linguistic skill should not be very important for the development of international contacts among MPs in the equality-oriented Nordic countries. If international contacts and the creation of international exchange can be facilitated without a simultaneous process of elitization, this should be evident from Nordic experiences in this area.

If, on the other hand, the Nordic countries prove not to have a large number of internationally oriented MPs, it would not seem reasonable to expect a high proportion of MPs in other Western democracies to have international contacts either. If we find that individual-level factors like education, economic standing, and linguistic skill are important for the development of international contacts among MPs in the Nordic countries, we may reasonably expect the same to apply to parliamentarians in general.

I shall focus on three questions in this chapter. First, I shall investigate how common international contacts are among Nordic MPs, the object being to ascertain the extent to which Nordic MPs fall into the internationally established pattern of parliamentarians with limited contacts across borders. Second, I shall investigate whether there is a specifically Nordic-oriented contact profile among parliamentarians in the region. With this approach, we can investigate whether a similar culture, history, and political environment further such contacts. Third, I shall seek to determine what explains the degree of international contacts among individual MPs: Is the frequency of such contacts determined by institutional or by individual factors?

Previous Nordic research has shown that, in general, international contacts among parliamentarians are weakly developed and rather uncommon (NOU 1982; Petersson 1989; Petersson et al. 1997). Peter Esaiasson and Sören Holmberg (1996:268–70) have shown that, at the end of the 1980s, the international contacts of Swedish parliamentarians were feebly developed. They observe that fewer than one MP in five reported having regular contacts with any international actor at all.[3] Esaiasson and Holmberg summarize their findings as follows: "Weakly developed international contacts should be added to the list of features characterizing the networks of elected representatives." What validity these results from the late 1980s have for the mid-1990s remains to be investigated. Therefore, the first question will focus on the period since the previous studies were carried out. This was a period characterized by rapid internationalization.

The specifically Nordic tradition of cooperation makes it reasonable to expect a special Nordic dimension in the contact patterns of parliamentarians. Cultural similarities and common historical experiences have been thought to promote the development of Nordic contact networks (see, e.g., Jerneck 1997:143). Cooperation between the Nordic countries has traditionally been strong. The second question posed in this chapter is therefore aimed at ascertaining whether or not there is a Nordic contact dimension. The existence of a specifically Nordic contact profile would show it is not impossible for international contacts to develop, at any rate if the conditions are good. On the other hand, the international research results— which show little in the way of far-reaching contacts among MPs from different nations—would be supported if the Nordic contact dimension proves to be weakly developed or not at all.

How the existence of international contacts is to be explained is the third question posed in this chapter. We can expect both institutional and individual factors to be important. We shall seek to ascertain which factors determine the shape and intensity of international contact patterns by comparing the impact of institutional and country-specific factors (e.g., the institutional arrangement in a given country) with that of individual-level factors.

We can test the first-mentioned explanatory factor with the help of the varying choices made by the Nordic countries in regard to association with the European Union. For a long time, the process of European integration has been a prominent element in a more general process of internationalization; thus we can use it as an indicator of internationalization (Sjöblom 1989:64; Petersson 1991a). In what follows, therefore, the integration process under way in Europe is treated as an aspect of a more comprehensive internationalization process. The implications for national parliaments of European integration have received attention among researchers (Smith 1996; Norton 1995; chapter 14 in this volume). All of the Nordic countries are affected by this process; Denmark has been a member of the union for many years, Sweden and Finland have recently joined, and Norway and Iceland have chosen to stay out.

Within the framework of the country-specific and institutional explanatory factors, we will test whether parliamentary size has any effect on the degree to which members of parliament keep international contacts. It might be thought that, since large parliaments provide for a more far-reaching specialization and division of labor among MPs, they will offer greater opportunities for the development of extra-national contacts. Small parliaments do not offer the same opportunities; it might therefore be expected that their members will be less internationally oriented. With its 349 elected members, the Swedish parliament diverges markedly in size from its Nordic counterparts. The other Nordic parliaments are much smaller. The hypothesis is therefore that Swedish parliamentarians will have more extensive international contact networks than their colleagues in the other Nordic countries.

The individual-level factors include educational background, previous work experience, and type of constituency. Sjöblom (1989) has earlier pointed out some characteristics influencing the degree to which international contacts are developed. According to him, such elite characteristics as good language skills and international knowledge and experience are associated most closely with extensive international contacts. In themselves, international contacts are of great importance in an internationalized democratic system. With internationalization may follow the necessity, therefore, for a growing proportion of politicians in general, and of parliamentarians in particular, to develop such characteristics. In this way, internationalization affects how decision-makers are recruited. The qualities highlighted by Sjöblom as critical for MPs' capacity to develop usable international contacts are all of such a character that an increased stress on such factors in the recruitment of decision-makers would lead to a distinct elitization of the elective institutions. Sjöblom also believes that election campaigns may be affected when internationalized MPs seek re-election (Sjöblom 1989:6–7). One purpose of this chapter is to study whether or not there is cause to expect such an process of elitization in the Nordic parliaments.

DATA

The analysis in this chapter is based on the materials presented in the introductory chapter of this book. Parliamentarians were asked to answer a specific question about their oral and written contacts over the last year with about twenty different actors—local, national, and international. The question put to MPs was formulated as follows: "This question deals with your contacts as a politician with various organizations, groups and authorities in the past year. Disregarding how the contact was taken, how often have you in the the past year, personally or by letter, been in touch with the organizations, groups or agencies below?"

The question provided five distinct headings under which the twenty or so actors were grouped: the labor-market interest organizations, executive actors, "your own" party organization, "other" interest organizations, and international actors. Employers' and wage-earners' organizations fell under the labor- market interest organizations, as did branch organizations for agriculture, business, and industry. Contacts with executive actors included contacts with cabinet ministers, senior civil servants, other governmental authorities, and local governmental authorities. Contacts inside the individual's own party organization included contacts with the local party structure in his or her district (both within and outside the MP's own constituency) and with national party organization. A number of other groups and organizations were listed in the question besides: for example, disabled persons' organizations, environmental organizations, women's organizations, and temperance/teetotaler organizations.

The three levels in the international hierarchy that we asked respondents to indicate were formulated as follows: foreign politicians/government agencies/organizations/companies in the Nordic countries, foreign politicians/government agencies/organizations/companies in the European Union,[4] and international organizations. The five replies with which MPs could indicate the frequency of their contacts ranged from at least once a week to never, with once or twice a month, a few times, and occasionally in between.

The question as we have framed it has certain limitations.[5] Studying MPs' real behavior on the basis of the answers they supply in a questionnaire is problematic. The risk is that the MPs will overestimate (or underestimate) the extent of their contacts. The problem is the same with all studies of human behavior that make use of questionnaires. Nor do the questions make it possible to distinguish which of the involved parties took the initiative for contact in the individual case. For the purposes of this study, however, it is not necessary to know who took the initiative. Other factors speaking for the usability of the question design are the low internal refusal rate and the earlier studies of panel stability in the available data (Esaiasson and Holmberg 1996:265).[6]

CONTACT PROFILES AMONG NORDIC PARLIAMENTARIANS

Earlier studies of the networks and contacts of parliamentarians have mainly taken their theoretical point of departure in the functional or sectorial structure of these networks. In functionally oriented network studies, the politically relevant networks are structured along the lines of various functions, such as legislation, the administration of justice, or the formation of opinion (Petersson 1989:19–22; Esaiasson and Holmberg 1996:268). Great attention has been devoted in social-science research to sectorial networks, with a focus on their political content. Sectorially structured networks and contacts lead to the drawing of boundaries between policy sectors, such as housing, agriculture, and education (Damgaard 1981; Hernes 1983; 1984; Nergaard 1988; Hernes and Nergaard 1989; Petersson 1989; Esaiasson and Holmberg 1996, ch. 12. See also Petersson et al. 1997).[7]

Fewer studies have chosen, like the present one, to stress the territorial structure of MPs' contacts and networks (see, e.g., Esaiasson and Holmberg 1996; Petersson et al. 1997). I shall investigate three levels in the territorial structure of the international contact patterns of Nordic MPs: the Nordic, the European, and the global. Such a division actually entails a gross simplification of international contact patterns. A larger number of levels could be specified in a more comprehensive territorial hierarchy. For the purpose, however, of increasing our relatively limited knowledge about the international contacts of Nordic parliamentarians, the division suggested above is sufficiently fine; nor is it especially uncommon in political science research (see, e.g., Heidar et al. 1997).[8]

That MPs' contacts are organized on a territorial basis of some kind emerges with great clarity from the studies that have been done of the parliaments of Nordic countries. With the help of a factor analysis, we can summarize MPs' contacts with some twenty different political institutions, organizations, and groups by means of six different contact profiles (see table 13.1).

One of the six contact profiles emerging from a factor analysis of the material is territorially structured.[9] The international (factor I) contact profile features contacts with national organizations involved in international questions; contacts with politicians, agencies, and companies in the Nordic region and the EU; and contacts with international organizations. This contact profile alone explains more than one-fourth of the variance in answers received to the question.[10] The results are the same in all five Nordic countries. In every Nordic country, we can distinguish an internationally oriented profile in the contact patterns of MPs. Moreover, this profile features the same four internationally oriented interfaces in all of the countries except Iceland.[11] It also explains a fairly large proportion of the variance in answers received to the question.[12]

From the rest of the material it follows that Nordic parliamentarians in the mid-1990s arrange their contacts on the basis of a further five factors as well. These contact dimensions each explain between 6 and 12 percent of the variance in answers received.

The contact dimension that, after the territorial dimension, explains the largest proportion of the variance in answers received is the executive

Table 13.1

Principal Component Factor Analysis of Nordic Members' Personal Contacts with Various Organizations and Official Bodies (orthogonal rotation)

	International (Factor I)	Executive Power (Factor II)	Interest Organizations (Factor III)	Trade Unions (Factor IV)	Own Party (Factor V)	Trade and Industry (Factor VI)
Labor market interest organizations						
Blue-collar	.11	.12	.09	**.81**	.12	.07
White-collar	.06	.04	.14	**.85**	.10	.14
Academics	.23	.04	.17	**.68**	.08	.30
Farmers' org.	.02	.11	.14	.04	.15	**.81**
Employers' Confed.	.17	.09	.05	.27	.06	**.77**
Executive actors						
Cabinet ministers	.28	**.77**	.00	.05	.00	.01
Senior civil servants	.24	**.84**	.05	.10	.03	.10
Other gov. authorities	.18	**.83**	.18	.02	.09	.08
Local gov. authorities	.25	**.45**	.35	.18	.29	.14
Party organizations						
Local party in own district	.14	.06	.05	.20	**.73**	.03
Other local party org.	.27	.06	.06	.05	**.79**	.09
National party org.	.37	.05	.00	.04	**.71**	.11

Interest organizations	Factor 1	Factor 2	Factor 3	Factor 4	Factor 5	Factor 6
Disableds' orgs.	.09	.09	**.81**	.24	.00	.00
Environmental orgs.	.23	.02	**.51**	.03	.38	.10
Pensioners' orgs.	.08	.17	**.80**	.21	.03	.08
Confessional orgs.	.12	.01	**.56**	.09	.03	.40
National orgs. working with international issues	**.66**	.06	.26	.03	.21	.03
International actors						
Foreign politicians/executive authorities/orgs./companies in Nordic countries	**.79**	.28	.01	.10	.10	.08
Foreign politicians/executive authorities/orgs./companies in the European Union	**.85**	.22	.04	.06	.04	.10
International orgs.	**.87**	.15	.14	.01	.10	.07
% variance	27	12	9	8	7	6
Eigenvalue	5.3	2.4	1.7	1.5	1.3	1.2

Notes: Varimax rotation. Kaiser's criterion has been used for determining the number of factors. All variables scored from 1 to 5. Number of respondents is 633.

power (12 percent, factor II). The factor analysis also underlines the importance of interaction between MPs and organizations on the labor market. Contacts with trade-union organizations (factor IV) add up to a distinct dimension of their own. Contacts with trade and industry (factor VI) also comprise a dimension of their own. A further dimension structures MPs' contacts along the lines of their own party organization (factor V). Another contact profile is tied to interest organizations (factor III). This latter contact profile features contacts with churches, religious organizations, associations for the promotion of temperance, and organizations devoted to pensioners and handicapped persons.[13]

The results show very clearly that MPs in the Nordic countries make a distinction between contacts with their own party organization and contacts with the executive power (the functional aspect). It also follows from the analysis that MPs structure their contacts in accordance with the sectorial aspect (since we found a distinct dimension tied to different interest organizations). The most interesting finding for this chapter, however, is that MPs in the Nordic countries structure their contacts and networks not just on the basis of *functional* and *sectorial* principles, but also on the basis of *territorial* ones (the territorial aspect).

INTERNATIONALLY ORIENTED CONTACTS

Previous international, Nordic, and, specifically, Swedish research has shown, as mentioned earlier in this chapter, that it is generally uncommon for parliamentarians to maintain international contacts. The first task in this chapter is to ascertain whether these results apply as well to Nordic MPs in the mid-1990s, or whether instead the Nordic countries diverge from the general international pattern regarding international contacts and thus constitute a model of their own.

Table 13.2 indicates how common it is for Nordic MPs to keep international contacts in the Nordic region, in the EU, and with international organizations. The table states the percentage of MPs who keep regular contacts with representatives for each international level. Contacts are "regular" if the MP has contacts with representatives for the level in question at least once or twice a month. The table also includes the mean value for the regularity of members' international contacts.[14] The regularity of contacts can vary from 1 to 5 for each territorial level; values under 4 correspond to irregular contacts or none at all, while values 4 and 5 correspond to regular contacts (at least once or twice a month).

Only one Nordic MP in five keeps regular contacts with actors on the

Table 13.2
Members' Contacts with Other Nordic Countries, the European Union, and International Organizations, Respectively, with an Index for Summed International Contacts (mean values, % regular contacts, and eta-square)

	All		Denmark		Finland		Iceland		Norway		Sweden		Eta²
	Mean	%	Mean	%	Mean	%	Mean	%	Mean	%	Mean	%	
To the Nordic countries	2.7	22	2.9	28	2.7	21	3.1	37	2.9	28	2.5	17	.04
To EU/Europe	2.5	19	2.8	28	2.6	20	2.6	9	2.6	22	2.3	16	.03
With international orgs.	2.5	18	2.8	26	2.8	18	2.7	9	2.6	21	2.3	16	.03
International orientation (index)	2.6		2.8		2.7		2.8		2.7		2.4		.04
N	721		102		114		43		141		321		

Notes: Contacts are considered "regular" if, during the last year, MPs had oral or written contacts twice a month or more often with politicians, government agencies, organizations, and companies in the Nordic countries or in the EU, or with international organizations. Each eta-square value in the right-hand column is based on a one-way analysis of variance with number of international contacts as the dependent variable and country as the independent variable.

Nordic, European, or broader international levels. There is thus reason to conclude that only a small proportion of the contacts of Nordic MPs are internationally oriented. Nordic MPs do not diverge from the international pattern mentioned earlier regarding parliamentarians' international contacts; they do not have more extensive international contacts than their colleagues in the world generally.

If we compare the situation of Swedish MPs at the end of the 1980s with that in the mid-1990s, we find that a certain increase in international contacts has probably occurred. We can compare the regularity of Swedish MPs' international contacts between 1988 and 1994 in two areas: with "foreign politicians/government agencies/organizations/companies in the Nordic countries," on the one hand, and with "international organizations," on the other. In both cases, the share of MPs with regular contacts (that is, at least once or twice a month) has increased. The proportion of MPs with regular contacts in the Nordic region has increased by 9 percentage points, from 8 to 17 percent. The proportion of MPs keeping regular contacts with international organizations has increased by 6 percentage points during the same period, from 11 to 17 percent.[15]

At the same time, the material in table 13.2 indicates that members of the Danish Folketing are more internationally oriented in general than are their counterparts in the other Nordic countries. As compared to the other Nordic parliaments, the Folketing has a higher share of members maintaining regular contacts on the EU/European level (28 percent), as well as with international organizations (26 percent). When it comes to contacts within the Nordic region, we find that the share of Danish and Norwegian MPs with regular contacts is the same (28 percent).

Iceland distinguishes itself through its high proportion of Nordic-oriented members (37 percent) and its relatively small share of MPs oriented to the EU (9 percent) or to international organizations (9 percent). No other Nordic country shows so high a proportion of MPs with Nordic contacts. The proportion of MPs who keep regular contacts varies greatly between the different levels in Iceland, more than in any other Nordic country. A higher proportion of Icelandic MPs have regular Nordic contacts than have comparable contacts at the EU/European level or with international organizations. In Norway, too, the proportion of MPs with Nordic contacts is higher (at 28 percent) than the proportion keeping contacts with actors in the EU (22 percent) or with international organizations (21 percent). In the remaining countries, differences between MPs' contacts at the various territorial levels are less apparent.

Thus, international contacts among Nordic MPs are not similarly structured in all of the Nordic countries. Quite the contrary; the differences are palpable. No common Nordic structure can be discerned in regard to territorially defined contacts. However, the statistical correlation (eta-square) between country and international contacts on the different levels is relatively weak.[16]

NORDIC-ORIENTED CONTACTS

The object of the following analysis is to investigate the possible existence of a Nordic contact profile among parliamentarians, and thus to answer the second question posed in this chapter. It was emphasized earlier that, in historical, cultural, and linguistic terms, there is much that unites the Nordic countries, even if many important differences also make themselves felt. With the favorable conditions existing for exchange between the Nordic countries, a result showing few contacts would be surprising. Our expection is rather that a clear Nordic contact profile will emerge.

We have divided Nordic MPs into four logically exhaustive categories on the basis of the regularity of their Nordic and European contacts. Both Nordic and European contacts have been dichotomized so as to separate MPs with regular contacts from those with irregular contacts or none at all. Hence four categories can be formed: "both Nordic and European contacts," "Nordic contacts, but not European ones," "European contacts, but not Nordic ones," and "neither European nor Nordic contacts." Table 13.3 shows how Nordic MPs distribute themselves in percentage terms among the four categories.

Except in the case of Iceland, the picture that emerges is both unambiguous and surprising. There appears not to be any specifically Nordic contact profile among MPs in Denmark, Finland, Norway, or Sweden. Iceland constitutes a distinct exception in this regard. Icelandic parliamentarians have substantial Nordic contacts and only sparse European ones. It bears recalling here that research has shown that the Nordic orientation has been strongest precisely in Iceland. In a study from 1983 on the subject of citizens' attitudes toward Nordic cooperation and the other Nordic countries, respondents in all Nordic countries averred that Nordic cooperation is important. This finding was strongest in the case of the Icelanders interviewed (Petersson 1991a:148). On the basis of the present study, moreover, it can be stated that this result applies to the members of the Althingi as well.

Perhaps the most interesting question to ask of the material is whether there are any MPs at all with specifically Nordic contacts. It can be stated that, with the exception of Icelandic MPs, it is more common for Nordic

Table 13.3
Nordic Members and Their Type of International Contacts (% with regular contacts)

	All	Denmark	Finland	Iceland	Norway	Sweden	EU[a]	Not EU[b]	Difference EU/Not EU
Both Nordic region and Europe	15	21	15	9	19	13	21	14	+7
Nordic region but not Europe	7	8	6	28	8	4	8	7	+1
Europe but not Nordic region	4	7	5	0	3	3	7	3	+4
Neither Nordic region nor Europe	74	64	74	63	70	80	64	76	-12
Total	100	100	100	100	100	100	100	100	
N	721	102	114	43	141	321	102	619	

Notes: The percentage of MPs with regular contacts refers to the proportion of parliamentarians who report having had contacts "once or twice a month" or more often with "foreign politicians/government agencies/organizations/companies in the Nordic countries" or with "foreign politicians/government agencies/organizations/companies in the European Union." Other respondents are considered to have irregular contacts or none at all.

[a] Countries with EU membership (Denmark).

[b] Countries without EU membership (Finland, Iceland, Norway, and Sweden).

parliamentarians to have both Nordic and European contacts than for them to have purely European contacts or purely Nordic contacts. However, the majority of members in all of the countries lack both European and Nordic contacts. The great majority of MPs are either internationally oriented on both the Nordic and European levels or not internationally oriented at all. Only a very small number of members choose to orient their contacts either to the Nordic region or to the EU. It is, to reiterate, mainly among Icelandic parliamentarians that a specifically Nordic contact profile can be found.[17]

No pronounced Nordic dimension and sense of community can, accordingly, be observed among Nordic parliamentarians. In view of our expectations of finding a Nordic contact profile, these results must be considered worth highlighting. Not even in a Nordic setting have we been able to observe or study such a regional profile in MPs' contacts. The material sooner indicates a unidimensional structure in MPs' territorially structured contacts. It is more a question of the degree of international orientation than of any definite geographical or territorial connection.

The finding that MPs' territorial contacts are structured in a unidimensional manner is something to bear in mind in the continued analysis. On the basis of this result, we can summarize the territorial contacts of MPs by means of a common index. The index embraces, on the one hand, contacts with politicians, government agencies, organizations, and companies in the Nordic countries and the EU; and, on the other, contacts with international organizations.[18] The index can vary from 1 to 5; values under 4 correspond to irregular contacts or none at all, while values 4 and 5 correspond to regular contacts, and are used for parliamentarians who have international contacts once a month or more often.[19]

INSTITUTIONAL OR INDIVIDUAL EXPLANATORY FACTORS

Certain differences emerged earlier in the chapter when it comes to how MPs in the Nordic countries orient their international contacts. A weak correlation between nationality and international orientation could be observed already from the material in table 13.2. In what follows, the reasons behind these differences will come under focus and investigation. By comparing the impact of national and institutional factors with that of a range of individual factors, I shall investigate the extent to which differences in the international orientation of MPs can be traced to differences between countries and thus to the differing institutional arrangements of the various parliaments.

In the following, I will examine different explanatory factors on both the national/institutional and the individual level. First, I shall study such factors as relate to the differing institutional solutions applied to international cooperation in the Nordic parliaments. Second, I shall explore such factors as relate to differences between individual MPs. Is the degree of regularity in MPs' personal contacts explained mainly by factors common to the entire parliament of a given country, or for the most part by factors specific to individual MPs? The two perspectives to be compared are the institutional perspective and the individual perspective. The different countries' varying degrees of association with the European Union, and the varying size of their parliaments as well, can be used as indicators of the first-mentioned type of explanatory factor.

European Union membership is an important way of organizing international cooperation. The variation in this regard between the countries featured in the study makes this factor usable for explaining the degree of international orientation in different countries. What primarily distinguishes each country from the others is whether it has been in the EU for a long time, for just a few years, or not at all. The Nordic countries group themselves into three categories in this regard. Denmark has been a member of the union for many years, Sweden and Finland have recently joined, and Iceland and Norway have chosen to remain outside the union.

If membership in the union has importance for the development of international contacts, then the international contact patterns of Danish MPs should diverge from that of their colleagues in the other Nordic countries. The Swedish and Finnish situations are virtually identical: the two countries entered the union at the same time. The Icelandic and Norwegian situations are similar as well. The study was carried out precisely during the transitional period to Swedish and Finnish membership in the union. It is relevant to investigate whether this aspect of international cooperation affects the international contacts of MPs. Does membership in the European Union have any significance for the degree of international orientation in members' contacts? This variable can be dichotomized in the present study. Danish MPs can be distinguished from MPs hailing from the other four Nordic countries.

The hypothesis can be formulated in the following fashion: if Danish MPs prove to have more international contacts than do their colleagues in Finland, Norway, Sweden, and Iceland, then the manner in which a country's international cooperation is organized has importance for the regularity of contacts. Tables 13.2 and 13.3 above suggest that this is the case, that the average degree of international orientation is higher for Danish MPs than for their counterparts in the other four countries. Before such a result can be established, however, it must be ascertained whether the observed difference persists even after individual-level explanatory factors are controlled for. Furthermore, the second institutional explanatory factor—parliamentary size—must be considered as well. The impact of two institutional factors—parliamentary size and the manner in which a country's international cooperation is organized vis-à-vis the EU—will therefore be measured against the impact of four groups of individual-level factors: parliament-related factors, like committee placement, leadership position, seniority, and international parliamentary assignments; party-related factors; person-related factors, like gender, occupation, and linguistic skill; and constituency-related factors.

Members with leading positions in their parliament may be assumed to keep more extensive contacts, both nationally and internationally. It has been shown, for example, that party-group leaders in the Storting have more regular contacts with ministers than do rank-and-file members of the same party group (Galtung 1966; Hernes and Nergaard 1989). Esaiasson and Holmberg present results indicating that Swedish MPs in leading positions have well-developed international contacts (Esaiasson and Holmberg 1996:272).

International research has shown that MPs' seniority has importance for the development of contacts (Aberbach et al. 1981). Members with lower seniority have more regular contacts with average citizens, with interest organizations, and with their own party organization on the local level (grass-roots networks, local party leaders, local officials). From this the authors draw the following conclusion: "In most parliamentary systems, especially where there is some measure of district representation, junior members are likely to specialize within their constituencies. More senior politicians seem to devote less time to such contacts" (Aberbach et al. 1981:227). Probably, therefore, the opportunity for international contacts is greater for senior MPs. Other research demonstrates the likelihood that junior members of parliament will have fewer international contacts than their more established colleagues, and a greater number of local contacts (Aberbach et al. 1981:211; Hernes and Nergaard 1989:196; Esaiasson and Holmberg 1996:272).

One earlier finding demonstrates a strong correlation between MPs' parliamentary position and their seniority (Hagevi 1995). Leading positions in parliament are held by members with high seniority. MPs' seniority also partly determines their placement on committees, especially those relating to foreign policy. Both of these features—leading position and internationally oriented committee placement—are normally associated with dense and recurrent international contacts.

Committees are important in Nordic parliamentary work (see chapter 10 in this volume; Damgaard 1994). It is therefore relevant to investigate whether members' committee placement has any significance for how they organize their contacts. Research on the sectorial structure of MPs' contacts has earlier ascribed great importance to committees. The territorial organization of contacts can also be affected by MPs' committee placement. There is reason to believe that committees are internationally oriented in varying degrees. Where Swedish conditions are concerned, Jerneck has argued that the international orientation is most pronounced in the Committee on Agriculture, the Committee on Industry and Trade, the Committee on Finance, and the Committee on Foreign Affairs. The same study shows the Committee on Housing to be the least internationally oriented (Jerneck 1987). One reasonable hypothesis is that members of the Committee on Foreign Affairs are more internationally oriented than other MPs (Esaiasson and Holmberg 1996:275). It is also reasonable to expect that parliamentarians with internationally oriented assignments to the Nordic Council, the Council of Europe, or the Interparliamentary Union are more internationally oriented than other members, and perhaps more so even than members of the Committee on Foreign Affairs.

Interest has increased in recent years in the internationalization of political parties and their contact networks. Most parties in the Scandinavian countries have reinforced and broadened their international commitments during the last ten years (see, e.g., Heidar and Svåsand 1997). Party affiliation, on the other hand, seems not to have any intuitively obvious effect on the degree of international orientation, inasmuch as no one party group can be seen as more internationally oriented than the others. How party affiliation affects the shape and structure of MPs' international contacts is sooner an empirical question. One analysis of the average degree of international orientation on the part of the various parties shows that centrist and rightist parties keep the most regular international contacts.[20] The question remaining to be answered is whether party affiliation has an independent impact on the degree of MPs' international orientation.

Cooperation in networks is often considered typically female. At the same, international cooperation, international relations, and international policy are commonly regarded as a typical male-dominated policy area (see, e.g., Tickner 1991). It is therefore difficult to judge what significance, if any, MPs' gender has for the development of international contacts. Studies of the international contacts of Swedish MPs give no guidance on this question (Esaiasson and Holmberg 1996:27).

MPs' educational background and occupational affiliation can be thought to have importance for the degree of their international contacts.

Gudmund Hernes and Kristine Nergaard have found, however, that background factors such as education and occupation have only a small importance for MPs' contacts with the executive power (Hernes and Nergaard 1989:197). In what follows, I shall investigate whether MPs' previous occupational affiliation has any impact on the degree to which they develop international contacts. The expectation is that parliamentarians who had previously been blue-collar workers will not develop extensive international contacts in the same way as parliamentarians who had previously been white-collar employees, self-employed, or farmers.

I shall investigate educational background mainly indirectly. One characteristic important for MPs in an internationalized world is proficiency in one of the major world languages. Such linguistic proficiency is closely associated with educational level. In what follows, I shall examine the extent to which linguistic proficiency explains the extent of MPs' territorially structured contacts. Gunnar Sjöblom has stressed the increased importance of good language skills in an period of internationalization (Sjöblom 1989:67). One purpose in this chapter is to ascertain whether MPs' linguistic proficiency influences the degree of international orientation in their contact networks. The question to be answered is whether linguistically talented MPs have more extensive international contacts than their colleagues.

I furthermore assume that MPs from the capital cities have fewer local contacts than do MPs from smaller towns and the countryside. Capital-city representatives thus have more time left over for international contacts. Capital cities are also a natural setting for international exchange. In the following analysis, we shall test whether representatives for Stockholm, Reykjavík, Oslo, Copenhagen, and Helsinki have more international contacts than do their colleagues from outside the capital cities.

We shall now look more closely at how these characteristics and factors on the part of individual MPs affect the degree of international orientation in their contacts. Table 13.4 presents a bivariate analysis and average mean value for MPs' contacts with politicians, government agencies, organizations, and companies in the Nordic countries and the EU, as well as for their contacts with other international organizations. The table also includes the mean value for the regularity of members' international contacts, using the index from table 13.2. All the explanatory variables mentioned earlier have been dichotomized: first, the index value is shown for parliamentarians with the relevant trait; second, the index value is shown for parliamentarians without the relevant trait. For every variable, the table shows the difference between the two groups at each territorial level, as well as the variance explained. It includes all of the Nordic

Table 13.4

International Contacts of Nordic Members by Various Determinants (mean scores and proportion of variance explained)

Determinants	Nordic		European		International		Overall		N
	Mean	R^2	Mean	R^2	Mean	R^2	Mean	R^2	
Parliament-related									
In leading position	3.2		2.9		3.0		3.0		56
Not in leading position	2.7		2.5		2.5		2.6		665
Difference	**+0.5**	.02*	**+0.4**	.01*	**+0.5**	.01*	**+0.4**	.02*	
High seniority	3.1		2.8		2.8		2.9		225
Low seniority	2.5		2.4		2.5		2.5		496
Difference	**+0.6**	.05*	**+0.4**	.03*	**+0.3**	.02*	**+0.4**	.04*	
Member of foreign affairs committee	3.3		3.2		3.3		3.3		70
Not member of foreign affairs committee	2.6		2.4		2.4		2.5		537
Difference	**+0.7**	.04*	**+0.8**	.06*	**+0.9**	.07*	**+0.8**	.06*	
International assignments	3.1		2.7		2.7		2.9		174
No international assignments	2.6		2.5		2.5		2.5		547
Difference	**+0.5**	.04*	**+0.2**	.01*	**+0.2**	.01*	**+0.4**	.02	
Party related									
Centrist or conservative party	3.0		2.9		2.8		2.9		207
Other party	2.6		2.4		2.4		2.5		506
Difference	**+0.4**	.03*	**+0.5**	.04*	**+0.4**	.02*	**+0.4**	.04*	
Person-related									
Female	2.6		2.4		2.5		2.5		262

Male	2.7	.00	2.6	.01*	2.6	.01	2.6	.01*	455
Difference	**-0.1**		**-0.2**		**-0.1**		**-0.1**		
Self-employed/farmer or not gainfully									
employed	2.8	.02*	2.6	.03*	2.6	.03*	2.7	.04*	631
Worker	2.2		1.9		2.0		2.0		71
Difference	**+0.6**		**+0.7**		**+0.6**		**+0.7**		
Language skills good	2.8	.08*	2.7	.11*	2.7	.10*	2.8	.12*	520
Langauge skills not good	2.1		1.9		1.9		2.0		146
Difference	**+0.7**		**+0.8**		**+0.8**		**+0.8**		
District-related									
Capital city	3.0	.01*	2.7	.00	2.7	.01*	2.8	.01*	85
Not capital city	2.6		2.5		2.5		2.5		522
Difference	**+0.4**		**+0.2**		**+0.2**		**+0.3**		

Note: Data derive in part from publicly registered data about MPs, in part from information obtained through the questionnaire. MPs are considered to hold *leading positions* if they are chairman or vice-chairman of their party group. Icelandic MPs with previous service as ministers are classified as part of this group, as are the so-called political chairpersons in the Danish Folketing. Members have also been classified according to their *seniority* in parliament. Those with nine or more previous years in parliament have high seniority; those with fewer than nine years have low seniority. *Committee placement* divides MPs who sit on their parliament's foreign affairs committee from those who do not. MPs selected to their parliament's delegation to the Nordic Council, the Council of Europe, or the Interparliamentary Union have been classified as having *international assignments*. MPs not so selected are treated as lacking international assignments. The parties have been divided into the following seven categories (see also appendix 3): left parties (Left Socialist Party, the Unity List, Left-Wing Alliance, Socialist Left Party, the Red Electoral Alliance, Left Party, People's Alliance), social democrats (Social-Democrats, Social Democrats, Social Democratic Party, People's Movement), centrist parties (Radical Party, Center Democrats, Swedish People's Party, Christian League, Liberals, Christian People's Party, People's Party, Christian Democrats), conservative parties (Conservatives, National Coalition, Conservatives, Moderate Unit Party, Independence Party), agrarian parties (Liberals, Finnish Center, Center Party, Center Party, Progressive Party), green/new parties (Green League, Ecology Party, Women's Alliance), and populist parties (Progress Party, Rural Party, Progress Party, Free Democrats). *Party affiliation* distinguishes center and conservative parties from the other parties. Where *occupational affiliation* is concerned, blue-collar workers have been contrasted with the other occupational categories (white-collar employees, farmers, and the self-employed) and with persons not gainfully employed. MPs have been classified according to whether or not they speak one or more (at most four) of the leading world languages. Members representing the constituencies of Stockholm City, Stockholm County, Oslo, Copenhagen, and Reykjavík are contrasted with those representing other constituencies.

*$p < .05$.

countries, and it provides a basis for further discussion of the significance of different explanatory factors for determining the territorial contacts of MPs.[21]

The main conclusion of the investigation is that all of the factors seem to have the expected effect on parliamentarians' contacts. The results also indicate that individual-level factors—such as linguistic proficiency, occupational background, and committee placement—have a somewhat stronger effect than the other factors. All of the differences in the table provide support, if rather weakly in certain cases, for the hypotheses earlier presented. It can be seen from the table that MPs with the following characteristics have more developed international contacts than do those of their colleagues without said characteristics: high seniority; a leading position in the party group; a place on the Committee on Foreign Affairs; or a place in a delegation to the Nordic Council, the Council of Europe, or the Interparliamentary Union.

The table further indicates that centrist and conservative parties have more regular international contacts than do other party representatives in the Nordic parliaments. At most, however, the variance explained comes to 4 percent. In addition, previous occupational affiliation, and to some extent gender and constituency affiliation, appear to affect the degree of international contacts. Linguistic proficiency has a large impact on the degree of international contacts—the largest of the variables shown in the table. Up to 11 percent (and 8 percent at the least) of the variance in international contacts on the three different levels is explained by the linguistic variable.

Viewing all three territorial levels together—as in the index—the variance explained ranges between 1 percent (gender and constituency affiliation) and 12 percent (linguistic proficiency). Committee placement explains 6 percent of the variance.

The conclusion we can draw from table 13.4, accordingly, is that committee placement and linguistic proficiency have the greatest impact on the degree of international orientation in MPs' contact networks. It is two factors associated with social exclusivity, then, which influence the degree of international orientation among individual members in the highest degree. To get an idea of the impact of the different individual-level explanatory factors in relation to each other, and above all in relation to the institutional factors, a multivariate regression analysis can be used. The results of such analysis are presented in table 13.5. All of the countries investigated except Finland are included in the analysis. The table also presents a corresponding multivariate analysis for each Nordic country, Finland again excepted.[22]

Table 13.5

Determinants of Members' International Contacts (unstandardized regression coefficients, OLS-estimates)

| | International Contacts coded (1–5) | | | | |
	All	Denmark	Iceland	Norway	Sweden
Country					
Denmark	.28*				
Iceland	.08				
Norway	.31*				
Parliament-related					
Leading position	.20	.37	.06	.03	.24
Seniority	.32*	.08	.32	.14	.44*
Committee placement	.59*	.24	.42	1.08*	.67*
International assignment	.22*	.02	.16	.18	.38*
Party related					
Party	.25*	.00	−.24	.12	.44*
Person-related					
Gender	.14	−.23	.43	.05	.24*
Occupation	.27*	.17	—	.48	.19
Linguistic proficiency	.64*	1.06*	.79	.83*	.47*
District-related					
Capital city	.18	−.42	.28	−.20	.40*
Constant	1.26*	1.86*	1.48*	1.39*	1.22*
Adjusted R^2	.26	.14	.08	.28	.31
No. of Respondents	558	97	43	123	295

Note: For information about the coding of variables, see table 13.4.

*$p < .05$.

The table shows that factors on both the national and the individual level explain the extent to which elected representatives in the Nordic countries keep international contacts. Taken together, the explanatory factors specified in the model explain 26 percent of the total variance found in Nordic MPs' international contact patterns. The explanatory power of the model varies somewhat between the countries: it is highest in Sweden and Norway (31 and 28 percent, respectively) and lowest in Denmark and Iceland (14 and 8 percent, respectively).

The results of this analysis clearly show that national affiliation affects the extent of international contacts on the part of Nordic MPs. Danish and Norwegian parliamentarians have more regular international contacts than do Icelandic parliamentarians. It is probably some other factor than a country's relationship to the European Union that determines the degree of international orientation on the part of its MPs. If the relationship to the EU had been the decisive thing, the results for Norway and Denmark would not have been so similar.

Nor does this result indicate that an institutional factor such as parliamentary size has any significance for the degree to which the MPs develop international contacts. If it did, the conditions for international exchange in the Norwegian Storting (with just 200 members) would be less favorable than those in the Swedish Riksdag (which is almost twice as large). It appears, then, that the opportunity for a division of labor presented by the larger Swedish parliament has no obvious effect on the degree to which members develop international contacts.

Linguistic proficiency and committee placement (e.g., on the Committee on Foreign Affairs) have the strongest impact on MPs' international contacts. This confirms the results produced by a bivariate analysis of the material. The international contacts of MPs are substantially increased by a seat on a foreign affairs' committee and a proficiency in one of the leading world languages. Interestingly enough, linguistic proficiency has a somewhat greater effect than committee placement.

None of the other parliament-related factors—for example, whether or not an MP occupies a leading position, has served for a long period, or holds an international parliamentary assignment—has as great an effect on MPs' degree of international orientation as does committee placement. The analysis also indicates, however, that MPs with assignments to the Nordic Council, the Council of Europe, or the Interparliamentary Union have more regular international contacts than do other MPs. The same applies to parliamentarians with high seniority. This result could be interpreted as meaning that it is usually later in their career that MPs have the opportunity to develop contacts over borders. The occupancy of a leading parliamentary position, on the other hand, has no statistically significant effect on the degree of international orientation among Nordic members of parliament.

Parliamentarians who represent centrist or conservative parties in Nordic parliaments generally have denser international contacts than do their colleagues from the other parties. Party affiliation thus has importance as an explanatory factor, albeit in a lesser degree than committee placement or linguistic proficiency. Moreover, the results in the case of the constituency factor—that is, the effect of representing the capital city—indicate no statistically significant impact on the density of MPs' territorially based contacts. Nor can MPs' gender be said with statistical certainty to have any effect on the extent of their international contacts. Occupational background, on the other hand, does have such an effect: white-collar employees, farmers, and the self-employed have more regular contacts on the international level than do blue-collar workers.

The effect of the language factor is visible in all of the countries save Iceland. In both Norway and Sweden, however, committee placement has a greater effect than linguistic proficiency. The decided conclusion one can draw on the basis of a multivariate analysis in each country is that the language factor has a distinct effect on the degree of extra-national contacts among parliamentarians in the Nordic region. Without a degree of proficiency in one of the leading world languages, it is not likely than an MP will build up a network of international contacts.

CONCLUSIONS

The main object of this chapter has been to ascertain whether or not Nordic MPs have a way of organizing their international contacts that resembles that of their counterparts in other countries, or whether instead they have developed a pattern of their own where international contacts are concerned. Our expectations, founded on earlier research, were that Nordic MPs would not have well-developed international contacts, that a specific and distinct Nordic profile would be observable in said international contacts, and that individual-level factors would explain variations in MPs' international contact patterns only to a limited extent.

The first question posed in this chapter concerned the prevalence of international contacts among Nordic MPs. It became clear that such an international dimension *was* present in their contacts: a pattern of dense international contacts proved to be one of seven common contact profiles among members of Nordic parliaments.

The results of our investigation into the international contacts of Nordic MPs accord closely with those of earlier studies. A large group of members in the five parliaments of the Nordic region have no regular international contacts at all. Parliamentarians in the Nordic countries do not diverge noticeably from their counterparts in other countries, where, research has shown, international contacts are not particularly common, either. Previous Nordic findings about MPs without international contacts are hereby confirmed. The present study, however, has shown Danish MPs to be an exception (albeit a modest one), with their relatively frequent and well-developed contacts on the international level.

One finding that must be reckoned surprising, in view of the expectations indicated, is that there does not seem to be any genuinely Nordic contact profile among Nordic MPs. If Danish MPs diverge from the others in respect of their level of international contacts in general, it is Icelandic MPs who are the exception where Nordic contacts are concerned. In Iceland, contacts oriented to the other Nordic countries are substantially more common than elsewhere in the Nordic region. (The results expected from the investigation had been that such specifically Nordic contacts would be common in the other countries, too.) The data indicate that, in large measure, parliamentarians with Nordic contacts have European and global contacts as well. The number of MPs with Nordic contacts but no regular European contacts is low to nonexistent.

Another important result is that factors on both the institutional and the individual level affect the regularity of international contacts. We may assume, therefore, that the institutional manner in which different nations organize their efforts at international cooperation has an effect on the degree to which their elected representatives develop cross-border contacts. However, elitist individual-level factors seem to have the stronger impact on the regularity of international contacts. Among such factors, several prove to have a strong effect: in particular, MPs possessing proficiency in a world language and/or sitting on an internationally oriented committee generally have denser international contacts than their colleagues.

The expectation that elite factors would have a limited influence on MPs' international contacts was not fulfilled. On the contrary, the effect of linguistic proficiency on MPs' ability to develop international contacts was great. The conceivable consequences of this circumstance are many. One could be that only members with good language skills will be able to make themselves felt in the international arena. If, moreover, MPs require advanced language skills in order to develop their international contacts, this could have repercussions for the way in which representative democracy works. There is a risk that international parliamentary work will be reserved to a small group of MPs who are favored in respect of both linguistic and other educational background, and who are exclusive in other respects as well. It is possible that such a process of elitization will affect the degree of social representation in parliament negatively. It is primarily, for instance, members with an advanced education and a white-collar background who report having good linguistic skills.[23]

The findings of this study can be summarized in the following manner: Elected representatives in the Nordic countries organize their contacts on a territorial basis. Judging from the material, the international contact profile is unidimensional; no specifically Nordic contact profile can be observed. Contacts should be viewed as more internationally oriented or less, rather than as directed toward any specific geographical unit or level.

Nordic parliamentarians prove not to differ from parliamentarians in general where international contacts are concerned. The proportion of Nordic MPs with regular extra-national contacts is low.

The degree of international orientation among individual members can in some measure be attributed to the manner in which each country organizes its efforts at international cooperation. Individual-level explanatory factors, however, are more important. Linguistic proficiency and committee placement are critical for the development of international contacts. It may be expected, therefore, that a process of ongoing and increasing internationalization, in which factors of this sort are significant for individual parliamentarians, will in turn lead to a process of elitization. National democracies are exposing themselves, in this perspective, to new and uncertain dangers. Who knows what a worsening fracture between voters and representatives can lead to?

NOTES

1. Political scientists Ulf Bjereld and Marie Demker have shown, adducing among others William R. Caspary and Olof Petersson, that this conception has been disputed. Their own study shows that foreign-policy questions do not determine voters' choices to any great extent (1995:77).

2. At the same time, it is possible to see the economic crisis, the questioning of the welfare state, and internationalization as examples of developments seriously threatening the Nordic model (Petersson 1995:35).

3. In Esaiasson and Holmberg's study, the following are included within the category of "international actors": "Swedish Embassies," "Foreign Embassies in Sweden," "Nordic Elite Actors," and "Other Foreign Elite Actors."

4. In the Finnish questionnaire, a distinction was made between "in the Nordic countries" and "outside the Nordic countries."

5. *Time-budget strategies* can provide an alternative way of studying the contacts and networks of elite actors and parliamentarians (Petersson et al. 1996; Christoffersson 1986).

6. The internal refusal rate on questions about international contacts varies somewhat between the different countries and lies within an interval of 3–7 percent.

7. An overview of the international research on international networks can be found in Knoke (1990).

8. The Democratic Audit of Sweden has chosen to investigate the contacts of the Swedish power elite using a greater number of territorial levels; in its 1997 report, it specifies six such levels: municipal, regional, national, Nordic, European, and extra-European (Petersson et al. 1997:104–10.). Researches on power and democracy in both Norway and Sweden have previously carried out studies of territorially structured contacts, but on the basis of fewer territorial levels (NOU

1982; Petersson 1989). In their book, *Representation From Above,* Esaiasson and Holmberg distinguish between the local and international contacts of Swedish MPs (Esaiasson and Holmberg 1996:268–70). In a similar fashion, Robert Merton has introduced a dichotomy between cosmopolitan and local contacts (Merton 1968).

9. The factor analysis is a so-called varimax-rotated principal-component analysis, in which no correlation between the ingoing factors is allowed (orthogonal rotation). All told, the six contact profiles account for 69 percent of the variance on the question.

10. The question one can ask oneself is whether contacts with national organizations working with international questions should be included in this dimension or not. Two points speak against considering contacts of this sort when investigating the international contacts of MPs. First, contacts with organizations of this type also form part of the profile featuring contacts with environmental, women's, refugees', and immigrants' organizations. Second, the correlations are weaker between these contacts and the other three contact surfaces. The correlation for contacts within the Nordic region, within the EU, and with international organizations varies between .70 and .77. The correlation for contacts with national organizations devoted to international questions is at highest .65 and at lowest .50 in connection with the other three contact surfaces. The analysis that follows concentrates instead on three aspects of MPs' international contacts.

11. The internationally oriented contact dimension of MPs from Iceland does not feature contacts with national organizations working with international issues.

12. The internationally oriented contact profile explains between 9 per cent (Iceland) and 29 per cent (Sweden). The percentage variance for the internationally oriented factor was 27 per cent in Finland, 26 per cent in Norway, and 13 per cent in Denmark.

13. The overall pattern of these contact dimensions is almost the same in all five countries in the study. In the following, I shall focus on the results for the Nordic countries taken together. See, for example, Aberbach et al. (1981) for an international study that has found significant similarities between different countries in regard to MPs' informal contacts.

14. The use of mean values is based on an interval-scale assumption concerning the five reply options used in the study.

15. The results of the *Riksdag Survey 1994* (the Nordleg study) have been compared with those of a corresponding parliamentary survey from 1988 (the *Riksdag Survey 1988*).

16. The measurement of correlation used in the table is the eta-square (eta^2), a measurement of variance that can vary between 0.00 (no correlation) and 1.00 (perfect correlation). The eta-square can be interpreted as the proportion of variance explained—in this case, the proportion of the variance in international contacts that can be statistically explained by MPs' national affiliation.

17. The results are roughly the same when contacts with international organizations are included in the analysis as well.

18. The three contact surfaces studied—the Nordic region, the EU, and international organizations—show strong correlations with each other (.70 at the lowest). The other two each amount to .78. Cronbach's alpha for the three contact surfaces comes to a full .90.

19. These conclusions about MPs' contacts are not altered by a look at how the index for these contacts varies among Nordic parliamentarians. Table 13.2 above presents the international contact patterns of MPs according to the index. The conclusion still holds, in sum, that MPs' international contacts are but little developed. The material rather shows that it is only a minority of elected politicians who maintain such international contacts.

20. The index values for centrist and conservative parties are somewhat higher in all of the countries. The comparison is based on an analysis in which the parties are divided into seven different party families (mean values in parentheses): *left parties* (Left Socialist Party, the Unity List, Left-Wing Alliance, Socialist Left Party, the Red Electoral Alliance, Left Party, People's Alliance) (2.5); *social democrats* (Social Democrats, Social Democrats, Labour Party, Social Democrats, Social Democratic Party, People's Movement) (2.4); *centrist parties* (Radical Party, Center Democrats, Swedish People's Party, Christian League, Liberals, Christian People's Party, People's Party, Christian Democrats) (2.9); *conservative parties* (Conservatives, National Coalition, Conservatives, Moderate Unity Party, Independence Party) (2.9); *agrarian parties* (Liberals, Finnish Center, Center Party, Center Party, Progressive Party) (2.6); *green/new parties* (Green League, Ecology Party, Women's Alliance) (2.5); and *populist parties* (Progress Party, Rural Party, Progress Party, Free Democrats) (2.6). (See also appendix 3.) This system of classification is not without problems. The category of agrarian parties, for example, contains parties with sharply contrasting views on the merits of membership in the EU. The agrarian party in Denmark (the Liberals) takes a positive view of the EU; the Norwegian agrarian party (the Center Party) is strongly opposed. This only affects the results, however, if members' attitude toward EU membership has an impact on how they develop their international contacts.

21. For two reasons, all of the explanatory factors in the following analysis will be dichotomized. With the use of this procedure, the readers' overview of the material is improved (*the pedagogical reason*), and we are able to employ more refined statistical methods at the same time (*the statistical reason*).

22. The reason for this is that the statistical material for Finnish MPs does not suffice for all of the variables in the multivariate analysis.

23. The opportunity for comparing these results with those provided by the Democratic Audit of Sweden is limited. The Audit's report contains no analysis of linguistic proficiency among MPs, save at a general level (Petersson et al. 1997).

14

Parliaments' Adaptation to the European Union

Tapio Raunio and Matti Wiberg

How have the Nordic legislatures adapted to membership in the European Union? What institutional reforms have these parliaments carried out? What future reforms need to be undertaken? How do Nordic legislators perceive the membership issue? Do they support intergovernmental or supranational decision-making?

The purpose of this chapter is twofold: to review the institutional adaptation of three Nordic parliaments to EU membership, and to analyze the views of Nordic members of parliament on the EU.

Our introductory discussion outlines the importance of national parliaments in EU governance. In the first part, we examine institutional changes within the respective legislatures. Comparing the Danish Folketing, the Finnish Eduskunta, and the Swedish Riksdag, we analyze parliament's involvement in the formulation of EU policy and its power to control the executive. We also briefly examine the participation of the two Nordic non-EU member states' parliaments, the Icelandic Althingi and Norwegian Storting in the decision-making of the European Economic Area (EEA).

In section two, we analyze Nordic MPs' perceptions of the Union with the help of survey data. We examine their views on the nature of the Union—including whether they favor an intergovernmental union or a supranational one.

In the concluding section, we offer some suggestions for institutional reforms to enhance the capacity of Nordic parliaments to deal with EU matters.

The main argument of this chapter is that, while Nordic MPs and parliaments are closely involved in EU issues, there is still much room for improvement. In particular, the legislatures should try to carve out a more pro-active role for themselves and to organize their work so as to benefit from the policy expertise of the standing committees. Survey evidence indicates there is much variation between the Nordic countries on the membership issue. Comparable differences are also found within party groups in each of the countries.

NATIONAL PARLIAMENTS AND EU GOVERNANCE

The role of national parliaments in the EU has recently attracted much scholarly interest.[1] But what should the role of the national legislatures be? Is there an ideal role for the parliaments of the member states? A critical factor and essential starting point is the recognition (however grudging) on the part of parliaments and MPs of two important facts: that certain powers—and by no means inconsequential ones—have been transferred to Brussels already and that this transfer of these powers has been ratified by the legislatures of the member states. Secondly, cooperation with EU institutions is not just necessary but mutually beneficial, too, if approached in a constructive manner. For example, the roles of the national parliaments and of the European Parliament should be regarded as complementary, even by those who do not favor a federal union.

Since the EU is composed of fifteen member states, each with its own political and parliamentary culture, it is not surprising that the role accorded parliament varies from one member state to another. In Italy, for example, the legislature plays but a marginal part in EU matters, while in others, such as Denmark, parliament has traditionally enjoyed a much stronger position. Comparable differences are found within the legislatures: the institutional solutions adopted by the member state parliaments exhibit considerable variation. In view of this diversity in institutional arrangements, Finland and Sweden had no particular blueprint to follow upon joining the Union in 1995.

National parliaments are the principal forums for discussion and scrutiny of EU policy at the national level. In order to contribute to the formulation of policy and the scrutiny of cabinet ministers in a meaningful manner, parliaments must seek and gain access to relevant information at the earliest possible stage of the decision-making process—that is, when the issues are still being prepared. Legislatures should not just passively wait for information either from the EU institutions or from the government, but should rather invest resources in producing and receiving information independently of the other actors. In order to be able to act—as opposed to just reacting—national parliaments must have the willingness and ability to formulate initiatives for further processing in the EU governance system.

One important aspect is procedural innovation: since they control their own Standing Orders, parliaments may introduce procedural changes to enhance their chances of participation. But how have the Nordic legislatures responded to the challenge? Is there variation between the legislatures or has a "Nordic" model emerged?

A NORDIC INSTITUTIONAL RESPONSE?

In this section, we analyze the institutional solutions adopted by the Danish, Finnish, and Swedish parliaments. We argue that the Finnish Eduskunta is stronger than the other two in dealing with EU issues, because Eduskunta is *pro-active,* and the *whole parliament* (including all its standing committees) is involved in preparing national EU policies before decisions are taken in the Council of Ministers.[2] Through its preparation of issues in advance and its decentralized processing of EU matters, the Finnish parliament is thus able to influence—on a routine and established basis—the position of the Finnish representative in the Council of Ministers. The Danish Folketing is renowned for its close scrutiny of ministers, but it is hampered by its late participation in the preparation of issues. The Swedish Riksdag is the weakest of the three legislatures: its influence on EU policies is rather limited and almost entirely *post-factum* in character.

We shall also analyze the Icelandic and Norwegian cases briefly. While neither country is a member of the Union, both are in the EEA, and European-level policy-making has significant consequences for both countries.[3]

The Establishment and Composition of the EU Committees

When Denmark began negotiations to join the European Economic Community in 1961, the Folketing decided to set up a special committee, the Markedsforhandlingsudvalg, to guarantee a dialogue between MPs and the government. De Gaulle vetoed enlargement, but the committee, now renamed the Markedsudvalg, resumed its normal functions in the early 1970s when membership negotiations were relaunched. When

Denmark became a member of the European Community in 1973, the Markedsudvalg became a permanent committee. On October 4, 1994, after the European Community had become the European Union, the committee changed its name from the Markedsudvalg (Market Relations Committee) to the Europaudvalg (European Affairs Committee).

Like other standing committees, the Europaudvalg has seventeen members. Normally it convenes on Fridays, each session lasting from two to five hours. Its meetings are not open to the public, but a decision was made in March 1993 to inform the press of the proceedings of the meetings, with information on the final negotiation position and on the views of political parties (Laursen 1995:48). It is estimated that around 95 percent of the memoranda received by the *udvalg* are accessible to the public and are routinely forwarded to the press corps (Arter 1995:113).

As far as the Eduskunta is concerned, adaptation to EU membership began during the EEA phase, which preceded membership in the Union. This manifested itself in the huge increase in new laws enacted annually. In early 1995, adaptation to membership faced a handicap in the form of general elections, which took place in March. The turnover of staff in both government and parliament meant that operational routines for the handling of EU issues were established during the summer of 1995.

The Eduskunta decided not to set up a special EU committee, opting instead to charge a previously existing body, the Grand Committee (Suuri valiokunta), with the main responsibility for EU-related matters. The composition of the Grand Committee (which has twenty-five members) reflects the parties' share of seats in the Eduskunta. The Grand Committee convenes behind closed doors on Wednesdays and Fridays.

The Riksdag followed Sweden's membership negotiations through an EU delegation consisting of eighteen MPs. It was important, in the view of the Constitutional Committee, that the Riksdag has an influential and pro-active role in preparing EU policy.[4] The Advisory Committee on EU Affairs, the EU-nämnd, was seen as providing the answer. The EU-nämnd is not a standing committee. It operates, however, much as a normal committee. It contains seventeen MPs and meets on Fridays, convening behind closed doors.

Mandate

The committees' general mandate refers to their powers and competences in dealing with EU issues.

In Denmark, the government must seek a mandate from the Europaudvalg on matters falling under the first pillar. On second-pillar issues

(Common Foreign and Security Policy), the government must keep both the Europaudvalg and the Foreign Affairs Committee informed. On matters falling under the third pillar (Justice and Home Affairs), both the *udvalg* and the Legal Affairs Committee are to be consulted.

In the Eduskunta, the Grand Committee deals with budgetary issues and with first- and third-pillar issues.[5] The Foreign Affairs Committee handles matters falling under the second pillar.

In Sweden, the EU-nämnd is charged with all EU questions save foreign and defense matters of particular importance, which are the preserve of the Foreign Affairs Committee.

Receiving Information

The legislatures may receive information at various stages of the decision-making process: for example, when a legislative proposal is first published, when it is being processed in the EU machinery, and prior to meetings of the Council. In all three countries, the government has the duty to inform parliament of legislative proposals, and it must consult the EU committee prior to the final decision.

In May 1994, the Europaudvalg decided to extend its scrutiny of EU proposals to the very start of the legislative process.[6] This means that Commission proposals for EU legislation, and other "important" documents too, must be sent by the foreign ministry to the *udvalg* as soon as they have been translated into Danish.[7] Specialized committees are to be sent material falling under their respective spheres of competence. Information on the effects of forthcoming EU legislation on Denmark must be included as well. When an issue appears on the Council's agenda, the *udvalg* must be sent factual notes about it at least one week before the relevant *udvalg* meeting. In the main, however, these factual notes are no more than brief summaries produced by the government. As far as meetings of the European Council are concerned, the procedure was clarified in a resolution adopted in August 1990, according to which the prime minister must inform the Europaudvalg of issues likely to be on the agenda of the meeting. If the government expects important decisions to be made, it must obtain a mandate from the committee.

The Eduskunta, for its part, must be informed without delay of any proposal for a Council decision, the substance of which, according to the constitution, falls within the remit of parliament. This usually involves legislative proposals by the Commission, but the Grand Committee has the right to require information on any issue relating to the EU. Prior to Council meetings, members of the committee are provided with the agenda in the form approved at the Committee of Permanent Representatives (COREPER), as well as with memoranda prepared by the ministries detailing Finland's position on the issues. The prime minister is obliged to inform the Grand Committee of questions arising in the European Council. He or she is also required to furnish information afterward on the deliberations of the European Council to the plenary session or the committee.

In Sweden, the government has the duty to inform parliament of EU proposals. The Riksdag must receive the relevant documents even if the Swedish translation is not yet available. The ministries must also submit statements on the effects of proposed EU legislation on Sweden. Before each Council meeting, moreover, members of the EU-nämnd are to be sent memoranda on the questions appearing on the agenda.

Plenary Debates

The preparation of EU matters in the Nordic legislatures is essentially based on the committee system, with the plenary session playing a less active role. Following a 1986 decision, the Europaudvalg may require—if two-fifths of its members so desire—that a proposal for EU legislation be taken to the plenary. These debates usually take place twice a year. They have attracted little interest, however, and are in no way binding on the Europaudvalg.

In Finland, the decision to delegate authority to the committees was based on the need to achieve maximum functional efficiency and to allow matters to be discussed away from the public eye. EU matters are debated and decided on the floor, but all the preparatory legislative work is done in the committees.

The EU-nämnd is the only European committee throughout the Union which cannot require that a particular issue be debated in the plenary.

Voting Instructions

As far as their ability to impose voting instructions on ministers is concerned, the three European committees may be placed in the following order: the Europaudvalg, the Suuri valiokunta, and the EU-nämnd.

The Europaudvalg is famous for its ability to impose a mandate on Danish ministers. Jacques Delors, the former Commission president, is alleged to have said that the European Community "has 13 members, 12 member states, and the Danish Market Relations Committee" (Fich 1993:69). However, while the Danes may be accused of delaying the actual negotiation process, they have had an impressive record throughout their

European Community/European Union membership in implementing European legislation, a fact no doubt linked to the role played by the Folketing.

The mandate is not legally binding, but in practice the government is bound by the committee's instructions. This practice dates from 1973, when the then-minister for agriculture, Ib Frederiksen, failed to bring home the expected "bacon," whereupon the opposition threatened a vote of no-confidence.[8] The cabinet remained in office by agreeing from then on to be bound by the instructions of the *udvalg*. To a great extent this informal norm has been followed.

The meetings of the *udvalg* are often very heated, with the cabinet's representative being subjected to close scrutiny. The so-called "negative majority" rule applies: the government's position is approved provided there is no parliamentary majority against it. It is important to note that the traditional "one man one vote" rule is not employed. One MP from each parliamentary party casts the votes for his or her party. These votes are then weighted according to the number of seats each party holds in the Folketing. The Europaudvalg has not hesitated to oppose the government. According to Peter Nedergaard (1994:308, cf. Hegeland and Mattson 1995:451), the *udvalg* has amended 2 percent to 5 percent of the government's positions in foreign policy questions, while in other policy areas it has demanded changes in 5 percent to 10 percent of the proposals. After each Council meeting, the government sends a written report to the *udvalg*. These reports have been public since 1993. The government or the *udvalg* can also decide that a minister appear before the *udvalg* to explain the proceedings of the Council meeting.

When explaining the strong role of the *udvalg*, Hegeland and Mattson (1995:449) stress the importance of minority government: "The power of the Europaudvalg vis-à-vis the executive is to a large extent dependent on the latter's strength in the Folketing: the larger the majority of the government, the less power will the *udvalg* have." Alas, "there is no doubt that the committee has been the driving force" in defining the relations between the government and the *udvalg* (Hegeland and Mattson 1995:438).

The Eduskunta does not issue any binding mandates to Finnish representatives. However, the comment by the finance minister, Sauli Niinistö (Conservative), illustrates well the close scrutiny to which ministers are subjected: according to him, waiting for committee meetings is "like waiting in the corridors of the district court" (*Helsingin Sanomat* 6/20/96). On two occasions, during the first two and a half years of EU membership, a minister voted in the Council against the wishes of the Committee. Following Council meetings, the committee is supplied with a report of the meeting and its decisions. Ministers must be prepared to appear before the committee, and to explain in detail any deviations from the given policy guidelines.

In Sweden, the government is not to adopt positions contrary to the wishes of the EU-nämnd. This is merely a recommendation, however: it is not legally binding. Decisions are taken by the negative majority rule. There has not been a single case so far in which the *nämnd* has opposed the government's line. The EU-nämnd has been rather easy on ministers and has refrained from criticizing them in the manner of its counterparts in Denmark and Finland. Another notable difference is that ministers have often failed to turn up in the EU-nämnd, sending another ministry representative instead. Following Council meetings, the government is required to produce a report stating Sweden's final position. These reports leave much room for improvement. Since the current Social Democratic–led cabinet faced a fragmented opposition in the Riksdag, at the time it appeared likely that Sweden's EU policy would remain government-driven at least until the next general elections (Hegeland and Mattson 1995:451). In retrospect, this prediction proved to be correct.

The Involvement of Standing Committees

Comparative analysis shows that only the Eduskunta makes efficient use of the cumulative expertise of the specialized standing committees.

In its May 1994 report, the Europaudvalg made it clear that other committees must be given a greater role in the handling of EU issues. There seems to be wide agreement in the Folketing on this change. While 73 percent of the MPs on the Europaudvalg wanted to preserve its monopoly on the issuing of mandates to ministers, 55 percent of the Folketing's remaining members agreed partially or totally with the idea of allowing the respective standing committees to exercise a similar function (T. Jensen 1995). As early as 1974, the *udvalg* had decided that the expertise of specialized committees should be used in processing EU matters in the Folketing. Decentralized decision-making of this sort never really took off, however; only the Environment and Regional Planning Committee became regularly involved in EU issues. Consultation usually takes place instead within the party groups, with each party's representative in the Europaudvalg (often a senior party figure) consulting his or her colleagues prior to *udvalg* meetings.

In the Eduskunta, the standing committees were assigned an influential role from the very beginning. When an EU legislative proposal arrives in parliament, it is simultaneously forwarded to the Grand Committee and to one or several specialized committees. The latter prepare an opinion, and it is rare for the Grand Committee to deviate from it. When several specialized committees have stated a position, the Grand Committee summarizes and mediates the result. This early and pro-active involvement on the part of specialized standing committees enables the whole Eduskunta effectively to influence the position of the government.

The role of standing committees in the Riksdag has so far remained limited. Each standing committee has the right to request information from the government on issues falling within its competence. The committees have made little use of this right, however, causing concern among the members of the EU-nämnd.

The Main Problems

The three legislatures face similar problems in handling EU issues. The constant flow of information from Brussels places a heavy burden on the MPs, the party groups, and the committees. The legislatures must be willing to allocate enough time and resources for themselves. Without such an investment, national policy formulation on EU issues will be severely weakened, at least in its parliamentary dimension.

Information from the EU often arrives far too late, leaving little time for discussion in the legislature. The situation is particularly bad regarding EU directives. The language problem exacerbates the situation further, with documents not being translated into the official languages soon enough. It is essential, therefore, to aim at making Council agendas public and binding and to ensure that the Brussels bureaucracy delivers the necessary information within time limits that are acceptable and clearly defined.

Comparative analysis suggests that institutional arrangements have a significant effect on the ability of Nordic parliaments to influence their countries' EU policies. The institutional choices adopted by the three legislatures are substantially similar. This is not surprising, since both Finnish and Swedish MPs studied the operation of the Danish Europaudvalg prior to setting up their own EU committees. But, despite this overall similarity, there are considerable variations between the three countries.

The Finnish Eduskunta is arguably the best equipped of the three to influence national policy formulation on European issues. The Danish Folketing is able to impose politically binding voting instructions on the government, but the legislature relies too much on information submitted by the government. It also needs to make better use of the standing committees. The latter problem is recognized in Sweden, too. The weakness

Table 14.1
Basic Information on the Nordic Parliaments' EU Committees

	No. of Members	Members per MPs (%)	Openness	Power
Denmark				
Europa-udvalget	17	9.5	2	1
Finland				
Suuri valiokunta	25	12.5	1	2
Sweden				
EU-nämnden	17	4.9	3	3

Notes: Name of committee is reported in native language. *Members* = number of members (excluding alternates). *Members per MPs (%)* = number of members as proportion of all representatives. *Openness* = the degree to which the documents and meetings of the committee are open to the public on an ordinal scale; 1 = max., 3 = min. (according to authors' best judgment). *Power* = the power of the committee vis-à-vis the executive on an ordinal scale (summing up all relevant aspects to be taken into consideration); 1 = max., 3 = min. (according to authors' best judgment).

of the Riksdag is exacerbated, moreover, by the strong position of the executive and by MPs' lack of constructive interest in EU matters.

Table 14.1 sums up the discussion with a review of basic information on the three European committees.

While Iceland and Norway have stayed outside the Union, membership in the EEA means taking on many of the rights and duties entailed by EU membership. Through the EEA, these two countries have adopted almost all the EU's legislation on the four freedoms, on competition, and on state aid. In Norway, for example, European Community legislation has been adopted at least as loyally as in the member states, and Norway is bound by the case law of the European Court of Justice. The EU has a weighty presence, therefore, in Norwegian and Icelandic politics.[9]

In the Storting, European issues have traditionally been the domain of the Foreign Affairs Committee. Prior to the 1994 referendum, there were plans to form a special EU committee in the event that Norway joined the Union. In May 1994, a special EEA Consultative Organ (ECO)—or the EEA Commission—was established. The ECO consists of the members of the Foreign Affairs Committee, supplemented by the six Norwegian representatives to the EEA Joint Parliamentary Committee.[10] As its name implies, the ECO is a purely consultative body. It does not vote or take formal decisions, and it does not submit written reports to the Storting. Normally it meets just once a month, on the Tuesday preceding the monthly meetings of the EEA Joint Committee. It is apprised of the government's negotiating position, and the representatives of the various parties indicate whether or not they accept this position. The government is usually represented by the foreign minister. There is no reporting back after meetings in Brussels. Specialized standing committees play a very limited role.

According to Sejersted (1996:137), the "ECO is an extended branch of the Foreign Affairs Committee, with the function of keeping the six special members of the EEA Parliamentary Committee informed, and drawing on whatever expertise they might possess." The Foreign Affairs Committee is the main forum for EU policy deliberations. This situation reflects the fact that European issues are still perceived in the Storting—and indeed in Norway at large—as foreign policy questions.

Unlike all the other Nordic states, Iceland has never applied for EU membership or held a referendum on whether or not to join. Highly dependent on the fishing industry, Iceland fears losing control of her natural resources. While actual membership is not on the daily agenda of Icelandic politics, there are differing views on the framework within which relations with Europe should be conducted. For instance, in the Althingi debate on the EEA, three out of five parties were divided on the issue.

When preparing for EEA membership, the Althingi considered establishing a special committee for dealing with EEA matters. This option was discarded in favor of assigning European questions to the Foreign Affairs Committee. This committee has nine members. It meets once a week for two hours and holds extra sessions when required.

The rules for parliamentary involvement were agreed in February 1994. If the relevant EU/EEA law must be ratified by the Althingi, the Foreign Affairs Ministry is obliged to send the text of the bill to the Foreign Affairs Committee. If the law is passed as an administrative regulation, a list of the measures involved is forwarded to the committee. The committee receives the materials prior to the meeting of the EEA Joint Committee. The Foreign Affairs Committee then submits the material to specialized standing committees for their opinion. Each such committee is responsible for scrutinizing forthcoming EEA laws falling within its field of competence. Finally, the Althingi transposes EEA legislation into Icelandic law in accordance with the normal law-making process.

In "matters of great importance," the Foreign Ministry produces reports for the Foreign Affairs Committee, and "once in a while" the foreign minister appears before the committee to give information (Bogason 1997:122). The Icelandic delegation to the EEA Parliamentary Committee serves as a channel of information between the Althingi and Brussels.

Since the EEA has only been operational since the start of 1994, the first years of membership have largely been spent in adopting the relevant

European legislation and in learning the rules of the new game. However, Iceland and Norway have both adjusted to EEA membership, and routines for handling European matters have now been established within the Althingi and the Storting. In both countries, integration issues are still largely regarded as foreign policy questions. Whether this is the right approach may be doubted, especially regarding the long term, since the volume and scope of EU/EEA legislation is likely to increase.

But how do Nordic MPs perceive the European Union? Do they support their country's membership in the EU? Would they like to see an intergovernmental union, or do they favor a United States of Europe marked by supranational decision-making? It is to these questions we now turn in the second part of the chapter.

A NORDIC VISION OF EUROPE?

Membership in the European Union has been, and still is, by no means a universally accepted fact of life in the three Nordic EU countries. While the Norwegians opted to remain outside, the "yes" side gained but narrow victories in membership referenda held in Denmark, Finland, and Sweden.[11] Evidence from other EU member states has shown that, while Europeans have in general favored the broad goal of integration, there is no consensus either on the European level or within the member states on the pace and form of the integration process (Niedermayer and Sinnott 1995). The Maastricht episode was an effective reminder of the importance of paying attention to public opinion when negotiating deals in the EU Council. As a result of the closely contested referenda in Denmark and France, the role of national parliaments came to the fore in debates on the democratic deficit. The idea was that public opinion could be better incorporated into EU policy planning by giving the national legislatures a greater say in EU decision-making.

But how do representatives in the five Nordic countries perceive the EU and its institutions? We focus on the following questions: To what extent do Nordic MPs support their country's membership in the EU? How many Althingi and Storting legislators would like to see their respective countries join the Union? To which EU institutions would MPs give more power, and to which less? Do Nordic representatives favor an intergovernmental or a supranational Union? Is there a Nordic vision of Europe?

Table 14.2 shows the views of Nordic MPs (save those from Finland) on the membership issue. The respondents had five choices: staying out

Table 14.2

Members Attitudes toward Own Country's Future Relationship with the EU (%)

	Neither EU nor EEA	Not EU, but Retain EEA	Join EU with Reservations	Join EU without Reservations	Work for a United States of Europe	Total
Denmark						
Left socialists	0	NI	100	0	0	100
Social democrats	0	NI	76	11	13	100
Liberals	0	NI	75	25	0	100
Agrarians	0	NI	0	42	58	100
Conservatives	0	NI	10	57	33	100
Populists	33	NI	67	0	0	100
All	6	NI	43	25	26	100
Iceland						
Left socialists	71	29	0	0	0	100
Social democrats	0	0	86	14	0	100
Agrarians	20	70	10	0	0	100
Conservatives	0	79	21	0	0	100
All	20	48	30	2	0	100
Norway						
Left socialists	92	8	0	0	0	100
Social democrats	1	32	7	52	8	100
Agrarians	93	7	0	0	0	100

Christians	20	80	0	0	0	100
Conservatives	4	5	14	77	0	100
Populists	0	17	50	33	0	100
All	29	23	9	36	3	100
Sweden						
Left socialists	30	65	5	0	0	100
Social democrats	1	9	31	57	2	100
Liberals	0	0	0	85	15	100
Agrarians	0	7	52	41	0	100
Christians	0	0	0	93	7	100
Conservatives	0	0	4	85	10	99
All	4	13	20	59	4	100

Notes: The question was worded as follows: "In the political debate, there exists different proposals concerning [country in question's] future relationship with the EU. Which of the proposals do you find most in accordance with your own opinion?" Response alternatives varied between countries. *Neither EU nor EEA*: "[Country] should not be a member of the EU, and the current EEA agreement should be canceled." In Denmark only: "Denmark should leave the European Union." *Not EU but retain EEA*: "[Country] should not be a member of the EU, but should keep an EEA agreement with the EU." Not included in the Danish study. *Join EU with reservations*: For Denmark, response alternatives referred to membership in the Union but with the opt-out clauses regarding the single currency and a possible common defense policy agreed at the Edinburgh Summit in 1992. For Iceland, response alternatives referred to joining the Union provided satisfactory exemptions from the common fisheries policy could be obtained. For Norway, response alternatives referred to joining the EU but without monetary integration. For Sweden, response alternatives referred to membership but without such things as cooperation in defense issues and a common currency. *Join EU without reservations*: To join the EU in accordance with the Maastricht Treaty (only minor variations between studies). *Work for a United States of Europe*: "[Country] should join the EU and work in the future for a United States of Europe." In Denmark only: "Denmark should be a member of the EU and work in the future for even closer coooperation between member states."

of both the EU and the EEA, joining the EEA, joining the EU with some opt-out clauses, joining the EU, and joining the EU and working for a "United States of Europe" (i.e., a full-fledged federal state). We use a party family approach here in searching for cross-national ideological patterns.

The results indicate clearly that the EU is a deeply contested matter throughout the Nordic region. The membership issue produces a significant cleavage in all five countries. This cleavage is found not just between parties but also within them.

In Denmark, no single category received the majority of votes. Of Danish MPs, 43 percent favor the current situation of membership with no commitment to a common currency or defense policy. Twenty-five percent favor taking on the full benefits and burdens of the Maastricht Treaty. As many as 26 percent would like to see the EU become a federal state. A small minority wants Denmark to withdraw from the Union or from the EEA. All party families with the exception of the left socialists—who favor the current situation—are divided on the matter. Most pro-integration are the conservatives and the agrarians, with a majority of the latter favoring a European federal state.

In Iceland, too, no one category commands majority support. Thirty percent favor membership in the EU, provided Iceland is given an opt-out clause from the common fisheries policy. Only 2 percent are willing to comply with the Maastricht terms, while federal Europe receives no support in Iceland. Forty-eight percent support the current situation, while one-fifth would like to withdraw from the EEA. No party speaks with one voice on this matter. The only pro-EU party is the social democrats, while the majority of conservatives and agrarians choose the EEA. The left socialists favor abandoning the EEA.

In Norway, 48 percent would like to see their country in the EU. This corresponds to the proportion of voters favoring membership in the 1994 referendum (47.7 percent). As many as 29 percent would like to withdraw from the EEA. The plan for a United States of Europe received only marginal support. All parties are divided in this question. The Labor Party in particular is clearly torn apart, with MPs from its ranks choosing all answer categories. Most anti-European are the left socialists and the agrarians, the overwhelming majority in both wanting Norway to leave the EEA. Most pro-European are the conservatives and the populists.

Sweden is the only country where a winning majority option is found. Fifty-nine percent of the respondents favor the current situation of full membership. One-fifth of MPs would like Sweden to receive opt-out clauses from common defense policy and the single currency. Seventeen percent support the idea of withdrawing from the Union or the EEA. Again, the federal option receives only marginal support. In Sweden, too, all the parties are internally split. The left socialists are firmly opposed to membership. A majority of the social democrats support full membership, but an internal conflict is evident here: MPs from this party choose all answer categories. The conservatives, the Christians, and the liberals are the most pro-integration parties.

While no data exist for Finland, the situation reflects the divisions highlighted by the 1994 referendum. The overwhelming majority of the National Coalition and the Swedish People's Party are in favor of integration. The social democrats also support membership. The Center, the Left Wing Alliance, and the Greens are internally split on the question. Only the Christian League and the True Finns are clearly against membership.

The results clearly indicate the conflict potential that integration carries across the five Nordic countries. Only in Sweden did we find a majority of respondents favoring full membership. In Denmark, Iceland, and Norway, no option enjoys the support of the majority. Almost all the parties in every country are divided—either over the pace of integration or over membership itself. Analyzed in terms of party families, the pattern that emerges is as follows: Left socialists oppose further integration in all five countries. Social democrats are supportive of membership but internally split over the depth of integration. There is strong cross-national variation among the agrarians. Among the Christian parties, the Norwegian and Finnish are against membership, while the Swedish are firmly in favor. The conservatives are the most pro-European party family, with clear majorities in every country except Iceland supporting moves toward further integration.

But where does power lie in the Union, and where should it lie? More information on the views MPs hold on Europe can be derived from their stated preferences regarding the powers of the following bodies: the European Parliament, the Commission, the Council of Ministers, and the European Court of Justice. We asked MPs a two-part question designed to ascertain their preferences on this matter: we asked them to state (a) their estimation of the current balance of power between the institutions, and (b) their preferences regarding the balance of power in the future. Among the four alternatives, the European Parliament, the Commission, and the European Court of Justice represent supranational decision-making, and they are widely recognized for their "European" bias. Thus, those MPs wishing to see these institutions play a more powerful role can be regarded as supporting the deepening of integration. Those eager to increase the power of the Council of Ministers, on the other hand, are interpreted either as favoring the status quo or as resisting further integration.

Table 14.3 shows the preferences of Danish, Finnish, and Swedish representatives on the powers of the four institutions. The findings in this

Table 14.3

Danish, Finnish, and Swedish Members' Attitudes toward the Influence of Various Institutions of the EU (% "influential")

	European Parliament		Commission		Council of Ministers		European Court	
	Actual	Preferred	Actual	Preferred	Actual	Preferred	Actual	Preferred
Denmark								
Social democrats	29	46	97	88	100	100	97	94
Radical Party	0	60	100	50	100	100	100	100
Conservatives	32	47	100	90	100	100	76	88
Center Democrats	67	100	100	100	100	100	100	100
Socialist People's P.	40	30	100	40	100	90	89	67
Liberals	37	79	100	84	100	100	74	77
The Unity List	75	25	100	50	100	100	50	75
Progress Party	40	0	100	0	100	6	80	0
Finland								
Social Democrats	66	90	97	95	97	100	92	92
Centre Party	32	36	100	96	100	96	68	60
National Coalition	42	68	100	84	95	95	78	72
Left Wing Alliance	44	90	100	100	100	100	90	80
Green League	50	50	100	75	100	100	100	67
Swedish People's Party	0	50	100	100	100	100	100	100
Christian League	33	67	100	100	100	100	100	100
Sweden								
Left Party	10	95	95	58	95	79	95	63
Social Democrats	40	81	96	80	98	92	92	79
Centre Party	52	96	96	91	100	96	96	91
People's Party	52	88	96	96	96	96	96	96
Moderate Unity Party	34	72	91	83	97	98	93	93
Christian Democrats	43	100	100	85	100	100	100	100
Greens	6	82	94	29	94	71	100	50

Notes: Respondents were asked to rank the actual level of influence as well as the preferred level of influence of each institution on decision-making in the EU on a scale reaching from 0 (very little influence) to 10 (very influential). Table entries are proportion of respondents that choose values 5 to 10 ("influential").

table reveal that a clear majority of Nordic representatives are ready to increase the jurisdiction of the Commission (81 percent), the Council (95 percent), the European Parliament (73 percent), and the European Court of Justice (82 percent). This means that Nordic legislators are willing to cede more sovereignty to Brussels. This generosity stands in striking contrast to public opinion throughout the Nordic region, as indicated in the referenda results.

Danish legislators want to keep the Council as the center of decision-making. MPs from the Center Democrats, the Liberals, and the Radical Party support increasing the power of the European Parliament, while all parties except the Progress Party want to see a more powerful European Court.

The situation is rather similar in Finland. All parties want to maintain the status quo in regard to the Council's mandate. Only Center Party MPs are opposed to strengthening the position of the European Parliament. All parties support increasing the weight of the Commission and the European Court of Justice.

In Sweden as well, the EU organs enjoy wide support among MPs. All parties want to give additional powers to the Council, the European Parliament, and European Court of Justice. Only the Ecology Party is prepared to reduce the role of the Commission.

The results indicate that an overwhelming majority of MPs in the three Nordic EU-member states are in favor of increasing the jurisdiction of the various EU organs. This stands in striking contrast to prevailing public opinion in these countries, and in partial contrast to MPs' own expressed views on the membership question (as shown in table 14.2). These results can be interpreted to mean that, while Danish, Finnish, and Swedish legislators want to maintain the intergovernmental dimension as manifested in the strong position of the Council, they also want to democratize EU decision-making by giving more weight to the supranational institutions.

THE INFLUENCE OF THE NORDIC PARLIAMENTS ON EU ISSUES

The EU's decision-making system has strengthened the position of the executive and weakened the parliamentary dimension. Many look to the national parliaments to reduce the much-lamented democratic deficit. This is a tall order, much too tall in our opinion. National parliaments and electorates must in any case accept the fact that, with the increasing use of majority rule in EU institutions, Denmark, Finland, or Sweden may end up on the losing side. Iceland and Norway, for their part, are heavily influenced by the integration process, even though they have stayed outside the Union; through their membership in the EEA, they face many of the commitments entailed by EU membership.

If a national parliament wants to influence EU policies, it must typically do this during the preparatory phase, and in a mediated way through its government. The formulation of national policy on Commission proposals involves a process of constant informing and consulting, which continues until the final decision has been taken by the Council and/or the European Parliament. The ability of the Nordic parliaments to have a meaningful impact depends first and foremost, however, on the availability of information from both Brussels and the government. The Council agendas must therefore be made public and binding, and they must be finalized in good time before the meetings take place (as the parliaments of the member states have repeatedly demanded; COSAC 1996). In order to facilitate useful policy deliberation, moreover, governments should provide parliaments with all relevant information at the earliest possible stage.

All parliaments are weak in dealing with EU issues, and some are weaker than others. EU issues present a formidable challenge to the Nordic legislatures. Each has responded to this challenge in its own way. The Finnish parliament is the strongest of the Nordic legislatures, for the entire body is involved in EU policy-making, and much of this involvement takes place already before the legislative processing of the issue in question begins at the European level. The strength of the Danish Folketing lies in its ability to impose a binding mandate on ministers. The Riksdag is clearly in the weakest position, a fact reinforced by the rather passive attitude of Swedish MPs toward the handling of EU matters. The same applies to Norway. But since European legislation has direct and far-reaching consequences for member states, national parliaments cannot afford to ignore EU issues.

The surveys reveal that a striking majority of Nordic MPs support the deepening of integration within the EU. Nordic representatives are willing to transfer more sovereignty to Brussels; in this they differ from Danish, Finnish, and Swedish voters. Experience from more established EU member states shows this to be a well-known phenomenon: parties tend to "move faster" than their supporters (Holmberg 1996a; Wessels 1995). Not only are there differences of opinion between party leaders and their supporters (as shown by membership referenda); party elites are divided on this matter as well. Practically all Nordic parties are internally split, both over the question of membership and (especially) over the process of integration. This may prove highly problematic for the parties as we move toward an economic and political union.

NOTES

We would like to thank Torbjörn Bergman (University of Umeå) for his perceptive comments on an earlier draft of this chapter.

1. See the Special Issue of the *Journal of Legislative Studies* 1:3; Judge (1995); Laursen and Pappas (1995); Smith (1996); and Bergman (1997).

2. All member states—except Austria and Finland—have created a special standing committee for the handling of EU issues (Norton 1995; Bergman 1997). While thirteen of the fifteen member-state legislatures have established a special EU committee, there is considerable variation between them. To quote Philip Norton (1995:187–88): "What constitutes a European Affairs Committee in one parliament may display little resemblance to a European Affairs Committee in another. . . . To talk of European Affairs committees is to convey an impression of a uniformity that does not exist." In our opinion, such centralized arrangements fail to benefit from the cumulative expertise of the standing committees. A decentralized system, on the other hand, forces all representatives—EU-skeptics as well—to engage in EU issues. The establishment of special EU committees obviously presents no obstacle to benefiting from the expertise of other standing committees. In Germany, Ireland, and the Netherlands, for example, the standing committees are closely involved in the processing of EU matters. Practice has shown, however, that most member-state legislatures have found it difficult to coordinate the activities of the EU committee and other standing committees.

3. The sections on the Folketing and the Riksdag draw heavily on research by Hegeland and Mattson (1995; 1996). Recent works on the Danish experience include Arter (1995), Fitzmaurice (1996a), T. Jensen (1995), Laursen (1995), and Sidenius (1997). Our analysis of the Finnish case is based on our previous work (Wiberg and Raunio 1996; Raunio and Wiberg 1997). An early account of the adaptation of the Eduskunta and the Riksdag is also found in Fitzmaurice (1996b). Data on the Storting are taken from Sejersted (1996) and Myhre-Jensen (1997), and on the Althingi from Bogason (1997). For further and more detailed information on the involvement of the Nordic legislatures in their countries' EU policies, see the volume edited by Wiberg (1997).

4. See *Konstitutionsutskottets betänkande* 1994/95 (KU22): Samverkan mellan riksdag och regering med anledning av Sveriges anslutning till Europeiska unionen; and *Konstitutionsutskottets betänkande* 1996/97 (KU2): EU-frågornas behandling i riksdagen.

5. See *SuVL* 3/1995 vp: Euroopan unionin asioiden käsittelystä suuressa valiokunnassa ja sille lausunnon antavissa erikoisvaliokunnissa, 11/22/95.

6. See *Beretning fra markedsudvalget* af 20. maj 1994 vedrørende regeringens orientering af Folketinget om EU-sager. Reprinted in English in Laursen (1995: 55–60).

7. According to Arter (1995:114–15), the imprecisely defined obligation to inform the *udvalg* leaves the government much room to maneuver. "Significantly, there is no formal provision enabling the EAC to take the initiative and request a statement from the Government or an administrative body—restriction which has been intermittently criticised by committee members, especially those opposed to the EU."

8. Mr. Frederiksen had given his consent to a compromise over Danish export bacon in the Council of Ministers which is thought to have cost the Danes 400–500 million kroner. The Social Democratic minority government survived the vote only with support from the Social Liberals and the Socialist People's Party (Laursen 1995:44).

9. The EEA Agreement does not include agriculture, fisheries, taxation, or commercial policy and tariffs. The EFTA (European Free Trade Area) countries have not agreed to the process leading toward economic and monetary union, nor are they signatories to the second and third pillars of the EU.

10. The EEA Parliamentary Committee consists of twelve representatives of the European Parliament and twelve from the EFTA states (six from Norway, four from Iceland, and two from Liechtenstein). The committee meets twice a year and is basically a forum for the exchange of information.

11. Denmark has held four referenda on the EU. In the first membership referendum in October 1972, 63.4 percent of those casting their vote supported entering the European Community. The yes-side gained 56.2 percent of the votes in the referendum on the Single European Act in February 1986. In the first referendum on Maastricht, held in June 1992, 50.7 percent of the votes went to the victorious no-side. After concessions from Brussels, a second referendum on Maastricht took place in May 1993, and this time 56.7 percent of the voters supported the treaty. In the membership referenda in Finland (10/16/94), Sweden (11/13/94), and Norway (11/28/94), the winning margins were very narrow, reflecting the controversial nature of the issue. Of the voters in Finland, 56.9 percent supported joining the Union. They were echoed by 52.2 percent of those in Sweden, while in Norway only 47.7 percent of those casting a vote supported EU membership.

15

What Kind of Future and Why? Attitudes of Voters and Representatives

Hanne Marthe Narud and Henry Valen

In a long-term perspective, representative democracy is a relatively new form of government that has emerged over an extended period of time. It involves a special type of relationship between citizens and leaders. By voting for parties in popular elections, citizens transfer political authority to representatives whose task it is to act on their behalf. The best guarantee that "the people's representatives" will make decisions corresponding to the "will of the people" consists, some theorists would claim, in representatives holding views essentially similar to those of their voters.

But political development never stops. Technological, social, and economic changes, as well as external forces, are likely to affect the conditions faced by democracy. In planning for the future, political decision-makers must take into account the possible impact both of political facts and of observed trends in current development. In so doing, they are bound to anticipate tomorrow's agenda and to consider the potential effects of policy decisions on their electorates. Voters, for their part, are able to hold their leaders accountable for policy decisions by means of popular elections. A mutual interdependence thus links the two levels.

Esaiasson and Holmberg's analysis (1996) demonstrates that Swedish members of parliament are skeptical of their ability to define the future, and that on the whole this skepticism is justified. Riksdag members are not able, to any great extent, to participate actively in the agenda-building process. They seldom see beyond the current situation, for their long-term issue priorities build on the assumption that present trends will continue. To a great extent, their long-term priorities are shared by their voters. As compared, then, to the situation in the 1960s (when congruence was poor), representatives and voters in the 1980s thought more alike about the future (Esaiasson and Holmberg 1996:171–94).

A lack of relevant data prevents us from examining changes in the pattern of responses over time. We can, however, study the perspectives held by representatives and voters about the future on the basis of the current situation. We will focus on two main questions: (1) How do political representatives perceive the future of the political system? (2) To what extent do the attitudes held by representatives regarding future society correspond to those held by the general public? We will examine both questions on a comparative Nordic basis. Since political parties play a critical role in parliamentary democracy in these countries, party affiliation will be a major independent variable in our analysis.

FUTURE PROBLEMS AND VOTER-REPRESENTATIVE LINKAGES

In the tradition of the "responsible party model," the national electorate passes on instructions to the national parties, who then convert the mandate they have received from their voters into policy. By transforming their electoral programs into public policies, parties honor their promises, which are presumed to match the preferences of the voters who supported them on election day (Pierce 1999).

The view that elected representatives should be "in tune" with their electorate seems most relevant in regard to contemporary political issues (see chapter 7, by Sören Holmberg). But in the process of defining future problems and policies, demonstrating leadership is equally relevant, because the question of voter-representative linkages also involves the question of elite domination over public opinion. The effectiveness of parties in the process of representation is linked to the role of representatives as opinion leaders and to their ability to influence the long-term agenda. Thus, a poor fit between representatives and voters when it comes to views about future problems and polices does not necessarily undermine the "responsible party model." It means only that a tension exists between representing the voters now and representing them in the future. The voters may eventually adopt the opinions of their representatives when informed of the parties' stands on new trends and policies.

Political development in the Nordic area has been marked by substantial diffusion in the area of ideas. Notwithstanding, however, several similarities in their pattern of social and political development, the five countries in question do indeed differ. Each has its own integrity and special character. They differ with regard to economic resources, and their foreign-policy orientations have traditionally differed as well, owing to variations in strategic location. (After World War II, for instance, the Nordic countries chose varying solutions to their defense problems.) In addition, economic developments, social pressures on the welfare state, and rapid changes in the international environment since World War II have posed new challenges for the Nordic representative systems in general and for their elected representatives in particular.

The question of membership in the European Union, however, is the most spectacular issue. The five Nordic countries have chosen differing forms of affiliation (see, e.g., Jenssen et al. 1998; Pesonen 1994; Jenssen and Valen 1995; Gilljam and Holmberg 1996). Denmark, Finland, and Sweden decided to join the EU, while Iceland and Norway chose to remain outside. Despite the range in their policies, however, all five countries will be greatly affected by the EU and by the process of European integration.

Furthermore, this process constitutes a challenge for representative democracy. Evidence from the Eurobarometer, as well as the findings in chapters 4 and 5 of this book, indicate that European elites are "out of tune" with their electorates on matters having to do with closer cooperation and the future implementation of important EU legislation. In general, elites and masses diverge from one another on questions having to do with European integration, national sovereignty, and democratic development.[1] When studying the political perspectives of representatives and voters in regard to the future, therefore, we must take the impact of the EU issue into account. Tapio Raunio and Matti Wiberg discuss this issue more extensively in chapter 14.

The organization of this chapter follows the two questions posed initially. The first part of the analysis is concerned with representatives' perceptions and attitudes, whereas the second part is preoccupied with voter/representatives comparisons. Of particular interest is the extent to which the globalization of politics is reflected in the perceptions of representatives and voters. For analytical purposes, therefore, we make a distinction between internal and external factors when comparing voter and representative opinion.

Altogether, four sets of dependent variables are the target for the empirical analysis: risks for the political system, views on the European Union, future problem areas, and ideological values. Thus the questions applied in the first part are designed to ascertain representatives' perceptions of future problems for the political system; for example, the growth of extreme movements, reduced national sovereignty, political indifference, citizen apathy, and so on. The items to which we refer in the text are similar for each country.

The purpose of the next set of questions is to uncover representatives' evaluations of the European Union, as well as their attitudes toward future cooperation and the development of the EU. We then switch to the question of representative/voter differences. First, by analyzing their perceptions of future problems in society;[2] then, by examining their ideological values with respect to society's future development. The latter part contains seven items in all; these bear on, among other things, economic and technological development, the development of moral values, and gender and racial equality.

THE POLITICAL SYSTEM OF THE FUTURE

In an attempt to measure perceptions of the future political system, we presented representatives with a series of threats or negative assertions drawn from current political debate. Recalling our distinction between external and internal factors, the question is what kind of issues are of particular concern to political representatives where the future is concerned. In all of the Nordic countries, opposition to EU membership was fueled by nationalistic concerns and by fears of granting foreign powers, including the EU bureaucracy, too much influence over domestic affairs. Supporters of membership, on the other hand, saw European integration as both politically and economically beneficial for all of the countries involved. So the question was: Are worries about reduced national sovereignty of major concern to representatives? Or are they more preoccupied with domestic policy issues? For each assertion, respondents were given a choice between four alternatives: "very worrying"; "fairly worrying"; "not very worrying"; and "not at all worrying." The responses for each country are presented in table 15.1.

Table 15.1 indicates that representatives are most worried about domestic aspects of the future political system. Five items are seen as particularly serious: populism or short-term solutions, citizen apathy, declining confidence in politicians, the increasing influence of journalists, and the declining power of parliament. Sizable proportions are also worried about the declining influence of political parties. On the other hand, external factors—such as a possible decline of national self-determination and an increase in the power of the EU—are not perceived as particularly threatening. Neither is the possibility of charismatic leaders' emerging.

Table 15.1

Members' Perceptions of the Future of Own Political System (% "worried about the problem")

Type of Problem	Denmark	Finland	Iceland	Norway	Sweden	Average	Eta^2
Increased populism/short-term solutions	89	83	91	87	85	87	.02*
Apathy among citizens	87	93	79	96	79	87	.03*
Increasing distrust in politicians	62	71	68	82	85	74	.05*
Growing influence of journalists	73	84	64	72	69	72	.01
Declining power of parliament	69	75	68	70	NI	71	.00
Increased influence of financial markets	43	74	61	69	72	64	.04*
Weakened political parties	72	42	50	67	67	60	.05*
Growth of extreme political movements	44	44	32	58	69	49	.06*
Increased power of the EU	39	51	55	46	NI	48	.01
Weakened national independence	38	43	46	47	27	40	.03*
Too strong and charismatic leaders	33	8	41	21	13	23	.06*

Notes: The question was worded as follows: "Thinking about the political system, how worrying for the future do you perceive the following?" The following response alternatives were offered: "very worrying"; "fairly worrying"; "not very worrying"; "not at all worrying." NI = the item not included in the survey. Each eta-square value in the right-hand column is based on a one-way analysis of variance, with country as the independent variable and perceptions of future problems as the dependent variable.

*p < .01

With a couple of exceptions, response patterns do not differ much from one country to another. Some of the deviating reactions probably reflect particular events in national politics. Thus, the very high figure for citizen apathy in Norway may reflect the extremely low turnout in the local elections held a few months before this study was carried out. Similarly, recent turmoil in Danish politics may explain why leaders in this country expressed particular concern with the declining influence of political parties.

The items included in table 15.1 have been subjected to a factor analysis for the five countries taken jointly. For this analysis the last two items in table 15.1 had to be dropped, since they were not included in the Swedish questionnaire. In table 15.2, we present a three-factor solution regarding perceived tendencies toward a future decline of the political system.[3]

The factor accounting for most of the variance explained relates to the evaporating legitimacy of the current political system: citizen apathy, declining confidence in politicians, and the declining influence of political parties. Moreover, representatives expect journalists and the mass media to become more influential. Another factor bears on declining democratic control. The perceived threat may come from extreme political movements and strong charismatic leaders. Representatives further discern a tendency for populism or short-term solutions to overtake long-term planning in the policy-making process. The final factor concerns the ability of the nation to make independent decisions in the face of threats from the international environment (e.g., the increased influence of financial markets). Thus, even though external forces were not perceived by political representatives as particularly threatening (cf. table 15.1), they emerge here as a separate factor accounting for about 12 percent of the variance explained. As noted already, the question of national self-determination was a hot topic in the EU debate in the 1990s. Clearly, moreover, the responses under this factor also relate to perceptions of the growing power of the European Union (cf. table 15.1).[4]

The factor analysis reported in table 15.2 has been repeated for all of the countries separately. The patterns prove to be similar throughout the Nordic area, although the weight of the different items tends to vary slightly.

A country-by-country comparison based on the factor scores indicates that practically no differences exist on the aggregate level.[5] A comparison of political parties across nations, however, leads to more interesting results.[6] Some variations are visible in regard to system legitimacy and democratic control, but they are not of a systematic character. Only one factor—the decline of national control—displays a relatively stable pattern from one country to the next. The traditional ideological orientations

Table 15.2
Structure of Members' Perceptions of the Future of Own Political System: Factor Analysis (varimax rotation)

	Factor 15 Decline of System Legitimacy	Factor 25 Decline of Democratic Control	Factor 35 Decline of National Control
Increasing distrust in politicians	.773	.002	.211
Apathy among citizens	.722	.178	.210
Growing influence of journalists	.622	.124	−.185
Wakened political parties	.532	.445	.151
Increasing populism	.252	.722	−.269
Too strong and charismatic leaders	−.005	.699	.179
Extreme political movements	.201	.633	.266
Influence of financial markets	.237	.001	.792
Weakened national independence	−.019	.207	.757
% variance	31.5	14.3	11.7
Eigenvalue	2.84	1.29	1.05

Note: The number of cases is 685.

Table 15.3
Members' Worries over Declining National Control in the Future, by Country and Party Family (mean scores)

Party Family	Denmark	Finland	Iceland	Norway	Sweden
Left socialists	−.81	−1.29	−.81	−1.17	−1.26
Social democrats	+.20	+.10	+.68	+.08	−.31
Liberals	−.04	+.33	NA	NA	+.40
Agrarians	+1.16	−.59	+.22	−1.38	+.12
Christians	NA	−1.09	NA	−.18	+.83
Conservatives	+.78	+.59	+.47	+.79	+.99
Populists	+.06	NA	NA	1.03	NA

Notes: Perceived threats to national control are lowest with high positive values and increase as we move in the negative direction. NA = not applicable.

of the "socialist" and "conservative" movements might lead us to expect left-wing parties to be most inclined to take an international direction and parties of the right to be ardent defenders of the nation-state. But table 15.3 demonstrates that this is not the case in the Nordic nations.

In all five of the countries, left-socialist representatives express great concern over national control; social democrats take up a middle position; and conservative representatives tend to be the least worried. Only Iceland deviates slightly from this pattern, inasmuch as social democrats in that country feel less threatened by international forces than conservatives do.

The most spectacular deviation, however, occurs in the case of the agrarian parties. In Denmark, the agrarians are the most pro-international party; in Norway and Finland they represent the other extreme; and in Iceland and Sweden they tend to occupy a middle position. As will be explained later, the patterns found in table 15.3 are consistent with the position taken by the respective parties toward the EU and European integration.

In general, the perceived threats to the political system tend to be universal in character, with little variation among political parties or from one country to the next. This result is consistent with Lane and Ersson's observation (1996:213) that "the European game of politics shows more and more similarities despite economic and social differences as well as lingering historical legacies." The main message is that forces of political change in modern society—for example, technological development and modern mass media—are perceived to have roughly the same impact among political parties throughout western Europe. As we have seen, however, the internationalization of the political and economic spheres constitutes a notable exception here. International market forces and the process of European integration loom large in the perceptions of Nordic leaders in particular.

EXTERNAL PRESSURES ON THE NATION-STATE

The preceding analysis suggests that representatives are strongly concerned with the relationship of their respective countries to the European Union. In fact, this particular issue seems to be the most divisive theme in Nordic representatives' perception of the future. The results reported by Tapio Raunio and Matti Wiberg in chapter 14 reflect substantial variations among the Nordic countries.

Most basic is the difference between Denmark, which joined the EU already in 1972, and the other four countries, which have debated their relationship to the organization recently. In the case of Denmark, the question asked of respondents was whether the country should leave the EU entirely. Only 6 per cent of MPs take this extreme position, while four in ten prefer to retain membership, provided the country is exempted from some of the provisions of the Maastricht Treaty (cf. table 14.2 above). Norwegians and Icelanders are the most inclined to reject EU membership, though sizable proportions in both countries regard the European Economic Area agreement (EEA) as an acceptable alternative. The proportion in favor of membership is one out of three in Iceland, one out of two in Norway, and four out of five in Sweden. But the data suggest a low commitment in these three countries to the idea of a United States of Europe; by contrast, one out of four Danes see this as a vision for the future.

Owing to differences in ideology and political predisposition, political parties respond variously to this challenge. Parties of the left—which more than others are favorable to a national planned economy and critical of the capitalist nature of the Union—are most skeptical of the internationalization of the financial markets. This pattern is consistent among the countries.

Equally interesting are the variations in policies and attitudes among agrarian parties, which are the prime defenders of the interests of the rural branches of the economy. Representing as they do relatively profitable agricultural sectors, the agrarian parties of Denmark and Sweden do not perceive European integration as a threat. By contrast, small-scale farming units prevail in the agricultural sectors of Norway, Finland, and Iceland; obviously, therefore, competition from large-scale European agriculture presents a more serious threat to these countries.

Polarization between the parties is most striking in Norway, which has experienced an exceptionally divisive EU debate. In that country, as in Finland and Iceland, opposition to the EU was based on an alliance between urban radicals and the primary sector of the economy in the countryside. Iceland, however, is an outlier, in that social democrats in that country are the ones most in favor of the EU while their counterparts in the other countries occupy a middle position.

VOTER VERSUS REPRESENTATIVE PERCEPTIONS OF FUTURE PROBLEMS

The next point to be considered is voter versus representative perceptions of future problems. A number of items were listed in the questionnaire about possible problems for future society, and respondents were asked to indicate the severity of the problem.[7] Table 15.4 lists a few of the items for all five Nordic countries. Observe that we lack voter data for Denmark and Finland, and that in the Swedish case we lack six of the listed items.

The column to the far right indicates that, as far as future problems in society are concerned, Nordic representatives are particularly worried about four aspects. The first two, unemployment and declining social concern, are of a domestic character. These worries likely relate to anticipated pressure on the welfare state and to the ability of the system to handle

Table 15.4

Perceptions of the Future of Own Society among Representatives and Voters (% "worried about the problem")

Type of Problem	Denmark	Finland	Iceland	Norway	Sweden	Average
The situation in Russia						
MPs	94	86	66	91	92	86
Voters	NA	NA	75	78	67	73
Less social care and consideration						
MPs	76	91	82	91	80	84
Voters	NA	NA	87	89	NA	88
Environmental crisis						
MPs	82	64	82	81	90	80
Voters	NA	NA	98	89	87	91
High unemployment						
MPs	84	100	89	84	96	73
Voters	NA	NA	84	78	96	86
The national debt						
MPs	60	91	84	11	96	68
Voters	NA	NA	NA	NA	NA	NA
Deterioration of norms and values						
MPs	41	52	71	72	61	59
Voters	NA	NA	82	68	NA	75
Corruption						
MPs	22	30	75	40	43	42
Voters	NA	NA	93	75	NA	84
Inflation						
MPs	42	16	39	13	59	34
Voters	NA	NA	48	34	NA	41
Nuclear war						
MPs	40	9	37	43	25	31
Voters	NA	NA	76	53	NA	65

Notes: The question was worded as follows: "Thinking about the [the country's] society, what do you yourself perceive as most worrying for the future?" The following response alternatives were offered: "very worrying"; "fairly worrying"; "not very worrying"; "not at all worrying." NA = question not included in the survey.

emerging social problems. Representatives are also greatly worried about the situation in Russia and about a possible environmental crisis. Least worrying is an issue related to external forces: namely, the threat of a nuclear war. Finnish representatives particularly are disinclined to regard this as a future problem.

A few country-specific differences on the leadership level are worth mentioning. First of all, increased corruption is ranked much higher as a future problem by Icelandic representatives than by other Nordic representatives. Second, government debt and inflation in the future are regarded as much less of a problem by Norwegian MPs than by their colleagues in the other four countries. The first result may reflect the fact that Iceland is a small country and possibly more transparent than the other Nordic countries. The results for Norway, on the other hand, are probably a reflection of the advantageous economic situation of that country due to its oil revenues. Finally—and we have no intuitive suggestion as to why this should be the case—the weakening of norms in the future is seen as a slightly more severe problem in Iceland and Norway than in the other three countries.

As far as voter/representative differences are concerned, there really is no consistent pattern. Voters in Norway and Iceland, however, are more worried than their representatives are about nuclear war, corruption and inflation, and they are slightly more worried about an environmental crisis. The perceptions of Swedish voters are very much in line with those of their MPs, except in regard to the future situation in Russia. On this item, Swedish representatives are more worried than their voters, and the pattern is similar in Norway.

FUTURE SOCIETY: VOTER AND REPRESENTATIVE ATTITUDES

Finally, we turn to the question of how representatives and voters evaluate future society. We are basically concerned here with (a) values that are controversial among representatives, and (b) values that separate voters from representatives. Seven items bearing on the development of future society were listed in the questionnaires. Respondents were asked to indicate their attitudes on a scale from 0 (a very bad proposition) to 10 (a very good one).[8] The contents of the various items are indicated in table 15.5, which presents the main results.[9] Observe that Finland has been left out of this portion of the analysis, since the relevant questions were not asked in that country.

The column to the far right indicates that Nordic representatives are enthusiastic about promoting more equality between men and women in the future. The notion of a multicultural society also seems to appeal to them, as does the idea of using advanced technology to enhance production. They are least enthusiastic about promoting Christian values, although a mean of 4.9 on this question can hardly be called negative (it indicates, rather, a fairly neutral position on the issue).

Where country-specific differences are concerned, the most interesting observation has to do with the two assertions concerning economic development. First of all, Norwegian representatives are much more negative toward a heavier reliance on private enterprise and the market economy in

Table 15.5
Views on Different Kinds of Future Societies among Representatives and Voters (mean scores)

Work toward a Society with . . .	Denmark	Iceland	Norway	Sweden	Average
More private enterprise and market economy					
MPs	6.1	6.5	3.8	5.6	5.5
Voters	NA	5.9	5.5	5.8	5.7
High economic growth and productivity					
MPs	7.0	7.7	4.8	7.4	6.7
Voters	NA	7.8	6.3	7.1	7.1
More environmental protection[a]					
MPs	6.1	5.0	6.2	5.0	5.6
Voters	NA	6.5	6.9	5.5	4.6
Use advanced technology to enhance production					
MPs	7.8	6.8	5.8	7.8	7.1
Voters	NA	6.1	5.1	5.4	5.5
Promote Christian values					
MPs	5.1	5.8	5.1	4.6	5.2
Voters	NA	NA	5.1	4.1	4.6
More equality between men and women					
MPs	7.9	8.9	7.9	8.8	8.4
Voters	NA	8.5	7.8	7.6	8.0
Multicultural society[b]					
MPs	6.1	7.9	7.6	8.4	7.5
Voters	NA	6.7	5.7	5.5	6.0

Notes: Respondents were asked to evaluate the future development of society on a scale from 0 (bad proposal) to 10 (good proposal). NA = question not included in the survey.

[a]The full wording of proposal was as follows: "Work toward an environmentally friendly society, even if it means little or no economic growth."

[b]The full wording of the proposal was as follows: "Work toward a multicultural society with much tolerance toward people from other countries with other religions and ways of life."

the future than are the leaders of the other three countries. Whereas Icelandic, Danish, and Swedish representatives hold opinions close to 6 on the scale, Norwegian leaders have a mean position of 3. 8. Compared to their Nordic colleagues, Norwegian representatives are also much more skeptical of promoting economic growth and productivity in the future. On this question, Icelandic representatives are the most positive ones.

On the question of environmental protection, on the other hand, Icelandic and Swedish representatives are the least enthusiastic, while Norwegian and Danish representatives are the most positive.

Differences among representatives on the question of promoting Christian values are not very great, and there is also little variation between them on the question of greater equality between men and women. When it comes to the idea of a multicultural society in the future, some differences are visible between Danish representatives and those hailing from the other three countries. While the latter are fairly enthusiastic about this idea, Danish representatives take a more neutral stand.

Table 15.5 also points to some interesting voter/representative differences. Again, Norwegian representatives deviate from the others. They are fairly "out of tune" with their voters on the question of a greater reliance on private enterprise and the market economy, as well as on the question of economic growth and productivity. While representatives are rather skeptical of these prescriptions for the future, voters take a more moderate position. Swedish representatives, for their part, are much more positive toward the use of advanced technology to enhance production than are voters.

In general, voter/representative differences are sizable. Most consistent are the discrepancies over the question of a multicultural society. Whereas political representatives have fairly positive attitudes toward this idea, voters tend to hold a more reluctant view. These results are consistent with the ones reported in chapter 7.

Let us look now at the question of party variations. Consistent with our previous research strategy, we have only included items in the table on which the parties hold systematically different ideological positions. These are listed in table 15.6.

The table indicates that the first two items have an ideological distribution compatible with that of the left-right axis, although item two also seems to tap a "green" dimension. Hence, the parties of the left are consistently more skeptical of a heavier reliance on private enterprise and the market economy, and more skeptical of economic growth and productivity as well. The only exception is the Icelandic Social Democratic Party, with a mean position of 7.0. The conservative and populist parties, together with the two liberal parties (in Denmark and Sweden), line up on the opposite side (all of them holding positive attitudes on the two issues).

By contrast, the Nordic agrarian parties are divided on these items. That is, the Norwegian agrarian party is very reluctant to accept a heavier reliance on the market economy in the future, and it opposes economic growth and productivity. Its skepticism is shared by the Norwegian Christian People's Party. By contrast, the other agrarian parties—the Danish one most notably—are favorably disposed to a heavier reliance on the market economy, and to economic growth and productivity, too. Their

Table 15.6
Views on Different Kinds of Future Societies among Representatives and Voters, by Party Family (mean scores)

	Party Family	Denmark	Iceland	Norway	Sweden
Work toward a society	Left socialists				
with more private	MPs	2.0	1.6	0.6	1.7
enterprise and	Voters	NA	4.1	3.4	3.6
market economy	Social democrats				
	MPs	3.9	7.0	2.2	3.7
	Voters	NA	6.3	4.9	4.6
	Liberals				
	MPs	7.0	NA	NA	8.4
	Voters	NA	NA	NA	7.0
	Agrarians				
	MPs	10.0	6.2	2.7	6.9
	Voters	NA	5.5	4.7	6.6
	Christians				
	MPs	NA	NA	4.3	7.9
	Voters	NA	NA	5.8	7.3
	Conservatives				
	MPs	9.5	9.1	8.3	9.4
	Voters	NA	6.8	7.1	8.0
	Populists				
	MPs	9.8	NA	9.2	NA
	Voters	NA	NA	6.9	NA
Work toward a society	Left socialists				
with high economic	MPs	3.4	5.3	1.2	4.3
growth rate and	Voters	NA	7.7	3.8	6.5
high productivity	Social democrats				
	MPs	6.5	8.0	5.0	7.4
	Voters	NA	7.9	5.3	6.9
	Liberals				
	MPs	7.3	NA	NA	8.5
	Voters	NA	NA	NA	7.1
	Agrarians				
	MPs	8.8	8.4	2.9	6.7
	Voters	NA	7.4	5.0	6.9
	Christians				
	MPs	NA	NA	2.9	7.2
	Voters	NA	NA	6.1	7.1
	Conservatives				
	MPs	8.7	9.0	7.7	9.2
	Voters	NA	8.1	6.8	8.2
	Populists				
	MPs	9.3	NA	8.8	NA
	Voters	NA	NA	7.8	NA

Table 15.6

Continued

	Party Family	Denmark	Iceland	Norway	Sweden
Work toward an	Left socialists				
environmentally	MPs	9.4	7.3	8.8	7.5
friendly society,	Voters	NA	7.1	7.3	6.1
even if it means	Social democrats				
little or no	MPs	7.1	4.2	6.0	4.7
economic growth	Voters	NA	6.6	6.9	5.5
	Liberals				
	MPs	8.2	NA	NA	4.3
	Voters	NA	NA	NA	5.6
	Agrarians				
	MPs	3.9	5.1	7.8	6.8
	Voters	NA	6.4	7.1	6.2
	Christians				
	MPs	NA	NA	7.8	5.7
	Voters	NA	NA	7.0	5.2
	Conservatives				
	MPs	4.0	2.9	3.7	3.2
	Voters	NA	6.3	6.4	4.7
	Populists				
	MPs	5.0	NA	3.2	NA
	Voters	NA	NA	6.8	NA
Work toward a	Left socialists				
multicultural	MPs	8.1	8.3	9.2	9.4
society with much	Voters	NA	7.6	7.1	6.4
tolerance toward	Social democrats				
people from other	MPs	7.4	8.7	7.9	8.6
countries with other	Voters	NA	6.8	6.0	5.4
religions and ways	Liberals				
of life	MPs	10.0	NA	NA	9.0
	Voters	NA	NA	NA	6.8
	Agrarians				
	MPs	3.8	7.2	7.8	7.3
	Voters	NA	6.4	4.8	5.4
	Christians				
	MPs	NA	NA	8.5	9.3
	Voters	NA	NA	5.5	5.5
	Conservatives				
	MPs	3.5	7.3	6.4	7.1
	Voters	NA	6.2	5.6	5.2
	Populists				
	MPs	1.2	NA	2.5	NA
	Voters	NA	NA	3.3	NA

Notes: Respondents were asked to evaluate the seven future societies on a scale from 0 (bad proposal) to 10 (good proposal). NA = data not available.

view is shared by the Swedish Christian Democrats and the Icelandic Social Democrats (and, in regard to productivity but not private enterprise, by the Swedish Social Democrats).

Turning to the bottom half of table 15.6 we find that, consistent with their skepticism toward economic growth and productivity, left socialists are much more in favor of environmental protection than are their colleagues on the right. Both conservative and populist parties are reluctant to give priority to environmental protection, should this mean little or no economic growth in the future. Social democrats take a middle position on this issue, with the Danish Social Democrats taking a slightly more favorable position than their ideological counterparts in the other countries. Again, parties of the "center" are divided, with the Danish and Norwegian agrarians staking out the two opposite poles on this question, with the Swedish and Icelandic agrarians in between. The two liberal parties also disagree on the issue, with the Danes very much in favor of environmental protection and the Swedes against (should it mean little or no economic growth).

Furthermore, left socialists are more favorable toward a multicultural society than are their colleagues on the right. These tendencies are hardly surprising, since they fit with "leftist" and "rightist" positions on similar *current* policy issues. Some interesting country variations are evident, however. These have to do with the attitudes of Danish right-wing and agrarian representatives, who are much more negative toward the idea of promoting a multicultural society in the future than are their colleagues in the other Nordic countries, especially Iceland and Sweden. The second interesting observation has to do with voter/representative differences. None of the party families are in line with their voters on the question of a multicultural society. Whereas, for example, representatives of the left and of the center are fairly enthusiastic toward this idea, their voters take a neutral position.

Consistent with the results in table 15.5, the figures in table 15.6 confirm the greater radicalism of Norwegian representatives—as compared with their colleagues in the other Nordic countries—on the two items bearing on private enterprise and economic growth. But the skepticism here is found in the parties of the left and—surprisingly enough—the parties of the center (the agrarians and the Christians). While agrarian representatives in Denmark, Iceland, and Sweden are quite positive toward a heavier reliance on private enterprise in the future, the Norwegian agrarians have a mean position of 2.7 on this question. And they are—together with the Christians—just as negative toward economic growth and productivity in the future. With a mean position of 2.9 on this item, they clearly deviate from their colleagues in Denmark, Iceland, and Sweden, all of whom look favorably on economic growth and productivity. Moreover, center representatives in Norway are not in line with their own voters on these issues. From table 15.6, we can see that agrarian and Christian voters have fairly neutral stands on the two questions. Norwegian agrarian voters have about the same profile as Icelandic agrarian voters on the first item, whereas on the second they are more negative.

Again, it is tempting to point to the EU issue as a possible explanation for the observed variations. We have earlier noted the differences between the Nordic nations regarding the impact of the EU on agriculture and fisheries. As the most ferocious opponent of membership prior to the 1993 elections, the Norwegian agrarian party (that is, the Center Party) adopted a clear anti-market attitude, thus entering into a strategic alliance with the left socialists. The radicalization of the party due to the EU issue is therefore reflected in the material presented here.

No doubt, the data reflect party-specific differences as well as country-specific differences. On several issues, parties belonging to the same party family—for example, left-socialist, conservative, or populist parties—hold similar opinions about how to organize future society. There is a consistent pattern in "leftist" attitudes toward market forces, economic growth, and environmental protection, and a similarly consistent pattern in "rightist" views on the same issues. But differences within party families are also evident, particularly in the case of agrarian and Christian leaders, and to some extent social democrats also.

Overall, Norwegian parties of the center have a more radical profile than do their Nordic cousins, and they take a more negative stance on market forces and economic growth in the future. However, the opinion profile of voters across national borders is more uniform than that of representatives. Conservative and populist parties, finally, have fairly similar patterns of opinion in all four countries.

CONCLUDING REMARKS

In this chapter, we have made an attempt at studying the political outlook regarding the future held by political representatives and voters in the Nordic countries. In so doing, we distinguished between external factors on the one hand and internal or domestic factors on the other. First, we considered the perceptions of political representatives about the future of the political system. According to our data, Nordic representatives feel that the system is endangered by internal forces. They fear a declining legitimacy on the part of the system and a declining ability to exercise control over traditional democratic institutions.

By and large, the main tendencies are similar across the five countries, as well as across party lines within individual nations. Leadership perceptions differ more in regard to threats from the international environment; that is, factors making for declining national control of the system. These perceived dangers have materialized in connection with the development of each nation's relationship to the European Union.

Representatives from nonmember countries tend to be the most worried about the increasing power of the EU. Similar tendencies are visible inside individual countries: representatives of pro-EU parties tend to be less worried than those representing anti-EU parties. This fear is not limited, though, to the question of the EU's future development. It also reflects worries about the increased internationalization of financial markets.

The second question posed in this chapter involves a comparison of attitudes—among both voters and representatives—toward future society in the Nordic countries. Again, we are struck by the similarity between the countries. However, the Norwegians tend to deviate concerning questions of economic development and the role of the market. In Norway, it is most especially the parties of the left and the agrarians who are restrictive toward private enterprise and economic growth in the future. These differences are largely restricted to representatives; voters in the various countries hold more similar views on these items.

As far as voter and representative perceptions of future development are concerned, respondents at both levels in all five countries see issues related to the welfare state—that is, unemployment and declining social concern—as a severe problem for future society. Norwegian representatives, however, are more optimistic than their Nordic colleagues about government debt and, to some extent, inflation. Icelanders, on the other hand, are more pessimistic than others about future corruption.

In general, the discrepancy between representatives and voters in regard to attitudes toward a multicultural society is sizable in all of the countries. The most notable voter/representative discrepancies are found in the Norwegian data and concern the development of market forces and economic growth.

As might be expected, the Nordic nations exhibit a great many similarities as regards views of politics and society in the future. The sharpest divisions seem to concern economic conditions and external forces. Country-by-country comparisons reveal a deviant pattern on the part of Norwegian representatives.

Two main reasons may be adduced for this. First, the Norwegian economy has benefited from substantial oil revenues during recent years. As a result, Norway has avoided a number of problems facing its neighbors, like budget deficits, public debt, and unemployment. Second, the EU debate in the 1990s was particularly bitter in Norway, and some of the reactions observed probably reflect hostilities occasioned by this debate; for example, negative attitudes toward financial markets and skepticism about the supranational decision-making entailed by the EU.

The question of how each country should deal with its future relationship to the EU poses the most important challenge to the Nordic representative systems. Decisions made within the EU will affect each Nordic country in numerous ways, whether it is a member of the organization or not. Some observers worry about the degree of democratic representation and accountability associated with European integration, and they have diagnosed a democratic deficit in European representative institutions. Others have pointed to the national parliaments as cornerstones in the process of integration, and have argued that European elections are fought primarily on the basis of national political concerns. The low level of turnout in these elections has become an increasingly important topic (see, e.g., Franklin et al. 1996), as has the seeming indifference of voters toward policy-making in the European Parliament.

One interesting question is how the development of the European Union will affect the relationship between political representatives and their voters. The analysis presented here demonstrates that representatives are worried about the future legitimacy of the political system, and that they fear increasing citizen apathy and declining trust in politicians (and perhaps in democratic institutions as well). Of great relevance to the process of political representation, then, is the capacity of political representatives to present voters with meaningful alternatives and to offer electorates some awareness of the political positions and decisions in the arena under consideration.

Another challenge for political representatives is the observed tendency among Nordic voters to adopt anti-immigrant attitudes. Although representatives are far more inclined than their voters to hold liberal views on this matter, the temptation to resort to populist solutions is clearly present on the leadership level. Representatives are thus faced with two options: either to submit to popular sentiments or to try to change the views of their followers. The latter option, however—which would be consistent with the top-down perspective of the "responsible party model"—is conditioned on the ability of candidates and parties to successfully communicate policy positions to their supporters.

NOTES

1. Parallel to the decisions taken by the EU in regard to the single market, results from the Eurobarometer in the winter of 1991–92 showed that a negative shift of opinion had occurred on the question of European integration. This shift showed up first among the larger and wealthier EU members; then, in 1993, it appeared within such countries as Portugal and Greece as well (Skjaak 1994). This shift of opinion was not registered by EU elites until the spring of 1993 (Skjaak 1994).

2. The items were identical for representatives and for voters. Respondents were asked to what extent they perceived the issue as "very problematic," "fairly problematic," "not very problematic," or "not problematic at all." Observe that, for Denmark and Finland, we do not have voter-level data on these items.

3. We have preferred this solution because, in a four-factor solution, the last factor had an eigenvalue of only .82.

4. We have done a separate factor analysis for the four countries that included the last two questions in table 15.1: increased power to the EU, and declining power to the national parliaments. Both items loaded strongly under the third factor in table 15.2, the one we have labeled "decline of national control."

5. As an alternative solution, we have constructed additive indexes based on the items that loaded under each separate factor. The results are similar, but less intuitively informative than the figures in table 15.3.

6. Throughout the chapter, we have divided the parties into seven party families, and we have excluded parties with three respondents (representatives) or less. The following parties have thus been excluded from the analysis: In *Denmark:* the Unity List, the Radical Left, and the Center Democrats. In *Finland:* the Greens. In *Iceland:* the Womens' Alliance and the Parliamentary Party. In *Norway:* the Red Election Alliance, the Liberals, and the Free Democrats. We have left out the Greens in Sweden.

7. The question was worded as follows: "Thinking about the (country in question) political system, how worrying, for the future, do you perceive the following?" The following response alternatives were offered: "very worrying"; "fairly worrying"; "not very worrying"; and "not at all worrying." The Finnish questionnaire also contained a middle category: "difficult to say." For purposes of comparability, we have excluded this category from the analysis.

8. The wording of the question was as follows: "We have listed a number of propositions that many people believe should be emphasized in the future. What is your opinion about them? You may indicate your answer by using the numbers on the scale presented here."

9. When factor analysis was applied on these items, no meaningful cluster emerged. We have therefore simply presented the mean values for each country on each item.

16

Risk Perceptions among Members of Parliament: Economy, Ecology, and Social Order

Torben K. Jensen

In this chapter, we shall analyze the perception of risk by members of Nordic parliaments—what they see, that is, as the most important threats to their respective societies. From one perspective, risk perception has to do with our *picture of the future:* what we have reason to *fear,* and what we may *hope* for. Conversely, our fears and expectations for the future reveal how we view our present situation. Thus, our possible or probable future scenarios contain elements of both causal and consequence analysis; revelations of which messengers and what kind of knowledge we trust; indications of whom we consider to be good guys, bad guys, heroes, victims, or friends in need; and descriptions of our respective political values.[1] So although risk perception seems to relate to the future, it relates still more to the present, in that it contributes to a *definition and portrayal of the current situation.* Our purpose in analyzing risk perception among Nordic parliamentarians, therefore, is first and foremost to shed some light on fundamental traits of political discourse and conflict in the Nordic political systems.

THEORY OF RISK PERCEPTION

The general consciousness of risk is sharply increasing, as is public attention to it. Research into risk perception is increasing as well (Nelkin 1989). We find numerous attempts in the literature to explain "who fears what and why." The perception of technology in particular has been the object of extensive studies. Correlations in this field have turned out to be highly complex, which is reflected in the research on risk perception. We can identify, roughly speaking, three traditions and three stages, each based on one of three factors: the risk-creating phenomenon as such, the individual, and culture and ways of life.

According to the first tradition, risk and risk evaluation are purely technical matters, which can only be elucidated and communicated to decision-makers and the public by experts. One problem, however, is that this conception of risk has never gained social acceptance. Another problem is that studies in this tradition have been unable to explain variations in the risk perception of different individuals (Nelkin 1989:100). In reaction, another tradition has focused on the subjective dimension of risk perception, attempting, on the basis primarily of psychological theory, to map thresholds of acceptance in different types of persons confronted with different types of risks. But research within this framework has been unable to explain variations in risk perception as between different social and cultural environments, a fact that in turn has formed the basis for a third generation within this field of research, taking its point of departure in theories of culture and ways of life (Nelkin 1989:100; Douglas and Wildavsky 1982).

In order to test a number of explanations produced by American risk-perception research, Karl Dake and Aaron Wildavsky have done an important study on the basis of comprehensive survey data (Wildavsky and Dake 1991). They find no evident statistical relationship between *individuals' knowledge of specific dangers* and their fear of them. Nor do they detect any unambiguous relationship between *individuals' personality* and either their perception of risks or their inclination to expose themselves to them. Politico-sociological variables, such as *gender, age,* or *social class,* do not account for very much either, whereas *ideological orientation* does give some indication of a specific pattern.

Wildavsky and Dake try to explain patterns of risk perception on the basis of a *cultural theory of different ways of life.* According to this theory—in the literature often referred to as Cultural Theory—risk and risk perception form part of the construction of social life. "The perception of risk is set in an ongoing cultural conflict in which the organization of rights and obligations, and of community loyalties and economic interests, matters at least as much as scientific evidence" (Nelkin and Pollack, quoted in Dake 1991:63) According to Cultural Theory, people can be expected to divide into *three main groups* according to their perception of risk: those who fear economic instability and breakdown most of all, those who mainly fear ecological instability and breakdown, and those whose foremost fear is of a breakdown of social order. According to Cultural Theory, these three risk perceptions are systematically related to individuals' perception of nature and society, and to their social relations as well.

Those *fearing economic breakdown* are bearers of an *individualistic way of life*. This group tends generally to look upon nature as a robust entity, to be in favor of economic growth, and to rely upon the market as a principal social institution. Where their social relations are concerned, such persons wish to live without too many (outside) rules and regulations, and to engage in many different social networks.

Those *fearing ecological breakdown* are bearers of an *egalitarian way of life*. This group perceives nature as fragile, for which reason (among others) they consider economic growth and the market economy to be irresponsible. Besides, they say, growth is unnecessary, for people can improve their quality of life just by distributing material goods more equally and by establishing well-defined communities with a high degree of (equal) participation in decision-making processes.

Finally, we have those who most of all fear the *breakdown of social order*. They cherish the *hierarchical way of life*. Lack of authority is seen as the main problem by this group. But opinions differ considerably within this group on the definition of "authority." Some demand more expertise. Others demand more central government and more regulation. Yet others call for more authority and social order in terms of the traditional civic virtues. Members of this group consider nature to be robust, though within certain limits that should be identified by science and controlled by the central government. In their opinion, the market must be equilibrated by means of regulation. Hierarchically minded persons prefer their social relations to be marked by well-defined communities that respect existing norms and rules.[2]

Thus, according to Cultural Theory, risk perceptions are explicable in terms of ways of life. Or, as Wildavsky puts it: "Individuals choose what to fear (and how much to fear it) in order to support their way of life" (Wildavsky and Dake 1991:135).[3]

The following analysis, therefore, is based on the assumption that we will have a key to the political culture of Nordic parliamentarians if we know something about what they fear. In what follows, we shall try to find answers to the following questions: (1) What issues are considered worrying by the democratically elected portion of the Nordic political elite? (2) Is it possible to identify specific patterns in MPs' risk perception? (3) Are any of the explanatory factors put forward in the literature applicable in a Nordic context? (4) What do the answers to these questions tell us about similarities and differences between the various political cultures of the Nordic countries and of the Nordic parliamentary parties? The analysis is guided by some of the basic assumptions of Cultural Theory, and it tries as well in some measure to test this theory.

The survey question used to measure risk perception among Nordic MPs is worded as follows: "Thinking about [Danish, Finnish, Icelandic, Norwegian, Swedish] society, what do you consider to be the most worrying issue for the future?" This question is then followed by seventeen items (see table 16.1 below). The inspiration for most of these items derives from Karl Dake's attempt to measure societal concerns among ordinary people as reported in the article "Orienting Dispositions in the Perception of Risk" (Dake 1991:71). Our analysis here is the first to put these questions to an elite political group.

WHAT WORRIES NORDIC PARLIAMENTARIANS, AND HOW MUCH?

In our survey, we presented Nordic MPs with a number of issues and asked them to indicate which of them they regarded as worrying for their society's future. The answers are shown in table 16.1. We were quite deliberate in asking MPs what worried them; our purpose was to make them weigh the gravity of the problem against the probability of its actually happening. It is just such a weighing of issues, in fact, that practitioners must always undertake when handling difficult questions.

There seems, on the whole, to be considerable agreement among parliamentarians about which risks are the most serious. *Unemployment* is considered the greatest problem by an overwhelming majority. Second on the list is *the situation in Russia*. Thirdly, respondents feel anxious about the way we treat nature (fearing *damage to the environment*), and, next, about *social solidarity*. The economy—or, to be more explicit, *the national debt*—seems also to give rise to considerable concern. Finally, a great many politicians are preoccupied with the possibility of increased *conflict between Western and Muslim countries*.

There are certain differences, however, in how respondents in the different *countries* rank these risks. The eta coefficients indicate that differences in the perception of risk associated with inflation, war in Europe, the national debt, the situation in Russia, and possible conflict between Western and Muslim countries are best explained in terms of country affiliation. Party affiliation, by contrast, seems to account best for differences in perception when it comes to environmental problems, nuclear power, the dissolution of norms, the lack of social consideration, and the increasing number of refugees.

Table 16.1

Members' Perceptions of the Future of Own Society, by Country and Party Family (% "worried about the problem")

	1. Large Unemploy.	2. Situation in Russia	3. Environ. Problems	4. Less Social Care and Consid.	5. National Debt	6. Confl. btw. Western and Muslim Count.	7. Dissolu. of Social Norms	8. Nucl. Power	9. Infla.	10. Incr. no. of Refug.	11. Corrupt.	12. Economic Competition from S.E. Asia	13. War in Europe	14. Economic Competition from Japan and the U.S.	15. Lack of Strong National Leadersip	16. Nucl. War	17. Techno. Devel.	Min. N
All	92	87	82	82	73	66	58	41	39	38	38	37	36	33	29	29	13	732
Country																		
Denmark	**84**	**94**	**82**	**76**	60	**79**	41	44	42	53	22	44	61	31	23	40	18	104
Finland	**99**	68	63	**82**	**90**	44	40	21	14	17	25	49	15	42	22	8	15	116
Iceland	**89**	66	**82**	**82**	**84**	**77**	**71**	42	39	39	**75**	41	46	25	30	37	7	43
Norway	**84**	**91**	**81**	**91**	11	**71**	**72**	55	13	NI	40	36	31	29	32	43	21	142
Sweden	**96**	**92**	**90**	**80**	**96**	NI	61	42	59	41	43	30	NI	NI	32	25	9	324
Eta	.23	.30	.24	.12	.72	.30	.24	.21	.41	.24	.26	.15	.36	.13	.09	.26	.15	
Party family																		
Greens	**98**	**83**	**100**	**89**	**93**	**67**	46	**78**	7	7	**67**	26	50	33	20	31	7	23
Left-Socs.	**100**	**73**	**91**	**90**	66	59	42	**68**	13	21	50	34	48	32	24	41	27	63
Soc-Dems.	**83**	**81**	**85**	**86**	65	63	45	43	36	30	36	35	30	34	24	31	14	302
Centrists	**94**	**89**	**85**	**87**	55	49	**71**	46	35	21	40	41	33	29	31	33	22	70
Agrarians	**92**	**81**	**81**	**84**	**76**	**73**	**71**	47	34	52	37	44	42	30	43	28	17	107
Conservs.	**88**	**89**	**67**	64	**71**	**78**	**67**	16	44	56	36	50	40	34	32	23	5	140
Populists	60	**100**	23	**70**	60	**95**	53	0	55	**100**	45	20	38	5	25	40	0	14
Eta	.18	.14	.31	.31	.14	.19	.30	.42	.25	.31	.15	.15	.14	.12	.27	.14	.19	

Notes: The question was worded as follows: "Thinking about the [Danish, Finish, Icelandic, Norwegian, Swedish] society, what do you yourself perceive as most worrying for the future?" The following response alternatives were offered: "very worrying"; "fairly worrying"; "not very worrying"; "not at all worrying." Problems mentioned by more than two-thirds of respondents are shown in bold print. Eta coefficients are calculated on the basis of unweighted data. NI = item not included in the survey.

For rather obvious reasons, having to do with oil and prosperity, *Norwegian MPs* are not anxious about national debt. On the other hand, they are more concerned than their Nordic colleagues about declining solidarity ("declining social consideration") and diminishing social cohesion ("dissolution of norms")—developments that may in part be the consequence of an impressive and protracted economic boom.

Danish parliamentarians are also less anxious about the national debt than are other Nordic politicians. They are more preoccupied, however, with foreign affairs: the situation in Russia, conflicts with the Muslim world, and the risk of war in Europe.

In *Finland,* unemployment and the national debt are both seen as problems of paramount importance, followed by the decline of social solidarity. Unemployment ranks high in *Sweden* as well, together with the national debt, and there is great concern about environmental problems, too.

Where social problems are concerned, *Icelandic* MPs, like their Norwegian colleagues, focus their attention on declining social consideration, the dissolution of social norms, and the threat of corruption. It is true that Icelandic politics has not been cursed with corruption and scandals, but the small size of Icelandic society may lead to a common feeling among people that the political elites are forming cliques.

If we examine the risk perceptions of individual *party families,* we discover significant variations. As a matter of fact, the only point on which there is general agreement across party lines is in regard to the situation in Russia, which everyone finds worrying. In addition, most parties (the populists excepted) agree that unemployment is among the most serious problems, followed by declining social consideration. (The latter point is not given priority by conservatives.)

Each party family seems to have its own profile on these matters. Thus *the greens* are particularly worried about the environment, nuclear power, and social solidarity, and they have a certain anti-establishment touch besides (as reflected in their concern with corruption). The *left-wing parties* worry more than others about unemployment and environmental problems, including the use of nuclear power. What makes *social democrats* anxious is first and foremost unemployment, followed by the situation in Russia, the environment, social solidarity, and the national debt. The most characteristic thing about MPs from *center* and *agrarian parties* is their particular concern with the dissolution of social norms and the decline in social solidarity. *Conservatives* share the concern about the dissolution of social norms, but they are unworried about the decline in social solidarity. *Populists* fear most of all an influx of foreigners into the country—whether Russians, Muslims, or others—and declining social solidarity thereafter.

THE IMPORTANCE OF GENDER, AGE AND EDUCATIONAL LEVEL

From table 16.2 it appears—quite predictably from a Cultural Theory perspective—that in most respects *gender* is not a very important factor in explaining differences in risk perception. At first sight, though, there does seem to be a few exceptions: women are considerably more worried than men about nuclear power, and relatively more women than men express concern about the environment. But more detailed analysis shows that this holds true only for social democratic women. We must accordingly conclude that ideology rather than gender explains attitudes to nuclear power and the environment.

Age does not appear, for most risk categories, to be an important explanatory factor either. However, older respondents do seem more anxious than young ones about economic competition from Southeast Asia, about the increasing number of refugees, and about technological development. When educational level is controlled for, the statistical relationship between age and the perception of technology dissolves, while the other two relationships still hold. A possible interpretation here is that, irrespective of education, older members of the parliamentary elite look upon the process of internationalization with greater concern than do younger members.

It is possible to formulate two intuitively plausible theses about the importance of a person's *educational level* for his or her perception of risk. The first is as follows: the higher your educational level, the more things you are able to survey and the fewer you have to worry about. The second thesis says instead that, the higher your educational level, the more precise is your knowledge of actual dangers and the greater your reason for feeling concerned about various factors.

Neither of these hypotheses is supported by the data (see table 16.2). A more detailed analysis, furthermore, shows that education generally has a very modest impact in Denmark, Norway, and Sweden (table 16.3). Moreover, in those cases where education does have an impact on risk perception, the effect tends be different in each of the three countries. Only on the question of refugees is there a clear tendency for people with less education to be more anxious than people with more.

At first sight, however, Iceland seems to be an interesting exception where the effect of education is concerned. The average percentage difference between people with high and low education is 13; in thirteen out of seventeen cases, moreover, respondents with a university degree feel less concerned than do respondents with less education. Thus the

Table 16.2
Members' Perceptions of the Future of Own Society, by Gender, Age and Education (% "worried about the problem" and eta)

	1. Large Unemploy.	2. Situation in Russia	3. Environ. Problems	4. Less Social Consid.	5. National Debt	6.[a] Confl. btw. Western and Muslim Count.	7. Dissolu. of Social Norms	8. Nucl. Power	9. Inflat.	10.[b] Incr. no. of Refug.	11. Corrupt.	12. Economic Competition from S.E. Asia	13.[a] War in Europe	14.[a] Economic Competition from Japan and the U.S.	15. Lack of Strong National Leadersip	16. Nucl. War	17. Techno. Devel.	Min. N
Total	90	82	80	82	68	68	57	41	33	38	41	40	38	32	28	31	14	732
Gender																		
Male	91	83	77	82	69	71	64	36	32	40	41	41	39	33	30	31	12	463
Female	91	80	87	83	69	62	61	48	35	32	40	37	38	30	24	28	18	266
Eta	.02	.01	.12	.03	.00	.10	.03	.16	.09	.02	.02	.07	.01	.03	.08	.05	.08	
Age[c]																		
Younger (−44)	87	87	82	84	70	61	50	44	37	31	31	32	37	29	22	30	10	183
Older (45−)	92	86	78	83	63	68	55	40	31	40	34	43	36	36	28	29	18	476
Eta	.08	.03	.04	.03	.02	.08	.07	.06	.02	.11	.03	.09	.01	.06	.07	.01	.08	
Education[d]																		
Below university	90	85	84	85	61	80	50	49	42	51	45	38	49	36	27	39	14	301
University-level	88	86	83	80	52	73	61	39	35	39	44	39	43	22	34	33	11	302

Notes: The question was worded as follows: Thinking about the [Danish, Finnish, Icelandic, Norwegian, Swedish] society, what do you yourself perceive as most worrying for the future? The following response alternatives were offered: "very worrying"; "fairly worrying"; "not very worrying"; "not at all worrying." Percentages are calculated on the basis of weighted data (all countries are given equal weight). Eta coefficients are calculated on the basis of unweighted data.

[a] Not included in the Swedish questionnaire.

[b] Not included in the Norwegian questionnaire.

[c] Icelandic MPs not included.

[d] Finnish MPs not included.

Table 16.3
Members' Perceptions of the Future of Own Society, by Education Controlling for Country (% "worried about the problem" and eta)

	1. Large Unemploy.	2. Situation in Russia	3. Environ. Problems	4. Less Social Consid.	5. Less National Debt	6. Confl. btw. Western and Muslim Count.	7. Dissolu. of Social Norms	8. Nucl. Power	9. Infla.	10. Incr. no. of Refug.	11. Corrupt.	12. Economic Competition from S.E. Asia	13. War in Europe	14. Economic Competition from Japan and the U.S.	15. Lack of Strong National Leadersip	16. Nucl. War	17. Techno. Devel.	Min. N
Denmark																		
Below university	87	97	79	74	60	84	41	50	42	57	21	47	65	36	22	41	20	61
University	80	91	85	78	61	72	41	36	42	48	24	39	57	26	24	39	15	46
Eta	.09	.12	.07	.05	.01	.14	.00	.14	.00	.09	.04	.08	.09	.10	.03	.02	.06	
Iceland																		
Below university	91	62	86	91	76	86	76	50	48	48	81	33	52	38	33	45	20	20
University	87	70	78	74	91	70	65	35	30	30	70	48	39	13	27	30	13	23
Eta	.06	.08	.10	.21	.21	.19	.12	.15	.18	.18	.13	.15	.13	.29	.07	.15	.26	
Norway																		
Below university	83	91	84	92	11	71	72	58	14	NI	40	35	29	29	29	43	24	116
University	89	92	76	89	12	76	77	42	12	NI	39	40	32	28	50	40	8	25
Eta	.06	.02	.07	.05	.00	.04	.05	.12	.03		.01	.04	.02	.01	.18	.02	.15	
Sweden																		
Below university	99	91	88	81	97	NI	60	38	64	47	39	35	NI	NI	25	27	11	104
University	95	92	92	80	95	NI	61	44	56	39	43	27	NI	NI	36	24	7	208
Eta	.10	.02	.06	.01	.04		.00	.06	.07	.07	.04	.08			.10	.04	.06	

Notes: The question was worded as follows: "Thinking about the [Danish, Finish, Icelandic, Norwegian, Swedish] society, what do you yourself perceive as most worrying for the future?" The following response alternatives were offered: "very worrying"; "fairly worrying"; "not very worrying"; "not at all worrying." NI = not included in survey.

Icelandic data seem to support the first thesis. Still, even if some of these relationships are pretty strong (the gamma coefficients are around .30), none of them are statistically significant at the 95 percent confidence interval level.[4] So while our general conclusion must be that educational level helps only marginally to explain differences in risk perception, we should for the present make a small reservation in the case of Iceland.[5]

THE IMPORTANCE OF NATIONAL
CONDITIONS AND PARTY AFFILIATION

Within each individual country, there seem to be certain situations that appear so unambiguous that they are judged alike by most parliamentarians. However, national differences in risk perceptions, like those seen in table 16.1, allow of several interpretations: Only 11 percent of Norwegian parliamentarians, for example, find the national debt to be worrying, which may be less than surprising, since Norway is experiencing the most rapid increase in its national income ever. No less than 90 percent of Finnish parliamentarians, by contrast, are concerned about the national debt; this must be seen against the background of the fact that Finland is still struggling with the repercussions of the serious economic crisis resulting from the fall of the Berlin Wall and the breakdown of commercial relations with the Soviet Union. *So, in some (few) cases,* it seems reasonable to see national differences in risk perception as *a reflection of "actual" or "objective" differences* in the risks being confronted.

In other cases, national differences in risk perception may be seen as reflecting a specific national interpretive filter. For example, Finnish parliamentarians are far less concerned about issues such as nuclear power, nuclear war, and war in Europe than are parliamentarians in the other Nordic countries. This is hardly due to "objective" conditions. *A certain national cultural factor must, therefore, be operational in the perception of risks—a national factor that "mediates" between actual conditions and risk perceptions.*

When analyzing the figures in table 16.4, we are astonished to see how are few the cases in which a specific situation is judged unanimously, across ideological barriers, by a country's MPs. All parliamentarians in Denmark, irrespective of party, agree that the situation in Russia and war in Europe constitute serious problems; in Finland, there is general agreement among the parties that unemployment and the national debt are weighty problems, whereas the prospect of war in Europe does not afford grounds for concern. In Iceland, MPs do not agree on *any* societal concerns across the political spectrum; in Norway, there is only general agreement on two

Table 16.4
Members' Perceptions of the Future of Own Society, by Party Family Controlling for Country (% "worried about the problem" and eta)

Country		1. Large Unemploy.	2. Situation in Russia	3. Environ. Problems	4. Less Social Consid.	5. National Debt	6. Confl. btw. Western and Muslim Count.	7. Dissolu. of Social Norms	8. Nucl. Power	9. Infla.	10. Incr. no. of Refug.	11. Corrupt.	12. Economic Competition from S.E. Asia	13. War in Europe	14. Economic Competition from Japan and the U.S.	15. Lack of Strong National Leadership	16. Nucl. War	17. Techno. Devel.	Min. N
Country	All	92	87	82	82	73	66	58	41	39	38	38	37	36	33	29	29	13	732
Denmark	Left socs.	100	100	100	100	40	53	7	87	0	13	20	33	67	20	0	67	50	15
	Soc. dems.	83	95	92	83	51	78	28	65	38	46	27	42	59	40	10	37	15	41
	Centrists	88	88	100	88	13	38	38	50	25	25	0	38	63	25	0	38	50	8
	Agrarians	85	90	70	63	95	95	70	11	65	85	20	60	65	32	68	21	5	19
	Conservs.	80	95	65	55	70	95	70	10	55	65	20	50	55	32	35	45	5	20
	Populs.	NA	NA	NA	NA	NA	NA	NA	NA	NA	NA	NA	NA	NA	NA	NA	NA	NA	
Eta		.25	.16	.44*	.37*	.48*	.44*	.48*	.61*	.47*	.49*	.21	.24	.10	.20	.58*	.27	.45*	
Finland	Greens	NA	NA	NA	NA	NA	NA	NA	NA	NA	NA	NA	NA	NA	NA	NA	NA	NA	
	Left socs.	100	67	89	100	100	44	44	56	11	33	44	67	22	56	22	0	22	9
	Soc. dems.	100	63	68	98	88	34	28	18	20	5	17	44	12	46	12	7	20	41
	Centrists	100	82	55	73	91	64	64	27	27	9	36	54	18	36	27	9	9	11
	Agrarians	96	50	58	92	86	35	58	19	8	27	19	56	15	35	39	4	12	26
	Conservs.	100	85	55	40	84	55	30	5	10	35	25	50	15	47	20	5	15	20
Eta		.17	.29	.23*	.58	.18	.23	.32*	.36*	.20	.34*	.20	.22	.11	.13	.25	.21	.14	
Iceland	Greens	NA	NA	NA	NA	NA	NA	NA	NA	NA	NA	NA	NA	NA	NA	NA	NA	NA	
	Left socs.	100	29	86	71	100	71	71	43	29	29	86	29	43	43	33	71	14	7
	Soc. dems.	80	70	90	70	80	70	60	30	50	30	60	30	20	20	60	40	10	10
	Centrists	90	80	80	90	90	90	80	40	20	40	70	30	50	20	20	20	10	10
	Agrarians	86	71	71	86	71	79	64	46	57	57	79	57	57	21	21	39	0	13
	Conservs.																		
Eta		.22	.35	.22	.25	.30	.19	.24	.18	.38	.32	.25	.29	.30	.19	.39	.39	.22	

Continued

Table 16.4
Continued

		1. Large Unemploy.	2. Situation in Russia	3. Environ. Problems	4. Less Social Consid.	5. National Debt	6. Confl. btw. Western and Muslim Count.	7. Dissolu. of Social Norms	8. Nucl. Power	9. Infla.	10. Incr. no. of Refug.	11. Corrupt.	12. Economic Competition from S.E. Asia	13. War in Europe	14. Economic Competition from Japan and the U.S.	15. Lack of Strong National Leadersip	16. Nucl. War	17. Techno. Devel.	Min. N
Norway	Left socs.	100	92	83	85	0	67	46	69	0	NI	39	25	58	8	39	62	42	13
	Soc. dems.	80	87	84	90	8	71	59	62	16	NI	39	32	30	31	25	44	15	51
	Centrists	91	91	100	100	18	46	100	73	27	NI	73	27	18	27	36	64	27	11
	Agrarians	89	89	96	96	0	70	85	78	7	NI	44	33	37	33	41	52	48	27
	Conservs.	82	100	73	86	32	82	86	18	14	NI	23	59	32	36	29	14	0	21
	Populs.	70	100	20	90	20	90	80	0	10	NI	40	40	0	10	50	30	0	10
Eta		.20	.18	.47	.15	.34	.22	.36*	.48*	.19		.24	.22	.27	.19	.18	.29	.42	
Sweden	Greens	94	83	100	**100**	78	NI	39	**100**	**22**	22	67	11	NI	NI	28	59	22	17
	Left socs.	100	75	95	**95**	91	NI	43	**86**	**24**	10	62	14	NI	NI	29	5	10	19
	Soc. dems.	99	92	95	**88**	97	NI	49	40	**55**	38	40	28	NI	NI	14	26	11	154
	Centrists	95	95	85	**88**	98	NI	81	34	**61**	29	49	42	NI	NI	59	22	2	41
	Agrarians	100	96	100	**77**	100	NI	62	**89**	**69**	56	32	40	NI	NI	46	44	12	25
	Conservs.	90	94	73	**51**	99	NI	87	3	**84**	65	35	35	NI	NI	54	13	3	70
Eta		.20	.18*	.31*	.40*	.25*		.36*	.58*	.35*	.31*	.19*	.18*			.41*	.28	.18*	

Notes: The question was worded as follows: "Thinking about the [Danish, Finnish, Icelandic, Norwegian, Swedish] society, what do you yourself perceive as most worrying for the future?" The following response alternatives were offered: "very worrying"; "fairly worrying"; "not very worrying"; "not at all worrying." Figures set off by bold print indicate items where risk perceptions tend to follow a left-right pattern. NA = not applicable. NI = not included in survey.

*p < .05

points: namely, that the situation in Russia and the decline in social consideration are worrying. In Sweden, finally, it is more or less agreed across party lines that unemployment, conditions in Russia, and the national debt are highly worrisome issues. Apart from these examples, the vast majority of risks are judged completely differently by different parliamentary groups.

The perception of a number of risks is clearly influenced by party affiliation. But there are also considerable national variations on this point (see the eta coefficients).

In political life, a few types of risk are obviously perceived in accordance with the traditional left-right dimension. In Denmark, this applies to environmental damage, social consideration, dissolution of norms, and nuclear power; in Iceland, to the question of refugees (the effect here is not statistically significant, however); and in Sweden to declining social consideration and the danger of inflation (see the bold print in table 16.4). In some other cases, risk perception is influenced by party affiliation, but the conflicts follow other lines than the left-right scale (see the italics in table 16.4). *So, while it is obvious that party affiliation does make a difference, the small extent to which the various risk perceptions can be arranged according to a left-right dimension is astonishing.*

It is also striking to see how greatly patterns differ from country to country. We find only one example where sister parties across frontiers have the same perception of risk: all members of left-wing parties in all five Nordic countries agree that unemployment is a problem that affords grounds for concern. *Sisterhood among the Nordic sister parties seems somewhat lacking when it comes to risk perception.*

In conclusion, the analysis so far reveals that risk perceptions are mediated—they are not mere reflections of objective factors; that the individual parliamentarian's perception is not a function of personal characteristics; that risk perceptions are clearly influenced by both a national and a party factor; and that these two variables are conditional as well as related in subtle ways.

CULTURAL BIAS AS AN UNDERLYING STRUCTURE IN RISK PERCEPTION

In order to simplify the further analysis of the many risk factors under review, as well as to find a possible underlying structure in risk perception (like the one described in Cultural Theory), we have done a factor analysis of answers to the questions bearing on risk.

The results of this analysis are reported in table 16.5, which reveals that the perceptions of ten different risks fall into three different frameworks of

Table 16.5
Structure of Members' Perceptions of the Future of Own Society:
Principal Component Factor Analysis of Risk Perceptions

Type of Problem	Factor 1 Ecology	Factor 2 Economy	Factor 3 Social Order
Environmental deterioration	**.76**	.11	−.13
Nuclear power	**.75**	−.09	−.06
Less social care and consideration	**.61**	.02	.25
Technological development	**.53**	−.27	.10
National debt	−.15	**.83**	.05
Inflation	−.12	**.67**	.21
Unemployment	.39	**.59**	.12
Deterioration of norms and values	.07	.00	**.81**
Lack of strong national leadership	−.09	.06	**.75**
Corruption	.38	.21	**.45**
% Variance	21.8	18.1	13.8

Notes: Number of respondents is 740 (missing values have been replaced by average values). Factor loadings above .40 in bold print. The procedure has been as follows: Thirteen items that were included in all surveys were selected for further analysis. Ten of these items tended to group under three factors, according to a fixed pattern. The item "the situation in Russia," however, turned out to load on several factors, whereas the items "nuclear weapons" and "competition from Southeast Asia" tended to get isolated, each under its own factor. We have, therefore, chosen not to include the latter three variables in the final stage of the analysis. Thus, the final factor analysis is based on ten variables. A factor analysis has been carried out for each national parliament and each relevant party family, and in practically all cases the variables group according to the same patterns. The only exception is the attitudinal structure among Icelandic members, which seems to differ slightly from that found in other parliaments. Iceland is, nevertheless, included in the analyses on a par with other countries.

understanding. The first of them—which I term *ecology*—stands for concern about the environment, technology, and nuclear power, as well as the exclusion of individuals from society. The second—which I call *economy*—stands for concern about classical economic parameters, such as national debt, inflation, and unemployment. Finally, we have a third framework, covering various expressions of concern about *social order*. The social-order factor includes what might be called a more or less communitarian concern for fragile civil society ("Dissolution of norms and values"), a slightly more authoritarian concern about lack of leadership and governance ("Lack of strong national leadership"), a dash of anti-establishment attitudes and mistrust ("Corruption"), and some xenophobic traits besides. If the item "Increasing number of refugees" is included in the factor analysis, it loads on the social-order factor.

Table 16.6

Members' Worries about the Future of Own Society, by Country and Party Family (% who score high on respective index)

	Economy	Ecology	Social Order	Minimum N
All	77	70	41	678
Country				
Denmark	68	66	19	103
Finland	94	61	25	71
Iceland	89	70	65	43
Norway	27	80	48	142
Sweden	96	70	45	318
Party family				
Greens	94	89	48	22
Left socialists	77	90	42	62
Social democrats	72	78	30	282
Centrist parties	71	77	52	65
Agrarians	80	75	52	95
Conservatives	74	41	40	132
Populists	60	10	30	14

Notes: Indices are defined as in table 16.5 above. Scores on individual items have been summed and converted into a scale running from 0 to 10, where 0 corresponds to "not at all worrying" and 10 corresponds to "extremely worrying." Scores of 5 and higher are classified as "high" and are thus reported in the table.

These three frameworks of understanding—which together account for much of the variance (54 percent)—are in perfect keeping with the Cultural Theory notion that it is possible to identify three fundamental discourses of risk perception.

The factor analysis forms the basis for the three indices on which we base the remaining part of our analysis.

ECONOMY, ECOLOGY, AND SOCIAL ORDER

It is the economic discourse that dominates the overall discussion of future problems and challenges among *Nordic MPs* (see table 16.6). But the table shows as well that environmental problems play an astonishingly important part. The political discourse about possible threats to social order is the least prominent, although it is far from totally absent.

There are conspicuous differences between the countries under examination. In *Norway* right now, the issues of ecology and social order are given higher priority than the economy. In *Iceland*, there is also a great deal of concern about social order, although the economy is still considered the most worrying issue of all. In *Finland,* the economic discourse is absolutely dominant. In *Sweden,* too, the economy is a top priority, but ecology is also a question of considerable importance. Compared with the others, *Denmark* is the country least preoccupied with the issue of social order, while ecological issues are given almost as much weight as economic ones.

If we look at how much importance the different parties attach to the economic discourse, there is general agreement across party lines. The members of the Nordic political elite seem to agree that it is one of their main responsibilities to give attention to the national economy. The ecological discourse, on the other hand, seems in some measure to follow the political left-right dimension: the further one is to the left, the greater is one's concern about the environment. With regard to the question of social order, finally, the center and agrarian parties express the most concern.

THE SIGNIFICANCE OF DIFFERENT DISCOURSES IN DIFFERENT COUNTRIES AND PARTIES

Politics is very much a question of setting priorities. So the question is: which of the three categories of risk do MPs consider the most serious? Which political discourse is given the highest priority? In order to measure this, we have sorted parliamentarians according to their scores on the three indices, each of which had been converted into a scale of 1 to 10 (table 16.7).

In general, a little more than half the parliamentarians scored higher on the economy index than on the other two. We interpret this as meaning that these MPs have the economy as their main concern. Nearly one-third of MPs think problems relating to ecology are the most urgent issue. Some 10 percent are most afraid of what they see as tendencies toward a dissolution of social order. Finland, Iceland, and Sweden follow this general pattern, in contrast to Denmark and especially Norway, where the ecological discourse is paramount.

It is still in Norway and especially Iceland that the question of social order comes high on the list of priorities. Looking at the distribution of parties over the whole Nordic region we now see—after the analysis has "forced" MPs to specify their priorities—a clear left-right dimension in the way respondents judge the importance of economic issues: the more right-wing a party is, the higher the proportion of its parliamentary party

Table 16.7
Members' Relative Worries about the Future of Own Society,
by Country and Party Family (% who score highest on respective index)

	Economy More Worrying than Ecology and Social Order	Ecology More Worrying than the Economy and Social Order	Social Order More Worrying than the Economy and Ecology	Total	N
All	59	31	11	100	591
Country					
Denmark	42	47	11	100	89
Finland	76	18	6	100	50
Iceland	69	15	15	100	39
Norway	12	64	24	100	131
Sweden	81	14	5	100	282
Party family					
Greens	24	71	6	101	21
Left socialists	32	65	3	100	56
Social democrats	52	37	11	100	251
Centrist parties	48	33	18	100	54
Agrarians	59	25	16	99	81
Conservatives	74	11	15	100	110
Populists	60	5	35	100	14

Notes: Indices are defined as in table 16.6. Scores on respective index have been transformed into a single variable, which is used as the dependent variable in this table.

that considers the economy a top priority. The ecological discourse still tends to follow the left-right dimension, though in reverse. Only a minor share of respondents—belonging mainly to the center and right-wing parties—see the challenges to social order as the most serious problem.

If we break down the data by country, we get a picture—albeit one based on very small numbers—of a varying composition in the political discourse of the different parties and countries. It turns out that the general image of the Nordic parties as "sister parties" does not apply to all of the countries (see table 16.8).

In *Denmark*, the ecological discourse is in a strong position, sustained by the left-wing parties, the center parties, and the social democrats. The economic discourse is kept alive chiefly by the agrarians and the conservatives, although a fourth of these parties' members mention social order as their main concern.

The discourses on social order and ecology are almost absent from the political debate in *Finland*. Only a negligible minority among Finnish conservatives regard threats to social order as the most important issue,

Table 16.8
Members' Relative Worries about the Future of Own Society, by Party Family Controlling for Country (% who score highest on respective index)

	Economy More Worrying than Ecology and Social Order	Ecology More Worrying than the Economy and Social Order	Social Order More Worrying than the Economy and Ecology	Total	N
All	59	31	11	101	591
Denmark					
Left socialists	0	100	0	100	13
Social democrats	28	69	3	100	32
Centrist parties	14	86	0	100	7
Agrarians	64	0	36	100	14
Conservatives	74	5	21	100	19
Finland					
Left socialists	29	71	0	100	7
Social democrats	88	12	0	100	17
Centrist parties	100	0	0	100	5
Agrarians	89	11	0	100	9
Conservatives	71	14	14	100	7
Iceland					
Left socialists	67	33	0	100	6
Social democrats	44	22	33	100	9
Agrarians	60	10	30	100	10
Conservatives	91	9	0	100	11
Norway					
Left socialists	0	92	8	100	12
Social democrats	11	72	17	100	54
Centrist parties	0	40	60	100	10
Agrarians	0	92	8	100	26
Conservatives	42	26	32	100	19
Populists	20	10	70	100	10
Sweden					
Greens	24	71	6	100	17
Left socialists	67	28	6	101	18
Social democrats	86	12	2	100	139
Centrist parties	78	9	13	100	32
Agrarians	82	14	5	100	22
Conservatives	91	0	9	100	54

Notes: Indices are defined as in table 16.6. Scores on respective index have been transformed into a single variable, which is used as the dependent variable in this table.

and only the small left party promotes the ecological discourse.

In *Iceland*, it is the social democrats and the agrarians who jointly support the discourse of social order. The economic discourse receives universal attention, whereas in particular the left-wing parties and the social democrats express some concern about the environment.

Not in a single *Norwegian* party is the economic discourse dominant. It is mainly to be found among conservatives. All Norwegian parties seem to focus relatively heavily on ecology, but the ecological discourse is backed most strongly by the left, the social democrats, and the agrarians. On this point, the Norwegian agrarian party deviates substantially from its Nordic sister parties. The discourse on social order is totally dominant among Norwegian centrist parties, on which point they diverge from their sister parties.

In *Sweden,* the economic discourse is absolutely dominant in all parties except the greens, who are alone in focusing on ecology. Hardly any Swedish MPs see the dissolution of social order as the most serious threat.

CONCLUSION

Rather than a glimpse into the future, the study of risk perception gives us an idea of contemporary political culture. Our analysis of Nordic MPs' perception of different societal risks reveals—in perfect accordance with Cultural Theory—that MPs' greatest concerns are centered on three categories of problem: (1) economic instability, (2) ecological and environmental problems, and (3) the dissolution of norms and of social order.

One of the main empirical findings is that, in the Nordic countries, ecological and environmental questions are "high politics." Nordic MPs taken together are nearly as worried about environmental problems as about economic ones, and about one-third of MPs rank environmental problems above economic ones. That environmental problems loom so large in Nordic political consciousness calls for an explanation.

Cultural Theory offers such an explanation. According to Cultural Theory, we should not expect the great interest in environmental matters among Nordic parliamentarians to be explicable in terms of "actual" facts/circumstances (e.g., a higher level of pollution in the Nordic countries than elsewhere). The explanation is rather to be found in the fact that the Nordic countries—as compared with most other societies—are much more equality oriented. In societies where egalitarian values are dominant, ecological arguments tend to be accepted far more readily.[6]

However, the figures might also allow of a supplementary explanation, seeing that the two countries most preoccupied with ecology are those with the healthiest economies, in terms of traditional economic parameters. This seems to indicate that consideration for the environment is also to some extent a question of financial capacity. So the distinct *combination* of egalitarian values and financial capacity seems a plausible explanation for the high priority given to ecological issues.

A second finding is that, although we have so far stressed the similarities in risk perception, our analysis also reveals amazingly different patterns of political discourse within the different Nordic countries. While economic issues are a top priority in the political debate in Sweden, Finland, and Iceland, the Danish debate is divided between economic and ecological discourses, while the Norwegian debate is dominated by discussions of ecology and of social order.

Thirdly, the different national patterns of political discourse heavily influence the parties. Parties that are commonly regarded as "sister parties" grouped into "party families" (and treated as such in much of our analysis) can only be classified that way with caution and with certain reservations.

At the theoretical level, Cultural Theory has proved very useful for discerning some patterns in the perception of societal risks and thus for detecting important patterns in political discourse among Nordic MPs. Throughout the analysis, therefore, Cultural Theory has first and foremost been used to specify the dependent variable. And both data and analysis confer some credibility on the theory.

On the other hand, it has not been our intention here to carry out a strong test of Cultural Theory's extensive and rather ambitious specifications of social relations, myths of nature, and risk perceptions as related phenomena. Our study has supported the idea of risk as a social construction. Risk perceptions are not a mere reflection of objective factors, nor are they a function of personal characteristics. Risk perceptions are mediated in subtle ways, primarily by ideology and national perspective. To what extent "ways of life" can be treated as an explanatory variable on a par with ideology and nationality is for future analyses to show.

NOTES

1. A special feature of concern and fear for the future is that you cannot take it away by means of knowledge alone. The phenomenon of the "future" has the inherent quality that knowledge and action are not simultaneous. We shall never be able to rely completely on our future scenarios, and we can never become 100 percent certain about the future implications of our present actions.

2. Besides the three ways of life mentioned here, Cultural Theory also defines a fourth—fatalism—that I do not expect to find among parliamentarians. For a more thorough discussion of the four ways of life described by Cultural Theory, see, e.g., Thompson et al. (1990); Grendstad and Selle (1996); Ellis and Thompson (1997). For a more specific description of the placement of persons with a communitarian attitude as a part of the hierarchic tradition, see Hendriks (1997).

3. An illustration of this may be seen in the different reactions to news of a hole in the ozone layer. Some people get extremely scared, regarding the hole as the final proof that our present lifestyle is totally irresponsible, that nature is fragile, and that is high time we change our behavior radically (the egalitarians). Others say we must demand more research and worldwide regulations in order to prevent problems from getting out of control ("the long, steady pull" favored by the hierarchically minded). Yet others think the hole must have been there all the time and simply has not been discovered until now; that nature will most likely close the hole again by itself; that the hole has probably been caused by other factors than human activities; and that the general situation is not at all alarming (the individualists). Most people have not seen that hole in the ozone layer. Only a negligible minority are qualified to interpret the data allegedly proving there is a hole and therefore a problem. But many have an opinion on the question.

According to Cultural Theory, our ways of life, including our risk perceptions, are taken for granted. Thus all of the reactions mentioned above are rational, each from its own perspective. Cultural Theory also explains, says Wildavsky, "how . . . the social filters enable people who possess only inches of facts to generate miles of preferences" (Wildavsky 1987:8).

4. This is an example of a problem that occurs very often when survey techniques are applied on elite groups: on account of the paucity of respondents, even strong statistical interdependence between variables may not be statistically significant. Even if we choose to treat the data as population data, which we strictly speaking cannot do because of dropout, we should be cautious. In the Icelandic case, for example, the statistical portrait could change considerably if a single person changed his/her mind or was replaced. We could, of course, refrain from doing this kind of study: alternatively, we could refrain from reporting data when the statistical rules are bent or even broken. But these options are not attractive, because the few people in question are also very important people. Here the strategy is to be very explicit about the statistical base, and then to hope for careful and prudent readers.

5. For a more developed reasoning, see Jensen (1998).

6. Numerous studies have concluded that, *compared* to most other countries, the social structures and value systems in the Nordic countries are very egalitarian. See, for example, Gunnar Grendstad's analysis of political culture in ten west European countries based on Eurobarometer data and Cultural Theory; Grendstad shows that Norway and Denmark are the two most egalitarian countries (Grendstad 1990). For an elite study, see for example, the comparative analysis of elite attitudes toward equality by Verba et al. (1987).

CONCLUSIONS

17

Learning from the Nordic Experience

Peter Esaiasson and Knut Heidar

How do democratic parliaments operate, and why do they operate as they do? Formidable though they be, these are the questions that have motivated a joint effort to carry out a highly standardized empirical study in the five similar and yet different Nordic parliamentary democracies. In this concluding chapter, we shall discuss what general conclusions might follow from the findings presented in the individual contributions to this volume.

This discussion will focus on two themes. The first bears on matters of description: What are the universal, what are the Nordic, and what are the unique characteristics of the Nordic parliaments? Can we reasonably claim that the Nordic parliamentary systems offer an *alternative model* to parliaments in the style of Westminster and the U.S. Congress? The second theme concerns the impact of *institutional arrangements* on parliamentary operations. What precise effects, if any, can we detect by comparing the parliaments of Denmark, Finland, Iceland, Norway, and Sweden with each other, as well as with other democratically elected parliaments?

Before turning to substantive topics, however, we would like to dwell briefly on two questions of research strategy on which we commented in the introductory chapter. The first relates to the obvious fact that parliaments operate in a complex manner. To do justice to that complexity, we have conceptualized the overall dependent variable in this study broadly and have divided it into various aspects. Our strategy has been to specify the operations of parliaments in four different dimensions: *the vertical* (how parliaments operate in relation to the electorate); *the internal* (how the decision-making process within parliament itself operates); *the horizontal* (how parliaments operate in relation to competing elite actors and institutions); and *the external* (how parliaments operate in relation to the

409

world outside the national polity, as well as how members of parliament perceive the political challenges of the future).

The specific point we wish to emphasize is that parliamentary research should not just be carried out within the boundaries of increasingly specialized subdisciplines. It should try as well to cover the totality of the process. What is important to us is not exactly how these relationships are conceptualized. We are not saying that our conceptualization of the operations of parliaments provides the ultimate analytical framework. But we do firmly believe that an increased understanding of representative democracies will be the result if scholars show a greater willingness to consider a broad array of parliamentary relationships simultaneously.

Yet developing a broad conceptualization of parliamentary relationships is just the first part of the job. It is equally important to operationalize the key concepts in a standardized fashion. The experience of this joint venture across countries speaks unequivocally in favor of standardization. As empirical evidence has materialized, most of us involved in the project have been forced to reconsider our favored ideas about representative democracies in general and about our "own" democracy in particular. This is so because a confrontation with good data tends to have a sobering effect even on strongly held convictions. We are certain that our experience in this matter is not unique. Standardized comparative studies are likely to detect both differences between parliaments that superficially appear to be rather similar and similarities between parliaments that appear to be quite different.

In this concluding discussion, we rely upon twenty-three empirical indicators of the multifaceted operations of parliaments. Table 17.1 offers a summary of these indicators. All have been operationalized in a standardized way across countries. Each one seeks to capture an aspect, moreover, of the four different parliamentary relationships proposed in the first chapter. With nine indicators, it is the vertical dimension (that vis-à-vis the electorate) which is the most thoroughly covered of the four. By contrast, the external dimension (that vis-à-vis the outside world and the future) is admittedly dealt with less extensively: only three indicators cover this dimension.

We readily concede that these twenty-three indicators do not come to grips fully with the operation of parliaments in representative democracies. Still, we would argue that all of them describe important aspects of parliamentary relations. Taken together, they can guide us toward a broader understanding of how parliaments operate.

Consider the following informal validity check of these propositions. Would knowing the parliamentary "score" on each of the twenty-three

Table 17.1
How the Operations of Parliament Have Been Conceptualized: Overview

Vertical Relations (with the electorate)	Internal Relations (within parliament)	Horizontal Relations (with other national institutions and actors)	External Relations (with the outside world and towards the future)
1. Social characteristics of representatives and represented (Chap. 4)	10. Degree of party cohesion (Chap. 9)	15. Perceptions of power (Chap. 12)	21. International contacts of individual representatives (chap 13)
2. Relevance of representatives' social characteristics (Chaps. 3, 4, 6)	11. Influence of parliamentary party groups (Chap. 8)	16. Views on proper role of parliament (Chaps. 11, 12)	22. Institutional adaptation to globalized politics (Chap. 14)
3. Attitude towards representation of social characteristics (Chaps. 3, 6)	12. Hierarchy of parliamentary party groups (Chaps. 8, 11)	17. Executive-legislative relations: interparty competition (Chap. 11)	23. Perceptions of future risks for representative democracies (Chaps. 15, 16)
4. Representatives' support of particular social groups (Chaps. 3, 6)	13. Strength of standing committees (Chaps. 8, 10, 11)	18. Executive-legislative relations: intraparty influence (Chaps. 8, 9, 11)	
5. Issue congruence (Chap. 7)	14. Process of committee assignment (Chap. 10)	19. Executive-legislative relations: cooperation across parties (Chaps. 9, 10, 11)	
6. Opinion balances among representatives and represented (Chaps. 7, 14, 15, 16)		20. Executive-legislative relations: conflicts between parliament and government (Chaps. 11, 12)	
7. Political tolerance of representatives and represented (Chaps. 7, 15)			
8. Representatives' definition of task (Chap. 3)			
9. Linkages between center and periphery (Chap. 5)			
No. of indicators 9	5	6	3

empirical indicators increase our understanding of the parliament in question substantially? Let us assume, for example, that we knew the following things: the social characteristics of representatives and represented (no. 1); the relevance of these social characteristics for the conduct of representatives (no. 2); the general attitudes of MPs toward the representation of social characteristics (no. 3); and the importance ascribed by MPs to the representation of particular social groups (no. 4). Would not our understanding of how this parliament operates vis-à-vis its electorate be enhanced if we knew these things?

Or assume that we knew the following: the degree of cohesion exhibited by parliamentary party groups (no. 10); the extent of influence wielded by parliamentary party groups in parliamentary decision-making (no. 11); the degree to which the internal power structure of parliamentary party groups is hierarchical in character (no. 12); the measure of influence enjoyed by standing committees in internal parliamentary decision-making (no. 13); and the manner in which the process of committee assignment is structured in parliament (no. 14). Would not our assessment of how this parliament works be more firmly grounded if we knew these things?

We could go on listing the specific indicators, but our general message is that someone with this knowledge has gained important insights into how *any* parliament operates. Moreover, by systematically comparing several parliaments on all of these points, we will be in a relatively good position to reach an informed conclusion about how and why parliaments differ.

A NORDIC ALTERNATIVE MODEL?

Do the Nordic parliaments offer not only an alternative experience but also an *alternative model* to parliaments in the style of Westminster and the U.S. Congress, the two most thoroughly scrutinized representative assemblies in parliamentary research? Admittedly, the concept of an "alternative model" is painfully vague unless specified further. Here, however, we take it to mean that the Nordic parliaments form a homogeneous and distinct unity within the universe of democratically elected legislative assemblies. If we are to venture an empirical assessment of our cases, then, we need to find out (a) whether the Nordic parliaments do indeed operate in a similar manner, and (b) whether this "Nordic" manner of functioning differs from the way in which other democratically elected legislative assemblies operate. Only if both of these questions are answered in the affirmative can we consider it meaningful to talk about a Nordic alternative model.

When comparing our findings on the five Nordic parliaments to those on other parliaments, we have mainly been looking for three empirical configurations: *the universal, the Nordic,* and *the intra-Nordic.* With respect to each indicator, we have asked the following: Is the characteristic in question operative in all parliaments; that is, outside the Nordic region as well? (The universal model.) Alternatively, is said characteristic common to the Nordic parliaments and *exclusive to them also* (such that it divides Nordic parliaments from legislatures in the style of Westminster and the U.S. Congress)? (The Nordic model.) Or is it instead the case, finally, that the operations of the five Nordic parliaments diverge with respect to said characteristic? (The intra-Nordic model.)

These three possibilities do not capture all relevant alternatives. One possibility not featured among them, for instance, is that all of the Nordic parliaments operate in much the same way as Westminster-style parliaments do; that is, that the Nordic parliaments belong to the group of Westminster parliaments. Such regularities would support the position that there are generally two types of parliaments: those functioning in presidential systems and those functioning in parliamentary systems. Another possibility would be that the Nordic parliaments form part of a "Continental" parliamentary model; we might be especially inclined to conclude this is the case if we stress the importance of the proportional (PR) voting systems widely used on the European continent, as opposed to the majoritarian electoral arrangements typical of Westminster parliaments (Verney 1959; Shaw 1979; cf. Lijphart 1990).

Our decision to highlight only three basic configurations is partly due to our ambition to present a parsimonious argument, and partly due to the patchy nature of relevant research on other parliamentary systems. As will become evident, these three configurations do provide a sufficient basis on which to form a judgment on whether or not an additional model—a "Nordic model"—exists. In our concluding discussion, moreover, we shall consider a broader spectrum of alternatives.

Table 17.2 summarizes, in a condensed form, the bulk of the empirical findings presented in the individual contributions to this volume. Our twenty-three different indicators have each been placed under one of three headings: *Universal Characteristics, Common Nordic Characteristics,* and *Intra-Nordic Differences.* (Depending, that is, on which empirical configuration the indicator in question supports.) In what follows, we discuss the merits of the "universal," the "Nordic," and the "different" configurations for each of the four parliamentary relationships, our aim being to come up with an answer to the simple question: do the data support the existence of a "Nordic model"?

Table 17.2

Summary Characteristics of the Operations of Parliaments: Empirical Configurations

	Universal Characteristics	*"Nordic" Characteristics*	*Intra-Nordic Differences*
Vertical Relations (with the electorate)	1. Socially exclusive representatives (chap. 4) 2. Relevance of representatives' social characteristics (chaps. 3, 4, 6) 5. Moderately high issue congruence (chap. 7) 7. Tolerance among MPs (chap. 7) 8. MPs' definition of task (chap. 3)	3. Attitude toward representation of social characteristics (chaps. 3, 6)	4. Representatives' support of particular social groups (chaps. 3, 6) 6. Opinion balances among representatives and represented (chaps. 7, 14, 15, 16) 9. Linkages between center and periphery (chap. 5)
Internal Relations (within parliament)		10. Degree of party cohesion[a] (chap. 9) 11. Influence of parliamentary party groups (chap. 8)	12. Hierarchy of parliamentary party groups (chaps. 8, 11) 13. Strength of standing committees (chaps. 8, 10, 11) 14. Process of committee assignment (chap. 10)
Horizontal Relations (with other national institutions and actors)	16. Views on proper role of parliament (chaps. 11, 12)	15. Perceptions of power[a] (chap. 12) 18. Executive-legislative relations: intra-party influence[a] (chaps. 8, 9, 11) 19. Executive-legislative relations: cooperation across parties (chaps. 9, 10, 11)	17. Executive-legislative relations: interparty competition (chap. 11) 20. Executive-legislative relations: conflicts between parliament and government (chaps. 8, 9, 11, 12)
External Relations (with the outside world and towards the future)	21. International contacts of individual MPs (chap. 13)	23. Perceptions of future risk for democracies (chaps. 15, 16)	22. Institutional adaptation to globalized politics (chap. 14)

[a]Feature is likely shared by one of the two competing models considered (Westminster or the United States Congress).

VERTICAL RELATIONS OF PARLIAMENTS

Turning first to the relationship of MPs to the electorate, we find a pattern that is clear but also partly surprising. Most of the nine empirical indicators covering this vertical relationship fall either within the universal characteristics (five indicators) or within the characteristics that differ substantially between the five parliaments (three indicators). Only one indicator is classified under the heading of "Nordic Characteristics." It is thus hardly relevant to speak of a unique Nordic alternative within this arena of parliamentary operations.

The list of *universal* characteristics starts with the widely accepted fact that elected representatives generally tend to be drawn from socially exclusive strata (no. 1).[1] Narud and Valen's analysis in chapter 4 demonstrates that this is true also in polities, such as the Nordic ones, that strongly emphasize egalitarian values. Thus, the proposition that the process of representation is inherently elitist has survived what might be characterized as a critical test.

Furthermore, the Nordic experience also confirms that social background matters for the conduct of representatives (no. 2). In particular, Wängnerud's study (chapter 6) shows that female politicians have played a key role in creating a more gender-neutral political milieu (see also Esaiasson, chapter 3; and Narud and Valen, chapter 4).

It is surprising, however, that the degree of issue congruence between representatives and represented also falls under the heading of "Universal Configurations" (no. 5). As Holmberg shows (chapter 7), no Nordic political system deviates substantially from the all-Nordic norm as regards issue congruence between electors and elected (see also Narud and Valen, chapter 15). Available empirical evidence suggests, moreover, that other institutional setups (the U.S. Congress included) produce a remarkably similar degree of issue congruence as well (see the analyses in Holmberg 1996b; 1999).

A further instance of a universal configuration may be seen in the notion of relatively tolerant political elites (no. 7). Previous research has concluded that elected representatives generally tend to hold more tolerant (or liberal) political views than do citizens (e.g. Sniderman et al. 1991; Sullivan et al. 1993). In accordance with this research, Holmberg's analysis (chapter 7) shows that Nordic MPs hold more tolerant views on questions pertaining to basic democratic rules of the game than do voters. The best example of this is the issue of immigration: differences between representatives and represented on this issue are greater than on any other issue, with representatives holding the more tolerant views.

Similarities across political systems also generally extend to the way in which individual representatives define their task as representatives (no. 8). In chapter 3, Esaiasson argues that representatives in different parliamentary contexts are guided in their actions by their personal views about which interests are the most important ones to champion.

Divergence is found among Nordic parliaments when the topic is the "opinion balance" among representatives and among represented (no. 6), the support of representatives for particular interest groups (no. 4), and political linkages between center and periphery (no. 9).

The five Nordic countries may be relatively homogeneous, yet Holmberg (chapter 7), Raunio and Wiberg (chapter 14), Narud and Valen (chapter 15), and Jensen (chapter 16) all demonstrate the existence of considerable differences among these polities in the balance and pattern of opinions (no. 6). Only rarely is it the case that representatives and represented in all five of the countries hold similar views on a political topic. A second example of divergence may be seen in the degree of support for various interest groups (no. 4). This is captured in Wängnerud's analysis in chapter 6, in which she argues that the high priority given to the interests of women in Iceland, Sweden, and Norway is the result of critical actions undertaken by political elites (see also Esaiasson in chapter 3). Finally, Valen, Narud, and Hardarson (chapter 5) show that a bias in favor of the periphery, like that found in the Icelandic and Norwegian constitutions, gives the periphery a stronger voice in parliament than does the strict proportionality characteristic of the electoral arrangements used in Denmark and Sweden (no. 9).

We have found only one example of a possibly unique *Nordic* configuration in the field: Nordic representatives strongly support the notion of descriptive representation; that is, the view that elected representatives should be drawn from a wide range of social strata (no. 3, see Wängnerud's chapter 6 especially). On the factual level, social characteristics matter for the conduct of representatives in most parliaments; in the egalitarian political culture of the Nordic countries, however, the idea of descriptive representation is accepted on the *normative* level as well (except, maybe, among conservative members). But not even on this point should we jump to conclusions regarding a unique Nordicness. Our conclusion has the character of an informed guess. In order to gain stronger validation, the proposition needs to be investigated in a wider set of polities.

INTERNAL RELATIONS OF PARLIAMENTS

Our examination of the internal affairs of parliaments has been restricted to the parliamentary party groups and the standing committees.[2] Five indicators were developed to discuss important aspects of these internal structures. Three were chosen to indicate the position of party groups: the degree of party cohesion (no. 10), the influence of parliamentary party groups (no. 11), and the internal hierarchy of parliamentary party groups (no. 12). Two were selected to indicate the position of committees: the strength of standing committees (no. 13) and the process of committee assignment (no. 14).

The internal profile of Nordic parliaments emerges in chapters 8 through 10 (by Heidar, Jensen, and Hagevi, respectively). The overall internal picture is radically different from that visible in connection with these parliaments' electoral relations. In the internal arena, "Nordic configurations" are revealed by two of five indicators, while the column for universal configurations (i.e., characteristics found in most legislative assemblies) is left empty. Moreover, the three indicators that have been classified as mainly displaying differences between the Nordic parliaments are all borderline cases; they might as well have been classified, very nearly, as showing mainly similarities between the Nordic parliaments.

The indicators placed under the heading of *Nordic Configurations* show a high degree of party cohesion (no. 10) and a large measure of influence for parliamentary party groups (no. 11). The influence of party groups is strong in all five of the countries (second only to that of government ministers; see Chapter 8), and there is a high level of party cohesion across the board (albeit somewhat lower in Finland; see chapter 9).

The three indicators found to document *Nordic differences* show that power hierarchies of parliamentary parties tend to be fairly weak, and that party groups function to a great extent as collective decision-making bodies (no. 12). Furthermore, a functional, permanent, and hence rather strong committee system is found in most Nordic parliaments (no. 13), and MPs are assigned to committees on the basis of leadership control, personal preferences, and seniority in all five countries (no. 14). The intra-Nordic differences revealed by these three indicators are as follows: party leaders in Finland and Iceland are stronger than their counterparts in the three Scandinavian countries; the Danish committee system is weaker than that in Sweden; and the seniority of representatives weighs more heavily in the process of committee assignment in the Swedish Riksdag than in the Norwegian Storting.

Turning to a larger set of legislative assemblies, we find that party cohesion in roll-call votes (no. 10) is clearly strong in most parliamentary systems, both Westminster-style and others (see the discussion in Jensen's chapter 9). This indicator does not, therefore, show a unique Nordic characteristic. But the particular mix of influential party groups, not-so-strong group hierarchies, and fairly strong standing committees is shared by neither Westminster nor the U.S. Congress. The question is whether this is a unique "Nordic feature," or whether it is also exhibited by other parliaments of a similar type outside this particular geographical region. Although our data on this matter is insufficient as yet for drawing conclusions, we believe that these characteristics of the internal operations of parliaments are typical for what is known as the Continental parliamentary model (cf. Verney 1959; Shaw 1979). Standardized comparative studies of (for example) the German, Dutch, and Austrian parliaments would probably show a difference in degree, not in kind.

HORIZONTAL RELATIONS OF PARLIAMENTS

The focus in our description of the horizontal dimension is on parliament-executive relations, on MPs' perceptions of the distribution of power in society, and on the views held by representatives on the proper role of parliaments in representative democracies. In the matter of legislative-executive relations, we find guidance in the modes proposed by Anthony King and developed by Erik Damgaard in chapter 11 (nos. 17–20). Ólafur Th. Hardarson (chapter 12), for his part, analyzes both the normative and factual aspects of MPs' views on power distribution (no. 15) and the role of parliaments in the political system (no. 16).

Where horizontal relations are concerned, there are substantial differences among parliaments; we argue that only one of six indicators reveals a universal configuration. But forming a judgment on the relative strength of the two remaining alternatives—Nordic or divergent—is more problematic. Three of the six empirical indicators have been classified under the heading of "Nordic Configurations," and two have been classified as displaying "Intra-Nordic Differences." Several of these indicators, however, are borderline cases that could easily have switched positions.

The *universal* trait found in horizontal relations has to do—not surprisingly—with the views held by MPs themselves regarding their proper position in democratic politics (no. 16). In chapter 12, Hardarson presents MPs' perceptions of the basic features of power in society and shows that parliamentarians believe governments to be more powerful than parliaments in the actual policy-making process. At the same time, elected representatives believe this ought to be the other way round. Parliamentarians want more power for parliament. Nor is it a diffuse kind of influence that representatives are demanding for their institution (and for themselves). They want a stronger say in deciding important policy matters because, they believe, this is the proper role of parliament in a democracy (see Damgaard's chapter 11; cf. Esaiasson and Holmberg 1996: 239–40). The general implications of this can be expressed in the following way: it is a universal characteristic of the chosen few entrusted with the right to make binding decisions on behalf of the many to show a certain degree of *institutional patriotism* (cf. Matthews 1960).

The first indicator showing *similarities* across the Nordic parliaments deals with MPs' views on the actual distribution of power in society (no. 15). As a description of factual power, a pluralist model for the distribution of societal power fits the data rather well; by contrast, the power structure MPs regard as ideal looks more like a "textbook democracy," with parliament at the summit of the power pyramid.

A further instance of similarity is found in the relationship between governmental ministers and parliamentary backbenchers of the parties in government (intraparty influence, no. 18). The government can rely on support from its own backbenchers in policy matters, but this support is nurtured through frequent personal contacts between ministers and members of the parliamentary party group. In terms of personal contacts, however, the Swedish Riksdag is an exception. Largely on account of the high ratio of MPs to ministers, relatively few representatives have regular contacts with ministers. From the perspective of cabinet ministers, however, the number of contacts with representatives in all five polities is roughly the same.

The third and final instance of a common Nordic configuration has to do with the importance of cooperation across parties (the cross-party mode, no. 19). In chapter 11, Damgaard furnishes many examples of how representatives from different parties work together to reach results on one or another policy issue. He concludes that the relatively influential parliamentary committees are crucial for many of these cross-party encounters. Once more, however, the Swedish Riksdag constitutes an exception. Cross-party initiatives on the part of individual representatives are less frequent in the relatively large and anonymous Swedish parliament than in the other Nordic parliaments.

Two indicators of parliamentary-legislative relations show mainly inter-Nordic *differences:* interparty competition (no. 17) and competition between parliament and government (no. 20). As regard the first (no. 17), it is clear that bargaining between parties is much more central within

Nordic parliaments than in single-party majoritarian Westminster systems or than in the U.S. Congress (with its weak parties). There is, however, a difference in parliamentary decision-making between, on the one hand, Denmark, Norway, and Sweden, and, on the other, Finland and Iceland. The difference is related to the fact that the three former countries are regularly governed by minority governments, whereas the latter two are usually governed by majority coalitions. In Denmark, Norway, and Sweden, interparty bargaining by necessity includes opposition parties, whereas bargaining in Finland and Iceland can be restricted in a higher degree to the governing parties themselves. Differences as regard the two-body relationship between parliament and government (no. 20) follow the same line. The government holds a stronger position vis-à-vis parliament in Finland and Iceland than it does in Denmark, Norway, and Sweden.

Of the four different modes of parliamentary relations discussed, it is the horizontal mode (vis-à-vis competing elite actors and institutions) that yields the best numerical case for the existence of a unique Nordic model (three of six indicators show Nordic similarities). This assertion does not, however, stand up to closer scrutiny. Most importantly, the type of intra-party influence found in Nordic parliaments (no. 18)—that is, a close relationship between the government and its parliamentary party group—is also found in Westminster-style parliaments, as well as in other parliaments operating in parliamentary systems.

Not even when we focus on the relative importance of different parliamentary modes can we reasonably claim the existence of a Nordic alternative (see Damgaard's chapter 11). It is true that the interparty mode of parliamentary bargaining (based on strong and cohesive party groups) is central to all Nordic parliaments, and that this mode clearly differs from the dominant modes at both Westminster (intraparty) and Congress (non-party). But the same applies, once again, in the case of the German, Dutch, and Austrian parliaments. Accordingly, rather than trumpeting the existence of a unique Nordic model, we find it more relevant to point out similarities with a more broadly based Continental (or "parliamentarian-PR") model for the operations of parliaments.

EXTERNAL RELATIONS OF PARLIAMENTS

As compared with the other kinds of parliamentary relations, those of the external type—vis-à-vis the outside world and the future—have attracted little scholarly attention. Given that the globalization of politics is a fairly recent phenomenon, and given that the politics of the present usually dominate legislative processes, it is not surprising that we observe some blind spots here. Moreover, the natural starting point for scholars with an interest in globalization may not be in institutions (like parliaments) tied so closely to traditional nation-states.[3] In this study, we have focused on three aspects of the external relations of parliaments: the personal networks of individual representatives (no. 21); the ways in which parliaments organize to cope with the challenges of the globalized world order (no. 22); and the centrality of external threats in MPs' thinking about future scenarios (no. 23). As it turns out, the three indicators are classified under different configurations in table 17.2.

Of these three indicators of parliamentary operations, we know most about representatives' international contacts (or rather their lack thereof, no. 21). Previous studies have found that MPs rarely develop close personal contacts at the international level (e.g., Aberbach et al. 1981; Esaiasson and Holmberg 1996). As Brothén shows in chapter 13, the Nordic experience confirms these findings. It is mainly a small group of MPs with elite personal qualifications that are active in international networking. It would appear that weakly developed international contacts should be added to the list of features characterizing the operations of *most parliaments.* Individual members of democratic legislatures are active mainly within the framework of the traditional nation-state.

An indicator pointing mainly to *similarities* between Nordic parliaments may be seen in the thinking of MPs about external threats to the future of their society (no. 23). Narud and Valen (chapter 15) and Jensen (chapter 16) show that external threats are generally ranked relatively low on a list of potential dangers. With the notable exception of perceptions concerning Russia's unclear future, representatives perceive serious threats as internal in character rather than external.[4]

Where effective parliamentary organization is concerned, however, there are differences between Nordic parliaments (no. 22). Raunio and Wiberg (chapter 14) argue that the Danish Folketing and the Finnish Eduskunta have devised better institutional arrangements than the Swedish Riksdag for integrating parliamentary operations into the decision-making processes of the European Union. This argument implies that the manner in which parliaments are organized affects their ability to adapt to the new globalized political order.

IS THERE A NORDIC MODEL?

This study was motivated in large part by a concern to correct for a bias in the selection of cases in parliamentary research. Among our basic questions was whether the Nordic parliamentary systems offered not only an alternative *experience* but also an alternative *model* to parliaments in the style of Westminster and the U.S. Congress. We know now that the answer to this question is basically negative. To the extent all of the Nordic parliaments display similar characteristics, these characteristics are also usually found (a) among most democratic parliaments (the universal model), (b) among most parliaments in parliamentary regimes (the parliamentary model as opposed to the presidential model), or (c) among most parliaments in parliamentary regimes based on PR voting systems (the Continental model as opposed to the Westminster model).

When scrutinizing the twenty-three empirical indicators separately, we find that only three rather disparate indicators show what are possibly unique Nordic experiences: overwhelmingly positive attitudes toward the representation of social characteristics (no. 3); a particular type of cooperation across parties (no. 19); and perceptions of threats to the future of a polity that focus primarily on internal rather than external factors (no. 23). Not even when we consider wider *combinations* of empirical indicators— such as the horizontal relations of parliaments to other elite actors and institutions—do we discover good reason to proclaim the existence of a unique Nordic model. According to our best judgment, there are quite simply many more similarities than differences between Nordic parliaments on the one hand and non-Nordic parliaments operating in representative democracies on the other.

This negative conclusion does not mean that our effort has been in vain. On the contrary, bringing the Nordic experience into the picture has emphasized the need for a continuing search for nuanced models of parliamentary operations. It is clear from our findings that attempts to categorize legislative assemblies will not be of much help if they simply outline a unidimensional, two-category typology inspired by thinly disguised versions of Westminster and Congress.

One shortcoming of the traditional typology of parliaments derives, of course, from the fact that parliaments operate differently within the family of parliamentary systems (as opposed to presidential systems). We have emphasized that the Nordic experience accords in much with a Continental model of parliamentary operations based on parliamentarism, proportional representation, multiparty systems, and coalition governments (particularly where horizontal and internal relations are concerned). But there is an additional reason to be skeptical of the old two-category typology. In our review of the Nordic experience, we have noticed several counts on which we can find *universal* traits of democratically elected legislative assemblies. The general lesson is that our search for differences between parliaments should not make us overlook their common features. An understanding of parliamentary operations should include an appreciation of what appears to be inherent characteristics of democratically elected legislative assemblies.

Certain implications for causal analysis follow from our reasoning about, on the one hand, universal traits of democratic parliaments, and, on the other, a prevalent Continental model of parliamentary operations. To say that democratically elected legislative assemblies share basic characteristics even when operating in radically different contexts is equivalent to saying that specific institutional arrangements do not affect these particular aspects of parliamentary operations. No matter what the specific institutional arrangements are, MPs will act in a particular way. Furthermore, emphasizing the relevance of a Continental model is equivalent to saying that the type of voting system—PR or majoritarian—affects aspects of parliamentary operations. These queries lead to our second theme in this concluding chapter: What can we learn from the Nordic experience as regards *why* parliaments operate the way they do? Or more precisely: which institutional arrangements matter in what way?

WHICH INSTITUTIONAL ARRANGEMENTS MATTER?

A basic lesson taught by sports psychologists is that athletes who want better results should learn to worry only about factors they can influence and to forget about the rest. Our decision to focus on the impact of institutional arrangements should be understood in this spirit. Our conceptualization of "institutions" is therefore a narrow one. We have taken the concept to refer to specific constitutional and structural arrangements that (in principle) are under the control of elected representatives. Our aim in this section is to search for more precise effects of institutional arrangements—effects that reformers of representative democracies can count on. More cautiously put: our purpose is to discuss what the Nordic experience can tell us about how institutional arrangements influence parliamentary operations.

Specifically, we will focus on three classes of constitutional arrangements: regime type, electoral system, and parliamentary organization. When discussing *regime type*, we will concentrate on the basic choice between a presidential and a parliamentary system (cf. Shugart and Carey 1992). *Electoral systems*, for their part, can vary along several dimensions (e.g., Grofman and Lijphart 1986; Tageepera and Shugart 1989; Lijphart

1994). Here we will look at four aspects of electoral systems for which the design of this study provides relevant information: (1) PR versus majoritarian voting systems; (2) candidate-preference voting versus party-list voting; (3) decentralized versus centralized nominating processes; and (4) having a formal bias in favor of peripheral regions versus not having such a bias. As regards *parliamentary organization,* constitutional reformers face even more numerous choices than they do in regard to electoral system (e.g., Döring 1995; Laver and Shepsle 1996; Mezey 1993). In the following, we focus on the consequences of (1) having a parliament with many seats versus having one with few; (2) various ways of organizing committee systems; and (3) different organizational measures taken to adapt to the globalized world order.

Scholars who discuss the effects of institutional arrangements do not always restrict themselves to factors under the control of representatives. An example may be seen in Weaver and Rockman's well-reputed study *Do Institutions Matter?*.[5]

Weaver and Rockman look at the effects of institutional arrangements on governmental effectiveness. A crucial category in their analysis is the type of *parliamentary regime*—that is, whether power is concentrated, as in single party-dominant governments, or checked, as in coalition governments (1993:448–51). Weaver and Rockman are clearly not "wrong" in discussing these effects. Obviously, a single-party dominant government and a coalition government have different positions in the policy-making process. We want to emphasize, however, that no direct causal link can be found between sets of constitutional arrangements and type of parliamentary regime. It is simply not clear which factors produce a single party-dominant government system and which a coalition government system.[6]

In the following analysis, we draw a line between "constitutional" and "political" determinants. What we mean by constitutional determinants should be clear by now. By political determinants we mean factors like "type of party system" (multiparty or not); "type of government" (coalition or single-party); and "parliamentary support of government" (majority or minority). In contrast to the case with constitutional arrangements, we treat these as political factors and also as factors that lie outside, in principle, the direct control of elected representatives.[7]

To undertake a systematic analysis, however, we will need further specifications. Comparative parliamentary research is not in such a state that scholars can concentrate on refining sophisticated theories on the effects of institutional arrangements. There is much basic work that needs doing before that.

Our analysis will focus on a limited set of propositions about constitutional effects found in the literature, and for which the Nordic experience provides relevant information. Some of these propositions are well founded in previous research and in practical experience; others are of the character of conventional wisdom. In addition, we shall discuss propositions that have emerged specifically from the individual contributions to this volume.

Table 17.3 summarizes a total of twenty-eight propositions about the effects of constitutional arrangements on parliamentary operations, along with our judgment in each case as to whether the proposition in question is supported when confronted with the Nordic experience. In what follows, we discuss the merits of the propositions for each of the three classes of constitutional arrangements: regime type, electoral system, and parliamentary organization.[8]

REGIME TYPE

Our evaluation of regime-type propositions is based mainly on comparisons between, on the one hand, Nordic parliaments, and, on the other, what we know about parliaments in the style of Westminster and the U.S. Congress. We also draw on internal Nordic variations, in the sense that there is a presidential element in Finnish politics (see chapter 2 above).

The type of regime (presidential or parliamentary) affects both the operations of parliamentary parties and the relationship between the legislative and executive branches of government. This is, of course, a staple in the scholarly literature on institutional arrangements. The standard argument goes roughly as follows: In contrast to presidential systems, parliamentary systems produce highly influential and cohesive party groups. Since governments depend on a parliamentary majority to survive, they must be based on the support of coherent groups in parliament. Presidential systems, with their separation of powers, do not require such party groups to the same extent in order to uphold stability, democratic accountability, and decision-making effectiveness (e.g., Daalder and Rusk 1972; Lijphart 1984; Damgaard 1994).

The Nordic experience does not in any way contradict these standard notions about differences between presidential and parliamentary systems. Claims to the effect that parliamentary party groups will be more cohesive and influential in parliamentary systems are thus generally supported (propositions 4 and 5). There is also support for the related proposition (no. 3) that the party will be a more central focus for individual representatives in parliamentary systems than in presidential ones. On all of these accounts, the Finnish Eduskunta differs slightly from other Nordic parliaments in a predicted way.

Table 17.3
Which Constitutional Arrangements Affect the Operations of Parliaments? An Overview of Tested Propositions

Type of Constitutional Arrangement	Proposition	Outcome
Regime Type Presidentialism vs. parliamentarism	1. Higher degree of issue congruence in presidential systems (#5)	Not supported
	2. Representatives are more locally oriented in presidential systems (#8, 9)	Not supported
	3. The party is a less central focus for representatives in presidential systems (#8, 10)	Supported
	4. More cohesive parliamentary party groups in parliamentary systems (#10)	Supported
	5. More influential parliamentary party groups in parliamentary systems (#11)	Supported
	6. Representatives recommend for parliament a more active role in the policy-making process in presidential systems (views on the proper role of parliaments, #16)	Not supported
	7. Initiatives of individual representatives are less relevant in parliamentary systems (nonparty mode, #20)	Not supported
Electoral System PR vs. first past the post (FPP)	8. Higher degree of issue congruence in PR systems (#5)	Not supported
	9. Representatives are more locally oriented in majoritarian systems (FFP) (#8, 9)	Not supported
	10. Less hierarchical parliamentary party groups in PR parliamentary systems (#12)	Supported
	11. Interparty bargaining is more crucial in PR parliamentary systems (#17)	Supported
	12. The government is less dominant in relation to its own parliamentary party group in PR-parliamentary systems (#18)	Supported
	13. Cross-party initiatives of individual representatives are more crucial in PR parliamentary systems (#19)	Supported
Candidate-Preference Voting vs. Party-List Voting	14. Representatives are more locally oriented in candidate-preference voting systems (#8, 9)	Not supported
	15. The party is a less central focus for representatives in candidate-preference voting systems (#8, 10)	Supported
	16. More cohesive parliamentary party groups in party-list voting systems (#10)	Partly supported
	17. More hierarchical parliamentary party groups in party-list voting systems (#12)	Not supported

Decentralized vs. centralized nomination processes	18. The party is a less central focus for representatives when nomination process is decentralized (#8, 10)	Supported
	19. Representatives are more locally oriented when nomination process is decentralized (#8, 9)	Undecided
	20. Less cohesive parliamentary party groups when nomination process is decentralized (#10)	Not supported
	21. Less hierarchical parliamentary party groups when nomination process is decentralized (#12)	Not supported
Formal bias in favor of peripheral regions or not	22. The linkage between representatives and represented in peripheral regions is tighter in electoral systems that provide a formal bias (in the form of additional seats) to the periphery (#9)	Supported
Parliamentary Organization	23. Better direct access for interest groups in large parliaments (#4,8)	Supported
Size of parliament: many seats vs. few seats	24. Representatives have fewer contacts with cabinet ministers in large parliaments (#17,20)	Supported
	25. Cross-party initiatives of individual representatives are less frequent in large parliaments (#19)	Supported
	26. Less influential individual representatives in large parliaments (nonparty model, #20)	Supported
Org. of Committees	27. Committees are more influential when they match the structure of ministers functionally (#13)	Supported
Adaptation to globalized politics	28. Parliaments are better equipped to successfully cooperate with the EU when all standing committees are involved in preparing national EU policies (#22)	Supported

Note: Figures in parentheses refer to the list of empirical indicators presented in table 17.1.

More interesting for the scholarly debate, perhaps, is the fact that other propositions about the effects of regime type on parliamentary operations are not as clearly supported. In fact, there are three propositions relating to the greater need in parliamentary systems for influential and cohesive parliamentary party groups which are not supported.

First, it could be expected that the initiatives of individual representatives will be more relevant in presidential than in parliamentary systems (proposition 7). The relatively great influence of individual U.S. congressmen would be an example of that. Judging from our findings, however, Finnish representatives—who must act in a presidential context—do not have a greater say in decision-making than do Danish and Norwegian representatives, who must do their job in a purely parliamentary system. (If anything, in fact, the relationship is the reverse.)[9] The Nordic experience would seem to indicate that forces other than regime type per se may determine the political importance of MPs' individual initiatives.

Second, it is generally assumed in the Anglo-Saxon literature that the relationship between representatives and their electoral constituency is closer in presidential systems than in parliamentary ones (proposition 2; e.g., Searing 1985; Cain et al. 1987).[10] This is thought to be the case because, in such systems, representatives meet with less pressure to stick to the party line, so they feel freer to orient themselves toward local interests and their re-election campaign. Third, it can be expected for similar reasons that issue congruence between voters and representatives will be higher in presidential systems than in parliamentary ones (no. 1). But, as reported above, the Nordic experience shows that representatives are also locally oriented in a high degree in parliamentary systems with strong and cohesive parliamentary parties. In addition, the Nordic experience demonstrates that different regime types produce remarkably similar degrees of issue congruence.

Our summary conclusion is that the effect of regime type is limited to such elements as the influence and cohesiveness of parliamentary parties. When the search for precise effects is extended to complementary aspects of parliamentary operations, the differences between presidential and parliamentary systems are much less substantial.

To undermine notions about the all-embracing effects of regime type further, we can add a fourth example of an unsupported proposition. It could be expected that MPs' views on the proper role of parliament in democratic politics is affected by the actual position of parliament in the policy-making process. Since parliaments in parliamentary systems are generally assumed to be less active in terms of lawmaking than are parliaments in presidential systems (see, e.g., Mezey 1979)—it is sometimes claimed, for example, that the U.S. Congress is the world's only example of a real legislature—we would expect Nordic representatives to ascribe a rather passive and supervisory political role to their own institution. Yet Nordic MPs reject this idea forcefully. According to them, their own institution should ideally be a major player in the policy-making process, second to no other institution including the government. Indeed, as concluded in an earlier section, we believe that this kind of institutional pride is a universal characteristic of elected representatives—one unaffected by specific constitutional arrangements.

ELECTORAL SYSTEM

The choice of electoral system is a central theme among constitutional engineers (e.g., Sartori 1994). The political effects of electoral systems figure prominently in classic studies like Duverger's *Les partis politiques* (1951), Lipset and Rokkan's *Party Systems and Voter Alignments* (1967), and Douglas Rae's *The Political Consequences of Electoral Laws* (1967). Recent years have seen the publication of several important new studies (e.g., Grofman and Lijphart 1986; Taagepera and Shugart 1989; Lijphart 1994). In this study, we deal with a relatively large number of propositions about the effects of electoral systems on parliamentary operations (fourteen of twenty-eight identified propositions in table 17.3).

We shall argue that the general lesson to be drawn is parallel to the one about regime type. It would be nonsensical to refute the notion that electoral systems matter, but the precise effects are surprisingly few and often conditioned by political factors that are not under the direct control of elected representatives. Paradoxically, moreover, the observed effects are related to parliament's internal affairs and its horizontal relations to other elite institutions, rather than to its vertical relations with the electorate (which are largely unaffected by the choice of electoral system).

A discussion on the consequences of the type of voting system employed (PR or majoritarian) illustrates our point. To begin with, we have identified two propositions about possible effects on parliament's relationship to the electorate, and both come up short of empirical support.

Our argument goes as follows. PR systems offer voters a larger menu of partisan choices from which to select, and they translate popular votes into legislative seats in a more nearly proportional fashion (Powell 1989; Lijphart 1994). The larger menus of partisan choices and the greater proportionality will result in a closer relationship between representatives and represented—which should, in turn, make for a higher degree of issue congruence in parliaments of the Nordic type than in those structured in the manner of Westminster (proposition 8). Second, majoritarian systems will arguably have the edge over PR systems as far as nurturing a strong local orientation on the part of individual representatives is concerned. This is because representatives elected in majoritarian systems can identify with a relatively small and clearly defined constituency (proposition 9; Searing 1985; Cain et al. 1987; Shugart and Carey 1992). Both propositions are contradicted, however, by two of the central findings of this study: namely, that different institutional setups produce remarkably similar degrees of issue congruence and that the interests of the geographical constituency are a major concern for representatives even in PR systems with strong and disciplined parliamentary parties.

Let us turn now to parliaments' internal and external relations. We have identified four propositions here (nos. 10 through 13). Note that all are conditioned by regime type; that is, by the fact that the system is parliamentary. The first is that parliamentary party groups will be less hierarchical in PR systems than in majoritarian parliamentary systems like that of Westminster (proposition 10). The reasons for this are that PR lowers the threshold for party splits and that whips are less effective under PR than under majoritarian systems. Second, interparty bargaining will be more crucial in PR systems (proposition 11). This is because it is less likely that a tradition of one-party governments will develop in which one party controls a majority in parliament. Parties will seek cooperation to a greater extent in order to gain power. Third, the government will be less dominant in relation to its own parliamentary party group in proportional parliamentary systems (proposition 12). The mechanism suggested here is that the government will be more dependent on its party group(s), which will have to work out the necessary compromises in parliament. Finally, cross-party initiatives on the part of individual representatives will be more crucial in such systems (proposition 13). This hypothesis combines the reasoning of propositions 10, 11, and 12: the claim is that proportional parliamentary systems tend to produce the kind of "working" parliaments that offer more space for individual political entrepreneurs.

All of these propositions are supported by the Nordic experience, but for at least three of them, the effects are conditioned by political factors that are not fully determined by the electoral system (or by any other constitutional arrangement, for that matter). Specifically, even though we find that the Nordic parliaments by and large operate as expected, we also find significant inter-Nordic differences between the parliaments of Denmark, Norway, and Sweden on the one hand and the Finnish and Icelandic parliaments on the other. It seems obvious that the frequency of minority and coalition governments plays its part in this respect. A plausible conclusion is that PR voting of the Nordic kind *interacts* with political factors to produce the observed empirical outcomes. Parliamentary operations will vary considerably according to whether the government commands a majority or just a minority, and whether it comprises a single party or a coalition.

The second aspect of electoral systems to be discussed is the choice between candidate-preference voting systems (as in Finland and, to a lesser degree, Denmark) and party-list voting systems (as in Norway and Sweden). (See chapter 2 above.) We would expect that representatives in electoral systems that allow voters to support a particular candidate at the polls will be less focused on their party than their counterparts in strictly party-oriented voting systems (proposition 15; Katz 1980). Moreover, if the electoral system in use contains a personal element, the result will be to strengthen the individual MP vis-à-vis the party leadership (Urwin 1987). This will decrease, in turn, the authority of the party leadership, making party-group cohesion less prevalent and hierarchies weaker (propositions 16 and 17). As a consequence of the weaker leadership control, we can also expect MPs to be more locally oriented in candidate-preference voting systems than in party-list systems (proposition 14).

Only two of these four propositions are supported wholly or in part by the Nordic experience. It does indeed seem that the degree to which a personal element is present in the electoral system affects the centrality of political parties in the representative process (proposition 15). The party is clearly a more central focus for representatives in Norway and Sweden, where strict party-list systems are in use, than it is for representatives in Finland, where voters are freer to choose among candidates. As predicted, moreover, parliamentary party groups are more cohesive in Norway and Sweden than in Finland (proposition 16). A troubling circumstance for the latter proposition, however, is that Danish parties are just as cohesive as their counterparts elsewhere in Scandinavia. As regard hierarchies in parliamentary party groups (proposition 17) and the local orientation of representatives (proposition 14), the Nordic parliaments do not operate as predicted. On the contrary, it bears noting that Finnish parliamentary parties are clearly more hierarchical than are party groups in Norway, Sweden, and Denmark, and that Swedish representatives are the most likely to define themselves as promoters of local interests.

The type of nominating process applied is the third aspect of electoral systems to be discussed here. As defined by us, the basic choice stands between centralized and decentralized processes for the selection of candidates. The decentralized nominating process can be expected to affect parliamentary operations in ways similar to those of the candidate-preference voting system. This is because representatives who rely on local forces for their political survival have a platform of their own that is not controlled by the central party leadership. Specifically, the following four propositions are confronted with the Nordic experience: the party will be a less central focus for representatives when the nominating process is decentralized (no. 18); representatives will be more locally oriented when the nominating process is decentralized (no. 19); parliamentary party groups will be less cohesive when the nominating process is decentralized (no. 20); and parliamentary party groups will be less hierarchical when the nominating process is decentralized (no. 21).

Nordic political systems offer a limited degree of internal variation in terms of type of nominating process. In four of five countries (Denmark, Finland, Norway, and Sweden), candidates are nominated according to a procedure that is common among Western democracies (Gallagher and Marsh 1988). That is, the nominating process is largely decentralized, with local party organizations watching jealously over their right of selection. The deviant case is Iceland. Icelandic nominations are *radically* decentralized, in the sense that all parties rely on decisive primaries (for some parties, in fact, the primaries are even open to nonmembers). The basic empirical test on this is whether the Icelandic Althingi operates differently from the other Nordic parliaments in a predicted way.

As it turns out, only one of the propositions is clearly supported by the Nordic experience. Icelandic MPs—just like their Finnish counterparts, who are elected on the basis of a candidate-preference voting system—consider the party to be a less central focus in the representative process than do Danish, Norwegian, and Swedish MPs. But the propositions which claim that nominations will affect cohesiveness and hierarchies in parliamentary party groups are not supported. Icelandic parliamentary parties are highly cohesive, and their internal hierarchies are stronger than those of their Scandinavian counterparts.

In the case of the fourth proposition—that MPs will be more locally oriented when the nominating process is decentralized—we find the evidence inconclusive. Icelandic representatives are not more locally oriented than their Scandinavian colleagues. Adding an extra dose of decentralization does not, when the nominating process is already decentralized, affect the local orientation of representatives. Still, the Nordic experience does not allow us to exclude the possibility that the relationship is curvilinear rather than linear: that the level of decentralization present in all of the Nordic nominating processes is sufficient to motivate representatives to give high priority to local concerns. A further test would require information from the few representative democracies where the selection of candidates is a centralized matter.[11]

The final aspect of electoral systems to be tested deals with arrangements that allow for the overrepresentation of peripheral areas (in the sense of providing additional seats to such areas). In the Nordic context, the Icelandic and Norwegian constitutions allow for such a geographical bias, whereas the Danish and Swedish constitutions are geographically neutral. According to our findings, arrangements of this kind affect the relationship between representatives and represented (proposition 22). In geographically biased electoral systems, the linkage between representatives and voters is closer in the peripheral areas than in the center. This internal difference between the center and the periphery does not show up in geographically neutral electoral systems. It should be noted that this is the only proposition about the effects of electoral systems on the vertical relations of parliaments which is systematically supported when confronted with the Nordic experience.

PARLIAMENTARY ORGANIZATION

It is generally accepted that parliamentary rules shape behavior to a degree. In *Parliaments and Majority Rule in Western Europe,* edited by Herbert Döring (1995), the support for this idea was effectively demonstrated in a comparative context. To name but a few such important factors: rules as regards constructive parliamentarism, investiture votes, and qualified-majority requirements will affect parliament-executive relations (King 1976; Mezey 1993; Andeweg and Nijzink 1995; Bergman 1995). Here we will accept the purported general relationship and try to be fairly selective in our discussion. We have decided to concentrate on a few propositions that have emerged from the individual contributions to this volume and that can be effectively tested in the Nordic context.

The one organizational factor proven to be of recurrent importance is parliamentary size, in the sense of *number of seats. First,* the size of parliament matters for the availability of channels for interest representation (proposition 23). Since mainly parliamentary backbenchers define themselves as champions of a particular interest group, a middle-sized parliament like the Swedish Riksdag provides better opportunities for direct group representation than do parliaments with relatively few seats, such as the Norwegian Storting, the Danish Folketing, and the Finnish Eduskunta. *Second,* parliamentary size matters for the frequency of personal contacts between MPs and government ministers (proposition 24). The size of the Swedish Riksdag makes it less likely that its members will maintain the level of contacts found in other assemblies. *Third,* it would appear that size affects the probability of cross-party initiatives on the part of individual representatives (proposition 25). Cooperation across parties is less frequent in the Swedish Riksdag than in the other Nordic parliaments. *Fourth*, the Swedish experience also indicates that size matters, in the sense that a high number of MPs decreases the power of the individual MP (proposition 26).[12]

The conclusion seems warranted that large parliaments make for relatively anonymous representatives and for good direct access for various interest groups.

Two final aspects of parliamentary organization will be discussed. The first relates to the proposition that committees are more influential when they match the structure of ministries functionally (proposition 27; Lees and Shaw 1979; Arter 1984). A careful examination of the committee structure of the five Nordic parliaments gives added support to this idea.[13] The final proposition relates to the question on parliamentary adaptation to the new globalized world order. Judging from the experience of the three Nordic members of the European Union, it make a difference for effective adaptation how parliaments organize the decision-making process (proposition 28). It can be argued that parliaments are better equipped to cooperate successfully with the European Union when all of their standing committees are involved in preparing national EU policies than when preparations are largely delegated to a specific committee.

INSTITUTIONAL ANALYSIS
REQUIRES CONTEXT

For enthusiastic adherents of constitutional engineering, this study should have a moderating effect. If we are right, institutional arrangements are not overly effective tools for controlling the operations of parliaments. Or, to put the argument more cautiously: reformers of representative democracies may have an almost unlimited number of constitutional options at their disposal, but they can count on relatively few precise effects. This book can be added to the growing number of studies arguing that institutional arrangements produce relatively few unconditioned effects (see, e.g., Weaver and Rockman 1993; Lijphart and Waisman 1996).[14]

There are two reasons that constitutional engineers face problems. The one is that all democratically elected legislatures function, in some respects, in a similar fashion. No matter what the specific institutional arrangements, MPs will act in a particular way. The other reason is that politico-cultural factors play such a crucial role for the operations of parliaments. How parliaments operate, therefore, is determined to a great extent by factors that are not easily changed.

We can also offer a somewhat more precise conclusion. Constitutional arrangements (as well as politico-cultural factors) matter the least when it comes to parliaments' vertical relations with the electorate. The five Nordic polities share important characteristics in regard to relations between those represented and those who represent. These findings square well, moreover, with what we know from studies of other democracies. Reformers of representative democracies should therefore not be too concerned about their parliament's relation to the electorate: whichever constitutional solution they suggest, the end result will be more or less the same.

Reformers would be well advised, rather, to focus on their parliament's internal relations, as well as on its external relations with other elite institutions and actors. These two dimensions of parliamentary relations are the most open to effective constitutional manipulation. For one thing, the Nordic experience confirms that the regime type (parliamentarism vs. presidentialism) affects the cohesiveness of parliamentary parties and also certain aspects of legislative-executive relations. Within the family of parliamentary regimes, moreover, there are differences in legislative-executive relations that can be tied to the difference between PR and majoritarian voting systems. Also, more specific institutional arrangements affect such matters as the centrality of political parties in the representative process (it matters whether or not the voting system allows for a personal vote) and cooperation between individual representatives across parties (the size of parliament matters).

We are not, accordingly, making the absurd argument that our findings in any way "refute" the institutional position. Institutions clearly matter, in the sense that they shape behavior. Our point is more that all things can be overdone, and that the real challenge lies in balancing the different forces at work and focusing our attention on the contextual conditions shaping a particular balance. Or, in other words: institutions operate within a political and cultural context, which affects the way in which they shape behavior.

It is our contention that constitutional engineers are generally helpless without an intimate knowledge of the political and cultural context. Single-minded institutionalists will easily meet the fate of the first wave of well-intentioned economic experts who set out to create Western-style economic enterprises in isolated enclaves of developing countries—without the infrastructure needed to sustain them. It will not work. Probably on account of our "trained professional incapacity," we would therefore make a plea for bringing politics closer to the center of parliamentary inquiries: the political process, the personal ambitions, the power struggles, the political history, the dominant ideologies—all need to be considered if the object is to figure out how institutions are working. This does not make the search for instrumental knowledge much easier; but then, we do not believe that parliamentary analysis is a quick fix.

END NOTE

We began this book by mentioning our concern for the discipline's capacity to produce well-founded advice to reformers of democratic societies. What solidly based recommendations from the experience of Nordic democracies could be offered reformers? Our thesis about the conditional nature of institutional effects may cast some light on why democratic reformers face such a difficult task.

While the tone of this argument may be a bit pessimistic—it would be much more inspiring, of course, to claim that the final solution is waiting just around the corner—we believe it is important to have realistic expectations about the prospects for institutional engineering. High expectations are certainly an important component in generating societal development, but it may be that a sustainable democratic system also demands that we learn to accept the limitations of institutional designs. From this perspective, it has been a rewarding endeavor to search for common denominators across political systems, in the form of core characteristics of the operations of democratic parliaments.

The set of universal characteristics that have been identified can be summarized in the following way. Imagine a person with no prior knowledge of democratic politics asking what kind of legislative assembly will emerge if his or her country turns into a representative democracy. An honest answer might be as follows:

We cannot give you a complete description, mostly because the operations of your parliament will be contingent on the political and cultural context of your country. Yet no matter what decisions the founding mothers and fathers of your nation make, you will most likely be confronted with elected representatives whose policy views are only moderately representative of those held by the voters; who defend relatively tolerant views on questions pertaining to basic democratic rights; who have much more frequent personal contacts nationally and locally than internationally; who are socially exclusive; who define their task as the defense of interests they personally consider important to champion; and who carry out their duties within the context of an institution that they believe ought to be a center for decision-making in society.

Those who dislike these characteristics and their political consequences have two options if they want to avoid further disappointment.

The one is to adjust their expectations. The other is to start promoting other forms of government than representative democracy.

NOTES

1. Recent research shedding new light on this aspect of representative democracies includes Norris and Lovenduski (1995), and Manin (1997).

2. We have here left out aspects of parliamentary life of such obvious importance as the formal institutional arrangements prevailing in regard to lawmaking and the formation of governments (see Döring 1995; Laver and Shepsle 1996; Mezey 1993).

3. A debate is rapidly emerging, however, in connection with the recent efforts at increased European integration. See, for example, Smith (1996), and Katz and Wessels (1999).

4. As regards other aspects of risk perception, of course, both Narud and Valen on the one hand and Jensen on the other find a more complex empirical pattern. One of their findings (and one central to our discussion in the following section) is that the observed empirical configurations probably cannot be tied to institutional arrangements. For instance, the formal relation of a country to the European Union matters only to a small extent. As for structural effects, it appears that MPs' risk perceptions are influenced mainly by politico-cultural factors that are partly common to the five Nordic countries and partly unique to each nation.

5. Indeed, we make use of this study in chapter 2 in order to structure our description of institutional and political variation in the Nordic countries.

6. For enlightening discussions of the limited effects of institutional arrangements on the Polish governmental type, see Gebethner (1996), and Lijphart and Waisman (1996).

7. Rule-making may affect these factors, however.

8. We will not review detailed empirical findings once more in this discussion. Readers interested in more information can start with the number of the empirical indicator associated with each proposition in table 17.3 and then go back to tables 17.1 and 17.2 to find out which chapter analyzes the topic in question.

9. Because of differences in parliamentary size, Sweden (with relatively many seats) and Iceland (with relatively few) are taken out of the comparison.

10. The complementary proposition that the local orientation of representatives will be stronger in majoritarian than in PR voting systems will be discussed in the next section.

11. The Swedish experience offers support for the proposition that the type of nominating process employed may be crucial. Representatives who are seeking re-election, and who were less careful to keep close contact with the local party organization during the original election period, become much more inclined to

put forward private member bills in support of local interests when the time for the final nominating process approaches (Esaiasson and Holmberg 1996:286).

12. Heidar's analysis in chapter 8 shows that group size also matters for internal debates and group hierarchy.

13. It should be added that the findings of this study also support the notion that political factors affect the influence of committees. The Nordic experience squares with the idea that committees are made stronger by coalitions or minority governments, which have the effect of weakening the executive in relation to parliament (Strøm 1990).

14. It may also be added to the general debate on the chicken and the egg. Which comes first in a causal sense—institutions or the political context within which they operate? See, for example, Rokkan (1968).

APPENDIXES

Appendix **1**

The Surveys

The analyses in this book draw mainly on two sets of data that were generated within the Nordleg project. The first covers the responses of representatives elected to the national parliaments of the Nordic countries Denmark, Finland, Iceland, Norway, and Sweden. The second set of data is surveys conducted with representative samples of eligible voters of all the Nordic countries except Finland.

The parliamentary surveys were mail questionnaires put to all members of respective national parliaments that were serving at the time of the study. The parliamentary surveys were conducted between November 1994 and May 1996.

The Danish Folketing study was conducted between April 1995 and July 1995. The preceding parliamentary election was held in September 1994. Response rate for the Danish study was 63 percent; that is, 110 responses out of 175.

The Finnish Eduskunta study was conducted between October 1995 and February 1996. The preceding parliamentary election was held in March 1995. The response rate for the Finnish study was 61 percent; that is, 122 responses out of 200.

The Icelandic Althingi survey was conducted between March 1996 and August 1996. The preceding parliamentary election was held in April 1995. The response rate was 72 percent; that is, 44 answers out of 63.

The Norwegian Storting survey was conducted between January 1996 and April 1996. The preceding parliamentary election was held in September 1993. The response rate in the Norwegian study was 88 percent; that is, 146 responses out of 165.

The Swedish Riksdag survey was conducted between November 1994 and January 1995. As was the case in Denmark, the preceding parliamentary election was held in September 1994. The response rate was 96 percent; that is, 336 responses out of 349.

The surveys were composed of a core of identically worded questions, or as identically worded as the languages and national contexts allow, and some country-specific questions for the national projects only. Not counting specified items, the core questionnaire consists of thirty-three questions. In addition, ten questions were posed in four of five countries and seven in three. Information about a number of background factors were also collected. The background information consists of bibliographical data as well as data on committee assignments and other political data. All in all, the common codebook for the project consists of more than five hundred variables. The wording of questions are reported where they are relevant in chapters of this volume. An English translation of the core questionnaire is available on request.

The other data set is a series of voter surveys, designed to be representative national samples of the electorates. In these we repeated some of the core questions put to the parliamentarians pertaining to left-right ideological self-placement, policy views, and perceptions of the future. The surveys also asked for basic background information. The voter surveys were carried out in the period between August 1994 and June 1996.

The Danish voter survey was conducted in June 1995. It was based on telephone interviews and was carried out by the Aim Nielsen Institute. With a response rate of about 80 percent, the final number of respondents was 981. The Icelandic voter survey was conducted in late May and early June 1996. Based on telephone interviews, it was carried out by the Social Science Research Institute, University of Iceland. With a response rate of 72 percent, the number of respondents was 1,064. The Norwegian study, which was carried out by the Central Bureau of Statistics, was conducted in March 1996. The response rate was 66.5 percent, and the number of respondents was 1,316 (from a total sample of two thousand respondents). Of the interviews, 61.5 percent were based on personal visits, the rest on telephone interviews. The Swedish voter survey was caried out in August 1994 and October 1994, as part of the Swedish National Election Studies Program. It was based on face-to-face interviews. With a response rate of 80 percent, the number of respondents was 2,336.

Complementary information on respective surveys are found in the following reports: Torben K. Jensen, "Rapport vedrørende data og dataindsamling i forbindelse med Spørgeskemaundersøgelsen i Folketinget i forsommeren 1995" (paper, Department of Political Science, Århus University, 1995); Matti Wiberg, "Report on the Eduskunta-Survey 1995" (paper, Department of Political Science, Turku University 1997); Ólafur Th. Hardarson, "Nordleg: Report on the Althingi Survey" and "Nordleg: Report on the Icelandic Voter Survey" (papers, Faculty of Social Sciences,

University of Iceland, January 1997); Knut Heidar, Hanne Marthe Narud, Henry Valen, and Frode Berglund, "Rapport om data og datainsamling for spørreskjemaundersøkelse med stortingsrepresentanterne 1996" (paper, Department of Political Science, University of Oslo, and Institute for Social Research, Oslo, 1996; Martin Brothén, Peter Esaiasson, and Sören Holmberg, "Riksdagsenkät 1994—en sammanställning" (paper, Department of Political Science, Göteborg University, 1995.

The Swedish voter survey is available at the Swedish Social Science Data Service (SSD) at Göteborg University. For reasons of data protection, however, the surveys of MPs will not be deposited at any data archive. Scholars interested in these data, and in respective voter surveys, should get in contact with Torben K. Jensen (Denmark), Matti Wiberg (Finland), Ólafur Th. Hardarson (Iceland), Knut Heidar or Hanne Marthe Narud (Norway), and Peter Esaiasson or Sören Holmberg (Sweden).

Appendix 2

Votes and Seats

DENMARK

Table A2.1
Percentage of Votes, Selected Years 1945–1997

Party	1945	1950	1960	1971	1973	1984	1987	1988	1990	1994
Communist Party[a]	12.5	4.6	1.1	1.4	3.6	0.7	0.9	0.8	—	—
Left Socialist Party[a]	—	—	—	1.6	1.5	2.7	1.4	0.6	—	—
Socialist People's Party	—	—	6.1	9.1	6.0	11.5	14.6	13.0	8.3	7.3
Social Democrats	32.8	39.6	42.1	37.3	25.6	31.6	29.3	29.8	37.4	34.6
Schleswig Party[b]	—	0.3	0.4	0.2	—	—	—	—	—	—
Radical Party	8.2	8.2	5.8	14.3	11.2	5.5	6.2	5.6	3.5	4.6
Common Course[c]	—	—	—	—	—	—	2.2	1.9	1.8	—
The Unity List[a]	—	—	—	—	—	—	—	—	1.7	3.1
The Greens	—	—	—	—	—	—	1.3	1.4	0.9	—
Justice Party	1.9	8.2	2.2	1.7	2.9	1.5	0.5	—	0.5	—
Liberals	23.4	21.3	21.1	15.6	12.3	12.1	10.5	11.8	15.8	23.3
Center Democrats	—	—	—	—	7.8	4.6	4.8	4.7	5.1	2.8
Christian People's Party	—	—	—	2.0	4.0	2.7	2.4	2.0	2.3	1.9
Conservatives	18.2	17.8	17.9	16.7	9.2	23.4	20.8	19.3	16.0	15.0
Progress Party[c]	—	—	—	—	15.9	3.6	4.8	9.0	6.4	6.4
Others[d]	3.1	0.0	3.3	0.0	0.0	0.1	0.4	0.1	0.3	1.0
Voter turnout (%)	86.3	81.9	85.8	87.2	88.7	88.4	86.7	85.7	82.9	83.3

Table A2.2
Percentage of Seats Won in the Parliament, Selected Years 1945–1997[e]

Party	1945	1950	1960	1971	1973	1984	1987	1988	1990	1994
Communist Party	12.2	4.7	0.0	0.0	3.4	0.0	0.0	0.0	0.0	—
Left Socialist Party	—	—	—	0.0	0.0	2.9	0.0	0.0	0.0	—
Socialist People's Party	—	—	6.3	9.7	6.3	12.0	15.4	13.7	8.6	7.4
Social Democrats	32.4	39.6	43.4	40.0	26.3	32.0	30.9	31.4	39.4	35.4
Schleswig Party[f]	—	0.0	0.6	0.0	0.6	—	—	—	—	—
Radical Party	7.4	8.1	6.3	15.4	11.4	5.7	6.3	5.7	4.0	4.6

Continued

445

Table A2.2

Continued

Party	1945	1950	1960	1971	1973	1984	1987	1988	1990	1994
The Unity List	—	—	—	—	—	—	—	—	—	3.4
Common Course	—	—	—	—	—	—	2.3	0.0	0.0	—
Justice Party	2.0	8.1	0.0	0.0	2.9	0.0	0.0	—	0.0	—
Liberals	25.7	21.5	21.7	17.1	12.6	12.6	10.9	12.6	16.6	24.0
Center Democrats	—	—	—	—	7.4	4.6	5.1	5.1	5.1	2.9
Christian People's Party	—	—	—	0.0	4.0	2.9	2.3	2.3	2.3	0.0
Conservatives	17.6	18.1	18.3	17.7	9.1	24.0	21.7	20.0	17.1	15.4
Progress Party	—	—	—	—	16.0	3.4	5.1	9.1	6.9	6.3
Others[d]	2.7	—	3.4	0.0	0.0	0.0	0.0	0.0	0.0	0.6
Total no. of seats in the Folketing	148	149	175	175	175	175	175	175	175	175

Sources: T. T. Mackie and R. Rose, *The International Almanac of Electoral History,* 3rd ed. (Washington, D.C.: Congressional Quarterly, 1991), pp. 87–90; S. Sauerberg, "The Danish Parliamentary Election of December 1990," *Scandinavian Political Studies* 1991, pp. 321–34; and L. Bille, "Denmark," *European Journal of Political Research* 1995, pp. 313–18.

[a] In 1990 and in 1994 a coalition of the Communist Party, the Left Socialist Party, and the Marxist-Lenninists contested the election.

[b] In 1973 the party ran with the Center Democrats.

[c] In 1990 the party's lists included Mogens Gilstrup and other former members of the Progress Party.

[d] In 1945 The Danish Union; in 1960 the Independent's Party.

[e] Two representatives from the Faroe Islands sit in the Danish Folketing. These are not included in the table.

[f] The Schleswig Party deputies were elected on Center Democrat lists.

FINLAND

Table A2.3
Percentage of Votes, Selected Years 1945–1997

Party	1945	1951	1962	1970	1975	1983	1987	1991	1995
Finnish Center[a]	21.4	23.3	23.0	17.1	17.6	17.6	17.6	24.8	19.8
National Coalition	15.0	14.6	14.6	18.0	18.4	22.1	23.1	19.3	17.9
Liberal People's Party[b]	5.2	5.7	5.9	5.9	4.3	—	1.0	0.8	0.6
Liberal League	—	0.3	0.5	—	—	—	—	—	—
Swedish People's Party[c]	8.4	7.6	6.4	5.7	5.0	4.9	5.6	5.8	5.5
Small Farmer's Party	1.2	0.3	—	—	—	—	—	—	—
Rural Party[d]	—	—	2.2	10.5	3.6	9.7	6.3	4.8	1.3
Christian League	—	—	0.8	1.1	3.3	3.0	2.6	3.1	3.0
Constitutional Party of Finland[e]	—	—	—	—	1.6	0.4	0.1	0.3	—
Finnish People's Unity Party[f]	—	—	—	—	1.7	0.1	—	—	—
Green League[g]	—	—	—	—	—	1.4	4.0	6.8	6.5
Social Democrats	25.1	26.5	19.5	23.4	24.9	26.7	24.1	22.1	28.3
Left-Wing Alliance[h]	23.5	21.6	22.0	16.6	18.9	14.0	9.4	10.1	11.2
Social Democratic League of Workers and Smallholders	—	—	4.4	1.4	—	—	—	—	—
Democratic Alternative	—	—	—	—	—	—	4.2	—	—
Young Finns[i]	—	—	—	—	—	—	—	—	2.8
Ecological Party[j]	—	—	—	—	—	—	—	0.1	0.3
Others	0.3	0.3	0.7	0.2	0.8	0.1	1.8	2.0	2.9
Voter turnout (%)[k]	74.9	74.6	85.1	82.2	73.8	75.7	72.1	68.4	68.6

Table A2.4
Percentage of Seats Won in the Parliament, Selected Years 1945–1997

Party	1945	1951	1962	1970	1975	1983	1987	1991	1995
Finnish Center[a]	24.5	25.5	26.5	18.5	19.5	19.0	20.0	27.5	22.0
National Coalition	14.0	14.0	16.0	18.5	17.5	22.0	26.5	20.0	19.5
Liberal People's Party[b]	4.5	5.0	6.5	4.0	4.5	—	0.0	0.5	—
Liberal League	—	0.0	0.5	—	—	—	—	—	—
Swedish People's Party[c]	7.5	7.5	7.0	6.0	5.0	5.5	6.5	6.0	6.0

Continued

Table A2.4

Continued

Party	1945	1951	1962	1970	1975	1983	1987	1991	1995
Rural Party[d]	—	—	0.0	9.0	1.0	8.5	4.5	3.5	0.5
Christian League	—	—	0.0	0.5	4.5	1.5	2.5	4.0	3.5
Constitutional Party of Finland[e]	—	—	—	—	0.5	0.5	0.0	0.0	—
Finnish People's Unity Party[f]	—	—	—	—	0.5	0.0	—	—	—
Green League[g]	—	—	—	—	—	1.0	2.0	5.0	4.5
Social Democrats	25.0	26.5	19.0	25.5	27.0	28.5	28.0	24.0	31.5
Left-Wing Alliance[h]	24.5	21.5	23.5	18.0	20.0	13.5	8.0	9.5	11.0
Social Democratic League of Workers and Smallholders	—	—	1.0	0.0	—	—	—	—	—
Democratic Alternative	—	—	—	—	—	—	2.0	—	—
Young Finns[i]	—	—	—	—	—	—	—	—	1.0
Ecological Party[j]	—	—	—	—	—	—	—	0.0	0.5
Others	0.0	0.0	0.0	0.0	0.0	0.0	0.0	0.0	0.0
Total no. of seats in the Eduskunta	200	200	200	200	200	200	200	200	200

Sources: T. T. Mackie and R. Rose, *The International Almanac of Electoral History,* 3rd ed. (Washington, D.C.: Congressional Quarterly, 1991), pp. 109–29; *Statistisk Årsbok för Finland 1991* (Helsingfors: Statistikcentralen), pp. 453–58; S. Berglund, "The Finnish Parliamentary Election of March 1991," *Scandinavian Political Studies* 1991, pp. 335–42; and J. Sundberg, "Finland," *European Journal of Political Research* 1996, pp. 321–29.

[a]Original name: Agrarian Union. Since 1965 the Center Party, and since 1988 Finnish Center.
[b]National Progressive Party until it was renamed the Finnish People's Party in 1951. Unified with the Liberal league in 1966 and renamed the Liberal People's Party. Ran with the Center Party in 1982–86.
[c]Including Aland Coalition and in 1945 the Swedish Left.
[d]Finnish Smallholders Party until 1966.
[e]Constitutional Peoples' Party until 1980.
[f]In 1983 Union for Democracy.
[g]The Greens until 1987.
[h]Finnish People's Democratic Union until 1990. Then the party was reunited with the Democratic Alternative.
[i]The Young Finns was founded shortly before the election by some well-known intellectuals.
[j]The Ecological Party appeared for the first time in elections in 1991. The founders came from the Green movement.
[k]Since 1975 citizens resident outside Finland have been eligible to vote; their turnout has averaged only 7 percent, thus depressing turnout overall.

ICELAND

Table A2.5
Percentage of Votes, Selected Years 1946–1997

Party	1946	1953	1963	1971	1978	1983	1987	1991	1995
Social Democrats	17.8	15.6	14.2	10.5	22.0	11.7	15.2	15.5	11.4
Progressive Party	23.1	21.9	28.2	25.3	16.9	18.5	18.9	18.9	23.3
Independence Party	39.5	37.1	41.4	36.2	32.7	38.5	27.2	38.6	37.1
People's Alliance[a]	19.5	16.0	16.0	17.1	22.9	17.2	13.3	14.4	14.3
National Preservation Party	—	6.0	—	—	—	—	—	—	—
Union of Liberals and Leftists	—	—	—	8.9	3.3	—	—	—	—
Candidature Party	—	—	—	2.0	—	—	—	—	—
Social Democratic Alliance	—	—	—	—	—	7.6	0.2	—	—
Women's Alliance	—	—	—	—	—	5.5	10.2	8.3	4.9
Citizens' Party[b]	—	—	—	—	—	—	10.9	1.2	—
Humanist Party[c]	—	—	—	—	—	—	1.6	—	—
National Party	—	—	—	—	—	—	1.3	1.8	—
Association for Equality and Justice	—	—	—	—	—	—	1.2	0.6	—
Christian Movement	—	—	—	—	—	—	—	—	0.2
Natural Law Party	—	—	—	—	—	—	—	—	0.6
People's Movement	—	—	—	—	—	—	—	—	7.1
Others	0.1	3.3	0.2	—	2.2	1.1	—	0.7	1.1
Voter turnout (%)	87.4	89.9	91.1	90.4	90.3	88.6	90.1	87.5	87.4

Table A2.6
Percentage of Seats Won in the Parliament, Selected Years 1946–1997

Party	1946	1953	1963	1971	1978	1983	1987	1991	1995
Social Democrats	17.3	11.5	13.3	10.0	23.3	10.0	15.9	15.9	11.1
Progressive Party	25.0	30.8	31.7	28.3	20.0	23.3	20.6	20.6	23.8
Independence Party	38.5	40.4	40.0	36.7	33.3	38.6	28.6	41.3	39.7
People's Alliance[a]	19.2	13.5	15.0	16.7	23.3	16.7	12.7	14.3	14.3
National Preservation Party	—	3.8	—	—	—	—	—	—	—
Union of Liberals and Leftists	—	—	—	8.3	0.0	—	—	—	—
Social Democratic Alliance	—	—	—	—	—	6.7	0.0	—	—
Women's Alliance	—	—	—	—	—	5.0	9.5	7.9	4.8
Citizens' Party[b]	—	—	—	—	—	—	11.1	0.0	—
Association for Equality and Justice	—	—	—	—	—	—	1.6	0.0	—

Continued

Table A2.6

Continued

Party	1946	1953	1963	1971	1978	1983	1987	1991	1995
Christian Movement	—	—	—	—	—	—	—	—	0.0
Natural Law Party	—	—	—	—	—	—	—	—	0.0
People's Movement	—	—	—	—	—	—	—	—	6.3
Others	0.0	—	0.0	—	0.0	0.0	—	0.0	0.0
Total no. of seats in the Althingi	52	52	60	60	60	60	63	63	63

Sources: T. T. Mackie and R. Rose, *The International Almanac of Electoral History*, 3rd ed. (Washington, D.C.: Congressional Quarterly, 1991), pp. 206–23; G. H. Kristinsson, "The Icelandic Parliamentary Election of April 1991: A European Periphery at the Polls," *Scandinavian Political Studies* 1991, pp. 343–54; Ó. Th. Hardarson, "Iceland," *European Journal of Political Research* 1996, pp. 367–76.

[a]Communist Party. Merged in 1938 with a Social Democrat splinter group to form the United Socialist Party. In 1956 the People's Alliance was formed by the United Socialist Party and another Social Democrat splinter group. It was joined by the National Preservation Party in 1963.
[b]The Liberal party in 1991.
[c]Has joined the National Party.

NORWAY

Table A2.7
Percentage of Votes, Selected Years 1945–1997

Party	1945	1953	1961	1969	1973	1981	1985	1989	1993	1997
Red Electoral Alliance[a]	—	—	—	—	0.4	0.7	0.6	0.8	1.1	1.7
Communist Party	11.9	5.1	2.9	1.0	—	0.3	0.2	—	—	0.1
Socialist Left Party[b]	—	—	2.4	3.5	11.2	4.9	5.5	10.1	7.9	6.0
Labor Party	41.0	46.7	46.8	46.5	35.3	37.2	40.8	34.3	36.9	35.0
Liberals	13.8	10.0	7.2	9.4	2.3	3.2	3.1	3.2	3.6	4.5
Liberal People's Party[c]	—		—	—	3.4	0.5	0.5	—	—	—
Center Party[d]	8.0	8.8	6.8	9.0	6.8	4.2	6.6	6.5	16.7	7.9
Christian People's Party	7.9	10.5	9.3	7.8	11.9	8.9	8.3	8.5	7.9	13.7
Joint Non-Socialist Lists	—	0.5	5.2	3.8	6.0	3.6	—	—	—	—
Conservatives	17.0	18.4	19.3	18.8	17.2	31.7	30.4	22.2	17.0	14.3
Progress Party[e]	—	—	—	—	5.0	4.5	3.7	13.0	6.3	15.3
Others	0.3	0.0	0.2	0.1	0.5	0.1	0.4	1.4	2.6	1.5
Voter turnout (%)	76.4	79.3	79.1	83.8	80.2	83.2	84.0	83.2	75.8	78.0

Table A2.8
Percentage of Seats Won in the Parliament, Selected Years 1945–1997

Party	1945	1953	1961	1969	1973	1981	1985	1989	1993	1997
Communist Party	7.3	2.0	0.0	0.0	—	0.0	0.0	0.0	—	0.0
Socialist Left Party[b]	—	—	1.3	0.0	10.3	2.6	3.8	10.3	7.9	5.5
Labor Party	50.7	51.3	49.3	49.3	40.0	42.6	45.2	38.2	40.6	39.4
Liberals	13.3	10.0	9.3	8.7	1.3	1.3	0.0	0.0	0.6	3.6
Liberal People's Party[c]	—	—	—	—	0.6	0.0	0.0	—	—	—
Center Party[d]	6.7	9.3	10.7	13.3	13.5	7.1	7.6	6.7	19.4	6.7
Christian People's Party	5.3	9.3	10.0	9.3	12.9	9.7	10.2	8.5	7.9	15.2
Conservatives	16.7	18.0	19.3	19.3	18.7	34.2	31.8	22.4	17.0	13.9
Progress Party[e]	—	—	—	—	2.6	2.6	1.3	13.3	6.0	15.2
Others[f]	0.0	0.0	0.0	0.0	0.0	0.0	0.0	0.6	0.6	0.6
Total no. of seats in the Storting	150	150	150	150	155	155	157	165	165	165

Sources: T. T. Mackie and R. Rose, *The International Almanac of Electoral History*, 3rd ed. (Washington, D.C.: Congressional Quarterly, 1991), pp. 356–71; O. C. Torp, *Stortinget i navn og tall.*

Continued

Table A2.8
Continued

Høsten 1989–våren 1993 (Oslo: Universitetsforlaget, 1990), pp. 189–94; B. Aardal, "The Norwegian Parliamentary Election of 1989," *Electoral Studies* 1990, pp. 151–58; B. Aardal, "The 1993 Storting Election: Volatile Voters Opposing the European Union," *Scandinavian Political Studies* 1994, pp. 171–80; K. Heidar, "Norway," *European Journal of Political Research* 1994, pp. 389–95.

[a]In 1989 the figure refers to "The County Lists for Environment and Solidarity," formed by the Marxist-Leninists and the Communists.

[b]Socialist People's Party until 1973. A joint list in Bergen is included in the figure of 1969. The 1973 figure refers to the Socialist Electoral Alliance, established by the Socialist People's Party, the Communist Party, and the Left Social Democratic organization.

[c]Before 1980 known as the New People's Party. Breakaway group from the Liberals. Reunited with the Liberals in 1988.

[d]Originally the Agrarian League, from 1921 the Farmer's Party; renamed Center Party in 1959.

[e]Anders Lange's Party until 1977.

[f]In the northernmost county, Finnmark, the top public servant, the Fylkesmann, Anders Aune left the Labor Party and formed his own party called "The People's Action for the Future of Finnmark." He was elected in 1989. In 1993 the Red Electoral Alliance won one mandate from Oslo, and in 1997 a whaling skipper won a seat from the Nordland constituency.

SWEDEN

Table A2.9
Percentage of Votes, Selected Years 1944–1997

Party	1944	1952	1960	1970	1976	1982	1988	1991	1994
Social Democrats	46.5	46.0	47.8	45.3	42.7	45.6	43.2	37.6	45.3
People's Party	12.9	24.4	17.5	16.2	11.1	5.9	12.6	9.1	7.2
Moderate Unity Party[a]	15.8	14.4	16.6	11.5	15.6	23.6	18.3	21.9	22.4
Center Party[b]	13.6	10.7	13.6	19.9	24.1	15.5	11.3	8.5	7.7
Left Party[c]	10.3	4.3	4.5	4.8	4.8	5.6	5.8	4.5	6.2
Christian Democrats[d]	—	—	—	1.8	1.4	1.9	2.9	7.1	4.1
Ecology Party	—	—	—	—	—	1.7	5.5	3.4	5.0
New Democracy	—	—	—	—	—	—	—	6.7	1.2
Others	0.7	0.1	0.1	0.5	0.4	0.3	0.7	1.2	1.0
Voter turnout (%)	71.9	79.1	85.9	88.3	91.8	91.4	86.0	86.7	86.0

Table A2.10
Percentage of Seats Won in the Parliament, Selected Years 1944–1997

Party	1944	1952	1960	1970	1976	1982	1988	1991	1994
Social Democrats	50.0	47.8	49.1	46.6	43.6	47.6	44.7	39.5	46.4
People's Party	11.3	25.2	17.2	16.6	11.2	6.0	12.6	9.5	7.4
Moderate Unity Party[a]	17.0	13.5	16.8	11.7	15.8	24.6	18.9	22.9	22.9
Center Party[b]	15.2	11.3	14.7	20.3	24.6	16.0	12.0	8.9	7.7
Left Party[c]	6.5	2.2	2.2	4.9	4.9	5.7	6.0	4.6	6.3
Christian Democrats[d]	—	—	—	0.0	0.0	0.0	0.0	7.4	4.0
Ecology Party	—	—	—	—	—	0.0	5.7	0.0	5.2
New Democracy	—	—	—	—	—	—		7.2	0.0
Others	0.0	0.0	0.0	0.0	0.0	0.0	0.0	0.0	0.0
Total no. of seats in the Riksdag[e]	230	230	232	350	349	349	349	349	349

Sources: T. T. Mackie and R. Rose, *The International Almanac of Electoral History*, 3rd ed. (Washington, D.C.: Congressional Quarterly, 1991), pp. 400–419; I. Wörlund, "The Swedish Parliamentary Election of September 1991," *Scandinavian Political Studies* 1992, pp. 135–43; *Dagens Nyheter, 9.20.94;* and A. Widfeldt and J. Pierre, "Sweden," *European Journal of Political Research* 1995, p. 477.

[a]Conservatives. Until 1969 the Right Party.
[b]Original name: Agrarian Party. In 1957 renamed the Center Party.
[c]Formed as the Social Democratic Left Party as a result of a split in the Social Democratic Party of Sweden. Changed its name to Communist Party in 1919. Renamed Left Party Communist in 1967, in 1990 it changed its name to Left Party.
[d]Kristen Demokratisk Samling until 1987, renamed Kristdemokratiska Samhällspartiet.
[e]Before 1970 Andra Kammaren (Lower Chamber).

Appendix 3

Classification of Party Families

Table A3.
Coding of Party Families

	Denmark	Finland[a]	Iceland	Norway	Sweden
Left parties	Left Socialist Party *Socialistik Folkeparti*; The Unity List *Enhetslisten* (15/19)	Left-Wing Alliance *Vasemmistoliitto* (f) *Vänsterförbundet* (s) (10/22)	People's Alliance *Althýdubandalag* (7/9)	Socialist Left Party *Socialistik Venstre* Red Electoral Alliance *Rød Valgallians* (13/14)	Left Party *Vänsterpartiet* (21/22)
Social democrats	Social Democrats *Socialdemokraterna* (40/63)	Social Democrats *Sosialidemokraattinen* (f) *Socialdemokraterna* (s) (41/63)	Social Democrats *Althýduflokkur* (10/11)	Labor Party *Arbeiderpartiet* (61/67)	Social Democrats *Socialdemokraterna* (153/161)
Centrist parties	Radical Party *Radikale Venstre*; Center Democrats *Centrum–Demokraterna* (8/13)	Swedish People's Party *Svenska folkpartiet* (s) Christian League *Kristillinen Liitto* (f) *Kristeliga Förbundet* (s) (11/19)	—	Liberals *Venstre*; Christian People's Party (CPP) *Kristeligt Folkeparti* (11/14)	People's party *Folkpartiet* Christian Democrats *Kristdemokraterna* (41/41)
Conservative parties	Conservatives *Konservative* (21/28)	National Coalition *Kansallinen Kokoomus* (f) *Samlingspartiet* (s) (21/39)	Independence Party *Sjálfstædisflokkur* (14/25)	Conservatives *Høyre* (24/28)	Moderate Unity Party *Moderata Samlingspartiet* (71/80)
Agrarian parties	Liberals *Venstre* (20/44)	Finnish Center *Suomen Keskusta* (f) *Centern* (s) (26/44)	Progressive Party *Fransóknarflokkur* (10/15)	Center Party *Senterpartiet* (27/32)	Center Party *Centerpartiet* (27/27)
Green/new parties	—	Green League *Vihreä Liitto* (f) De Gröna (s) (4/9)	Women's Alliance *Kvennalisti* (3/3)	—	Ecology Party *Miljöpartiet* (18/18)
Populist parties	Progress Party *Fremskridtspartiet*; Jacob Haugard (4/12)	—	—	Progress Party *Fremskrittspartiet*; Free Democrats *Fridemokraterna* (10/10)	—

Notes: Only parties where at least one MP responded have been included. Numbers in parentheses are number of respondents out of all representatives.

[a](f) means the name in Finnish, (s) in Swedish.

References

Aardal, B. 1994. "Hva er en politisk skillelinje? En begreppsmessig grenseopp-gang." *Tidskrift for samfunnsforskning* 35:218–49.

Aardal, B., and H. Valen. 1995. *Konflikt og opinion.* Oslo: NKS-forlaget.

Aberbach, J. D., R. D. Putnam, and B. A. Rockman. 1981. *Bureaucrats and Politicians in Western Democracies.* Cambridge, Mass.: Harvard University Press.

Abram, M., and J. Cooper. 1968. "The Rise of Seniority in the House of Representatives." *Polity* 1:52–85.

Adelsohn, U. 1987. *Partiledare: Dagbok 1981–1986.* Malmö: Gedins.

Allardt, E. 1956. *Social struktur och politisk aktivitet.* Helsinki: Söderström.

Allardt E., ed. 1981. *Nordic Democracy.* Copenhagen: Det Danske Selskab.

Almond, G. A. 1960. *The American People and Foreign Policy.* New York: Praeger.

Anckar, D. 1972. *Några anteckningar kring riksdagsutskottens ålderstruktur.* Åbo: Meddelanden från institutionen för samhällsforskning.

———. 1990. "Nordens folkförsamlingar: jämförande synpunkter." In K. Ståhlberg, ed., *Parlamenten i Norden.* Åbo: Åbo Akademi.

———. 1992. "Finland: Dualism and Consensual Rule." In E. Damgaard, ed., *Parliamentary Change in the Nordic Countries.* Oslo: Scandinavian University Press.

Andersson, L.-G. 1984. "Utskottsledamöterna i den svenska riksdagen: tidigare erfarenheter och utskottsplacering." Paper, Nordic Political Science Association Meeting, Lund.

Andeweg, R. B. 1992. "Executive-Legislative Relations in the Netherlands: Consecutive and Coexisting Patterns." *Legislative Studies Quarterly* 17:161–82.

———. 1997. "Role Specialisation or Role Switching? Dutch MPs between Electorate and Executive." *Journal of Legislative Studies* 3:110–27.

Andeweg, R. B., and L. Nijzink. 1995. "Beyond the Two-Body Image: Relations between Ministers and MPs." In H. Döring, ed., *Parliaments and Majority Rule in Western Europe.* Frankfurt: Campus Verlag.

Arter, D. 1984. *The Nordic Parliaments: A Comparative Analysis.* London: C. Hurst & Company.

———. 1995. "The Folketing and Denmark's 'European Policy': The Case of an 'Authorising Assembly.'" *Journal of Legislative Studies* 1:110–23.

Aydelotte, W., ed. 1977. *The History of Parliamentary Behavior.* Princeton: Princeton University Press.

Bachrach, P., and M. Baratz. 1962. "Two Faces of Power." *American Political Science Review* 56:947–52.

————. 1963. "Decisions and Nondecisions: An Analytical Framework." *American Political Science Review* 57:632–42.

Barnes, S. 1977. *Representation in Italy: Institutional Tradition and Electoral Choice.* Chicago: University of Chicago Press.

Bellquist, E. 1959. "Congressionalism and Parliamentarism." In J. Wahlke and H. Eulau, eds., *Legislative Behavior: A Reader in Theory and Research.* Glencoe: Free Press.

Bendix, R. 1964. *Nation-Building and Citizenship.* New York: Wiley.

————. 1977. *Nation-Building and Citizenship.* Berkeley & Los Angeles: University of California Press.

Berglund, S., and U. Lindström. 1978. *The Scandinavian Party System(s): A Comparative Study.* Lund: Studentlitteratur.

Bergman, T. 1995. *Constitutional Rules and Party Goals in Coalition Formation: An Analysis of Winning Minority Governments in Sweden.* Department of Political Science, Umeå University.

————. 1997. "National Parliaments and EU Affairs Committees: Notes on Empirical Variation and Competing Explanations." *Journal of European Public Policy* 4:373–87.

Bergman, T., and G. Gidlund, 1996. "Den demokratiska legitimiteten—de folkvalda parlamentens roll i EU." In *Demokrati och öppenhet: Om folkvalda parlament och offentlighet i EU.* SOU 1996:42. Stockholm: Allmänna förlaget.

Beyme, K. von. 1985. *Political Parties in Western Democracies.* Aldershot: Gower.

Bille, L. 1993. "Candidate Selection for National Parliament in Denmark 1960–1990: An Analysis of the Party Rules." In T. Bryder, ed., *Party Systems, Party Behaviour, and Democracy.* Copenhagen: Copenhagen Politial Studies Press.

————. 1999. "A Power Centre in Danish Politics. Danish Parliamentary Party Groups." In K. Heidar and R. Koole, eds., *Parliamentary Party Groups in European Democracies: Behind Closed Doors.* London: Routledge, 1999.

Birch, A. H. 1964. *Representative and Responsible Government.* London: George Allen and Unwin.

————. 1971. *Representation.* London: Macmillan.

Bjereld, U., and M. Demker. 1995. *Utrikespolitiken som slagfält: De svenska partierna och utrikesfrågorna.* Stockholm: Nerenius & Santérus Förlag.

Bjørklund, T. 1997. *Om Folkeavstemninger: Norge og Norden 1905–1994.* Oslo: Universitets-forlaget.

Björnberg, A. 1946. "Riksdagsutskottens rekrytering." *Tiden* 38:193–98.

Bjurulf, B., and I. Glans. 1976. "Från tvåblocksystem till fraktionalisering. Partigruppers och ledamöters röstning i norska stortinget 1969–1974." *Statsvetenskaplig Tidskrift* 79:231–53.

Blondel, J. 1973. *Comparative Legislatures.* Englewood Cliffs, N.J.: Prentice Hall.

Bogason, T. 1997. "Althingi and EEA Rules in the Making." In M. Wiberg, ed., *Trying to Make Democracy Work: Nordic Parliaments and the European Union.* Stockholm: Gidlunds.

Bollen, K. A., B. Entwisle, and A. S. Alderson. 1993. "Macrocomparative Research Methods." *Annual Review of Sociology* 19:321–51.

Borg, S., and R. Sänkiaho. 1995. *The Finnish Voter.* Helsinki: Finnish Political Science Association.

Borre, O., and J. Goul Andersen. 1997. *Voting and Political Attitudes in Denmark.* Århus: Århus University Press.

Brady, D. W., and C. S. Bullock. 1985. "Party and Factions within Legislatures," in G. Loewenberg et al., eds., *Handbook of Legislative Research.* Cambridge, Mass.: Harvard University Press.

Brusewitz, A. 1929. "Vad menas med parlamentarism? Ett försök till typologisk bestämning." *Statsvetenskaplig Tidskrift* 32:323–34.

Bullock, C. 1976. "Motivations for U.S. Congressional Committee Preferences: Freshmen of the 92nd Congress." *Legislative Studies Quarterly* 1:201–12.

———. 1985. "U.S. Senate Committee Assignments: Preferences, Motivations, and Success." *American Journal of Political Science* 29:789–808.

Burke, E. 1827. "Speech to the Electors of Bristol." In *Speeches and Letters on American Affairs.* London: Everyman (1961 edition).

Cain, B., J. E. Ferejohn, and M. P. Fiorina. 1987. *The Personal Vote. Constituency Service and Electoral Independence.* Cambridge, Mass.: Harvard University Press.

Christophersen, J. A. 1963. "Representant og vælger I." *Tidskrift for Samfunnsforskning* 4:215–40.

———. 1964. "Representant og vælger II." *Tidskrift for Samfunnsforskning* 5:85–110.

———. 1969. *Representant og vælger.* Oslo: Universitetsforlaget.

Christoffersson, U. 1986. "Riksdagsledamöternas arbetsveckor." In *Folkets främsta företrädare.* SOU 1986:27. Stockholm: Allmänna förlaget.

Collier, M. P. 1985. "Voting Behavior in Legislatures." In G. Loewenberg et al., *Handbook of Legislative Research.* Cambridge, Mass.: Harvard University Press.

Congressional Quarterly. January 27, 1996: 199–201, 236, 245–48.

Converse, P. E. 1964. "The Nature of Mass Beliefs Systems." In D. Apter, ed., *Ideology and Discontent.* New York: Wiley.

Converse, P., and R. Pierce. 1986. *Political Representation in France.* Cambridge, Mass.: Harvard University Press.

Copeland, G., and S. Patterson, eds. 1994. *Parliaments in the Modern World.* Ann Arbor: University of Michigan Press.

COSAC. 1996. Report on the 15th COSAC (Conference of European Affairs Committees), in Ireland.

Cox, G. C., and M. D. McCubbins. 1993. *Legislative Leviathan: Party Government in the House.* Berkeley & Los Angeles: University of California Press.

Crook, S., and J. Hibbing. 1985. "Congressional Reform and Party Discipline: The Effects of Changes in the Seniority System on Party Loyalty in the House of Representatives." *British Journal of Political Science* 15:207–26.

Crowe, E. 1983. "Consensus and Structure in Legislative Norms: Party Discipline in the House of Commons." *Journal of Politics* 45:907–31.

———. 1986. "The Web of Authority: Party Loyalty and Social Control in the British House of Commons." *Legislative Studies Quarterly* 11:1611–83.

Daalder, H., and J. G. Rusk. 1972. "Perceptions of Parties in the Dutch Parliament." In S. C. Patterson and J. C. Wahlke, eds., *Comparative Legislative Behavior: Frontiers of Research*. New York: John Wiley and Sons.

Dahl, R. A. 1961. *Who Governs?* New Haven: Yale University Press.

———. 1989. *Democracy and Its Critics*. New Haven: Yale University Press.

Dahl, R. A., and E. R. Tufte. 1973. *Size and Democracy*. Stanford, Calif.: Stanford University Press.

Dahlerup, D. 1988. "From a Small to a Large Minority: Women in Scandinavian Politics." *Scandinavian Political Studies* 11:275–98.

———. 1989. *Vi har väntat länge nog: Handbok i kvinnorepresentation*. Copenhagen: Nordiska Ministerrådet.

Dahlerup, D., and K. Hvidt. 1990. *Kvinder på Tinge: Kvinder i landspolitik i 75 år*. Copenhagen: Rosinante.

Dake, K. 1991. "Orienting Dispositions in the Perception of Risk." *Journal of Cross-Cultural Psychology* 22:61–82.

Dalton, R. 1985. "Political Parties and Political Representation. Party Supporters and Party Elites in Nine Nations." *Comparative Political Studies* 18:267–99.

Damgaard, E. 1973. "Party Coalitions in Danish Lawmaking 1953–1970." *European Journal of Political Research* 1:35–66.

———. 1977. *Folketinget under forandring*. Copenhagen: Samfundsvidenskabeligt Forlag.

———. 1979. *Folketingsmedlemmer på arbejde*. Århus: Forlaget Politica.

———. 1981. "Politiske sektorer: Jerntrekanter eller løse netværk?" *Nordisk administrativ tidsskrift* 62:396–411.

———. 1982a. *Partigrupper, representation og styrning*. Copenhagen: Schultz Forlag.

———. 1982b. "The Public Sector in a Democratic Order. Problems and Non-Solutions in the Danish Case." *Scandinavian Political Studies* 5:337–58.

———. 1983. *Magt i et pluralistisk demokrati: Notat om opfattelser af magtforhold i Danmark*. Århus: Institut for statskundskab.

———. 1987. "Ændringer i den parlamentariske kultur." *Politica* 19:280–89.

———, ed. 1992a. *Parliamentary Change in the Nordic Countries*. Oslo: Scandinavian University Press.

———. 1992b. "Denmark: Experiments in Parliamentary Government." In E. Damgaard, ed., *Parliamentary Change in the Nordic Countries*.

———. 1992c. "Nordic Parliamentary Government." In E. Damgaard, ed., *Parliamentary Change in the Nordic Countries*.

———. 1992d. "Parliamentary Change in the Nordic Countries." In E. Damgaard, ed., *Parliamentary Change in the Nordic Countries*.

———. 1994. "The Strong Parliaments of Scandinavia: Continuity and Change of Scandinavian Parliaments." In G. Copeland and S. Patterson, eds., *Parliaments in the Modern World.* Ann Arbor: University of Michigan Press.

———. 1995. "How Parties Control Committee Members." In H. Döring, ed., *Parliaments and Majority Rule in Western Europe.* Frankfurt: Campus Verlag.

Damgaard, E., and P. Svensson. 1989. "Who Governs? Parties and Policies in Denmark." *European Journal of Political Research* 17:731–45.

Davidson, R. 1969. *The Role of the Congressman.* New York: Pegasus.

Deutsch, K., and W. J. Foltz. 1963. *Nation-Building.* New York: Atherton.

Döring, H., ed. 1995. *Parliaments and Majority Rule in Western Europe.* Frankfurt: Campus Verlag.

Douglas, M., and A. Wildavsky. 1982. *Risk and Culture: An Essay on the Selection of Technological and Environmental Dangers.* Berkeley & Los Angeles: University of California Press.

Ds 1993:44. *Statsförvaltningens internationalisering: En vitbok om konsekvenser för den statliga sektorn i Sverige.* Stockholm: Finansdepartementet.

Duverger, M. 1951/1954. *Les partis politiques.* Paris: Armand Cohn (English trans. 1954).

Eckstein, H. 1975. "Case Study and Theory in Political Science." in F. I. Greenstein and W. P. Nelson, eds., *Handbook of Political Science.* Reading, Mass.: Addison-Wesley.

Eisenstadt, S. N., and S. Rokkan, eds. *1973–74: Building States and Nations.* 2 vols. Beverley Hills: Sage.

Elder, N., A. H. Thomas, and D. Arter. 1988. *The Consensual Democracies? The Government and Politics of the Scandinavian States.* Rev. ed. Oxford: Basil Blackwell.

Eliassen, K. 1985. "Rekrutteringen til Stortinget og regjeringen 1945–85." In T. Nordby, ed., *Storting og Regjering 1945–1985.* Oslo: Kunnskapsforlaget.

Eliassen, K., and M. Pedersen. 1978. "Professionalization of Legislatures: Long-Term Change in Political Recruitment in Denmark and Norway." *Comparative Studies in Society and History* 20:286–318.

Elklit, J. 1993. "Simpler than Its Reputation: The Electoral System in Denmark since 1920." *Electoral Studies* 12:41–57.

Ellis, R. J., and M. Thompson. 1997. *Culture Matters: Essays in Memory of Aron Wildavsky.* Boulder, Colo.: Westview Press.

Esaiasson, P. 1999. "Not All Politics Is Local—The Geographic Dimension of Policy Representation." In W. Miller et al., *Policy Representation in Western Democracies,* Oxford: Oxford University Press.

Esaiasson, P., and S. Holmberg. 1990. "Makten i Riksdagen." *Statsvetenskaplig Tidskrift* 93:137–47.

———. 1996. *Representation from Above: Members of Parliament and Representative Democracy in Sweden.* Aldershot: Darthmouth.

Esping-Andersen, G. 1990. *The Three Worlds of Welfare Capitalism.* Cambridge: Polity.

Eulau, H. 1984. "Legislative Committee Assignments." *Legislative Studies Quarterly* 9:587–633.

———. 1985. "Committee Selection." In G. Loewenberg et al., eds., *Handbook of Legislative Research.* Cambridge, Mass.: Harvard University Press.

Eulau, H., and P. D. Karps. 1977. "The Puzzle of Representation: Specifying Components of Responsiveness." *Legislative Studies Quarterly* 2:233–54.

Eulau, H., J. C. Wahlke, W. Buchanan, and L. C. Ferguson. 1959. "The Role of the Representative: Some Empirical Observation on the Theory of Edmund Burke." *American Political Science Review* 53:742–56.

Fenno, R. F. 1973. *Congressmen in Committees.* Boston: Little, Brown and Company.

———. 1978: *Home Style: House Members in Their District.* Boston: Little Brown.

Fich, O. 1993. "Markedsudvalget—dets styrke og svagheder." *Udenrigs* 48:59–69.

Fitzmaurice, J. 1996a. "Denmark." In R. Morgan and C. Tame, eds., *Parliaments and Parties: The European Parliament in the Political Life of Europe.* Basingstoke: Macmillan.

———. 1996b. "National Parliamentary Control of EU Policy in the Three New Member States." *West European Politics* 19:88–96.

Francis, W. 1985. "Leadership, Party Caucuses and Committees in U.S. State Legislatures." *Legislative Studies Quarterly* 10:243–57.

Franklin, M., and P. Norton, eds. 1993. *Parliamentary Questions.* Oxford: Clarendon Press.

Franklin, M., C. van der Eijk, and E. Oppenhuis. 1996. "The Institutional Context: Turnout." In C. van der Eijk and M. Franklin, eds., *Choosing Europe?* Ann Arbor: Michigan University Press.

Gahrton, P. 1983. *Riksdagen inifrån: En studie av parlamentarisk handfallenhet inför ett samhälle i kris.* Stockholm: Prisma.

Gallagher, M., and M. Marsh, eds. 1988. *Candidate Selection in Comparative Perspective: The Secret Garden of Politics.* London: Sage.

Galtung, J. 1966. "East-West Interaction Patterns." *Journal of Peace Research* 3:146–77.

Gebethner, S. 1996. "Proportional Representation versus Majoritarian Systems: Free Elections and Political Parties in Poland 1989–1991." In A. Lijphart and C. Waisman, eds., *Institutional Design in New Democracies: Eastern Europe and Latin America.* Boulder, Colo.: Westview Press.

Gertzog, I. 1976. "The Routinization of Committee Assignments in the U.S. House of Representatives." *American Journal of Political Science* 20:693–712.

Gilljam, M., and S. Holmberg. 1993. *Väljarna inför 90-talet.* Stockholm: Norstedts Juridik.

———. 1995. *Väljarnas Val.* Stockholm: Norstedts Juridik.

———. 1996. *Ett knappt ja till EU: Väljarna och Folkomröstningen 1994.* Stockholm: Norstedts Juridik.

Gladdish, K. 1990. "Parliamentary Activism and Legitimacy in the Netherlands." *West European Politics* 13:102–19.

Goldmann, K. 1993. "Internationalisering, internationalism och nationell självständighet." in B. von Sydow, G. Wallin, and B. Wittrock, eds., *Politikens väsen: Idéer och institutioner i den moderna staten*. Stockholm: Tiden.

———. 1994. "Sverige, EG och politikens internationalisering." In *EG-konsekvensutredningarna: Suveränitet och demokrati, bilagedel med expertuppsatser*. SOU 1994:12. Stockholm: Fritze.

Goldmann, K., G. Sjöstedt, and S. Berglund. 1986. *Democracy and Foreign Policy: The Case of Sweden*. Aldershot: Gower Publishing Company.

Goodwin, G. 1970. *The Little Legislatures: Committees of Congress*. Amherst: University of Massachusetts Press.

Graubard, S. R., ed. 1986. *Norden—The Passion for Equality*. Oslo: Norwegian University Press.

Grendstad, G. 1990. *Europe by Cultures: An Exploration in Grid/Group Analysis*. Department of Comparative Politics, University of Bergen.

Grendstad, G., and P. Selle, eds. 1996. *Kultur som levemåte: Hierariki, egalitarianisme, individualisme, fatalisme*. Oslo: Det nordiske samlaget.

Grímsson, Ó. R. 1976. "The Icelandic Power Structure 1800–2000." *Scandinavian Political Studies* 11:9–33.

Grofman, B., and A. Lijphart, eds. 1986. *Electoral Laws and Their Political Consequences*. New York: Agathon Press.

Gudmundsson, E. R. 1997. "Making the Government Behave. The Control Function of the Icelandic Parliament 1970–1995." Manuscript. Department of Political Science, Århus University.

Gustafsson, A., and C.-G. Carlsson. 1968. "Anciennitetsprincipen och utskottsväsendet." *Statsvetenskaplig Tidskrift* 71:139–46.

Hagevi, M. 1993. "Utskottsförflyttningar—ett steg i riksdagskarriären?" Paper, Nordic Political Science Association Meeting, Oslo.

———. 1994. "Först till kvarn får först mala— Riksdagsledamöternas utskottskarriär och anciennitetsprincipen." *Statsvetenskaplig Tidskrift* 97:175–205.

———. 1995. *Riksdagen utifrån: En gahrtonsk teori synas i sömmarna*. Department of Political Science, Göteborg University.

———. 1996. "Party Activity among Swedish Riksdag Members." Paper, European Consortium for Political Research, Joint Workshop Session, Oslo.

———. 1997. "Med tiden gör riksdagsledamöterna karriär. Riksdagsutskotten och anciennitetsprincipen." In I. Mattson and L. Wängnerud, eds., *Riksdagen på nära håll*. Stockholm: SNS Förlag.

———. 1998. *Bakom riksdagens fasad*. Göteborg: Akademiförlaget Corona.

———. 1999. "Party Groups in the Swedish Riksdag." In K. Heidar and R. Koole, eds., *Parliamentary Party Groups in European Democracies: Behind Closed Doors*. London: Routledge.

Hall, R., and L. Evans. 1990. "The Power of Subcommittees." *Journal of Politics* 52:335–55.

Hansen, A. M. 1897. *Norsk Folkepsykologi*. Christiania: Jacob Dybwads Forlag.

Hansson, G., and L.-G. Stenelo, eds. 1990. *Makt och internationalisering*. Stockholm: Carlsson.

Hardarson, Ó. 1995. *Parties and Voters in Iceland.* Reykjavik: University of Iceland, Social Science Research Institute University Press.

———. 1997. "Iceland." In D. A. Kaple, ed., *World Encyclopedia of Political Systems and Parties.* 3rd ed. New York: Facts on File.

Heckscher, G. 1984. *The Welfare State and Beyond: Success and Problems in Scandinavia.* Minneapolis, Minn.: University of Minnesota Press.

Hedlund, R. 1985. "Organizational Attributes of Legislative Institutions: Structure, Rules, Norms, Resources." In G. Loewenberg et al., eds., *Handbook of Legislative Research.* Cambridge, Mass.: Harvard University Press.

Hegeland, H., and I. Mattson. 1995. "Att få ett ord med i laget. En jämförelse mellan EU-nämnden och Europaudvalget." *Statsvetenskaplig Tidskrift* 98: 435–57.

———. 1996. "To Have a Voice in the Matter. A Comparative Study of the Swedish and Danish European Committees." *Journal of Legislative Studies* 2:198–215.

Heidar, K. 1995. "Partigruppene på Stortinget." *Norsk Statsvitenskapelig Tidsskrift* 11:277–97.

———. 1997. "Roles, Structures, and Behavior: Norwegian Parliamentarians in the Nineties." *Journal of Legislative Studies* 3:91–109.

Heidar, K., and E. Berntzen. 1995. *Vesteuropeisk politikk: Partier, Regjeringsmakt, Styreform.* Oslo: Universitetsforlaget.

Heidar, K., and R. Koole, eds. 2000. *Parliamentary Party Groups in European Democracies: Behind Closed Doors.* London: Routledge.

Heidar, K., and L. Svåsand, eds. 1997. *Partier uten grenser?* Oslo: Tano Aschehoug.

Heidar, K., H. C. Petterson, and L. Svåsand. 1997. "Internasjonalt partisamarbeid." In K. Heidar and L. Svåsand, eds., *Partier uten grenser?*

Helander, V. 1997. "Finland." In P. Norris, ed., *Passages to Power.* Cambridge: Cambridge University Press.

Held, D. 1991. "Democracy, the Nation-State and the Global System." In D. Held, ed., *Political Theory Today.* Cambridge: Polity Press.

———. 1995. *Democracy and the Global Order: From the Modern State to Cosmopolitan Governance.* Cambridge: Cambridge University Press.

———. 1999. "The Transformation of Political Community. Rethinking Democracy in the Context of Globalization." In I. Shapiro, ed., *Democracy's Edge.* Cambridge: Cambridge University Press.

Hellevik, O. 1969. *Stortinget—en sosial elite?* Oslo: Pax Forlag.

Helsinginki Sanomat. June 20, 1996.

Hendriks, F. 1997. "Politics, Culture, and the Post- Industrialising City." Paper, European Consortium for Political Research, Workshop on Cultural Theory, Bern.

Hernes, G. 1971. *Interest, Influence, and Cooperation: A Study of the Norweigan Parliament.* Ann Arbor: University Microfilms.

———. 1973. "Stortinget komitésystem og maktfordelningen i partigruppene." *Tidskrift for samfunnsforskning* 1:3–29.

————. 1975. *Makt og avmakt.* Bergen: Universitetsforlaget.

————. 1977. "Interests and the Structure of Influence: Some Aspects of the Norweigan Storting in the 1960s." In W. Aydelotte, ed., *The History of Parliamentary Behavior.* Princeton: Princeton University Press.

————. 1983. *Makt og styrning.* Oslo: Gyldendal Norsk Forlag.

————. 1984. "Segmentering og samordning", in O. Berg and A. Underdal, eds., *Fra valg till vedtak.* Oslo: Aschenhoug.

Hernes, G., and W. Martinussen, W. 1980. *Demokrati og politiske ressurser.* Oslo: Norges Offentlige Utredninger.

Hernes, G., and K. Nergaard. 1989. *Oss i mellom. Konstitusjonelle former og uformelle kontakter Storting—Regjering.* Oslo: Fafo.

Hernes, H. 1987. *Welfare State and Woman Power: Essays in State Feminism.* Oslo: Norwegian University Press.

Herzog, D., H. Rebenstorf, C. Werner, and B. Wessels. 1990. *Abgeordnete und Burger.* Opladen: Westdeutscher Verlag.

Hibbing, J. R. 1991. *Congressional Careers: Contours of Life in the U.S. House of Representatives.* Chapel Hill: University of North Carolina Press.

Hinckley, B. 1971. *The Seniority System in Congress.* Bloomington: Indiana University Press.

————. 1976. "Seniority 1975: Old Theories Confront New Facts." *British Journal of Political Science* 6:383–99.

————. 1988. *Stability and Change in Congress.* New York: Harper & Row Publishers.

Holmberg, S. 1974. *"Riksdagen representerar svenska folket": Empiriska studier i representativ demokrati.* Lund: Studentlitteratur.

————. 1981. *Svenska väljare.* Stockholm: Liber.

————. 1989. "Political Representation in Sweden." *Scandinavian Political Studies* 12:1–36.

————. 1996a. "Lagom makt till EU." *Statsvetenskaplig Tidskrift* 99:257–68.

————. 1996b. "Svensk åsiktsöverensstämmelse." In B. Rothstein and B. Särlvik, eds., *Vetenskap om Politik: Festskrift till professor emeritus Jörgen Westerståhl.* Department of Political Science, Göteborg University.

————. 1997. "Dynamic Opinion Representation." *Scandinavian Political Studies* 20:265–83.

————. 1999. "Policy Congruence Compared." In W. Miller et al., *Policy Representation in Western Democracies.* Oxford: Oxford University Press.

Holmberg, S., and P. Esaiasson. 1988. *De folkvalda: En bok om riksdagsledamöterna och den representativa demokratin i Sverige.* Stockholm: Bonniers.

Hunter, F. 1953. *Community Power Structure.* Chapel Hill: University of North Carolina Press.

Inter-Parliamentary Union. *Women in Parliaments 1945–1995: A World Statistical Survey.* Geneva: Series "Reports and Documents" No. 23.

Isberg, M. 1982. *The First Decade of the Unicameral Riksdag: The Role of the Swedish Parliament in the 1970s.* Department of Political Science, University of Stockholm.

————. 1984. *Riksdagens roll under 1970-talet.* Stockholm: Förlaget Akademikerlitteratur.

Jansson, J.-M. 1992. *Från splittring till samverkan: Parlamentarismen i Finland.* Borgå: Söderström.

Jensen, H. 1995. *Arenor eller aktører? En analyse af Folketingets stående udvalg.* Frederiksberg: Samfundslitteratur.

Jensen, J. A. 1996. "Prior Parliamentary Consent to Danish EU Policies." In E. Smith, ed., *National Parliaments as Cornerstones of European Integration.* London: Kluwer Law International.

Jensen, T. K. 1993. *Politik i praxis: Aspekter of danske folketingsmedlemmers politiske kultur of livsverden.* Frederiksberg: Samfundslitteratur.

————. 1994. "The Danish Political Elite. Recruitment, Style, and Culture." Paper, European Consortium for Political Research, Joint Sessions of Workshops, Madrid.

————. 1995. "Partierne, Europaudvalget og europæiseringen." *Politica* 27: 464–79.

————. 1996. "Partidisciplin of indflydelsesstrategier i partigrupperne i Folketinget." Paper, Nordic Political Science Association Meeting, Helsinki.

————. 1998. "Party Cohesion and Cooperation across Party Lines in Nordic Parliamentary Parties." Department of Political Science, Århus University.

Jenssen, A. T., and H. Valen, eds. 1995. *Brüssel midt i mot: Folkeavstemningen om EU.* Oslo: Ad Notam.

Jenssen, A. T., P. Pesonen, and M. Gilljam, eds. 1998. *To Join or Not to Join.* Oslo: Universitetsforlaget.

Jerneck, M. 1987. "Den internationaliserade riksdagen." In L.-G. Stenelo, ed., *Statsvetenskapens mångfald: Festskrift till Nils Stjernquist.* Lund: Lund University Press.

————. 1990. "Internationalisering och svensk partidiplomati." In G. Hansson and L.-G. Stenelo, eds. *Makt och internationalisering.* Stockholm: Carlsson.

————. 1997. "De svenska partiernas utlandsförbindelser från internationalisering till europeisering." In K. Heidar and L. Svåsand, eds., *Partier uten grenser?* Oslo: Tano Aschehoug.

Jerneck, M., A. Sannerstedt, and M. Sjölin. 1988. "Internationalization and Parliamentary Decision-Making: The Case of Sweden 1970–1985." *Scandinavian Political Studies* 10:169–94.

Jónasdóttir, A. 1991. *Love Power and Political Interests.* Örebro: Örebro Studies 7.

Judge, D. 1995. "The Failure of National Parliaments." *West European Politics* 18:79–100.

Kaartvedt, A. 1964. "Fra Riksforsamlingen til 1869." in *Det norske Storting gjennom 150 År.* Vol. 1. Oslo: Gyldendal.

Kaiser, K. 1971. "Transnational Relations as a Threat of the Democratic Process." *International Organization* 4:790–817.

Katz, R. 1980. *A Theory of Parties and Electoral Systems.* Baltimore: Johns Hopkins University Press.

———. 1986. "Party Government: A Rationalistic Conception." In F. G. Castles and R. Wildenmann, eds., *Visions and Realities of Party Government.* Berlin: Walter de Gereyter.

Katz, R., and P. Mair. 1992. *Party Organizations: A Data Handbook.* London: Sage.

Katz, R., and B. Wessels. 1999. *The European Parliament, the National Parliaments, and European Integration.* Oxford: Oxford University Press.

Kim, C. L., J. D. Barkan, I. Turan, and M. E. Jewell. 1984. *The Legislative Connection: The Politics of Representation In Kenya, Korea, and Turkey.* Durham, N.C.: Duke University Press.

King, A. 1976. "Modes of Executive-Legislative Relations: Great Britain, France, and West Germany." *Legislative Studies Quarterly* 1:11–16.

———. 1992. "Modes of Executive-Legislative Relations: Great Britain, France, and West Germany", in P. Norton, ed., *Legislatures.* Oxford: Oxford University Press.

Kirchheimer, O. 1959. "The Waning of Opposition in Parliamentary Regimes." In J. Wahlke and H. Eulau, eds., *Legislative Behavior: A Reader in Theory and Research.* Glencoe: Free Press.

Knoke, D. 1990. *Political Networks: The Structural Perspective.* Cambridge: Cambridge University Press.

Koch, H., and A. Ross, eds. 1949. *Nordisk Demokrati.* Oslo: Halvorsen og Larsen Forlag.

Kristinsson, G. H. 1996. "Parties, States, and Patronage." *West European Politics* 19:433–57.

Kristjánsson, S. 1994. *Frá flokksræði til persónustjórnmála.* Reykjavik: Félagsvísindastofnun Háskóla Íslands.

Kuhnle, S. 1972. "Stemmeretten i 1814." *Historisk Tidskrift* 51:373–90.

Kurian, G., ed. 1997. *World Encyclopedia of Parliaments and Legislatures.* Baldwin Place: Congressional Quarterly Publications.

Kuusela, K. 1995. "The Finnish Electoral System: Basic Features and Developmental Tendencies." In S. Borg and R. Sänkiaho, eds., *The Finnish Voter.* Tampere: Finnish Political Science Association.

Lane, J. E., and S. Ersson. 1996. *European Politics.* London: Sage.

Lane, J. E., T. Martikainen, P. Svensson, G. Vogt, and H. Valen. 1992. "Scandinavian Exceptionalism Reconsidered." *Journal of Theoretical Politics* 5:195–230.

Lanfranchi, P., and R. Lüthi. 1995. "Cohesion of Party Groups and Interparty Conflict in the Swiss Parliament: Roll Call Voting in the National Council." Paper, European Consortium for Political Research, Joint Sessions of Workshops, Bordeaux.

Larsson, T. 1986. "Att vara riksdagsledamot." In *Folkets främsta företrädare.* SOU 1986:27. Stockholm: Allmänna förlaget.

Laursen, F. 1995. "Parliamentary Bodies Specializing in European Union Affairs: Denmark and the Europe Committee of the Folketing." In F. Laursen and

S. A. Pappas, eds., *The Changing Role of Parliaments in the European Union.* Maastricht: EIPA.

Laursen, F., and S. A. Pappas, eds. 1995. *The Changing Role of Parliaments in the European Union.* Maastricht: EIPA.

Laver, M., and B. Hunt. 1992. *Policy and Party Competition.* New York: Routledge.

Laver, M., and K. Shepsle. 1996. *Making and Breaking Governments: Cabinet and Legislatures in Parliamentary Democracies.* Cambridge: Cambridge University Press.

Laver, M., and N. Schofield. 1991. *Multiparty Government: The Politics of Coalitions in Europe.* Oxford: Oxford University Press.

Lees, J., and M. Shaw. 1979. *Committees in Legislatures: A Comparative Analysis.* Durham: Duke University Press.

Lewin, L. 1970. *Folket och eliterna.* Stockholm: Almqvist & Wiksell.

―――. 1996. *Votera eller förhandla? Om den svenska parlamentarismen.* Stockholm: Fritzes.

Lijphart, A. 1971. "Comparative Politics and Comparative Method." *American Political Science Review* 65:682–98.

―――. 1975. "The Comparable-Cases Strategy in Comparative Research." *Comparative Political Studies* 8:158–77.

―――. 1984. *Patterns of Majoritarian and Consensus Government in Twenty-One Countries.* New Haven: Yale University Press.

―――. 1990. "The Political Consequences of Electoral Laws 1945–85." *American Political Science Review* 84:481–96.

―――. 1994. *Electoral Systems and Party Systems.* Oxford: Oxford University Press.

Lijphart, A., and C. Waisman. 1996. "The Design of Democracies and Markets: Generalizing across Regions." In Lijphart and Waisman, eds., *Institutional Design in New Democracies: Eastern Europe and Latin America.* Boulder, Colo.: Westview Press.

Lindström, U., and L. Karvonen, eds. 1987. *Finland en politisk loggbok.* Stockholm: Almqvist & Wiksell International.

Lipset, S. M., and S. Rokkan. 1967. "Cleavage Structures, Party Systems, and Voter Alignments: An Introduction." In S. M. Lipset and S. Rokkan, eds., *Party Systems and Voter Alignments.* New York: Free Press.

Loewenberg, G. 1972. "Comparative Legislative Research." In S. C. Patterson and J. C. Wahlke, eds., *Comparative Legislative Behavior: Frontiers of Research.* New York: John Wiley.

―――. 1995. "Legislatures." In V. Bogdanor, ed., *The Blackwell Encyclopedia of Political Institutions.* Oxford: Blackwell.

Loewenberg, G., and C. L. Kim. 1978. "Comparing the Representativeness of Parliaments." *Legislative Studies Quarterly* 3:27–50.

Loewenberg, G., and S. C. Patterson. 1979. *Comparing Legislatures.* Boston: Little Brown.

Loewenberg, G., S. C. Patterson, and M. E. Jewell, eds. 1985. *Handbook of Legislative Research*. Cambridge, Mass.: Harvard University Press.

Lovenduski, J., and P. Norris. 1993. *Gender and Party Politics*. London: Sage.

Lukes, S. 1974. *Power: A Radical View*. London: Macmillan.

Magnusson, T. 1987. *The Icelandic Althingi and Its Standing Committees*. Exeter: University of Exeter.

Manin, B. 1997. *The Principles of Representative Government*. Cambridge: Cambridge University Press.

Mann, T. E. 1986. "United States Congressmen in Comparative Perspective." In E. N. Suleiman, ed., *Parliaments and Parliamentarians in Democratic Politics*. New York: Helmer and Meier.

Master, N. 1961. "Committee Assignments in the House of Representatives." *American Political Science Review* 55:345–57.

Matland, R. 1995. "Kjønnsstereotype forestillinger om politikere: en eksperimentell studie av likestillingen i Norge." In N. Raaum, ed., *Kjønn og politikk*. Bergen: Tano A.S.

Matland, R., and D. Studlar. 1996. "The Contagion of Women Candidates in Single-Member District and Proportional Representation Electoral Systems: Canada and Norway." *Journal of Politics* 58:707–33.

Matthews, D. 1960. *U.S. Senators and Their World*. Chapel Hill, N.C.: University of North Carolina Press.

Matthews, D., and H. Valen. 1999. *Parliamentary Representation: The Case of the Norwegian Storting*. Ohio: Ohio State University Press.

Mattson, I. 1994. "Parliamentary Questioning in the Swedish Riksdag." In M. Wiberg, ed., *Parliamentary Control in the Nordic Countries: Forms of Questioning and Behavioural Trends*. Helsinki: Finnish Political Science Association.

———. 1996a. *Förhandlingsparlamentarism: En jämförande studie av riksdagen och folketinget*. Lund: Lund University Press.

———. 1996b. "Negotiations in Parliamentary Committees." In L.-G. Stenelo and M. Jerneck, eds., *The Bargaining Democracy*. Lund: Lund University Press.

Mattson, I., and K. Strøm. 1995. "Parliamentary Committees." In H. Döring, ed., *Parliaments and Majority Rule in Western Europe*. Frankfurt: Campus Verlag.

Mattson, I., and L. Wängnerud. 1997. *Riksdagen på nära håll*. Stockholm: SNS Förlag.

Mayhew, D. R. 1974. *Congress: The Electoral Connection*. New Haven: Yale University Press.

McAllister, I. 1991. "Party Elites, Voters, and Political Attitudes: Testing Three Explanations for Mass-Elite Differences." *Canadian Journal of Political Science* 24:237–68.

Merton, R. 1968. "Patterns of Influence: Local and Cosmopolitan Influentials." In Merton, *Social Theory and Social Structure*. New York: Free Press.

Mezey, M. L. 1979. *Comparative Legislatures*. Durham, N.C.: Duke University Press.

———. 1993. "Legislatures: Individual Purpose and Institutional Performance." In A. W. Finifter, ed., *Political Science: The State of the Discipline*. Vol. 2. Washington D.C.: APSA.

Michels, R. 1968. *Political Parties: A Sociological Study of the Oligarchical Tendencies of Modern Democracy*. New York and London: Free Press, Collier-Macmillan.

Mikkelsen, H. C. 1994. "Udviklingen i partisammenholdet." *Politica* 26:1, 25–31.

Miller, W., and D. Stokes. 1963. "Constituency Influence in Congress." *American Political Science Review* 57:45–56.

Miller, W., R. Pierce, B. Wessels, S. Holmberg, R. Herrera, and P. Esaiasson. 1999. *Policy Representation in Western Democracies*. Oxford: Oxford University Press.

Molin, B. 1965. *Tjänstepensionsfrågan*. Göteborg: Akademiförlaget.

Müller, W. C. 1993. "Executive-Legislative Relations in Austria: 1945–1992." *Legislative Studies Quarterly* 18:467–94.

Müller, W. C., and K. Strøm, eds. 1997. *Regierungskoalitionen in Westeuropa*. Vienna: Signum.

Myhre-Jensen, K. 1997. "The Storting and the European Union." Speech given at Conference on Nordic Parliaments and the European Union, Hässelby, Sweden.

Naroll, R. 1965. "Galton's Problem: The Logic of Cross-Cultural Analysis." *Social Research* 32:428–51.

Narud, H. M. 1994. "Nominasjoner og pressen." In K. Heidar and L. Svåsand, eds., *Partiene i en brytningstid*. Bergen: Alma Mater.

———. 1996. "Electoral Competition and Coalition Bargaining in Multi-Party Systems." *Journal of Theoretical Politics* 8:472- 99.

———. 1997. "Professionalization of the Norwegian Storting: Party Based and District Oriented." In J. Borchert, ed., *Politics as a Vocation: The Political Class in Western Democracies*.

Nedergaard, P. 1994. *Organiseringen af Den europæiske Union. Bureaukrater i beslutningsprocessen: EU-forvaltningens effektivitet og legitimitet*. Copenhagen: Handelshøjskolens Forlag.

Nelkin, D. 1989. "Communicating Technological Risk: The Social Construction of Risk Perception." *Annual Review of Public Health* 10:95–113.

Nergaard, K. 1988. "Tingmenn og talsmenn. En analyse av stortingsrepresentantenes organisasjonskontakt med utgangspunkt i segmenteringshypotesen." *Tidsskrift for Samfunnsforskning* 29:107–29.

Niedermayer, O., and R. Sinnott, eds. 1995. *Public Opinion and Internationalized Governance*. Oxford: Oxford University Press.

Nijzink, L., and P. Kopecky. 1995. "Party Discipline and the Relations between Ministers and MPs: A Comparison between the Netherlands and the Czech

Republic." Paper, European Consortium for Political Research, Joint Sessions of Workshops, Bordeaux.

Nordal, J., and G. H. Kristinsson. 1996. "Government and Foreign Relations." In J. Nordal and G. H. Kristinsson, eds., *Iceland: The Republic*. Reykjavik: Central Bank of Iceland.

Norris, P. 1985. "Women's Legislative Participation in Western Europe." *West European Politics* 8:90–101.

———. 1996a. "Legislative Recruitment." In L. LeDuc, R. G. Niemi, and P. Norris, eds., *Comparing Democracies: Elections and Voting in Global Perspective*. London: Sage.

———. 1996b. "Women Politicians: Transforming Westminster?" In J. Lovenduski and P. Norris, eds., *Women in Politics*. Oxford: Oxford University Press.

Norris, P., and J. Lovenduski. 1993. "'If Only More Candidates Came Forward': Supply-Side Explanations of Candidate Selection in Britain." *British Journal of Political Science* 23:373–408.

———. 1995. *Political Recruitment: Gender, Race, and Class in the British Parliament*. Cambridge: Cambridge University Press.

Norton, P. 1981. *The Commons in Perspective*. New York: Longman.

———. 1990a. "Legislatures in Perspective." *West European Politics* 13:141–52.

———. 1990b. "Parliaments: A Framework for Analysis." *West European Politics* 13:1–9.

———. 1991. "Parliament I—The House of Commons." In B. Jones, ed., *Politics UK*. London: Philip Allan.

———. 1992a. "General Introduction." In Norton, ed., *Legislatures*.

———, ed. 1992b. *Legislatures*. Oxford: Oxford University Press.

———. 1992c. "Parliament and Policy in Britain: The House of Commons as a Policy Influencer." In Norton, ed., *Legislatures*.

———. 1995. "Conclusion: Addressing the Democratic Deficit." *Journal of Legislative Studies* 1:177–93.

———, ed. 1996. *National Parliaments and the European Union*. London: Cass.

———. 1997. "Roles and Behaviour of British MPs." *Journal of Legislative Studies* 3:17–31.

———. 1999. "The United Kingdom: Exerting Influence from Within." In K. Heidar and R. Koole, eds., *Parliamentary Party Groups in European Democracies: Behind Closed Doors*. London: Routledge.

NOU. 1982. *Maktutredningens slutrapport*.

Nurmi, H. 1990. "A Theoretical Review of the Finnish Parliamentary and Presidential System." In J. Sundberg and S. Berglund, eds., *Finnish Democracy*. Jyväskylä: Finnish Political Science Association.

Nyholm, P., and C. Hagfors. 1968. *Ryhmäytenäisyyden kehityksestä eduskunnassa 1930–1954*. Helsinki: Helsingin Yliopisto.

Øidne, G. 1957. "Litt om Motsetninga mellom Austlandet og Vestlandet." *Syn og Segn* 63:97–114.

Olsen, J. 1983. *Organized Democracy: Political Institutions in a Welfare State—the Case of Norway.* Oslo: Universitetsforlaget.

Olson, D., and M. Hagevi. 1998. "The Parliament of Sweden: Riksdagen." In G. Kurian, ed., *World Encyclopedia of Parliaments and Legislatures.* Washington, D.C.: Congressional Quarterly Press.

Olson, D., and M. Mezey. 1991. *Legislatures in the Policy Process: The Dilemmas of Economic Policy.* Cambridge: Cambridge University Press.

Oscarsson, H. 1994. "Ett krympande partisystem?" *Statsvetenskaplig Tidskrift* 97:141–74.

Oskarson, M., and L. Wängnerud. 1995. *Kvinnor som väljare och valda: Om betydelsen av kön i svensk politik.* Lund: Studentlitteratur.

Ostrogorski, M. 1902. *Democracy and the Organization of Political Parties.* Vol. 2. New York: Macmillan.

Ozbudun, E. 1970. *Party Cohesion in Western Democracies: A Causal Analysis.* Sage Professional Papers in Comparative Politics. Beverley Hills, California: Sage.

Pateman, C. 1989. *The Disorder of Women.* Cambridge: Polity Press.

Pedersen, M. 1972. "Lawyers in Politics: The Danish Folketing and American Legislatures." In S. Patterson and J. Wahlke, eds., *Comparative Legislative Behavior: Frontiers of Research.* New York: John Wiley.

Perkins, L. 1980. "Influences of Members' Goals on Their Committee Behavior: The U.S. House Judiciary Committee." *Legislative Studies Quarterly* 5:373–92.

Pesonen, P., ed. 1994. *The 1994 EU Referendum in Finland: A Report on Voters' Opinion and Behavior.* Helsinki: Finnish Political Science Association.

Pesonen, P., R. Sänkiaho, and S. Borg. 1993. *Vaalikansan äänivalta.* Helsinki: Werner Söderström.

Petersson, O. 1982. *Väljarna och världspolitiken.* Stockholm: Norstedts.

———, ed. 1987. *Maktbegreppet.* Stockholm: Carlssons.

———. 1989. *Maktens nätverk.* Stockholm: Carlssons.

———. 1991a. *Nordisk politik.* Stockholm: Allmänna Förlaget.

———. 1991b. "Democracy and Power in Sweden." *Scandinavian Political Studies* 14:173–91.

———. 1993. *Svensk politik.* Stockholm: Publica.

———. 1994. *The Government and Politics of the Nordic Countries.* Stockholm: Fritzes.

———. 1995. *Nordisk politik.* 3rd ed. Stockholm: Publica.

Petersson, O., J. Hermansson, M. Micheletti, and A. Westholm. 1996. *Democracy and Leadership: Report from the Democratic Audit of Sweden.* Stockholm: SNS Förlag.

———. 1997. *Democracy across Borders: Report from the Democratic Audit of Sweden.* Stockholm: SNS Förlag.

Phillips, A. 1995. *The Politics of Presence.* Oxford: Oxford University Press.

Pierce, R. 1999. "Mass-Elite Issue Linkages and the Responsible Party Model of

Representation." In W. Miller et al., *Policy Representation in Western Democracies*. Oxford: Oxford University Press.

Pitkin, H. 1967. *The Concept of Representation*. Berkeley & Los Angeles: University of California Press.

Polsby, N. W. 1963. *Community Power and Political Theory*. New Haven: Yale University Press.

———. 1968. "The Institutionalization of the U.S. House of Representatives." *American Political Science Review* 62:144- 68.

———. 1975. "Legislatures." In F. I. Greenstein and N. W. Polsby, eds., *Handbook of Political Science*, vol. V. Reading, Mass.: Addison-Wesley.

———. 1992. "Legislatures." In P. Norton, ed., *Legislatures*. Oxford: Oxford University Press.

Polsby, N. W., M. Gallaher, and B. Rundquist. 1969. "The Growth of the Seniority in the U.S. House of Representatives." *American Political Science Review* 63:787–807.

Powell, G. B. 1989. "Constitutional Design and Citizen Electoral Control." *Journal of Theoretical Politics* 1:107–30.

Przeworski, A., and H. Teune. 1970. *The Logic of Comparative Social Inquiry*. New York: Wiley.

Putnam, R. 1976. *The Comparative Study of Political Elites*. New Jersey: Prentice-Hall.

Rae, D. 1967. *The Political Consequences of Electoral Laws*. New Haven, Conn.: Yale University Press.

Ragin, C., D. Berg-Schlosser, and G. de Meur. 1996. "Political Methodology: Qualitative Methods." In R. E. Goodin and H.-D. Klingemann, eds., *A New Handbook of Political Science*. Oxford: Oxford University Press.

Ranney, A. 1951. "Toward a More Responsible Two-Party System: A Commentary." *American Political Science Review* 45:488–99.

Rasch, B. E. 1995. "Party Discipline in Parliament: A Note on the Case of the Norwegian Storting." Paper, European Consortium for Political Research, Joint Sessions of Workshops, Bordeaux.

Rasmussen, E. 1972. *Komparativ politik*. Copenhagen: Gyldendal.

Raunio, T., and M. Wiberg. 1997. "Efficiency through Decentralisation: The Finnish Eduskunta and the European Union." In M. Wiberg, ed., *Trying to Make Democracy Work: Nordic Parliaments and the European Union*. Stockholm: Gidlunds.

Refsgaard, E. 1990. "Tæt vid toppen." In D. Dahlerup and K. Hvidt, eds., *Kvinder på Tinge: Kvinder i landspolitik i 75 år*. Copenhagen: Rosinante.

Rice, Stuart A. 1928. *Quantitative Methods in Politics*. New York: Alfred A. Knopf.

Rieselbach, L. 1992. "Purposive Politicians Meet the Institutional Congress." *Legislative Studies Quarterly* 17:95–110.

Rodrigo-Blomqvist, P. 1996. "Vem representerar invandrare? En studie av kommunalpolitiker i Göteborg." M. A. thesis, Department of Political Science, Göteborg University.

Rohde, D., and K. Shepsle. 1973. "Democratic Committee Assignments in the House of Representatives: Strategic Aspects of a Social Choice Process." *American Political Science Review* 67:889–905.

Rokkan, S. 1968. "Electoral Systems." In *International Encyclopedia of the Social Sciences.* New York: Macmillan.

————. 1970. *Citizens, Elections, Parties.* Bergen: Universitetsforlaget.

————. 1975. "Dimensions of State Formation and Nation-Building." In C. Tilly, ed., *The Formation of National States in Western Europe.* Princeton: Princeton University Press.

————. 1981. "Territories, Nations Parties: Towards a Geo-economic—Geopolitical Model for the Explanation of Variations within Western Europe." In R. Merrit and B. M. Russett, eds., *From National Development to Global Community: Essays in Honor of Karl W. Deutsch.* London: George Allan and Unwin.

Rokkan, S., and D. Urwin. 1982. *The Politics of Territorial Identity.* London: Sage.

————. 1983. *Economy, Territory, Identity: Politics of West-European Peripheries.* London: Sage.

Rokkan, S., and H. Valen. 1960. "Parties, Elections, and Political Behavior in the Northern Countries." In O. Stammer, ed., *Politische Forschung.* Köln: Westdeutscher Verlag.

————. 1962. "The Mobilization of the Periphery." In S. Rokkan, ed., *Approaches to the Study of Political Participation.* Bergen: Chr. Michelsens Institutt.

————. 1964. "Regional Contrasts in Norwegian Politics." In E. Allardt and Y. Littunen, eds., *Cleavages, Ideologies, and Party Systems.* Helsinki: Westermarck Society.

Rommetvedt, H. 1991. *Partiavstand og partikoalisjoner.* Stavanger: Rogalandsforskning.

————. 1997. "Norwegian Parliamentary Committees: Performance, Structural Change, and External Relations." In G.-E. Isaksson, ed., *Inblickar i nordisk parlamentarism.* Åbo: Åbo Akademi.

Rose, R., ed. 1974. *Electoral Behavior: A Comparative Handbook.* New York: Free Press.

Rosenau, J. N. 1961. *Public Opinion and Foreign Policy.* New York: Random House.

Roth, P. A. 1996. *Riket, valkretsen och hemkommunen.* Göteborg: Department of Political Science, Göteborg University.

Rothstein, B. 1996. "Political Instututions: An Overview." In R. E. Goodin and H.-D. Klingemann, eds., *A New Handbook of Political Science.* Oxford: Oxford University Press.

Rothstein, B., P. Esaiasson, J. Hermansson, M. Micheletti, and O. Petersson. 1995. *Demokrati som dialog.* Stockholm: SNS Förlag.

Rule, W. 1987. "Electoral Systems, Contextual Factors, and Women's Opportunity for Election to Parliament in Twenty-three Democracies." *Western Political Quarterly* 40:477–86.

Ruostetsaari, I. 1993. "The Anatomy of the Finnish Power Elite." *Scandinavian Political Studies* 16:305–37.

————. 1997. "An Amateur Politician, Political Professional, or Expert Representative? Recruitment of the Parliamentary Elite in Finland 1863–1995." Manuscript.

Rustow, D. 1956. "Scandinavia: Working Multiparty Systems." In S. Neumann, ed., *Modern Political Parties.* Chicago: University of Chicago Press.

Rydenfelt, S. 1954. *Kommunismen i Sverige.* Lund: Gleerup.

Saalfeld, T. 1990. "The West German Bundestag after 40 Years: The Role of a Parliament in a 'Party Democracy.'" *West European Politics* 13:68–89.

Sainsbury, D. 1987. "Class Voting and Left Voting in Scandinavia." *European Journal of Political Research* 15:507–26.

————. 1993. "The Politics of Increased Women's Representation: The Swedish Case." In J. Lovenduski and P. Norris, eds., *Gender and Party Politics.* London: Sage.

————. 1996. "Suffrage, Mobilization, and the Australian Welfare State." Paper, Swedish Political Science Association Annual Meeting, Lund.

Sandberg, N. 1992. "Stabilitet for eksistensen av segmenter. Hvor stabil er kirke- og undervisningskomitéen i forhold til de andre fagkomiteene?" Paper, Institute for Social Research, Oslo.

Sannerstedt, A. 1992. *Förhandlingar i riksdagen.* Lund: Lund University Press.

————. 1996. "Negotiations in the Riksdag." In L.-G. Stenelo and M. Jerneck, eds., *The Bargaining Democracy.* Lund: Lund University Press.

Sannerstedt, A., and M. Jerneck, eds., 1994. *Den moderna demokratins problem.* Lund: Studentlitteratur.

Sannerstedt, A., and M. Sjölin. 1992. "Sweden: Changing Party Relations in a More Active Parliament." In E. Damgaard, ed., *Parliamentary Change in the Nordic Countries.* Oslo: Scandinavian University Press.

————. 1994. "Folkstyrets problem." In A. Sannerstedt and M. Jerneck, eds., *Den moderna demokratins problem.*

Särlvik, B. 1970. *Electoral Behavior in the Swedish Multiparty System.* Department of Political Science, Göteborg University.

————. 1983. "Scandinavia." In V. Bogdanor and D. Butler, eds., *Democracy and Elections.* Cambridge: Cambridge University Press.

Sartori, G. 1965. *Democratic Theory.* New York: Praeger.

————. 1994. *Comparative Constitutional Engineering.* London: Macmillan.

Schattschneider, E. E. 1942. *Party Government.* New York: Holt, Rinehart & Winston.

Schmitt, H., and J. Thomassen. 1999. *Political Representation and Legitimacy in the European Union.* Oxford: Oxford University Press.

Schumpeter, J. 1942. *Capitalism, Socialism, and Democracy.* New York: Harper and Row.

Searing, D. 1985. "The Role of the Good Constituency Member and the Practice of Representation in Great Britain." *Journal of Politics* 47:348–81.

————. 1991. "Roles, Rules, and Rationality in the New Institutionalism." *American Political Science Review* 85:1239–60.

———. 1994. *Westminster's World: Understanding Political Roles.* Cambridge, Mass.: Harvard University Press.

Sejersted, F. 1996. "The Norwegian Parliament and European Integration—Reflections from Medium-Speed Europe." In E. Smith, ed., *National Parliaments as Cornerstones of European Integration.* London: Kluwer Law International.

Shaffer, W. R. 1991. "Interparty Spatial Relationships in Norwegian Storting Roll Call Votes." *Scandinavian Political Studies* 14:59–83.

Shaw, M. 1979. "Conclusion." In J. D. Lees and M. Shaw, eds., *Committees in Legislatures: A Comparative Analysis.* Durham, N.C.: Duke University Press.

Shepsle, K. 1978. *The Giant Jigsaw Puzzle.* Chicago: University of Chicago Press.

Shugart, M., and J. Carey. 1992. *Presidents and Assemblies.* Cambridge: Cambridge University Press.

Sidenius, N. 1997. "Problems Searching a Solution: The Role of the Folketing in Danish European Community Politics." In G.-E. Isaksson, ed., *Inblickar i Nordisk parlamentarism.* Åbo: Meddelanden från Ekonomisk-Statsvetenskapliga fakulteten vid Åbo Akademi A:470.

Siegfried, A. 1913. *Tableau politique de la France de l'Ouest.* Paris: Armand Collin.

Sigelman, L., and G. H. Gadbois. 1983. "Contemporary Comparative Politics: An Inventory and Assessment." *Comparative Political Studies* 16:275–305.

Sinclair, B. 1983. "Purposive Behavior in the U.S. Congress: A Review Essay." *Legislative Studies Quarterly* 8:117–31.

———. 1989. *The Transformation of the U.S. Senate.* Baltimore: Johns Hopkins University Press.

Sjöblom, G. 1968. *Party Strategies in a Multiparty System.* Lund: Studentlitteratur.

———. 1989. "Notater om politiska partier och internationalisering." In B. Heurlin and C. Thune, eds., *Danmark og det internationale system: Festskrift till Ole Karup Pedersen.* Copenhagen: Politiske Studier.

Sjölin, M. 1991. "'Decline of Parliaments'-tesen och den svenska riksdagens makt under 1970—och 1980—talet." *Statsvetenskaplig Tidskrift* 94:125–48.

———. 1993. *Coalition Politics and Parliamentary Power.* Lund: Lund University Press.

Skard, T. 1980. *Utvalgt til Stortinget: En studie i kvinners frammarsj og menns makt.* Oslo: Gyldendal Norsk Forlag.

Skard, T., and E. Haavio-Mannila. 1986. "Equality between the Sexes—Myth or Reality in Norden?" In S. Graubard, ed., *Norden—the Passion for Equality.* Oslo: Norwegian University Press.

Skare, A. 1996. "Kandidatutvelging—mer enn riktig kjønn fra rett sted. Politiske utvelging og politiske endringer i en brytningstid." *Tidsskrift for Samfunnsforskning* 37:328–62.

Skjaak, K. K. 1994. "Omlegging av Eurobarometer." Bergen: NSD.

Skjæveland, A. 1997. *Partidisciplin og brug på partidisciplinen i partigrupperne i Folketinget.* Århus: Institut for Statskundskab.

Skjeie, H. 1992. *Den politiske betydningen av kjønn: En studie av norsk topp-politikk.* Oslo: Institutt for Samfunnsforskning.

Smith, E., ed. 1996. *National Parliaments as Cornerstones of European Integration.* London: Kluwer Law International.

Smith, S. 1986. "The Central Concepts in Fenno's Committee Studies." *Legislative Studies Quarterly* 11:5–18.

Smith, S., and C. Deering. 1983. "Changing Motives for Committee Preferences of New Members of the U.S. House." *Legislative Studies Quarterly* 8:271–81.

———. 1984. *Committees in Congress.* Washington D.C.: Congressional Quarterly Press.

Sniderman, P., J. Fletcher, P. Russell, P. Tetlock, and B. Gaines. 1991. "The Fallacy of Democratic Elitism: Elite Competition and Commitment to Civil Liberties." *British Journal of Political Science* 21:349–70.

SOU. 1986. *Folkets främsta företrädare.* SOU 1986:27. Stockholm: Allmänna förlaget.

SOU. 1990. *Demokrati och makt i Sverige, Maktutredningens huvudrapport.* SOU 1990:44. Stockholm: Fritze.

Stavang, P. 1964. *Parlamentarisme og maktbalanse.* Oslo: Universitetsforlaget.

Steed, M. 1985. "The Constituency." In V. Bogdanor, ed., *Representatives of the People: Parliamentarians and Constituents in Western Democracies.* London: Gower.

Stenelo, L.-G., and M. Jerneck, eds. 1996. *Bargaining Democracy.* Lund: Lund University Press.

Stjernquist, N. 1966. *Samhälle och riksdag IV. Riksdagens arbete och arbetsformer.* Stockholm: Almqvist & Wiksell.

Strøm, K. 1986. "Deferred Gratification and Minority Governments in Scandinavia." *Legislative Studies Quarterly* 11:583–605.

———. 1990. *Minority Government and Majority Rule.* Cambridge: Cambridge University Press.

Strøm, K., and L. Svåsand. 1997. *Challenges to Political Parties. The Case of Norway.* Ann Arbor: University of Michigan Press.

Sullivan, J., P. Walsh, M. Shamir, D. Barnum, and J. Gibson. 1993. "Why Politicians Are More Tolerant: Selective Recruitment and Socialization among Political Elites in Britain, Israel, New Zealand, and the United States." *British Journal of Political Science* 23:51–76.

Sundberg, J. 1994. "Nationalized Parties, Professionalized Organisations." In R. S. Katz and P. Mair, eds., *How Parties Organize: Change and Adaptation in Party Organizations in Western Democracies.* London: Sage.

———. 1995. "Organizational Structure of Parties, Candidate Selection, and Campaigning." In S. Borg and R. Sänkiaho, eds., *The Finnish Voter.* Tampere: Finnish Political Science Association.

———. 1996. *Partier och partisystemer i Finland.* Saarijärvi: Schildts.

Sundberg, J., and C. Gylling. 1992. "Finland." In R. S. Katz and P. Mair, eds.,

Party Organizations: A Data Handbook on Party Organizations in Western Democracies, 1960–1990. London: Sage.

Sundström, G. 1994. "Riksdagen: Ett transportkompani? En studie över riksdagsledamöternas inflytande i samband med propositionsskrivandet." Manuscript. Department of Political Science, University of Stockholm.

Svallfors, S. 1992. "Dimensions óf Inequality: A Comparison of Attitudes in Sweden and Britain." Working Paper, Department of Sociology, Umeå University.

———. 1993. "Policy Regimes and Attitudes to Inequality: A Comparison of Three European Nations." In T. P. Boje and S. E. Olsson-Hort, eds., *Scandinavia in a New Europe.* Oslo: Scandinavian University Press.

Svåsand, L., K. Strøm, and B. E. Rasch. 1997. "Change and Adaptation in Party Organization." In K. Strøm and L. Svåsand, eds., *Challenges to Political Parties: The Case of Norway.* Ann Arbor: University of Michigan Press.

Svensson, P. 1981. "Partiernes 'krise' of deres sammenhold." *Politica* 13:102–19.

———. 1982. "Party Cohesion in the Danish Parliament during the 1970s." *Scandinavian Political Studies* 5:17–42.

———. 1988. "Parliament and Foreign Policy Making in Denmark." *Irish Studies in International Affairs* 2:19–39.

———. 1996. *Demokratiet i krise? En system- og debatanalyse af dansk politik i 1970'erne.* Århus: Forlaget Politica.

Sydow, B. von. 1991. "Sweden's Road to a Unicameral Parliament." In L. D. Longley and D. M. Olson, eds., *Two into One: The Politics and Processes of National Legislative Cameral Change.* Boulder, Colo.: Westview Press.

———. 1995. "Parlamentarismen i Sverige—en introduktion." In N. Stjernquist, ed., *Parlamentarismen i de nordiska länderna—en egen modell?.* Stockholm: Riksbankens Jubileumsfond och Gidlunds Förlag.

Taagepera, R., and M. S. Shugart. 1989. *Seats and Votes.* New Haven: Yale University Press.

Thomas, S. 1994. *How Women Legislate.* Oxford: Oxford University Press.

Thomassen, J. 1976. *Kiezens en gekozen in een representatieve demokratie.* Alphen aan den Rijn: Samson.

———. 1988. "Political Representation in France and Beyond." Paper, XIV World Congress of the International Political Science Association, Washington D. C.

———. 1991. "Empirical Research into Political Representation." In H.-D. Klingemann et al., eds., *Politische Klasse und Politische Institutionen.* Opladen: Westdeutscher Verlag.

———. 1994. "Empirical Research into Political Representation. Failing Democracy or Failing Models?" in M. K. Jennings and T. E. Mann, eds., *Elections at Home and Abroad.* Ann Arbor: University of Michigan Press.

Thompson, M., R. Ellis, and A. Wildavsky. 1990. *Cultural Theory.* Boulder, Colo.: Westview Press.

Tickner, J. A. 1991. "Hans Morgenthau's Principles of Political Realism. A Feminist Reformulation." In R. Grant and K. Newland, eds., *Gender and International Relations*. Milton Keynes: Open University Press.

Tingsten, H. 1966. *Från idéer till idyll: Den lyckliga demokratien*. Stockholm: Norstedt & Söner.

Togeby, L. 1994. *Fra tilskuere til deltagere*. Århus: Politica.

Underdal, A. 1984. "Internasjonalisering og offentlig politikk: problemer, muligheter og svar." *Statsviteren* 1:4–22.

Urwin, D. 1987. "Electing Representatives: Proportional Systems." *Social Studies Review* 3:1–12.

Uslaner, E. M. 1985. "Casework and Institutional Design: Reedeming Promises in the Promised Land." *Legislative Studies Quarterly* 10:35–52.

Valen, H. 1966a. "Den sosiale og politiske bakgrunn for rekrutteringen av det politiske lederskap." *Tidsskrift for Samfunnsforskning* 2/3:175–98.

———. 1966b. "The Recruitment of Parliamentary Nominees in Norway." *Scandinavian Political Studies* 1:121–66.

———. 1976. "National Conflict Structure and Foreign Politics: The Impact of the EU Issue on Perceived Cleavages in Norwegian Politics." *European Journal of Political Research* 4:47–82.

———. 1981. *Valg og politik—et samfund i endring*. Oslo: NKS- Forlaget.

———. 1988. "Norway: Decentralization and Group Representation." In M. Gallagher and M. Marsh, eds., *Candidate Selection in Comparative Perspective*. London: Sage.

———. 1990. "Vælgere, politisk avstand og koalisjoner." *Norsk Statsvitenskapelig Tidskrift* 6:17–32.

———. 1994. "List Alliances: An Experiment in Political Representation." In M. K. Jennings and T. E. Mann, eds., *Elections at Home and Abroad*. Ann Arbor: University of Michigan Press.

Valen, H., and H. M. Narud. 1998. "Professionalization, Political Representation, and Geography." Research Report 98/15. Oslo: Institute for Social Research.

Valen, H., and S. Rokkan. 1974. "Norway: Conflict Structure and Mass Politics in a European Pheriphery." In R. Rose, ed., *Electoral Behavior: A Comparative Handbook*. New York: Free Press.

Valgordningskommisjonen av 1917 (The Norwegian Electoral Commission of 1917).

Verba, S., S. Kelman, G. Orren, I. Miyake, J. Watanuki, I. Kabashima, and D. Ferree, Jr. 1987. *Elites and the Idea of Equality. A Comparison of Japan, Sweden, and the United States*. Cambridge, Mass.: Harvard University Press.

Verney, D. V. 1959. *The Analysis of Political Systems*. London: Routledge and Kegan Paul.

Wahlke, J., and H. Eulau. 1959. *Legislative Behavior: A Reader in Theory and Research*. Glencoe: Free Press.

Wahlke, J. C., H. Eulau, W. Buchanan, and L. Ferguson. 1962. *The Legislative System: Explorations in Legislative Behavior*. New York: John Wiley and Sons.

Wängnerud, L. 1997. "Varannan damerans och riksdagen utskott." In I. Mattson and L. Wängnerud, eds., *Riksdagen på nära håll*. Stockholm: SNS Förlag.

―――. 1998. *Politikens andra sida: Om kvinnorepresentation i Sveriges Riksdag*. Göteborg: Göteborg Studies in Politics.

Weaver, R. K., and B. A. Rockman. 1993. *Do Institutions Matter? Government Capabilities in the United States and Abroad*. Washington, D.C.: Brookings Institution.

Wessels, B. 1995. "Evaluations of the EU: Elite or Mass-Driven?" In O. Niedermayer and R. Sinnott, eds., *Public Opinion and Internationalized Governance*. Oxford: Oxford University Press.

Westefield, L. 1974. "Majority Party Leadership and Committee System in the House of Representatives." *American Political Science Review* 68:1593–1604.

Westerståhl, J. 1985. "Om Representation." In *Makten från folket*. Folkstyrelseskommitten. Stockholm: Liber.

―――. 1993. "Personbedömning som motiv för röstsplittring." In Westerståhl, *Person och parti*. SOU 1993:63. Stockholm: Allmänna förlaget.

Westerståhl, J., and F. Johansson. 1981. *Medborgarna och kommunen: Studier av medborgerlig aktivitet och representativt folkstyre*. Report 5, Kommunaldemokratiska forskningsgruppen. Ds Kn 1981:12. Stockholm.

Westlund, Å. 1998. "Politikerna och gnosjöandan." Undergraduate thesis, Department of Political Science, Göteborg University.

Wetterqvist, B. 1996. "Partisammanhållingen i Riksdagen—en voteringsanalys av partisammanhållingen riksmötet 1994/95 i jämförelse med riksmötet 1969." Undergraduate thesis, Department of Political Science, Göteborg University.

Wiberg, M., ed., 1994a. *Parliamentary Control in the Nordic Countries: Forms of Questioning and Behavioral Trends*. Jyväskylä: Finnish Political Science Association.

―――. 1994b. "To Keep the Government on Its Toes: Behavioural Trends of Parliamentary Questioning in Finland 1945–1990." In M. Wiberg, ed., *Parliamentary Control in the Nordic Countries*.

―――, ed. 1997. *Trying to Make Democracy Work: Nordic Parliaments and the European Union*. Stockholm: Gidlunds.

―――. 1999. "The Partyness of the Finnish Eduskunta: Parliamentary Party Groups in Finland." In K. Heidar and R. Koole, eds., *Parliamentary Party Groups in European Democracies: Behind Closed Doors*. London: Routledge.

Wiberg, M., and M. Mattila. 1997. "Committee Assignments in the Finnish Parliament 1945–1994." In G.-E. Isaksson, ed., *Inblickar i Nordisk parlamentarism*. Åbo: Åbo Akademi.

Wiberg, M., and T. Raunio. 1996. "Strong Parliament of a Small EU-Member State: The Finnish Parliament's Adaptation to the EU." *Journal of Legislative Studies* 2(4):302–21.

―――. 1997. "Where's the Power? Controlling Voting Outcomes in the Nordic Parliaments 1945–95." In G.-E. Isaksson, ed., *Inblickar i Nordisk parlamentarism*. Åbo: Åbo Akademi.

Wieslander, B. 1994. *The Parliamentary Ombudsman in Sweden.* Stockholm: Bank of Tercentenary Foundation & Gidlunds Bokförlag.

Wildavsky, A. 1987. "Choosing Preferences by Constructing Institutions: A Cultural Theory of Preference Formation." *American Political Science Review* 81:3–21.

Wildavsky, A., and K. Dake. 1990. "Theories of Risk Perception: Who Fears What and Why." *Dædalus: Journal of the American Academy of Arts and Sciences* 119:41–59.

———. 1991. "Theories of Risk Perception: Who Fears What and Why." In A. Wildavsky, *The Rise of Radical Egalitarianism,* Washington, D.C.: American University Press.

Worre, T. 1970. "Partigrupperne i Folketinget. Et magtcentrum i det danske politiske system." *Økonomi og Politikk* 44:143–88.

Contributors

Martin Brothén is finishing his doctoral thesis at Göteborg University, Sweden. His research interests include the internationalization of national parliaments, public trust in parliament, and the European Parliament.

Erik Damgaard is professor at the University of Århus, Denmark. He is editor and coauthor of *Parliamentary Change in the Nordic Countries* (1992) and has published widely on Danish and Nordic parliaments and politics.

Peter Esaiasson is professor of political science at Göteborg University, Sweden. His publications include *Representation from Above* (1996), with Sören Holmberg.

Magnus Hagevi is a project leader at the Center for Public Sector Research at Göteborg University, Sweden. His research interests include parliamentary party groups, committees, and individual MPs.

Ólafur Th. Hardarson is an associate professor of political science at the University of Iceland, Reykjavík. His publications include *Parties and Voters in Iceland* (1995).

Knut Heidar is professor at the University of Oslo, Norway. He has been editor of *Scandinavian Political Studies* and is the editor, with Ruud Koole, of *Parliamentary Party Groups in European Democracies* (1999).

Sören Holmberg is professor of political science at Göteborg University, Sweden. Since 1979 he has been director of the Swedish National Election Studies Program. His publications include *The Political System Matters* (1988), with Donald Granberg; and *Representation from Above* (1996), with Peter Esaiasson.

Torben K. Jensen is associate professor at the University of Århus, Denmark.

Hanne Marthe Narud is senior researcher at the Institute for Social Research, Oslo. Her publications include *Voters, Parties and Governments* (1996).

Tapio Raunio is a postdoctoral researcher in the Program on European Policy-making at the University of Helsinki. He is the author of *The European Perspective: Transnational Party Groups in the 1989–94 European Parliament* (1997).

Henry Valen is senior researcher at the Institute for Social Research, Oslo. He has been director of the Norwegian Electoral Research Program since 1957. Among his publications are *Political Parties in Norway* (1964), with Daniel Katz; *Electoral Change* (1992), edited with Mark Franklin and Thomas Mackie; and *Parliamentary Repesentation: The Case of the Norwegian Storting* (1999), with Donald Matthews.

Lena Wängnerud works at Göteborg University under a research grant from the Swedish Council for Planning and Coordination of Research.

Matti Wiberg, professor of political science at the University of Tampere, Finland, has published six monographs, edited a dozen books, and published more than a hundred articles. ·

Index

Page numbers referring to tables are followed by (*t*).

Other books in the series

Citizens as Legislators: Direct Democracy in the American States
   Shaun Bowler, Todd Donovan, and Caroline J. Tolbert

Party Cohesion, Party Discipline, and the Organization of Parliaments
   Shaun Bowler, David M. Farrell, Richard S. Katz, eds.

Cheap Seats: The Democratic Party's Advantage in U.S. House Elections
   James E. Campbell

Coalition Government, Subnational Style: Multiparty Politics in Europe's
   Regional Parliaments
   William M. Downs

Parliamentary Representation: The Case of the Norwegian Storting
   Donald R. Matthews and Henry Valen

Creating Parliamentary Government in Bulgaria: The Transition to Democracy
   Albert P. Melone

Senates: Bicameralism in the Contemporary World
   Samual C. Patterson and Anthony Mughan, eds.

Politics, Parties, and Parliaments: Political Change in Norway
   William R. Shaffer